Essays in Regional Economics

Benjamin Chinitz

William Alonso

Gerald Kraft

Alan R. Willens

John B. Kaler

Daniel Shimshoni

Roger E. Bolton

William H. Miernyk

George H. Borts

Mahlon R. Straszheim

Joseph J. Persky

Stanley L. Engerman

J. W. Milliman

James C. Burrows

Charles E. Metcalf

Essays in Regional Economics

Edited by John F. Kain and John R. Meyer

Harvard University Press, Cambridge, Massachusetts / 1971

Preface

Several years ago the Economic Development Agency of the Department of Commerce awarded a grant to support a program of teaching and research in regional and urban economics at Harvard (Program on Regional and Urban Economics, PRUE). This and subsequent grants from EDA have permitted the development of that program, the publication of more than seventy working papers dealing with various aspects of regional and urban economics, support of numerous doctoral dissertations, and the enrichment of the educational experiences of countless Harvard students. Virtually all PRUE discussion papers have been published in professional journals and many are widely used in universities and by government officials at all levels of government.

The initial grant from EDA included funds to commission a number of survey papers on various aspects of regional economic development. Six of these survey papers by Chinitz, Bolton, Borts, Miernyk, Engerman, and Milliman, were prepared specifically for the Harvard regional economics seminar; these papers have not been published previously, and are the core of this volume. Of the remaining papers in this volume, four (Shimshoni, Alonso, Straszheim, and Kain and Persky) present findings of EDA sponsored research done as part of the PRUE program. The papers by Kraft *et al* and Burrows and Metcalf were not supported by grants to PRUE, but were done in close association with PRUE and report on previously unpublished research sponsored by ARA and EDA.

We believe that the relationship between PRUE and EDA has been unusually productive. Much of the credit is due to the continued support of EDA personnel, who have demonstrated their belief in the value of university research for the policy process. This includes all three individuals who served as Assistant Secretary of Commerce for Economic Development during the six year period: Eugene Foley, Ross D. Davis, and Robert A. Podesta. It also includes all four Directors of the EDA's Office of Economic Research—Anthony Pascal, Harvey E. Garn, John Kaler, and Samuel M. Rosenblatt—as well as those staff members responsible for monitoring our research and providing support and encouragement for our Program, such as Gerald L. Duskin, Caryl Holiber, Roger Prior, Charlotte Breckenridge, and Chi-ta W. Chen. Our, and PRUE's debt to all these and many other persons is extensive, and we acknowledge their help with gratitude and with our sincerest thanks.

JOHN F. KAIN

JOHN R. MEYER

Contents

The Authors

Professor William Alonso
Institute of Urban and Regional Development
University of California, Berkeley

Associate Professor Roger E. Bolton
Department of Economics
Williams College

Professor George H. Borts
Department of Economics
Brown University

Dr. James C. Burrows
Senior Research Associate
Charles River Associates
Cambridge, Massachusetts

Professor Benjamin Chinitz
Department of Economics
Brown University

Professor Stanley L. Engerman
Department of Economics
University of Rochester

Professor John F. Kain
Department of Economics
Harvard University

John B. Kaler, Economist
U.S. Department of Commerce
Economic Development Administration
Office of Development Research
Washington, D.C.

Gerald Kraft, President
Charles River Associates
Cambridge, Massachusetts

Assistant Professor Charles E. Metcalf
Department of Economics
University of Wisconsin, Madison

Professor John R. Meyer
Department of Economics
Yale University
President, National Bureau
of Economic Research

Professor William H. Miernyk
Professor of Economics and Director,
Regional Research Institute
West Virginia University, Morgantown

Professor J. W. Milliman
Center for Urban Affairs
University of Southern California, Los Angeles

Assistant Professor Joseph J. Persky
Department of Economics
University of Alabama in Birmingham

Professor Daniel Shimshoni
Department of Economics
Tel-Aviv University, Israel

Associate Professor Mahlon R. Straszheim
Department of Economics
University of Maryland, College Park

Alan R. Willens, Vice President and Treasurer
Charles River Associates
Cambridge, Massachusetts

Essays in Regional Economics

JOHN F. KAIN and JOHN R. MEYER

Introduction

Regional Economics, like most applied fields in economics, is concerned with the application of the tools of economic analysis to a particular class of policy problems. The central issue of regional economics is understanding the processes of economic growth in a geographic area which is a subdivision of a larger national economy. Although those processes can be expected to be more or less the same as those that condition the growth of the larger national economy, regional economists also wish to know how and why those larger growth processes distribute by geographic area. Accordingly, their ambition is extensive: they seek to know and forecast some of the distributional as well as the aggregative aspects of economic development.

Given the scope of that ambition, it is hardly surprising that regional economics is a difficult-to-define and highly diverse field. In microcosm, it embodies some aspect of virtually every aspect of applied economics. The papers in this volume, by intention, reflect that diversity. Only some very broad and rather arbitrary groupings are discernible. These are: (I) The Objectives of Regional Development Policy; (II) The Impact of Industrial Development; (III) Regional Growth and Capital Flows; (IV) Special Problems of Southern Development; and (V) Regional Models.

The three papers comprising Part I are concerned with the objectives of regional development policies. Of these, the first was written by Benjamin Chinitz, former Deputy Assistant Secretary for Economic Development, several months after he left the agency in 1967. In large measure, his paper is a retrospective look at the problems of formulating a consistent and effective policy for regional economic development under the terms of the Economic Development Act (EDA). Chinitz discusses whether programs designed to assist certain areas can be justified on the grounds of improving the conditions of the affected populations. Specifically, he grapples with the economists' argument that, if the objective is to increase the well-being of an area's population, programs directed at *persons* are more efficient than programs directed at *places*. He concludes that "it is possible to define a meaningful and socially desirable program in . . . [area-directed] terms, but the existing legislation does not do justice to this sort of mandate."

Following his evaluation of the rationale and objectives of regional development programs, Chinitz discusses the difficulties created by Congress's imposition of highly specific criteria for designating areas as qualified for benefits under redevelopment programs. He sees these legislative provisions as excellent examples "of how economics is tempered by politics in our form of government." He maintains that the specific character of these eligibility criteria so limit the discretion of program administrators as to make it virtually impossible to design meaningful economic development programs for depressed areas.

Chinitz also reviews the agency's efforts to foster local participation in the development planning process. It is, he concludes, an excellent example of good legislative intentions failing to work well in practice. Experience has shown that the *actual provisions* of the legislation are "extremely cumbersome to administer and greatly complicate the essential task of evolving and administering a sensible plan for an area." A particularly unsuccessful requirement in his view is the Overall Economic Development Plan (OEDP), a planning document which areas must complete before receiving EDA assistance. The OEDP was conceived by its legislative sponsors as a device to foster careful planning and coordination at the local level. Local officials, however, instead of viewing the preparation of the OEDP as central to formulating a meaningful development strategy, typically regarded it as a bothersome bit of red tape. This discrepancy between intention and practice led Chinitz to conclude that most OEDP's were virtually worthless and that they imposed heavy administrative costs on the agency and the applicants.

In considering the tools provided by the EDA legislation, Chinitz contrasts them with earlier economic development programs, as for example, the Area Redevelopment Administration (ARA) and such short-term public works employment stimulants as the Accelerated Public Works Administration (APWA). To a greater extent than its predecessors, the Economic Development Act depends on the subsidization of public capital to achieve long-term economic development. This strategy, he notes, is based on the still unverified assumption that large subsidies to public capital can foster economic development. The greatest part of the agency's research budget was devoted to trying to identify this complex and elusive link. Even so, Chinitz's final judgment is that "programs to stimulate local economic development do have a definite place in an overall federal strategy to improve welfare," but that "we do not yet know how to use federal dollars efficiently to promote local economic development."

The second paper in Part I, William Alonso's "Equity and Its Relation to Efficiency in Urbanization," although more abstract and theoretical, deals with many of the same questions as those discussed by Chinitz. Specifically, Alonso is concerned with the trade-offs that may exist between aggregate national efficiency and regional equity. Like Chinitz, he eschews income transfers as a means of making regions more equal in per capita income or in other measures of well-being.[1] As an alternative to income transfers, Alonso evaluates migration as a means of increasing national income growth (efficiency) and regional equality (equity). To analyze the effects of migration, he constructs a paradigm which divides the nation into two realms: an advanced and prosperous region (the

1. Chinitz ignores income transfers because he believes there has been a political decision, expressed in area redevelopment legislation, in favor of economic development. Alonso never states his reasons for not considering this alternative.

metropolitan area, or city) and a depressed and backward region (the periphery). Four different consequences of migration both to and from the metropolitan area are defined in terms of the growth of aggregate and regional per capita income. These depend on the marginal product of an additional worker at the periphery and in the city, and on the initial level of per capita income of each region.

Alonso also devotes considerable attention to the problems of measuring equity. He argues that whereas the goal of aggregate efficiency is generally understood and accepted, the goal of (regional) equity is not. In his opinion this is because there is no commonly accepted measure of equity, regional inequality being measured by both income and unemployment.

This problem of measuring or defining equity is, of course, central to designating a specific area as "deserving" of special developmental aids. As a practical matter, quite obviously, any program directing itself to improvement of places or areas has to have some means of defining a "needy" area. The commonly accepted criteria of need are unemployment and low income. If these two phenomena always occurred in close conjunction, no special problems of designation would arise; quite clearly a classification on one would encompass and do as well as the other.

Unfortunately, such is not the case. This is aptly illustrated by data presented in the third paper of Part I, "On the Definition of a Depressed Area" by Gerald Kraft, Alan Willens, John Kaler, and John Meyer. Their data show that U.S. counties that ranked in the lower third by various per capita or household income measures are to a quite surprising degree *not* the same counties as those in the upper one-third of counties ranked by unemployment. Low income tends to be associated with agricultural counties, mainly in the southeastern United States, while high unemployment seems to be associated with the heavy and extractive industries. To a considerable extent, unemployment is a cyclical manifestation while low income is more permanent or trend-related. Definitional problems may also be involved: there is some evidence that low-income status may be associated with indicators of disguised unemployment (e.g., part-time employment at some distance from a person's place of residence).

Kraft and associates explore in some depth how various indices or measures of "welfare need" might be constructed and used to designate areas for economic redevelopment. These indices range from those almost exclusively derived from income criteria to those based mainly on unemployment measures. The authors quite clearly prefer the more income-oriented measures, contending that economic development is a long-term process best directed as government policy to areas in long-term need. As noted, low incomes in an area seem a more durable problem than high unemployment. Further strengthening the case for defining the need of an area on the basis of income rather than unemployment is the simple and quite practical fact that area income can be measured with much greater accuracy than unemployment.

Industrial development, the subject matter of Part II, is a commonly advanced technique for promoting economic improvement and illustrates the long gestation periods involved in such policies. The first paper in II, by Daniel Shimshoni, considers the oft-advocated panacea of promoting the economic development of lagging regions by attracting science-based industry to such areas. In his paper, Shimshoni analyzes those factors which have influenced the establishment and growth of science-based industry in various regions of the United States. Relying heavily on an intensive survey of science-based firms in the Boston area and a somewhat less detailed investigation of the San Francisco Bay Area complex, Shimshoni concludes that "there is a recognizable pattern in the way in which the leading centers of scientific industry, or "complexes" have grown."

Specifically, he feels that the ability of a region to attract scientists and engineers is a necessary prerequisite to the development of science-based industry. Universities usually are identified as the magnet that draws high-technology firms to a region. In general Shimshoni agrees, concluding that universities are important as a force in attracting and keeping industry leaders and highly skilled personnel, as an amenity, as a source of entrepreneurs, and as an attraction for government investment.

Shimshoni reviews in depth the generally accepted argument that government spending for research and development has been a critical factor in the development of science-based complexes and in the formation of many individual firms. He concludes that merely attracting government R & D spending to a region is not a sufficient condition for the development of a science-based complex and, moreover, that such spending cannot be obtained unless the region already possesses extensive technical leadership and skills. Again he emphasizes the importance of acquiring or developing those amenities which will attract and hold highly skilled professionals. Thus, in his view, the appropriate strategy for a region hoping to develop a major complex of science-based industries is to invest heavily in general and higher education systems and in the other amenities which make a locale a desirable place to live. Simultaneously the region should seek federal help in improving the quality of the local universities and should assist local firms and laboratories in procuring federal R & D contracts. As Shimshoni points out, however, the extent to which any area can expect to realize immediate gains from these strategies will depend to a considerable extent on the base of existing amenities, such as good schools or an attractive climate.

Roger Bolton's paper, "Defense Spending and Policies for Labor-Surplus Areas," is concerned with the impact of defense spending on regional economic growth and the advantages and disadvantages of using defense procurement to combat underemployment in labor-surplus areas. Bolton first outlines the reasons why national policy makers should be concerned about the regional impact of defense spending and why they might consider some deviations from a "least-cost criterion" for defense procurement.

Although Bolton considers the arguments for subsidizing depressed regions as fairly persuasive, he is much less certain about the desirability of using defense spending for this purpose. He notes that the volatility of defense spending is a major disadvantage in using it to aid distressed regions. Moreover, placing defense moneys in depressed areas may create additional political resistance to subsequent efforts to reduce defense spending. In his view, the furor that has surrounded Department of Defense efforts to close a number of obsolete military bases should give pause to those who propose using defense contracts for area development.

The final section of Roger Bolton's paper is concerned with the conceptual and methodological problems of measuring the direct and indirect impacts of defense activities. The great interdependence among specialized parts of the economy creates serious problems in attempting to evaluate the regional impact of defense spending. To trace the impact of a defense order requires detailed knowledge of interindustry and interregional trading patterns. Description of these interrelations requires better analytical methods and far more data than are presently available.

In the third paper of Part II, "Local Labor Market Effects of New Plant Locations," the impact of new plants on labor-surplus areas is evaluated by William Miernyk. His analysis draws on the findings of several case studies for a variety of local labor markets. The first case study deals with the experience of five small manufacturing plants that located in rural areas without any subsidy. The workers hired by these five plants are compared to the local labor force as a whole; the comparisons indicate that these manufacturers, like employers elsewhere, generally favor young and relatively well-educated workers.

The experience of these plants and others locating without subsidy is then compared to that of thirty-three new plants induced to locate in labor-surplus areas by ARA loans. Miernyk concludes that there were some important differences in the hiring done by subsidized and unsubsidized firms. Subsidized firms locating in labor-surplus areas tended to hire a larger proportion of formerly unemployed workers than plants locating without benefit of subsidy in more prosperous areas. Like the unsubsidized firms, however, they tended to be selective in their hiring, choosing the young and better educated.

Both the subsidized and unsubsidized new firms appear to have had a larger impact on local employment than on local unemployment. This seems due to several factors. First, the new employment opportunities increase the rate of labor force participation in the area; that is, more local residents are drawn into the labor force. In addition, however, some workers are attracted to the areas from outside, and the rate of migration out of the area is diminished. The net effect, again, is not necessarily to reduce unemployment but to increase employment. Clearly, Miernyk's findings also suggest some additional reasons why unemployment may be a poor indicator of area welfare or need, thereby reinforcing the finding of Kraft and associates that low income is preferable as a criterion for making such decisions.

Miernyk also considers the indirect employment or multiplier effects of new plant locations. He notes that many projections of the effects of new plant locations on local employment and unemployment in depressed areas have been unduly optimistic because they are based on unrealistically large estimates of the employment multiplier. Often the trade and service establishments in depressed areas operate well below capacity. When new plants locate in the area, these establishments often are able to accommodate the increased demand for their services without significant increases in employment. This could be construed, of course, as a very positive argument for area redevelopment under circumstances of full employment and widespread pressures on productive capacity elsewhere in the economy.

Miernyk ends his evaluation on a somewhat pessimistic note. He concludes that even a stepped-up program of investment in labor-surplus areas will not reduce unemployment in depressed areas to its purely frictional component, and that a serious effort to eliminate structural unemployment will require more radical policies, such as making government the employer of last resort.

Regional capital flows and markets, the subjects of Part III, have long played a prominent role in studies of regional economic development. George H. Borts, in the first paper of this section, has adapted neoclassical growth models, of the type first used by T. W. Swan and Robert Solow, to the analysis of external borrowing and lending among regions of the U. S. economy. From them he derives time-path solutions for investment, balance of payments on current account, and net factor income. Assuming a perfect national capital market, Borts develops two specific growth models and uses them to describe the long-run flow of capital between borrowing and lending regions of the United States. These solutions are functions of parameters such as the interest rate, the marginal propensity to save, the growth rate, and the capital coefficient. From numerical estimates of these parameters, Borts obtains numerical solutions for the 48 states in 1953 and compares them with actual behavior for the same year. Borts determines from these empirical tests that growth models are potentially very valuable in analyzing the behavior of regional economies.

The assumption of perfect capital markets is crucial to Bort's analysis and empirical estimates. Mahlon R. Straszheim examines this perfect capital market hypothesis in the second paper in Part III, "An Introduction and Overview of Regional Capital Markets." He also describes the nature and extent of regional compartmentalization of U. S. money markets and evaluates the regional impact of changes in aggregate credit conditions.

Measurement and analysis of the regional dimensions of U.S. capital markets have received only slight attention from economists. Straszheim believes that this neglect is traceable to the formidable data and methodological problems inherent in such analysis. An even more important factor is the widespread acceptance of the view that regional variations in interest rates and in other measures of borrowing and lending terms are empirically insignificant. In his paper Straszheim sets out to examine this widely held hypothesis. The task is a difficult one. Data on regional lending rates are limited; indeed, they are altogether nonexistent for all but a few of the different markets. Therefore he relies heavily on an examination of the characteristics of borrowers and lenders operating in regional capital markets and their ability to use national and secondary markets.

Reflecting on the nature of capital markets, Straszheim decides that information costs are the most significant restraint on the movement of capital between regions. Because of these information costs, there are significant economies to "local" placement and administration of capital transactions. These economies are particularly important for small and heterogeneous transactions. This potential source of regional differentials, however, is largely offset by secondary markets in a number of important credit instruments, by methods for regional pooling and sharing of lending and borrowing opportunities, and by extensive participation of "local" lending institutions and financial intermediaries in national markets.

It remains true, however, that a fairly significant portion of total borrowing is done "locally" and that significant costs would be imposed on many borrowers if they were forced to obtain their funds in other regions. This is much less true of lenders and for certain classes of specialized, but quantitatively quite important, securities. As a result, the adjustment of capital markets to different regional rates of return occurs mostly on the lending side and operates through relatively standardized securities, such as government-insured FHA mortgages and certificates of deposits (CD's).

Examining the changes in capital markets since the end of World War II, Straszheim finds that they have become increasingly complex and that this greater complexity has generally helped to make capital markets more "perfect." Regional differences in the cost and availability of credit are currently small, are continuing to decline, and are largely associated with periods of credit stringency. In part this is because regional capital markets are accounting for a smaller portion of the total flow of investment funds, as more lenders and borrowers participate in national markets and as various local restrictions on lending or borrowing are eliminated.

In summarizing his findings for particular markets, Straszheim states that significant, though small, differentials exist for 1-4 family mortgages, consumer credit, and bank loans of small denomination. By comparison, corporate bonds and stocks, government securities, and large commercial mortgages are usually traded in national markets and therefore exhibit little or no regional variation. All in all, only about 10 percent of the total flow of funds in the capital market is subject to regional variations in rates of 10 percent or more. Whether these small differentials deserve much consideration depends on the purposes to be served.

Straszheim concludes that the assumption of perfect capital markets used by Borts and others in analyzing long-term regional growth, while not precisely correct, is reasonable and will usually provide satisfactory results.

It is impossible to spend much time studying regional economic development in the United States without becoming aware of the large and persistent differential between the per capita incomes of the South and the rest of the nation. Analysis of this differential is the central topic of Part IV. Of the estimated 9.6 million U.S. families living in poverty in 1960 (having incomes of less than $3,000 per year), 4.5 million lived in the South. By almost any measure the South is the largest and most populous underdeveloped region in the U.S. and, at the same time, the region with the greatest potential for economic development. Despite its desperate poverty and its undisputed potential for economic growth, the South has received surprisingly little attention from national planners. Regional economic development programs have concentrated to a considerable extent on regions that are better off, at least in terms of per capita income, and that may have much less potential for development.

In recent years there has been a growing awareness that the problems spawned by southern poverty are not confined to the South. The higher wages and better opportunities available outside the South have produced a massive shift of population from the South to the major metropolitan areas of the North and the West. Since 1910, the South has never failed to run a net migration deficit of more than one million in any decade. This deficit reached a high of two and a quarter million migrants for the decade 1940-1950. These migrations streams, particularly those linking the largest metropolitan areas of the North and West with the rural South, have become increasingly Negro.

The first paper in Part IV, "The North's Stake in Southern Poverty" by John F. Kain and Joseph J. Persky, examines the pattern of migration between rural areas of the South and metropolitan areas of the West. This paper, a revised and shortened version of a policy paper prepared for the President's Commission on Rural Poverty, contends that the fortunes of the metropolitan North and the rural South are closely linked by migration. Many problems of urban poverty have their roots in southern rural poverty. Concluding that much more should be done to deal with these problems at their origin, the authors propose a two-pronged strategy of migrant improvement and southern economic development. The highest priority should be given to improving southern education, in particular that received by the rural population, especially rural blacks whose achievement levels are by far the lowest in the country.

The authors also propose a major program of southern economic development. The resulting expansion of opportunities would complement improved educational and equal employment programs. Indeed, they argue that such a growth of opportunities might well be the most effective equal employment program of all. If a decision is made to accelerate the already rapid economic development of the South, the next question becomes—how to do it. Kain and Persky favor geographically neutral subsidies within the South as a whole. It is claimed that subsidies to firms willing to establish plants anywhere within the South would produce a varied pattern of new development. Some of this new employment growth would occur in rural low-wage areas, but an increasing share would occur in the rapidly growing metropolitan areas of the South. The basic premise is that new development anywhere within the South will help to narrow the gap between northern and southern incomes which lies at the heart of so many of our current social problems.

The gap between northern and southern per capita incomes is not a recent development. It has existed for more than a century. Indeed, eighty years ago the South lagged even further behind the rest of the country than it does today. In 1960 southern per capita income was about 77 percent of the U.S. average; in 1880 it was only an estimated 51 percent of the U.S. average. Except for some retardation during the 1930's, the differential between northern and southern income levels has narrowed throughout the century since the Civil War.

The causes of southern underdevelopment, important for both regional analysis and economic history, are considered at length by Stanley L. Engerman in the second paper of Part IV, "Some Economic Factors in Southern Backwardness in the Nineteenth Century." Answering such questions as those examined by Engerman is never easy. However, it is even more difficult in this case because of the unavailability of all but the most fragmentary data needed to determine the levels of per capita income and to analyze the causes of southern decline.

In considering the origins of southern backwardness, historians previously argued that on the eve of the Civil War the South was a stagnant economy with little potential for future growth. There were a variety of explanations for this, but most focused on the supposedly debilitating aspects of the slave system. Easterlin's data on antebellum regional incomes, discussed by Engerman, effectively undermine this position and pinpoint the deterioration of the southern income position as having occurred in the twenty-year period from 1860 to 1880.

Interpretation of South–North per capita income differentials before the Civil War is complicated by the existence of slavery in the antebellum period. The question, stated simply, is whether or not in calculations of per capita income slaves should be considered people or capital goods. Humanitarian motivations argue for regarding them as people, but most antebellum property owners, in making their locational and investment calculations, certainly regarded slaves as capital goods. However, even if slaves are counted as people in computing per capita income, southern per capita income *before* the Civil War was about 80 percent of that for the United States as a whole, and it was not until 1950 that the relative income position of the South again reached this level. For analyses of regional growth and development, Engerman argues that it is more correct to compute southern per capita income in the antebellum period by subtracting an estimate for slave subsistence from regional income and then computing the per capita income of only the free population. This computation reveals that the per capita income of the southern free population before the Civil War may have exceeded that of the North. Thus, from the point of view of the free population, it is hard to argue that the South was less developed than the North prior to the Civil War.

In addition to analyzing Easterlin's regional income estimates, Engerman examines three common hypotheses relating to southern backwardness: (1) that southern agriculture was inefficient because slaves were less productive than free labor; (2) that slavery and the social and economic system it produced discouraged industrialization and capital formation; and (3) that the slave system caused the South to underinvest in human capital. Using a variety of historical evidence and economic analyses, Engerman concludes that there is little evidence for any of these hypotheses. Then, extending his analysis to the more direct effects of the war, he concludes that "the first instance of [income] divergence can be attributed to wartime destruction and to social upheaval which prevented rapid recovery from the impact of the Civil War, and not directly to the southern antebellum economic position." Thus, Engerman provides an important answer to the riddle of what first caused the large discrepancy between the South and the rest of the nation: the devastation visited upon the South by the Civil War and the inadequacy of postwar reconstruction.

Regional economics has borrowed heavily from techniques and models originally developed to analyze national economies. For example, input-output models, now a stock-in-trade for regional analysts, were first developed by Wassily Leontief as a means of describing interindustry relationships in the national economy. In the last decade regional economists have shown great interest in developing and further refining these and other tools into regional forecasting models. Part V is essentially concerned with reporting and evaluating these efforts.

Several complex and costly studies have been undertaken to develop large-scale models for forecasting the levels of employment, population, and income in particular regions. Unfortunately, the enthusiasm for designing and constructing such models has not been matched by an equal interest in assessing and auditing their performance. Indeed, many of these models are so poorly documented as to make such assessments almost impossible. In spite of these obstacles, several of the most significant of these large-scale regional models are discussed and evaluated by J. W. Milliman in his paper, "Large-Scale Models for Forecasting Regional Economic Activity." Specifically, he considers: (1) the New York Metropolitan Region Model; (2) the Upper Midwest Economic Model; (3) the Ohio River Basin Model; (4) the California Development Model; (5) the Oahu, Hawaii, Model; (6) the Lehigh Basin Simulation Model; and (7) the Susquehanna Basin Simulation Model.

Milliman's paper would be valuable if it did no more than provide brief summaries of these often fugitive or difficult-to-obtain models. He does more than this, however. He also provides a highly useful discussion of several conceptual and empirical problems encountered in nearly all attempts to forecast economic activity in particular regions. Among the most important of these problems is the inherently conditional character of regional planning and forecasting. In order to devise meaningful plans, planners need some kind of forecast. Yet presumably the purpose of planning is to permit conscious decisions about future development. Therefore, plans should change the future. Similarly, in order to make projections, the forecaster must know or assume future government policies and programs and their consequences. That is, he must know the plan. Where particular government decisions and policies are expected to have only limited consequences, this problem may not be too serious, and the forecaster may be able to make his projections without serious concern about government policies or investments. However, many large-scale regional models are developed to assist in evaluating the impact of major public investments, such as dams. These projects are intended to, and usually do, make major changes in the region's economy. In these circumstances, the interrelations between the plan and the forecast is critical, and there is a need for the closest articulation of forecast and plan. In discussing this issue, Milliman observes that "no generally accepted procedures or rules of conduct for combining forecasting and planning have been devised," but that the "refinement of plans and forecast is usually the result of an interactive process."

Milliman also discusses the often troublesome problem of specifying goals for regional development. He notes that while this may at first appear to be a simple problem, it is often very difficult. Regions may have multiple goals, and these are not always consistent. Even if the individual goals do not conflict, there may be no consensus about which are the more important. Finally, in those instances where regional goals have been agreed upon, they may be inconsistent with national goals.

The problem of specifying regional goals, as Milliman points out, is not unrelated to the choice of methodology for regional models. Specifically, the difficulty of formulating a single goal for regional development, or even a consistent set of weights for multiple goals, may mitigate against the use of optimizing techniques, such as linear programming, which have considerable appeal on other grounds. Such methods are best applied with the specification of a unique objective, although some subsidiary goals often can be introduced into programming models as constraints.

In Milliman's view, the difficulty of achieving agreement on goals prior to the analysis increases the attractiveness of computer simulation models. Such models permit the efficient evaluation of a great many alternative goal sets under different assumptions about future developments and policies. Specifically, analyses of alternative sets of goals may indicate where conflict exists and where it does not, thereby narrowing the ultimate range of disagreement on objectives.

Milliman also provides a lengthy discussion of the relative merits of "sophisticated" and "naïve" methods of forecasting. Naïve models are usually, although not invariably, cheaper than more sophisticated ones, a consideration that naturally favors their use. Moreover, there is some question whether the more sophisticated models provide forecasts which are enough superior to justify their higher costs. Indeed, where forecasting accuracy is the only criterion, naïve models may work better than more sophisticated and costly ones.

Incredible as it may seem, evaluation has been so meager that it is often impossible to state how well a particular model forecasts or to compare the accuracy of two or more models. As Milliman points out, however, there is often more at stake than forecast accuracy. For many purposes it is necessary to have a model that depicts the impact of certain projects or policies on the structure of the economy and on particular sectors. Where this is the case, there may be no choice except to attempt to construct a complex structural model of the economy with full recognition of the difficulties involved.

The second paper in Part V, "The Determinants of Industrial Growth at the County Level: An Econometric Analysis," by James C. Burrows and Charles E. Metcalf, summarizes the results of a large-scale regional forecasting study. In this respect it is similar to the studies surveyed by Milliman; but it also differs in a number of important respects. The Burrows-Metcalf study develops employment forecasts by industry groups for all regions, whereas the models surveyed by Milliman forecast the levels of employment, population, and income in specific regions. In fact, the Burrows-Metcalf model is designed to forecast employment in 1970 for all 3,097 counties in the contiguous United States. The model contains 63 equations, utilizes 168 variables, and makes 74,328 separate employment projections (24 industries in 3,097 counties). This task is a staggering one. Indeed, if the authors are to be criticized, it must be for attempting a task so ambitious!

The Burrows-Metcalf forecasting model employs four equations for each industry. Together, these four equations are used to forecast 1970 employment levels by industry group and county from 1960 data. The equations are estimated econometrically using 1960 employment in each industry and county as the dependent variable and 1950 employment and socio-economic characteristics as explanatory variables.

Counties, particularly rural ones, are often rather small units of aggregation. As a result, there are many instances where a particular industry was not present in a county in one or both years, 1950 and 1960. Since the dependent (or predetermined) variable assumes a zero in such cases, the authors resorted to discriminant analysis to identify those counties in which an industry was unrepresented.

Two discriminant functions were needed. It was necessary to have an equation for determining which counties having no employment in a particular industry in 1960 would acquire employment in that industry by 1970. In a parallel fashion, a method was needed to select those counties which would go from positive employment in 1960 to zero employment in 1970.

For those counties having positive employment in a particular industry in 1960, one of two regression equations was used to explain 1960 employment. For those counties that previously had employment in the industry, an equation was used containing 1950 employment in the same industry and 1950 socio-economic characteristics as explanatory variables. Where the industry was represented in the county in 1960 but not in 1950, the regression equation was of the same general form but included only the socio-economic variables, not the previous (zero) employment.

The sum of the 1970 forecasts by industry and county, obtained by solving these four equations using 1960 data, was then scaled to conform to industry-control totals for the nation. These industry-control totals were based on the aggregate forecasts of the Almon input-output model of the U.S. economy.[2] Briefly, the authors made

2. Clopper Almon, Jr., *The American Economy to 1975—An Interindustry Forecast,* (New York: Harper & Row, 1966).

proportional reductions or increases of the county forecasts depending on the extent to which the sum of county employment by industry exceeded or fell short of Almon's forecast for the nation.

The Burrows-Metcalf study is an impressive one by any criteria. The authors show great ingenuity in dealing with a frightening array of estimation problems. These methodological contributions make the paper required reading for anyone with a serious interest in the development of regional forecasting models. Nevertheless, there are a number of serious difficulties with the study, nearly all of which arise from the initial definition of the problem.

Perhaps the most serious drawback in using counties in estimating the model is that comprehensive employment data are not available for counties. The stated objectives of the study and the formulation of the model are concerned with industry location. However, the employment data used in estimating the models were obtained from the 1950 and 1960 Censuses of Population and report employment by place of residence rather than place of work. This produces serious errors when there is significant commuting across county lines.

Intercounty commuting is most prevalent within metropolitan areas. The decade 1950-1960, used by the authors in estimating their model, was one of rapid suburbanization of both employment and population. Although closely linked, suburbanization of workplaces and residences may not proceed identically. Indeed, important policy issues are concerned with imbalances between the rates of decentralization of households and firms.

Owing to the obvious weaknesses of the data in portraying the location of employment within metropolitan regions, a strong argument can be made for using Standard Metropolitan Statistical Areas (SMSA's) as the unit of aggregation. Commuting across SMSA boundaries is proportionately much less significant than commuting across county lines within the same metropolitan area. Since there would have been fewer measurement errors and since the metropolitan area is the more meaningful economic unit, it seems likely that better results would have been obtained if SMSA's had been used as the units for estimating and forecasting for all urban counties. If county forecasts were essential, a primitive allocation model which distributed SMSA forecasts among metropolitan-area counties might have produced better results. A similar, but somewhat weaker, argument can be advanced for using SEA's (Standard

Economic Areas) as the unit of aggregation for areas located outside of metropolitan areas.

As Metcalf and Burrows illustrate, regional economics faces many substantive technical problems not the least of which is simply defining a meaningful regional economy. Such a seemingly straightforward question can arise in connection with basic policy questions, as noted by Chinitz, or from technical considerations, shown by Kraft and associates, or from data requirements as in the paper by Burrows and Metcalf. One marvels, in fact, that a field of study facing such fundamental definitional problems can continue to thrive. The probable explanation of this phenomenon is that it meets a perceived need at the policy and planning level—as we hope these highly diverse essays do as well.

Part I *The Objectives of Regional Development Policy*

BENJAMIN CHINITZ

National Policy for Regional Development

Introduction

In 1961 Congress enacted the Area Redevelopment Act (ARA), the first piece of legislation that provided federal funds for the stimulation of economic activity in the nation's depressed areas. This was followed in 1962 by the enactment of additional legislation, the Accelerated Public Works Act (APWA), to finance the construction of public facilities in such areas. In 1965, under the banner of the Great Society, the earlier legislation, which had expired, found new expression in the Appalachian Regional Development Act and the Public Works and Economic Development Act, both of which are still in effect in early 1971. For the fiscal year 1969, beginning July 1, 1968, Congress appropriated on the order of $500 million to implement these programs.

From the very beginning, which really dates back to the 1950's when Senator Paul Douglas first proposed such programs during the Eisenhower administration, the notion that the federal government could and should intervene to combat localized economic anemia has been the subject of considerable controversy. The most unequivocal judgment we can render at this moment is that seven years of legislative and administrative experience have failed to assure a place for this form of federal activity in the nation's overall strategy for dealing with domestic social and economic problems. In short, Congress probably will not renew the relevant legislation when it expires at the close of the 1960's. This may happen despite a stronger commitment today than prevailed at the beginning of the sixties to use the powers and the resources of the federal government to improve individual and social welfare.

If Congress allows these programs to lapse, it will not be because they have failed to reduce unemployment or raise incomes in some of the nation's distressed areas. Then why would the Congress turn its back on a program with a demonstrable record of success? While success, in these simple terms, is a sufficient barometer of performance, it is hardly a necessary one. In fact, I would argue that it ought not to be regarded as a performance criterion even in principle. Seven years may be a long time in a ten-year program to land on the moon, but it is a very short time in the life of an economic development program.

If the Congress and the nation are tired of area programs, it is because after seven years of experience no clear direction has emerged. Fundamental questions relating to rationale, objectives, and strategy have not been resolved in the legislative mandate or in the administrative process. The simplest questions of "what," "why," and "how" still beg for unequivocal answers.

My purpose here is to articulate the anguish that has permeated the activity of the federal government in this field and to suggest a more constructive formulation of objectives and policies that might lead to progress in the future. My comments will be organized around the major features of the legislation: rationale and objectives; the delineation of areas and the criteria for designation; the role of planning and local participation therein; and, finally, the tools—that is, investment in public facilities, loans to business, and technical assistance.

Rationale and Objectives

The troubles of the program began with rationale and objectives, as one might expect. Superficially, the mandate of the Congress was to reduce the rate of unemployment where it was relatively high and to increase the average (median) level of income where it was inordinately low. At first glance this may seem to have been a fairly unambiguous set of objectives with a sound rationale. The common denominator of high unemployment and low income is the potential for greater output, in the one case, through fuller utilization of resources, and in the other, through higher levels of productivity.

But this simple view of the matter becomes murky when the legislation and the rationale are examined more carefully. Clearly, a consistent approach to reducing unemployment and increasing income would include measures that do not entail the direct stimulation of the local economy. The best example of such a measure is a concerted effort to relocate the unemployed (perhaps, also, the poor) to areas where they could find employment or better-paying jobs. Yet this kind of action is clearly out of bounds under these legislative mandates.

Recognizing the political constraints that preclude certain kinds of policies, we may have to reconcile ourselves to measures that expand the demand for labor in the area, creating more jobs or better-paying jobs. Certainly the theme of job creation permeates the legislation and the administration of the program. Even so, there are serious problems with this interpretation of objectives.

What happens if an expansion of the demand for labor in the local area does not reduce the number of unemployed or the number of poor people, but reduces the rate of unemployment by increasing the size of the employed labor force and raises the average income by increasing the incomes of the rich? The local economy has been properly stimulated but the potential for greater output residing in the unemployed and underemployed resources remains untapped. Are we happy with this outcome? Or do we care about the distribution of the gains within the community?

It is only fair to ask, from an analytical standpoint, whether such a thing can happen. One can easily conjure up a set of circumstances, not wholly atypical, in which it can clearly happen: A plant is induced to locate in an area by the provision, at federal expense, of low-interest long-term capital and some requisite public capital such as a road or a sewer system. The increased demand for land benefits the already well-to-do landowner. The labor employed in the plant is drawn from other locations because the locally unemployed do not possess the requisite skills. The impact of the additional purchasing power in the community is absorbed in local shops and factories that are operating below capacity. Some locally unemployed people may get caught up in the process but the number is so small that the cost per job is extremely high when measured in terms of jobs for the unemployed. Ironically, the higher the rate of unemployment the more likely this is to happen, because it is likely to be associated with a higher level of underutilized capacity.

Yet the Economic Development Act does not provide financial assistance contingent upon the employment of those presently poor or unemployed in the area. Within limits it is possible to exercise administrative initiative and discretion in this regard, but the limits are narrow in practice. For example, it is virtually impossible to constrain a grant to a community in this way if the project is intended to fill a gap in the area's "infrastructure" without reference to specific potential employers. The latter may not require additional inducements and will therefore not be subject to further scrutiny of any kind.

As reluctant as one might be to abandon the notion that the legislation is intended to bring jobs and higher incomes to unemployed and underemployed workers, it is difficult to avoid the conclusion that the area rather than the people is the immediate target of the legislation. Stated in this fashion, the legislation is put in its worst possible light in the opinion of many observers. Economists particularly cringe at the notion that federal policy should promote the growth of particular areas. With so little to be gained in terms of human welfare, they can see no greater waste of national resources anywhere in the system. Administrators also find this posture uncomfortable, and they continually affirm that their objective is to help people, not places. Unfortunately, this only arouses skepticism because the real thrust of the program *is* directed at areas.

The question to focus on, therefore, is whether an area-directed program can serve the national interest. If the ultimate concern is with people, does not the emphasis upon area interfere with defining and coming to grips with the problems? Why should it matter if there is 3 percent or 8 percent unemployment in the area if the target group is the long-term unemployed? If the focus is on poor people, what difference does it make whether the median income of the area is above or below the national average? And if a *place* is somehow rationalized as an appropriate focus for policy, how can one justify programs which do not operate directly on the people who make up the statistics which qualify the place for special treatment?

Unless and until the Congress confronts these questions, the area development programs and their administrators are not likely to develop a sense of identity and purpose. It is entirely possible, in my opinion, to define a meaningful and socially desirable program in these terms, but the existing legislation does not do justice to a mandate of this sort.

The fundamental proposition on which this conclusion is based is that of welfare of an individual—that is, his income and employment status—depends on the environment in which he lives as well as his own attributes, assets, and skills. The relative importance of personal environmental influences varies over time and place. We have no compunction about using macro-economic policies to stimulate aggregate demand in order to help unemployed people find jobs when the national rate of unemployment is 6 percent. Likewise, we use foreign aid to help poor people in the underdeveloped countries of the world. We find it difficult, however, to aid depressed regions in an advanced country during periods of full employment. In this case we ignore the *environmental* variable and devote all of our attention on the *personal* variable. Hence, the philosophical preference for antipoverty programs, such as the Office of Economic Opportunity (OEO), rather than area development programs.

The fallacy in this attitude is the assumption that all poor people (and all unemployed people) have equal access to the healthy "national" environment. Recent events have made us keenly aware of racial barriers that inhibit mobility. Spatial barriers also inhibit mobility. A white child born and reared in a poor county has no access to a superior public education. When he grows up he will be judged to have personal disabilities that are unambiguously a product of his environment. This is now recognized as a problem, and there are federal programs to assist poor school districts even though the aid is not directed exclusively at the poor students in those districts. In other words, we are ready to extend assistance to bolster the environment as a way of helping the poor who are caught in those environments.

There was a time when we believed that federal assistance to urban renewal rested on the same rationale. We would help the poor by improving their environment. In that case we made the opposite error; we assumed that the enriched environment would remain the environment of the poor.

Can a case be made in these terms for federal assistance to stimulate the local economic environment? The answer depends on whether economic development is regarded as a particularly potent remedy for environmental deficiencies when compared to two other more obvious kinds of assistance: direct payments to the poor and direct transfers of federal revenues to local governments without reference to specific projects. Neither alternative entails a direct commitment to economic development as an intermediate mechanism for improving welfare, yet both would increase the effective demand for resources in the community through the familiar multiplier process.

The unique aspect of an economic development program is the encouragement of private enterprise in the community. One should not have to argue too hard that the presence of a vigorous private sector is valuable, even if the vigor can only be generated through subsidy. All the beneficiaries—the local government which collects property taxes, the local industries which supply the new firm, the workers who are employed there—can legitimately have the normal feeling of economic achievement which would prevail in the absence of the subsidy, and this carries with it a greater assurance that the forward momentum will be sustained. To put it somewhat cynically, a "derived" subsidy is not as bad for morale as a "direct" subsidy. The normal processes of growth can be simulated better by the stimulation of private enterprise than by direct transfers either to people or to local governments.

But is it worth the cost? In the next section I will discuss the problems of area delineation and criteria for designation and show how these features of the legislation undermine the basic rationale by creating a presumption that the stimulation of private enterprise is a feasible tool for improving the environment in all circumstances. Clearly, the cost of invigorating the private sector may be so high in many depressed areas that it becomes prohibitively expensive by comparison to direct transfers. However, it will not necessarily be cost-ineffective in all circumstances.

Implicit in the latter judgment are two assumptions which I suspect are still accepted by a majority of economists—even "regional" economists. The first is that the nation as a whole has a momentum for growth that is essentially independent of the regional distribution of economic activity; in other words, the total available for all regions is determined outside the regional context altogether. The second, and corollary, assumption is that the fortunes of a specific region ultimately depend upon the location preferences of the nation's business enterprises. It follows from this that (a) a region's rate of growth can only be altered by making the region more competitive in its locational pull; and (b) in this competition one region can only grow at the expense of the other. Hence, a subsidy to stimulate the growth of industry where it would not "naturally" grow, is bound to reduce total national output. The loss might be justified on distributional grounds, but why not maximize output and achieve redistribution through transfers?

My own experience in regional analysis has led me to question this conventional view of the interaction between national and regional economic development. In looking first at Pittsburgh and later at the Appalachian Region, I found the conventional view to be inadequate. The impact of "national" forces was dramatically clear: changes in technology and in demand patterns had undermined the natural resource advantages of these regions. The conventional view was compatible and even convincing, except that it did not explain the shape of the regional response to these external shocks. This response seemed to be conditioned very heavily by internal rather than external factors. The sociopolitical-economic superstructure that had been erected on the natural resources base was faulty in many respects. Local government had failed to siphon off enough wealth to create community and public facilities essential to a more diversified pattern of development. The profitable exploration of the region's natural wealth had not bred a more ubiquitous spirit of entrepreneurship. The profits were not fed into the financial streams that could nourish new enterprises in new fields. The labor force had been trained in specific skills, but had not been taught to be receptive to the learning of new skills and new occupations.

Ex post facto, one could still look at the region and, in the conventional view, attribute its decline to an unfavorable competitive posture. But this begged the question. A more sensible approach was to turn the problem around and say that the region had declined because, like the underdeveloped nations of the world, it had failed to develop those assets—human, social, and political—which are essential in fostering a self-sustaining process of economic development. The challenge, therefore, was not to grow by becoming competitive, but rather to become competitive by growing. The objective was not to grab a bigger piece of the nation's economic pie, but to make the pie bigger by unleashing the potential that lay dormant in the region's resources. In these terms, local efforts could be additive and not cancel out each other, and the nation as a whole could have a legitimate interest in the development of specific regions.

In short, circumstances may occur where the stimulation of local economic activity through subsidy may expand regional output without reducing national output. In such circumstances, the need for subsidy is likely to be temporary rather than permanent. When both conditions prevail, a strong case may be made for using economic development as a tool to correct environmental deficiencies.

Delineation of Areas and Criteria for Designation

If the poor articulation of rationale and objectives in the legislation reflects some underlying unresolved economic issues, the detailed maze of provisions relating to the delineation and designation of areas is a monument to the special flavor of the American political process. The spirit of compromise is all-pervasive. As the legislation has evolved, new ideas and new concepts have been added, but very few old ones have been abandoned. Progress seems to be achieved in our system only by addition, not by subtraction.

The most important unit in both the new and the old acts is the county. If the county has the requisite statistics, all parts of the county qualify for the program. But the county is not a necessary building block. In a labor market consisting of a number of counties, the requisite statistics for the entire labor market would qualify all counties in the labor market regardless of their individual statistics. A city of 250,000 or more people within a county could be qualified on the basis of the city's own statistics. Indian reservations, provided they have a population of 1,000 or more, can qualify regardless of the condition of the larger entity that surrounds them. A place like Harlem, however, is neither a county nor a city of 250,000 nor an Indian reservation, and therefore is not eligible by the terms of this legislation.

The current legislation has two additional geographic layers. The Development District is a multi-county area consisting of at least two counties with the requisite statistics and what is referred to as a "growth center." The latter is a vaguely defined community, not to exceed 250,000 in population, which offers considerable potential for growth. The criteria for delineating the boundaries of the District and identifying the growth center are vague enough to require considerable administrative initiative in implementing this feature of the program.

Finally, there is the multi-state region. This is an area that stretches across state boundaries and is defined via political and administrative processes as a collection of contiguous counties. The region is, of course, central to the Appalachian Regional Development ment Act, which introduced the district concept. It was incorporated into the Public Works and Economic Development Act under which five additional regions have been designated throughout the country: New England, Upper Great Lakes, Ozarks, Coastal Plains, and Four Corners. A region need not pass any specific quantitative test to qualify as one. The language of the legislation is such as to create a potentially eligible region almost anywhere in the country. At the moment, New England, for example, has only one claim: it has not grown in the aggregate at the national average. Anticipating a bit, it should be pointed out that counties (and variations thereof), districts, and regions qualify for different packages of financial assistance. Most of the dollars flow to the county, the oldest area in terms of legislative history, where specific projects are financed through grants and loans. The district receives a limited amount of project support, but it is mainly a planning unit for the present. The region, with the exception of Appalachia, which has direct authority from Congress, is exclusively a planning activity under the terms of the Public Works and Economic Development Act.

My comments on the district and the region have already alluded to criteria for designation. In strictly formal terms, the current legislation (Public Works and Economic Development Act of 1965) defines seven independent criteria of eligibility for the county (and variations thereof):

1. Substantial unemployment
2. Persistent unemployment
3. Low median family income
4. High out-migration
5. Indian reservations
6. Prospect of sudden rise in unemployment
7. At least one eligible area in every state

The last provision is an excellent example of how economics is tempered by politics in our form of government. It means that the state of Rhode Island, which consists of little more than the Providence-Pawtucket Labor Market, is perpetually eligible regardless of the rate of unemployment or the level of median income.

The first three criteria are delineated quantitatively in the current legislation. "Substantial" unemployment means 6 percent or more in the last calendar year. "Persistent" unemployment is achieved by a combination of depth and breadth: 100 percent above the national average for one year, 75 percent above the national average for two years, or 50 percent above the national average for three years. Persistent unemployment qualifies a county for all forms of financial assistance. Substantial unemployment only qualifies a county for Public Works grants, which will be discussed later. Low median family income means a number less than 40 percent of the national median family income. The precise definition of high out-migration was left to the administrative process, and what emerged was a double criterion—median income less than 50 percent of the national average combined with 25 percent or more out-migration in the 1950-1960 decade. The sixth criterion of "sudden rise" is an extremely flexible instrument in the hands of a skillful administrator and has led, for example, to the designation of the immediate area around the Brooklyn Navy Yard following the announcement by the Department of Defense that it would be phased out.

The law also provides for an annual review of eligibility to take account of shifting economic circumstances. Regions and districts are almost entirely protected from this hazard except that a district would be technically disqualified if it contained only two eligible counties and one dropped out. The force of this provision is felt mainly at the county level. Since the only kinds of annual data currently available relate to unemployment at the county level and are of questionable accuracy, the process of annual review is fraught with inequities and a variety of other problems.

In reviewing this maze of provisions one wonders about the validity of the famous remark, "Politics is the art of the possible," and rather leans to the view that politics is the art of making life impossible for a public administrator. Under this scheme the number of distinct entities that can reach out for federal assistance is about 1,000, depending on the vigor of the national economy. The budgets of the government Agencies have never been large enough to take even one action in each of these places each year, let alone implement a whole plan with an interdependent set of projects. For example, in a recent year a total of 527 projects of all kinds were approved for 343 areas. The administrative cost of saying *no* to an eligible area is not trivial: all projects must be processed to a point and reviewed before they are denied. When the cost borne by the applicant is included, it adds up to horrendous waste.

One wishes it were possible for Congress to give administrators the following mandate: "The entire nation is eligible for this program. Your job is first to identify the circumstances in which the stimulation of local economic development will improve the environment of the poor and the unemployed and thereby increase their welfare. Then compare the cost of achieving improvements in various localities and allocate your budget accordingly. If you think your limited budget will force you to pass up some very good opportunities, come back for more."

The introduction of the district and the region might be interpreted as a move in this direction. Unfortunately, the move was half-hearted because Congress would not relinquish the county as the basic unit, would not abandon the rigid statistical criteria for designation, and would not direct the bulk of the resources to the districts and the regions. Nor would Congress offer the administrator the chance to test his program in the ghettos of our large cities unless the city as a whole met the criteria for designation. True, the administrator can, within the constraints of the legislation as it is now structured, exercise considerable discretion in the allocation of his resources, but to use an overworked adage, "He can't see the forest for the trees."

The most charitable interpretation of the existing legislation would charge the Congress with having presumed that it could identify the circumstances in which this program made sense and that its prescriptions for delineating areas and qualifying them reflect this wisdom. Unfortunately, if knowledge cannot be legislated, it ought to precede legislation; in this case, as in so many others, the state of the art lags behind the aspirations of the country. This may be safely regarded as inevitable; but a much more workable mandate should exist to allow for the knowledge to evolve with the practice.

Undoubtedly, an unqualified mandate such as I have suggested would expose the administrator to random pressures from all parts of the nation regardless of their economic circumstances. These pressures are greater when the law specifically includes some areas while it excludes others. In the latter case, the recitation of area statistics goes a long way to establish a prima facie case for the applicant, because the law itself endows such statistics with power. Under a generalized mandate, the case could only be made in terms of the fundamental rationale and objectives of the Act.

Planning and Local Participation

The attempt to foster local economic development inevitably calls for a certain amount of planning. Although defining planning in a universally acceptable fashion might be difficult, if not impossible, its basic ingredients are readily identified. Planning involves a process of measuring and metering local economic performance, articulating a strategy for improving that performance, and pinpointing the investments and related activities by which the strategy can be implemented over time. In greater detail, planning involves the identification of financial and related resources and the sequencing and phasing of activities.

Congress, in its wisdom, recognized the need for planning in a local economic development program. In fact, the current legislation puts even more emphasis on planning than the earlier legislation. This is manifested in extremely generous authorizations of funds to support planning in various ways. Regional commissions, district commissions, and even local area development groups can receive federal funds in direct support of their own planning staffs and for studies procured from private contractors. The Economic Development Administration itself is amply funded to carry on an extensive research program in-house and through grants and contracts with private organizations. The budget also calls for a large staff to work with the various area and regional groups in the field.

In the absence of any further complications, all these resources and more could be productively engaged in improving the science and the art of local economic development planning. The legislation is, after all, only a hypothesis in the present state of our knowledge. It is entirely appropriate, indeed essential, that an Act of Congress such as this should not only divert resources to finance projects but should also divert skilled manpower to develop the tools to improve the program as time goes on.

Unfortunately, there are serious obstacles to the successful transformation of resources into concrete progress. The recognition of planning as an indispensable element in the program is mixed in with the requirement for local responsibility in the preparation of plans. The legislation requires the formation of a local organization which adequately represents the interests of the area, and the preparation by that organization of an Overall Economic Development Plan (OEDP). When that plan is certified by the federal agency, the area becomes eligible for financial support for specific projects that are "consistent" with the plan.

These provisions of the legislation are extremely cumbersome to administer and greatly complicate the essential task of evolving and administering a sensible plan for an area. The legislation creates the pretense that planning is initiated in the area by representatives of the area and that the federal agency can and does protect the integrity of the plan. All of this confronts a typically unsophisticated view of planning at the local level, in which the OEDP is regarded as an arbitrary exercise required to establish eligibility for projects. The area in a hurry to qualify will "procure" an OEDP from an outside consultant that begins with a collection of published statistics and concludes with fairly standard but vague prescriptions for action. The document is typically faulty, to put it mildly, both as a diagnosis and as an action program.

Meanwhile, at the federal level, where hundreds of these documents have to be reviewed in a short period of time, it is difficult to maintain the pretense of a careful screening procedure that will weed out the good plans from the bad ones. The administrator is loath to withhold qualification from too many areas which are statistically eligible; he wants to initiate projects and get on with the program. Moreover, if he wishes to go ahead with a particularly attractive project, he is reluctant to get bogged down in upgrading the local OEDP. He therefore approves the project along with hundreds of others of very poor quality, thereby making a sham of the whole concept of planning.

Again, it is not difficult to identify the pressures and the considerations that give rise to such legislative provisions. First of all, an area might not take kindly to being designated as "depressed" by the federal government. The advantages of federal assistance might, in the minds of its leaders, be offset by the adverse publicity of calling attention to its poor economic performance. So somehow the area must request designation, but it is not clear who should speak for the basic unit, the county, in these matters. At a later stage, when the county is designated, every municipality within the county is eligible for project support, and even a private business may apply for a loan. It is not surprising therefore that Congress chose to create a new mechanism to serve the needs of this program.

The emphasis on local organization also reflects the hypothesis that local initiative is a critical ingredient in the success of these programs. To rely on an existing unit of local government would deprive the community of a great opportunity to organize itself and go through the steps entailed in the preparation of an Overall Economic Development Program. Organization, per se, becomes a force to encourage economic development. Also, there is the concern for the poor, the unemployed, and the minority groups. The proper representation of these groups in the community's economic development effort could only be achieved within the framework of a new organization specifically designed for this purpose.

All things considered, one can sympathize with the desire of Congress to make local participation an integral part of the program, but the presumption of effective local planning is one that undermines the integrity of the whole program. Federal approval of local plans as a prerequisite for financial support is not an effective means of screening out bad projects. For understandable reasons the client is interested in obtaining assistance for specific projects, and the federal government ought not to pretend otherwise. The OEDP requirement should be abandoned, and the energy of the local area should be channeled into improving the quality of project applications. These should serve as inputs into a planning process to be conducted at the federal level, except when and where a complete integration of area and district, or area and region, is achieved. In these cases effective planning in district and regional commissions could be sought. The unique capacity of the man in the street for perceiving opportunities that may be unique should not be sacrificed, and administrators should be alert to capture those perceptions in fashioning a strategy for an area. However, given the complexities of the economic development process, it is a mistake to endow that capacity with the halo of "planning."

The Tools

In the final analysis the underlying philosophy of the legislation is best reflected in the tools that it places at the disposal of the administrator. Under ARA the emphasis was clearly on business capital; public capital could be subsidized only when there was an industry ready and waiting to locate in the area. Under APWA the emphasis was entirely on public capital, and the whole purpose of the program was to create jobs in the process of constructing the capital.

In the Economic Development Act, the short-term employment effects are of only marginal interest. Strictly speaking, a public capital project that has a very low labor input will not be adversely judged on that count alone. In this respect the goals are similar to those of ARA, but the subsidization of public capital emerges as the dominant strategy for achieving long-term economic development. No longer is a public works project necessarily related to a "bird in hand." Rather, the case to be made is that it will facilitate private development in a general sort of way. The business loan remains as a subsidiary tool to exploit specific opportunities for private investment.

The primary role of public capital is also reflected in the fact that areas of "substantial" unemployment, but not "persistent" unemployment (as defined above), do not qualify for business loans at all. Their eligibility is restricted to public works projects.

Business capital formation is subsidized by making available a long-term loan of 40 years at favorable rates of interest, to cover as much as 65 percent of the initial capital costs of a new facility or an expansion of an existing facility. A strict reading of the law would require evidence from the applicant that credit was not available through normal channels. The law also prohibits the extension of assistance if the applicant is relocating his plant from one area to another. Finally, the law specifies that the plant must be in an industry that does not already have unused efficient excess capacity, the latter being determined by the government.

The spirit of these provisions is compatible with the rationale described above. If the growth of region "A" is to be maximized at minimum cost in terms of the growth of all other regions, then the ideal "happening" is the creation of a new enterprise that might not otherwise exist in an industry which needs additional capacity. Unfortunately, these restrictions leave the administrator with a very feeble tool, especially if the national economy is not expanding vigorously. During most of the ARA period (1961-1965) the demand for loans did not exhaust the appropriation. When capital is readily available and business investment is generally depressed, it is not easy to find customers who can meet all the conditions set down in the law and who can be judged to be reasonable risks. This was the economic environment experienced by EDA during the mid-sixties.

The constraints on direct subsidies to private business to locate in depressed areas reflect again the half-hearted commitment of Congress to local economic development as a means of improving human welfare. In part, they too are a product of the American political process: to get enough votes from congressmen in healthy areas the medicine had to be diluted. The constraints also may reflect a fundamental failure to come to grips with the relationship between spatial distribution of economic activity and aggregate welfare. Congress, in fashioning the legislation, never thought that the interest of the growing areas, especially the large metropolitan areas with heavy inmigration from the rural areas, might be served by fostering the economic development of lagging areas.

As the summers became "hotter" and the financial crisis in our major cities deepened, the dialogue began to have a spatial dimension. The feeling grew that local development policy ought to be used as a more deliberate tool to change the flow of migration, as well as a means of relieving local economic distress. The urban areas of the North are now seen to have a stake in the economic stimulation of rural areas in Appalachia and the South. In these terms the business loan program as it is now constrained by law will hardly be adequate to the task.

The current legislation, however, emphasizes development of the infrastructure. The implicit rationale is that the capacity of an area to attract industry depends critically on the availability of public capital in the form of roads, water and sewer systems, and similar social overheads. In a healthy economic environment such facilities are financed by local revenues which flow from a robust private sector. In a depressed area difficulties develop in raising needed revenue locally; hence the need for federal grants and/or loans to cover a substantial proportion of the cost.

Probably no other question in this field has received more attention than this basic one of the relation between investment in public capital and development. A large fraction of EDA's research budget has been allocated to this problem. So far, it is hard to point to results that would help the administrator predict with confidence the developmental consequences of particular investments.

The problem is inherently difficult for the customary reasons. Many things are happening to affect the course of economic development in an area which is "open" with respect to the movement of goods, capital, and people. Despite our increasing sophistication in the application of statistical techniques to identify the influence of a particular variable in a multivariate system, it has not been possible to distill from the data a reliable estimate of the relation between infrastructure and development. It is not a simple matter to perceive the impact of a pebble thrown into a pool into which rocks are being thrown at the same time. Similarly, income and unemployment in particular areas are affected by the national rate of growth, shifts in technology and demand, and major governmental programs in other fields. Identifying the impact of a single investment *ex poste*, let alone *ex ante*, seems almost hopeless. Therefore, the economic development program tends to be evaluated in terms of the jobs created by business loans where at least a first-order approximation of impact is evident.

Yet, the uncertainty surrounding the impact of public investment projects could be reduced if the administrator were able to take greater initiative in planning for an area and in making investments toward fulfillment of a plan. The concentration and focus of his actions would enhance the objective as well as the subjective perceptions of impact. However, the Economic Development Act as it is now written, greatly inhibits the pursuit of this kind of strategy.

Technical assistance is the third tool authorized by the legislation—a mixed bag of supports to research and planning. Strictly speaking, no legal requirements for eligibility are needed as with public works and business loans. Here the legislation does give the administrator maximum latitude in the disbursement of funds, and it would be difficult to quarrel with the precise terms of the mandate. Nevertheless, the administrator is constrained in making efficient use of these resources in other ways.

For one thing, there is the inevitable pressure to respond to the demands of areas that are eligible for the grant and loan components of the program. A favorite form of technical assistance is the feasibility study to explore the economic potential of a project that will then be presented for financial support. Typically this results in a contract between an outside consulting firm and the government to perform a study on behalf of the area. Once again, a fragmentation of effort precludes a systematic accumulation of knowledge about the development process. The in-house staff of the agency has its hands full in processing applications and monitoring contracts, and there is little time or energy left to sift the reports and carefully glean whatever insight they might provide into the subject.

This brings us to the final point, which is the lack of adequately trained manpower within the agency to carry on a productive research program. As matters now stand, the only way to employ an experienced professional at competitive rates is to saddle him with heavy administrative duties so that he has little or no time to think. The alternative is to let him remain at his university or institute under a grant or contract, but this does not adequately meet the research needs of the agency. There is the inevitable gap: the insider who is less of a professional is often cowed by the superior outsider or deeply suspicious of his commitment to the agency's problems, a suspicion which is usually well grounded.

Administrators have reason to be suspicious of researchers, but they allay their anxieties in ways that are not conducive to productivity. Similarly, the fellow who is most patient with the delays and abuses of government does not necessarily produce the best results. The more effective alternative requires a more serious commitment to research within the agency so that contractor, in-house research staff, and "paper pushers"—are all geared to serving the objectives of the agency. If the administrator is concerned with the researcher's awareness of priorities, he should confront the researcher in precisely these terms.

Communication of research findings is a related problem that tends not to take care of itself. Reports come in, that have something meaningful to say to the decision maker, but they are not going to be read by him because he cannot find enough free time to read more than a few pages. Somebody on the research staff must make it his personal responsibility to communicate the findings—by memoranda, briefings, or other devices. Unless the agency is authorized to hire high-level professionals in research positions, little hope exists that these gaps can be successfully bridged.

Conclusion

Programs to stimulate local economic development have a definite place in an overall federal strategy to improve welfare, but it is clear that we do not yet know how to use federal dollars efficiently to promote local economic development. This would not be at all disturbing if the congressional mandate were such as to permit and even encourage a learning process. Unfortunately, aside from a generous appropriation for research, the legislation is so structured as to inhibit a cumulative process of policy formation and action.

WILLIAM ALONSO

Equity and Its Relation to Efficiency in Urbanization*

Introduction

The first part of this paper is a discussion of the goals of national policies for regional development, focusing primarily on the conceptual and operational difficulties of dealing with the goal of equity. The second part is a paradigm of the interplay between the goals of efficiency and equity in interregional migration. Many simplifications are made to highlight this interrelation, which has been the source of considerable confusion.

*The work reflected in this paper was done under a grant from the Economic Development Administration of the U.S. Department of Commerce.

National Goals for Regional Policy

National regional policy may respond to many goals. Most commonly, in addressing itself to the issues of urbanization and depressed areas, policy focuses on the goals of national economic growth and the regional distribution of income and unemployment. Recent academic literature has concentrated on these, usually under the names of efficiency and equity, but it must be recognized that several other goals for regional policy are commonly encountered. These include the occupation of territory for defense purposes,[1] the occupation of frontier regions to create national consciousness, identification, pride, and purpose,[2] and policies aimed at civil stability or political gain.[3] Related to this last, but ultimately distinct goal, are policies directed to supporting or weakening the solidarity of ethnic or cultural groups, usually but not always in response to the tension between the national interest in socio-cultural unity and the group's desire to maintain their solidarity and promote their interests as a group.[4] We shall return to this issue in the discussion of the concept of equity.

This paper is concerned solely with the relation of the goals of growth and income distribution, and attempts to clarify their interplay. Public debate and academic discourse have had a great deal of trouble dealing clearly with this interrelation. One often reads statements, for example, that population movements from rural areas to urban centers should be discouraged for two reasons: first, that urban centers are subject to diminishing returns as the result of congestion and other factors and that further movements of population to these centers are consequently inefficient. Second,

1. Instances of this are the policies of India with respect to its Chinese and Pakistani borders, Israel's settlement policy, Thailand's Northeast development efforts, and many well-known instances in the history of the United States.
2. Among the best known of these are the contemporary efforts of Brazil, Peru, and Venezuela to occupy and develop their interiors.
3. Perhaps the most interesting current instance of this is the common experience of most nations that have tried to use growth poles for regional development. Although the logic behind this strategy is the concentration of energy and investment, political pressures, usually associated with the territorial representation embodied in the legislative branch, lead almost invariably toward the proliferation of the centers.
4. Instances of this include the tragic experience of tribal conflict in African nations, the Iranian handling of the Kurdish question, and Spain's enduring separatist Basque and Catalonian movements. Needless to say, this issue in many different forms has become a central one in America's racial situation.

that cities are already rich and powerful, whereas the out-migration from the rural areas is draining the countryside of its best young people, thereby increasing the inequality among regions. Although both of these positions are often held simultaneously, though seldom stated with precision, a moment's thought will raise doubts as to whether both can be true at the same time. We shall see that although one statement does not necessarily contradict the other, both can be true only in unlikely circumstances.

The goal of *efficiency* is, most simply, a goal of national economic growth. It is commonly accepted both at the level of political statements and of technical analysis. Slight variations exist as to how to measure performance. The most easily understood and commonly used criterion is the rate of growth of the Gross National Product; more technical measurements use the sum of the discounted values of future levels of consumption. These distinctions, however, are not fundamental to the argument in these pages. The goal is generally understood and accepted, and specific statements are possible about performance which, in one form or another, are intelligible to most people and thus affect political decisions.

Equity does not enjoy such clarity. Public policy accepts the desirability of assisting the less fortunate, but there is no commonly accepted basis of conventional or scientific wisdom on which to base operational judgments of need or performance. It is extraordinary that there has been so little technical discussion of a concept so central to political economy. In ordinary usage, equity is the quality of being equal or fair. The idea, in some form, is at the root of the concept of social justice. But equity is not mere equality. "To each according to his needs" implies that these needs may differ. If a man has greater capacity for enjoyment than his brother, is it more equitable to give them both the same income or the same enjoyment? Our concept of what is fair is an evolving one, as we slowly forge an economic bill of rights consisting of guaranteed income, access to education, compensation to victims of discrimination, crime, sickness, and so on. Similarly, our idea of who is our brother is an evolving one. American democracy long considered the slave as a non-person. The contemporary Negro movement in this country demands parity with white America, not with Haiti or black Africa. Equity is intuitively accepted as a goal by people and governments, but it remains full of ambiguity and problems of meaning and technical measurement, especially in matters having to do with regional issues. Although the paradigm presented later in this paper will revert to simplifications, a brief discussion of some of the more technical issues may be useful.

The geographic scale of regional definition is crucial to the evaluation of inequality. It is well known that a fine-grained regionalization will result in higher measures of inequality than one that is coarse-grained. In other words, the same index of inequality for the United States computed by state will be lower than if computed by county because much of the intercounty variation (that is, inequality) is averaged out when the larger unit is used. The use of smaller and smaller regions is not the solution to this problem, for the logical result would be one-person regions, and the index would be for the nation and would not be a regional index. When a regional measure is used, it is because it is believed that there is a meaningful spatial association of the phenomenon. If there is no such association, or if the association is not meaningful for the purpose at hand, there is no particular sense in using a regional index.

In brief, a *regional* measure of inequality or of concentration depends on the variable of regional scale, and a meaningful measure should be based on divisions of the territory that reflect the spatial structure of the socioeconomic system.[5] Consider a possible case in which certain depressed regions can develop only by an internal specialization which increases the inequalities within the region. Then equalization of average incomes among regions could occur while inequality increased for the nation. National interest in equity might well accept this convergence in average incomes among regions in spite of the associated divergence of incomes within the region. This would be particularly plausible if increases in the intraregional inequality were the result of some of the people in the poor regions being better off without worsening the condition of others.

5. This problem has begun to receive some attention, particularly among geographers, in a slightly different formulation: that of spatial intercorrelation. It is the two-dimensional equivalent of the problem of serial correlation in time series. The use of smaller and smaller regions in computing the index runs into the problem of ignoring the tendency of a small area to be like its neighbors or, more technically, it ignores the problem of spatial autocorrelation. A recent illustration of this problem is found in Karl E. and Alma F. Taeuber, *Negroes in Cities* (Chicago: Aldine Publishing Co., 1965). The authors compute indices of segregation for American cities, using the city block as their unit. Indices of segregation are indices of inequality by another name. The deficiency of this procedure is that a city with many small Negro districts might receive the same index score as a city with one massive ghetto.

The use of relative numbers, such as rate of unemployment, as measures of equity leads to similar problems. Areas that are to receive aid frequently are identified by such criteria. But comparison of the average income of a high-income area (such as the New York metropolitan area) with that of a low-income area (such as one of the southern states) may hide the fact that there may be more poor people in the prosperous area than in the poor one.[6] This problem does not arise in the measurement of efficiency because in that case the performances of subdivisions of the national territory add up to national performance. In the case of equity, measurement is relational and therefore not additive in a straightforward sense, so that the measure will be extremely sensitive to the scale and manner of regionalization.

The definition of equality depends on the terms of reference. Thus, a low-income region may specialize in low-wage industries but have higher-than-average wages for those industries. Measured simply on the basis of per capita income, that region would appear disadvantaged. But if its industrial composition is taken into account, the opposite conclusion would follow. Comparative statements usually carry a heavy baggage of implicit assumptions as to the basis of comparison. The previous example pointed to the effects of composition, but similar problems arise in the definition or perception of the universe within which we make our comparisons. Thus, Appalachia appears to be a low-income region within the United States, but it would be a high-income region if it were considered within the context of the Western Hemisphere.

Indices of inequality, concentration, localization, and segregation are really the same indices by different names. There are surprisingly few techniques that have been used in the construction of these indices. Among the principal ones are the relative mean deviation, the standard deviation, the Lorenz and Gini indices, and, most recently, measures of entropy.[7] They all share the same underlying

6. An interesting treatment of this question is found in G. Davies, "Regional Underemployment, Labour Availability, and Redeployment," *Oxford Economic Papers* (March 1967).

7. See H. Theil, *Economics and Information Theory* (Amsterdam: North Holland Publishing Co., 1967). This work is of particular interest because it is based on information theory and therefore may be used to relate expectation explicitly to observed values. However, Theil limits himself to the mean as the *ex ante* expectation.

logic: an *ex ante* expectation is compared to the observed value for each unit, and the difference or ratio between expected and observed values by units is combined according to some formula. The literature has treated almost exclusively the choice among combinatorial formulae, and the expected value has been taken as a matter of course as the mean of the universe's distribution.[8] Very little theoretical work has been done on the setting of expected values, yet this is the key to the meaning of the index. The importance of how expectations are defined was shown in the example above of the low-income region with relatively high wages in its specific industries.

Because of spatial autocorrelation, the use of the national mean as the expected value in territorial or regional indices is not desirable in every case. It presumes that we make no use of information of regional location (or spatial association), and its use in geographic research is equivalent to ignoring the information of the sequence of observations in time series analysis. Use of the national mean is suitable for some purposes but deceptive for others. Techniques based on spatial association, such as potential mapping, map generalization, and geographic spectral analysis, hold great promise as alternative ways of generating sets of expected values for which useful statements can be made, which link explicitly the level of inequality with regional scale.

These techniques have a further interest. Generating an expectations surface by running some version of a two-dimensional moving average over the observed values provides a controllable regional scale (the range or some measure of dispersion of the weighting function used) without dividing the national territory into discrete regions. This feature is particularly attractive because a conventional division into discrete regions will suffer from a necessary arbitrariness in the setting of boundaries. Human interaction seldom respects hard boundaries, and inequality and concentration are usually studied as problems of lack of social or economic integration. These techniques are all based on some form of distance decay function that simulates the friction of space. When the rate of decay is nil, we say that distance plays no role. In this case, the

8. The Gini index proves to be very subtle, relating expected value not to the mean, as do the other measures, but rather to the weighted distribution of values in the rest of the universe as a probability function.

expected value by these techniques becomes the mean, which is therefore a limiting special case.

An interesting development is the increasing governmental practice of setting expectations on normative rather than statistical grounds. Thus, we have definitions of poverty based on society's notions of adequacy rather than measures of relative income in terms of the overall distribution of income. Needy regions are normally defined in terms of the proportion of their population below the poverty line. Such bench marks are necessarily arbitrary and often poorly constructed; still, measures of equity or inequity based on a concept of what ought to be have considerable appeal. Equity is the quality of being *equal* or *fair*. Measures based on statistical distributions describe what is and take equity to mean equality. Normative measures indicate how close we come to our concept of fairness, to what we expect of ourselves. However, once the expected values are set, the index measure is constructed in the usual way by relative deviations, and so on. Analysts have become sophisticated in dealing with the time dimension of efficiency measures by the use of discounting procedures. By comparison, equity is difficult enough to measure at one point in time, and few have ventured to consider intertemporal comparisons. How much inequality in the short run can be tolerated for greater equality in the long run?[9] The much-debated problem of trade-offs between efficiency and equity, and their reduction to a common metric which might enable us to combine them into a common measure, must await development of some theory to discount inequality streams.

So far, most of the discussion has dealt with the equity problem from the point of view of income inequality, and this is the common approach of economists. Politicians and others have usually spoken of the problem as if it had to do with high rates of unemployment. Recent work has shown that both are right: United States counties characterized by low income are not usually the same counties with

9. H. Peter Rydell, in the only treatment of this problem of which I am aware, suggests treating each component region as concerned exclusively with its own efficiency goal, and combining their discounted consumption levels into an equity index which would thus be interregional and intertemporal. It may be objected that this procedure does not take sufficient account of the perception of inequality at the time. Thus, two discounted income streams may be equal, but incomes in the two regions may be unequal at virtually all times and this may be perceived as inequality. Alternatively, the suggested procedure seems to depend on the starting date of the comparison. (See H. P. Rydell, "The Shape of Optimal Consumption Paths in a Two-Region, Single-Sector Economy," unpub. diss., University of Pennsylvania, 1966.)

high unemployment.[10] Yet both types of areas are troubled and are the proper objects of equity policy. Equality and inequality turn out to be multidimensional. We have only arbitrary ways of relating low income and high unemployment. Existing programs rely on rough-and-ready methods that consider low income and high unemployment as well as a third dimension, sustained outmigration to identify areas that are in need of aid. A single, theoretically sound criterion is nowhere in sight.

A fundamental problem remains untouched. From its foundations in the eighteenth-century rationalism of Locke and Bentham, economics views the world atomistically, as if the level of satisfaction of an individual related exclusively to his own well-being and was unaffected by the circumstances and companionship of his fellows. On the other hand, the discussion outside of technical journals frequently takes what may be termed an organic view of groups and regions. Some of this is clearly a semantic trap, which may be termed "the fallacy of place," whereby territories are personalized and endowed with feelings.[11] It is perfectly possible for the per capita income of a depressed region to decline, while all individuals become better off. It is only necessary that the region be subject to diminishing returns and that the high-income members leave for other regions where they receive even higher incomes. Since the region is, in a sense, overpopulated (diminishing returns), the departure of some raises the incomes of those who remain. Those who leave and those who stay are better off, but many will argue that the region has declined because its average income has dropped.[12]

10. *Area Welfare: Eligibility for Development Assistance,* report prepared for the Area Redevelopment Administration of the U.S. Department of Commerce (Cambridge, Mass.: Regional & Urban Planning Implementation, Inc., May, 1965), vol. I, chap. vii.

11. For an excellent discussion see L. Winnick, "Place Prosperity vs. People Prosperity: Welfare Considerations in the Geographic Redistribution of Economic Activity," in *Essays in Urban Land Economics,* (University of California at Los Angeles, Real Estate Research Program, 1966). The same issue is addressed in the U.S. Supreme Court ruling (in *Baker vs. Carr*) that "legislators represent people, not acres or trees. Legislators are elected by voters, not farms or cities or economic interests. . . . The weight of a citizen's vote cannot be made to depend on where he lives." Here the Court comes on the side of atomism, reflecting the eighteenth-century rationalism of the Constitution of the United States.

12. The most common forms of the geographic fallacy seem to relate to our urban problems. Simplified statements about the decline of our cities ignore the fact that populations move across municipal boundaries (suburbanize), and compare measurements that refer to constant areas to shifting populations. Conversely, many of the positive evaluations of earlier attempts at urban renewal were based on keeping the same geographic base, but ignoring the change of population in the cleared area.

The classic position of the economist is that this is an excellent development because everyone is better off. But, in a sense that I have never seen well articulated, many seem to feel that this represents a decline of *a people,* although, it may represent improved conditions for *persons.* Pride, self-image, a valued way of life, a sense of identity with a people or a cultural tradition, are reflected in this perception, which is opposed to the rationalism of economists.

This latter viewpoint assumes many guises: Limiting ourselves to the contemporary scene in the United States, we find expressions of it not only in the public discussion of depressed areas, but in some of the propositions of black power, in the cries of ethnic or cultural communities threatened by urban clearance, and in the language of those concerned with Indian reservations. Economics has had little to offer here.[13] Sociology may provide a more useful framework in terms of its classic distinction between organic and mechanistic solidarity (*Gesellschaft* and *Gemeinschaft*). The descendants of Adam Smith, dealing only with questions of a contract society, use conceptual instruments more suited to a modern, developed society and therefore miss some of the considerations that apply to the less developed societies that characterize many distressed areas.[14] In the economist's language, it might be said that the *Gemeinschaft* of a region or a people is a merit good, but this does not advance us a great deal.

Finally, any consideration that will help frame decisions that affect the lives of people must be intelligible to more than a small fraternity of experts. Since equity is relational, its definition and measurements are quite naturally abstruse. Statements about the

13. The proposition that the utility function of individuals can be made to include as independent variables the levels of consumption of others, weighted by the degree of concern of the individual for these others, does not seem to do justice to the question.

14. The concepts of B. Bellassa and J. R. P. Friedmann about economic integration are particularly relevant here (see B. Bellassa, *The Theory of Economic Integration* [New York: R. D. Irwin, 1961]; J. R. P. Friedmann, *Regional Development Policy* [Cambridge, Mass.) M. I. T. Press, 1966]). Lack of integration is an irrational immobility of factors in spatial or sectoral terms, judged by the standards of rationalism. To the extent that economic development may be viewed as the rationalization of production and consumption, it represents a shift from organic to mechanistic solidarity (from tradition to contract), and much of the problem of distinguishing between depressed areas and their populations may be viewed as a conflict between the two types of solidarity. Analysis and proposals framed entirely in terms of one or the other frame of reference will obviously be insufficient for consensus.

root-mean-square deviation or about the complement of entropy are unlikely to invite political support or to engage the hearts of men. There is a lesson to be learned from the effectiveness which the simplified measures of performance of the efficiency goal (principally, rate of growth of the economy) have had in mobilizing support for this objective. In spite of their statistical limitations, two measures of equity stand out as being understandable and therefore effective guides to political action. One is the use of normative bench marks discussed above: the number or proportion above or below some standard such as poverty level or unemployment rate. The other measure, the relative weighted mean deviation from the mean, is rarer, but very promising. In cases of unemployment, income, or racial distribution, it measures the number of workers, cents per dollar, or people in the population that would have to be moved in order to equalize conditions. Nontechnical persons can easily understand that, whereas some years ago we would have had to move X cents per dollar from the rich to the poor to equalize material welfare, we now have to move Y cents per dollar. To influence and inform policy, it is frequently important to present findings in measures that have vividness and intelligibility.

A Paradigm of Efficiency and Equity in the Migration to Cities

The interplay between considerations of efficiency and equity is fairly simple if considered systematically. Yet there is enough complexity to give rise to considerable confusion, and at times equivocation, among scholars and national and international agencies. The reasons for this confusion seem to be twofold. On the one hand, where a particular policy favors one goal over the other, its advocates are tempted, in seeking support, to represent it as serving both. On the other hand, the semantic shorthand by which we use the name of some piece of territory to speak of a population has led to untold confusion because people can move, whereas real estate cannot. We have referred to this under the label of the fallacy of place. It must be admitted, however, that the following attempt at clarification ignores many of the considerations raised in the preceding pages.

We shall conceive of a simplified country composed of two realms,

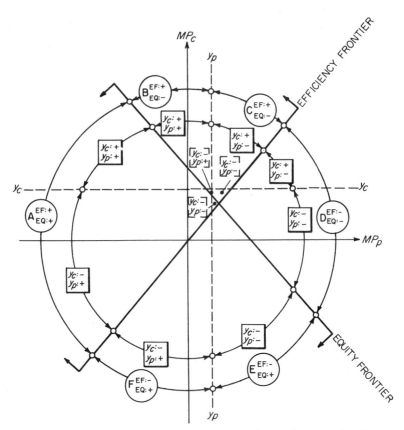

Figure 1. Effects of a migrant's moving from the rural area to the city.

$+$ = increase	EF = efficiency goal performance
$-$ = decrease	EQ = equity goal performance
MP_c = marginal urban product	y_c = mean urban income
MP_p = marginal rural product	y_p = mean rural income

one advanced and prosperous, the other depressed and backward.[15] We pose the question of a national government that is evaluating, from the point of view of its goals of efficiency and equity, a possible move by a worker from a poorer area (periphery) to a city (center). To keep matters simple, we ignore movements of capital and, for the time being, we do not distinguish among types of migrants.

Figure 1 embodies the core of the argument. On the vertical axis

15. On this we follow many precedents, notably A. Hirschman's distinction between North and South (*Strategy of Economic Development* [New Haven: Yale University Press, 1958]) and J. Friedmann's center and periphery (*op. cit.*), whose terminology we borrow.

we measure the marginal product of labor in the city, MP_c, and on the horizontal axis we measure the marginal product of labor in the periphery, MP_p.[16] We extend both axes beyond the zero point to admit negative values. A point on the graph represents the objective consequences of the movement of an individual in terms of marginal product, and the national government may evaluate the consequences in terms of its objectives. Clearly, if the marginal product of a worker is greater in the center than in the periphery, the contemplated migration will increase national product and serve the goal of efficiency. We can therefore draw a 45-degree line sloping upward through the origin, which we call an *efficiency frontier,* such that any point above the line represents circumstances where the efficiency goal would be served by the move. This obtains even in the negative quadrant. As sometimes happens in developing countries under conditions of labor surplus both in the center and the periphery, surplus workers may have a negative effect on product both in the city and in the countryside, and the national goal of efficiency would best be served by the worker being in the region where his or her presence does the least harm.

Also on Figure 1 are plotted dashed lines y_c and y_p, which represent the per capita incomes[17] in the center and the periphery, respectively, before the move. It will be noted that in the illustration, urban per capita income, y_c, is greater than rural per capita income, y_p, as is true in all countries that I know of. If the point that represents the marginal product contribution of the worker is above the y_c line, marginal urban product is greater than per capita urban income (a condition of increasing returns to scale for the city), and the move will result in a rise in per capita urban income.[18] Similarly, if the point is to the right of y_p, the periphery also enjoys increasing returns to scale, and the departure of the individual will lower rural

16. Marginal product may be thought of as increases of value added in a region or changes in the contribution to regional product from a marginal change in labor force at that location. It should be stressed that this does not necessarily mean that this marginal product is equivalent to the wages of the marginal worker. Even should institutional conditions result in wages being equal to marginal product within the firm, the contribution to regional product takes into account the net effect of external economies and diseconomies of the increase in population, many of which do not enter into the internal calculations of the firm.

17. For verbal simplicity, we shall equate regional per capita product with regional per capita income, and use the words "product" and "income" interchangeably.

18. We are assuming, of course, that there are no transfer payments among regions.

per capita income. In such a case it is obvious that the equity goal will not be served, because the rich region becomes richer and the poor, poorer.

At this point we can reduce the laborious analysis by plotting an *equity frontier*, a line to one side of which the equity goal is served, and to the other side of which it is not. The line has been calculated on the "cents per dollar to be moved" criterion of equity,[19] and takes into account the shift of population. Most alternative definitions of equity will also yield a straight line, differing slightly in slope, and passing through the intersection of the y_c and y_p lines or just under it. Figure 2 shows the equity frontier for five alternative definitions.[20] In all cases, if the point that represents the marginal product of the individual at both locations is below the equity frontier, the move will increase equity. The argument that follows is not affected by the measure of equity which may be chosen.

The equity and efficiency frontiers on Figure 1, together with the lines y_c and y_p, define a number of sectors and subsectors. Each sector has been labeled by a letter, A through F, and in each sector it is shown whether efficiency and equity are increasing or decreasing. In addition, for each of the subsectors we have indicated in small rectangular boxes the direction of change of the per capita incomes.

Sector A represents a condition in which the move would improve both equity and efficiency, and there can be no doubt that the move is desirable. The upper subsector corresponds to a situation in which the urban realm enjoys increasing returns to scale, so that further increases of urban population result in higher levels of welfare in the cities. This implies that the economies of agglomeration exceed the diseconomies. On the other hand, this subsector corresponds to a condition of rural overpopulation (as, for instance, those regions undergoing rationalization of agricultural production or rapid rates

19. The equation for the constant relative deviation is:

$$MP_p = \frac{(p_p y_p + p_c y_c)^2 - MP_c[p_p y_p(p_p + p_c) + p_p y_p + p_c y_c]}{p_p y_p(p_p + p_c) - p_p y_p - p_c y_c},$$

where the notation is as in the diagram, and p_c and p_p are the populations of the center and the periphery, respectively, before the move.

20. It will be noted that the three absolute measures of difference, A, B, and C, share the same inclination, while the relative measures, D and E, have a slightly different one. This is an indication of the structural similarity of the relative mean deviation to the ratio of per capita income, which is, of course, a highly intelligible measure but is limited to the comparison of pairs of regions. The "cents per dollar to be moved" measure can be used for any number of regions.

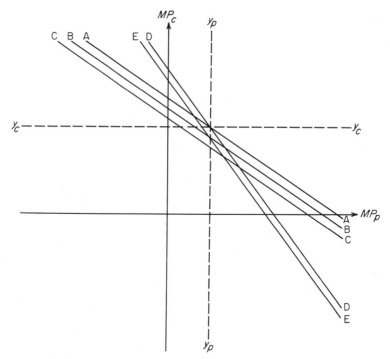

Figure 2. Five equity frontiers.
A. Constant difference in per capita regional products
B. Constant standard deviation in per capita regional products
C. Constant dollars to be moved to equalize per capita incomes
D. Constant ratio of per capita incomes
E. Constant relative deviation (cents per dollar of GNP to be moved
   to equalize per capita incomes)

of natural population growth). Those who argue that people should be moved to jobs imply the situation in the United States may be depicted as being in this sector. The lower subsector corresponds to a case of declining returns to labor in the city, resulting in a drop in average urban income, and of even greater overpopulation in the countryside. In other words, the upper subsector depicts situations in which migration from the countryside to the city has a very positive consequence, whereas the lower subsector permits only making the best of a bad situation. Unfortunately, the conditions portrayed by the lower subsector are all too imaginable where economic development is flagging.

Just to the right of the y_p line there is a small subsector of A that is of some interest. The average incomes of both city and periphery drop, but total average income for the nation increases, and the goal of equity as well as that of efficiency is served. This represents a circumstance in which the returns to labor in the city are decreasing while those to rural labor are increasing, but where the returns to urban labor are still larger than those to rural labor. Still, in a sense it is surprising that the efficiency goal should be served when the mean incomes in both regions are dropping. This is the result of the shift of population from the poorer to the richer region. In general, as can be seen from the diagram, this apparent paradox will occur in other cases where marginal product is very near to average product, that is, where both regions are close to constant returns to scale.

Sector D is close to being symmetrically opposed to sector A. Throughout sector D, marginal returns to labor are higher in the periphery than at the center, and therefore efficiency is served by not moving. Similarly, through this sector the move would also reduce national equity. In the upper subsector of D, city incomes would go up and rural incomes would go down. Both the city and periphery can use more labor, but there is a higher marginal return to rural manpower. In the lower subsector of D, the city is too big, in the sense of diminishing returns (and at the very bottom of the subsector, below the *MP* axis, too big in the sense of an absolute decline in urban product), while the rural sector still enjoys increasing returns. The frequent assertions that urban-to-rural migration is inefficient and leads to greater inequality can be true only if national circumstances are represented by a point in this sector. These circumstances may be typified as (1) rural production would increase more than proportionately with increases in population, and (2) urban returns to population growth are lower than rural returns. The first proposition would be true only in rare cases. If, as frequently happens, a nation finds itself in sector D, it might try to encourage migration from the cities to the rural areas. Worldwide experience shows, however, that it is difficult to move people back to rural areas once they are in the cities.

Sector C and F represent circumstances of genuine conflict between the two goals. If the nation finds itself in sector C, migration will increase the national product but will also increase inequality. Over the upper part of the subsector, both city and countryside are characterized by increasing returns to labor, but marginal product is greater in the city. In the lower part of sector C there is a small area containing the apparent paradox of a drop in the per capita income in both regions, but a rise in national per capita income. The explanation of the paradox has already been mentioned. Sector F is an unfortunate situation for a nation. It is overpopulated, both city and countryside have declining returns, and over most of the sector (to the left of MP_c) additional workers reduce production. In this plight the most efficient solution results in an increase of inequality, and there is genuine conflict between the two goals. The choice in both sectors C and F must be made by whatever political processes are available.

Sectors B and E are perhaps the most interesting. Sector B appears to satisfy the efficiency criterion, but to deny that of equity. On closer examination it proves to be a Pareto optimum. Efficiency is served, of course, and though equity is not, everyone is better off than before. This is not a quirk of the particular index used, but common to all measures of equity. In practice it represents a situation, met fairly frequently, of surplus labor in the periphery and increasing returns to the urban realms. If the national policy permits or encourages migration, incomes in the cities and the rural areas rise. However, the growth in per capita income is faster in the city, and inequality increases. The opposite policy adopted—that of restricting migration—makes the regions more equal but national income grows more slowly, and the per capita incomes in the rural region are lower (as is the per capita income in the urban region) than if migration were permitted. This situation described by Sector B may arise if dynamic manufacturing and service sectors in the cities result in increasing returns to scale and if structural transformations in the rural primary sector produce a labor surplus. The best-documented case of this condition is that of southern Italy, where early policy called for an equalization of incomes between North and South, but where experience prevailed in setting the more modest objective of raising southern incomes while recognizing that northern incomes might rise faster.[21]

Sector E, by contrast, might be called an invidious Pareto situa-

21. A particularly clear account of this shift in objectives is found in H. Chenery, "Development Policies for Southern Italy," *Quarterly Journal of Economics* (November 1962). Of course, in the reality of the Italian case, many other factors were operating, such as the movement of capital, skilled labor, and entrepeneurship. Nonetheless, the basic shift resulted from the realization that a Pareto optimum might be possible which violated the *prima facie* concept of equality.

tion. Although contemplated migration might serve the goal of equity at the expense of efficiency, everyone would in fact be worse off after the move since the per capita income in both regions would be lower. It would take a rather bitter concern for formal equity to insist on migration under these circumstances. If migration from the city to the countryside were possible, it would result in an increase in efficiency, and, whereas everyone would be better off, formal inequality would increase. It must be noted that the conditions for this dilemma are that marginal returns to labor be very high in the rural areas and very low in the cities.

Throughout this analysis we have considered the migration of a worker as if all workers were alike. However, it is clear, that in any nation, people with different skills and attitudes will place differently in the diagram. For instance, a very good farmer might place in the right side of the diagram, and if he were unable to adapt to city life, in the lower right. A skilled machinist might place in the upper part of the diagram. A poet, a physicist, a laborer, an accountant, a shaman, would each place differently. Similarly, the consequences of an individual's move are not likely to be so certain that they can be represented by a point. Rather, the diversity of individuals, even within a class, and the uncertainty of prediction would require that the conclusions be stated in probabilistic terms, especially if the area fell into more than one sector.

Where do We Stand? Consequences For Policy

The paradigm presented in these pages is only a systematic classification for evaluating the consequences of the act of migration with respect to the goals of efficiency and equity. The remaining question is the important one, and it is one of fact: Where is the United States located on the diagram? It is remarkable that there is so little practical knowledge about the marginal product of populations in various regions, considering the importance of this issue and the radical policies (usually opposed to urbanization) advocated in Western Europe, socialist countries, and in developing nations. Rather, it would seem that the flood of pronouncements on this issue by politicians, economists, aesthetes, and assorted urbanologists has created a sort of self-reinforcing conventional wisdom supported primarily by a well-polished rhetoric that has discouraged not only empirical inquiry but even the examination of its logical basis. Without knowing (or asking) whether the urban or rural realm is subject to increasing or decreasing returns, most countries have adopted at least the rhetoric associated with policies of decentralization and the advancement of backward regions. The necessary factual assumption is that cities are inefficient (diminishing returns), and that there are many unexploited opportunities in the periphery (increasing returns), placing them in sector E or in the lower part of sector D. A conscientious search of the literature reveals no persuasive empirical evidence for this opinion.

This is not the place to review the limited evidence which exists. On the marginal products of different areas, it may be expected that circumstances will differ from country to country and from period to period. This should not be interpreted as a plea that no policy be adopted while years are spent on research which may prove inconclusive. Rather, we should get on with research while framing our policies more consistently with current estimates of economic reality.

GERALD KRAFT, ALAN R. WILLENS, JOHN B. KALER, AND
JOHN R. MEYER

On the Definition of a Depressed Area*

Introduction

At the very heart of any program for the economic development
or rehabilitation of an area must be some process by which such
areas are selected. This study, in very broad outline, is an effort to
improve the selection criteria by attempting to specify more rigorously the welfare implications of different selection procedures and
to analyze the qualitative characteristics of the quantitative or
empirical data on which such selection procedures almost invariably
must be based.

Broadly speaking, the problems of area designation can be classified under two major headings: (1) determining the welfare criteria
or objectives implicit or explicit in the legislation establishing a

*This paper is largely adapted from *Area Welfare–Eligibility for Development
Assistance,* a study performed by the authors for Regional and Urban Planning Im-
plementation, Inc., for the Area Redevelopment Administration, U.S. Department of
Commerce.

redevelopment effort; and (2) attempting to specify these welfare criteria in an empirical way, that is, in terms of actually observable and available quantitative measures. For the purposes of this study it is accepted that both unemployment and low-income status are usually intended as criteria to be taken into consideration when designating areas for redevelopment. It is not so obvious, however, what relative weights are to be attached to these two different criteria when, as is often the case, they do not occur simultaneously or neatly paired by conventional rankings.

It is reasonably easy, in fact, to demonstrate that a high unemployment rate in an area is not invariably associated with the more common manifestations or measures of low-income status.[1] Furthermore, the persistency of low-income or unemployment status by areas seem to be rather different; specifically, low income seems to be a considerably more persistent phenomenon in a particular area than high unemployment rates. As persistence of low-income or unemployment status by geographic areas must underlie any sensible rationalization of area redevelopment as a public policy, these observed differences in the persistency characteristics of low income and unemployment have important policy implications.

The data available for measuring low-income and unemployment status on an areal basis are somewhat less than those optimally desirable for policy decisions. Such a comment, of course, can almost invariably be made of almost any economic data or measures. Still, the discrepancy between what is available and what would be optimally desirable for implementing or designing an area redevelopment program is almost notorious. In broad characterization, the area unemployment data are more available on a time series basis than the income data but are of inferior quality. Specifically, the area income data are of reasonably good quality but are available only once every 10 years. The unemployment data, by contrast, seems to be internally inconsistent (and also inconsistent with alternative measures of corresponding phenomena)

1. Unemployment seems to be a phenomenon mainly associated with areas in which the extractive industries have played a prominent role (including forestry as an extractive industry). Moreover, there seems to be little distinction to be made between the different types of extractive industries: coal, iron, forestry and hard-rock mining all have been well represented in the areas of major unemployment. Low-income status, on the other hand, seems to be primarily concentrated in the northern counties of the southeastern states. The only important overlap between low-income and high-unemployment areas occurs in Kentucky and Tennessee.

but have the advantage of being available in varying degrees on an annual or even a monthly basis. It is worth emphasizing again that, to the extent that an area redevelopment program is intended primarily to deal with persistent, localized economic problems, the fact that the unemployment data are available more frequently should not necessarily be an important consideration.

The Classification Problem

The basic problem of area classification can be described as follows: for each area a set of n measured characteristics $(x_1, \ldots, x_n)$ are available. In the legislation establishing redevelopment programs, areas or groups of areas are referred to as *eligible* or as *ineligible*. Assume that if an area belongs with the group of areas eligible for assistance, the joint probability density of the observed x's is $p\,(x_1, x_2, \ldots, x_n|\text{E})$. On the other hand, if the area does not belong to the eligible group (i.e. hopefully belongs to the economically healthy group) the density is $p(x_1, x_2, \ldots, x_n|\text{H})$.[2]

Assume further that the fraction of all areas that are, in fact, eligible is q_E and those not eligible is q_H [equals $(1 - q_\text{E})$]. This assumption is not critical and could be made on the basis of policy considerations, such as a desire to help the poorest third of the areas in the country, i.e., $q_\text{E} = 1/3$.

The decision process we wish to apply is one that will minimize the cost of errors. For example, there is a cost associated with classifying an area as eligible when, in fact, it is not. The cost consists in reducing available funds to assist truly needy areas and perhaps a reduction in total benefits derived from the financial or other assistance provided. Similarly, there is a cost associated with classifying an area as healthy, when it is truly eligible for aid. In this case no assistance is provided to the area, and any benefits that might arise from assistance will be lost; furthermore, the particular economic situation of the area may become progressively worse, requiring substantially more assistance at a later time when the area becomes more obviously eligible.[3]

2. The specific form of these density functions and their parameters are unimportant at this stage. We can derive a general result independently of these specifications.

3. One may wish to offset these costs of misclassification with benefits of proper classification—for example, the benefit achieved by properly classifying an area that is, in fact, eligible; the same methodology can be applied with only a slight increase in complexity, but the derivation here will not consider these offsets.

Let the cost of classifying an area as eligible when it is, in fact, healthy be $C(E|H)$, and let the cost of classifying an area as healthy when it should, in fact, be eligible as $C(H|E)$. These costs, in general, may depend on characteristics of the area in question, such as its size or industrial base; however, for purposes of this analysis we assume that the costs are the same for all areas.

We wish to find a classification procedure that minimizes the expected loss from costs of misclassification decisions.[4] In other words, we wish to divide all possible sets of characteristics $x_1, \ldots, x_n$ into two mutually exclusive regions or subspaces, R_E and R_H. R_E will designate the subspace of areas that have a set of characteristics falling in the class designated as eligible and R_H will designate the subspace of areas regarded as healthy.

Let $X = (x_1, \ldots, x_n)$ and $dX = (dx_1, dx_2, \ldots, dx_n)$; then following probabilities may be defined:

1. the probability of *correctly* classifying an area as belonging to the population of eligible areas is

$$P(E|E) = \int_{R_E} p(X|E)dX;$$

2. the probability of misclassification of an area that belongs to the population of eligible areas as healthy is

$$P(H|E) = \int_{R_H} p(X|E)dX;$$

3. the probability of *correctly* classifying an area as belonging to the population of healthy areas is

$$P(H|H) = \int_{R_H} p(X|H)dX;$$

and finally,

4. the probability of misclassification of an area that belongs to the population of healthy areas as eligible is

$$P(E|H) = \int_{R_E} p(X|H)dX.$$

Since the probability that an area selected at random belongs to the eligible population is q_E, the probability of selecting an area from the eligible population and correctly classifying it is $q_E P(E|E)$; and the probability of selecting an area from the eligible population

4. Other objective functions could be used, but this one is relatively simple in concept and, in particular, is tractable.

and misclassifying it is $q_E P(H|E)$. Similar probabilities for selecting an area from the ineligible group and classifying it correctly or misclassifying it are $q_H P(H|H)$ and $q_H P(E|H)$, respectively.

The expected loss from cost of misclassification, L, is then the sum of the individual costs of misclassification weighted by their appropriate probabilities:

$$L = C(H|E)P(H|E)q_E + C(E|H)P(E|H)q_H.$$

The problem is to find regions, R_E and R_H, that minimize L. We have:

$$L = C(H|E)q_E \int_{R_H} p(X|E)dX + C(E|H)q_H \int_{R_E} p(X|H)dX. \qquad (1)$$

Since the regions R_E and R_H exhaust the space and the integral of a probability density over the entire space is unity, equation (1) can be written:

$$L = C(H|E)q_E \left[1 - \int_{R_E} p(X|E)dX \right] + C(E|H)q_H \int_{R_E} p(X|H)dX$$
$$= \int_{R_E} \left[C(E|H)q_H p(X|H) - C(H|E)q_E p(X|E) \right] dX + C(H|E)q_E. \qquad (2)$$

In equation (2), the second term, $C(H|E)q_E$, is a constant. Consideration of the first term indicates that L will be minimized if we select, for region R_E, those X's for which the term in brackets is negative or zero. In other words, an area having property X belongs to the set of eligible areas, $X \epsilon R_E$ if:

$$C(E|H)q_H p(X|H) - C(H|E)q_E p(X|E) \leq 0. \qquad (3)$$

The criterion for classifying an area having characteristics $X = (x_1, x_2, \ldots, x_n)$ can then be rewritten using inequality (3) as $X \epsilon R_E$ if

$$\frac{p(X|H)}{p(X|E)} \leq \frac{C(H|E)q_E}{C(E|H)q_H} = k. \qquad (4)$$

A similar derivation can be used to find the criterion for the ineligible region; however, considering that the entire region is divided into only two subregions, it is obvious that the criterion for the ineligible region is obtained from inequality (4) by changing the direction of the inequality $X \epsilon R_H$ if

$$\frac{p(X|H)}{p(X|E)} > \frac{C(H|E)q_E}{C(E|H)q_H} = k. \qquad (5)$$

The criteria for classification thus far developed are independent of the form of $p(X|H)$ or $p(X|E)$. By assuming specific forms for these probability density functions, an explicit criterion or discriminant function can be derived. For this purpose we have assumed a multivariate normal distribution because of its relative tractability in the analysis and because of its widespread use in problems of this sort.[5] In addition, it was assumed that the two normal distributions, for the two groups, had equal covariance matrices.[6]

Under the assumptions of normality and equal covariance matrices, we may construct an explicit discriminant function. Let

$\mu^{(E)} = [\mu_1^{(E)}, \mu_2^{(E)}, \ldots \mu_n^{(E)}]$ be the vector of population means for the eligible areas;

$\mu^{(H)} =$ the vector of population means for the ineligible areas; and

$\Sigma =$ the matrix of variances and covariances for each population.

Then, assuming normality,

$$p(X|E) = \frac{1}{(2\pi)^{n/2}|\Sigma|^{1/2}} \exp\left[-\frac{1}{2}(X - \mu^{(E)})'\Sigma^{-1}(X - \mu^{(E)})\right]. \quad (6)$$

and

$$p(X|H) = \frac{1}{(2\pi)^{n/2}|\Sigma|^{1/2}} \exp\left[-\frac{1}{2}(X - \mu^{(H)})'\Sigma^{-1}(X - \mu^{(H)})\right]. \quad (7)$$

The criteria for designation of an area as eligible can then be written—from inequality (4)—as $X\epsilon R_E$ if

5. With respect to the types of variables actually used in our analysis, such as the percent of children of age 14-17 in school, the data do not exactly fit a normal distribution. The possible range of variation in the percent of 14–17-year-olds in school, for example, is between zero and 100 percent, a finite range, while the multivariate normal distribution has an infinite range at both ends of the distribution. Other characteristics have subtler problems in that the distributions may be skewed to the left or to the right. While these particular problems can often be corrected by transforming the measurement of the characteristic, other problems arise in their interpretation. Although the true distributions are not exactly normal, they do not seem to represent such a serious departure from normality that the results would be impaired.

6. While it would be possible to relax this assumption and still develop a method of classifying areas as to their eligibility, the techniques would be more difficult to apply and the previous theoretical work performed with respect to the normal distribution would be of little value. Furthermore, application of results when this assumption is relaxed, would require much more difficult mathematical manipulations than are required when the equal covariance matrices are assumed.

$$\frac{p(X|H)}{p(X|E)} = \exp\left\{-\frac{1}{2}\left[(X-\mu^{(H)})'\Sigma^{-1}(X-\mu^{(H)})\right.\right.$$
$$\left.\left.-(X-\mu^{(E)})'\Sigma^{-1}(X-\mu^{(E)})\right]\right\} \leq k. \quad (8)$$

We can take the natural logarithm of each side to obtain $X\epsilon R_E$ if

$$\left[-\tfrac{1}{2}(X-\mu^{(H)})'\Sigma^{-1}(X-\mu^{(H)})\right.$$
$$\left.+\tfrac{1}{2}(X-\mu^{(E)})'\Sigma^{-1}(X-\mu^{(E)})\right] \leq \ln k. \quad (9)$$

Inequality (9) can then be expanded and simplified with considerable manipulation to obtain the relationship $X\epsilon R_E$ if

$$[X'\Sigma^{-1}(\mu^{(H)}-\mu^{(E)})-\tfrac{1}{2}(\mu^{(H)}+\mu^{(E)})'\Sigma^{-1}(\mu^{(H)}-\mu^{(E)})] \leq \ln k. \quad (10)$$

The first term on the left is the ordinary discriminant function; the second term is a constant. If we use expressions (4), (5) and (10) the criteria for classification for this case can be stated: $X\epsilon R_E$ if

$$X'\Sigma^{-1}(\mu^{(H)}-\mu^{(E)}) \leq \ln k + \tfrac{1}{2}(\mu^{(H)}+\mu^{(E)})'\Sigma^{-1}(\mu^{(H)}-\mu^{(E)}),$$

and $X\epsilon R_H$ if

$$X'\Sigma^{-1}(\mu^{(H)}-\mu^{(E)}) > \ln k + \tfrac{1}{2}(\mu^{(H)}+\mu^{(E)})'\Sigma^{-1}(\mu^{(H)}-\mu^{(E)}).$$

In summary, we have described the classification problem as a problem to minimize the expected loss from costs of misclassification. For the special case when the probability densities of the two populations are multivariate normal with equal covariance matrices, the criteria can be simplified to obtain a relatively simple function, i.e., the discriminant function:

$$X'\Sigma^{-1}(\mu^{(H)}-\mu^{(E)})$$

and a critical value:

$$\ln\left[\frac{C(H|E)q_E}{C(E|H)q_H}\right] + \frac{1}{2}(\mu^{(H)}+\mu^{(E)})'\Sigma^{-1}(\mu^{(H)}-\mu^{(E)}).$$

As can be seen, the critical value is independent of the values of the variable, X. Furthermore, the critical value is a monotonic function of the cost ratio and of the ratio of probabilities. Because the test for classification is an inequality—that is, R_E is made up of those observations to the left of the critical value and R_H is made up of observations to the right—it is easily seen that the values of the discriminant function can be ordered in terms of likeness to the population of eligible areas. The ability to order areas is an essential result of the discriminant analysis. The particular values selected for the costs of misclassification and for the prior probabilities are not important if we are only concerned with ranking areas.

Samples and Variables

To implement the discriminant analyses just outlined, three initial tasks were performed:

1. Sets of areas to be analyzed were selected representing contrasting conditions of economic welfare. For example, areas of highest rates of unemployment were contrasted with areas of lowest rates of unemployment.

2. A set of variables was selected that was likely to explain or be related to these contrasting economic conditions.

3. The contrasting sets of areas and explanatory variables were analyzed to determine which explanatory variables best accounted for area welfare.

The complexity of the phenomena dictated a rather large list of explanatory variables. Furthermore, consideration of the two characteristics, income and unemployment, and the ways in which they are measured and reported, indicated that it would be desirable to consider a variety of welfare measures in the initial analyses.

Income and unemployment are, of course, logically linked: employment is a principal mode of acquiring income. The linkages, though, are not simple or obvious. This is particularly true in view of the fact that unemployment is a complicated phenomenon in its relationship to the population and the labor force. Factors such as disguised unemployment and underemployment further complicate the situation. Income differences among areas of high unemployment, therefore, may be best explained by one set of explanatory variables, and income differences among areas of low unemployment by another set. Further, even if income differences in the two types of areas are explained by the same set of variables, the variables may have different levels of relative importance in the two cases.

As noted previously, there is little dispute regarding the welfare significance of income and unemployment. Thus it is generally agreed that, in two otherwise similar areas, the one suffering the higher unemployment rate is *prima facie* in a less desirable welfare condition. The same applies to income.

There are, however, different ways of measuring income and different ways of measuring unemployment. It may be puzzling to decide which of two areas is in the poorer welfare condition, for example, when one of the areas has a higher percentage of low-income families but a higher median income. Hence, the choice of any particular measure for each of these welfare characteristics appears to be somewhat arbitrary. For the discriminant analyses, three representations of area income were used: (1) percent of families with income under $2000; (2) number of families with income under $2000; and (3) median family income. Two representations of unemployment were used: (1) percent unemployed; and (2) number unemployed. The data were taken from the 1960 Census of Population for the over three thousand counties in the United States. The county was used as the basic unit of observation because designation as a depressed area has generally been done by county or a group of counties in the United States.[7]

7. It was our objective in creating the master data file to produce a complete record with a uniform set of selected variables for every county in the United States. However, complete lagged data (1950 and earlier) were not available for the states of Alaska and Hawaii. Therefore, all state and county data relating to these states were deleted from the master data file. Similarly, there are three county-like records in the *1962 County–City Data Book* relating to the parts of Yellowstone National Park that lie in Idaho, Montana, and Wyoming. As these counties are nearly empty of permanent residents and industry, and are unlike counties in most other respects, they were also deleted from the master data file. In the same vein, three areas that existed as counties in 1950 were consolidated into other political units between 1950 and 1960. In these cases, the 1950 data were consolidated to correspond with the 1960 definitions. Finally, five new independent cities were created in Virginia between 1950 and 1960 by separating parts of six counties. In these cases, the 1960 data for the independent cities involved were recombined with data for the counties from which they had been separated, resulting in the deletion of five independent cities from the master file. The "complete" U.S. data file thus included 3097 counties, derived as follows:

Total U.S. counties per *County and City Data Book, 1962*		3137
Plus:		
District of Columbia, treated as a county		1
		3138
Less:		
Alaska (including 4 Judicial Divisions)	28	
Hawaii	5	
Yellowstone National Park Counties	3	
New Virginia Counties	5	41
		3097

Table 1. Two-Way Joint Membership of 300 Most Distressed Counties

	300 counties with:					
	Highest percent unemployed	Highest number unemployed	Highest percent of families with income under $2,000	Lowest median income	Highest number of families with income under $2,000	300 most populous areas
300 COUNTIES WITH:						
Highest percent unemployed	300	33	33	32	30	13
Highest number unemployed	33	300	0	0	211	255
Highest percent of families with income under $2,000	33	0	300	291	22	0
Lowest median income	32	0	291	300	20	0
Highest number of families with income under $2,000	30	211	22	20	300	213
300 most populous areas	13	255	0	0	213	300

Source: *Census of Population, 1960*, U.S. Department of Commerce, Bureau of the Census.

The effects of using different unemployment measures and different income measures are summarized in Table 1. Shown are the number of counties that can be found in the most distressed 300 when the welfare measures are considered jointly, two at a time. For example, in 1960 there were 32 counties that were among the 300 with the highest unemployment rates and also were among the 300 with the lowest median family income. For reference, comparisons with the most populous 300 counties are also included.

Clearly a substantial overlap exists between the 300 counties highest in numbers of unemployed and the 300 highest in numbers of low-income families (211 counties). If the overlap of both of these sets with high-population areas is considered (255 and 213 counties, respectively), it appears likely that sheer size is an important factor determining the overlap in the welfare measure. Thus, in explaining measures based on numbers of unemployed persons or on numbers of low-income families, care is necessary to ensure that the explanatory variables selected are truly causal factors of area welfare rather than simply a measure of area population.

By contrast, the set of 300 counties with the highest unemployment *rates* appears to be relatively independent of all the other sets. The fact that the set of counties with the highest unemployment rates had little overlap with the sets based on any of the other measures indicates that unemployment will not serve as a substitute for other indicators of welfare.

A major objective was to compare groups of counties having high income with groups of counties having low income; similarly, we wanted to compare groups of counties having high unemployment with groups of counties having low unemployment. These comparisons were made for all five representations of welfare characteristics listed in Table 1. For reference, the samples involved in these comparisons will be called *unconditional samples*. Here, low- and high-income areas were selected without reference to any precondition or to any other characteristics of the areas. Three hundred counties were selected to be members of each group. To illustrate, one pair of unconditional samples compared the 300 counties having the lowest unemployment rates with the 300 counties having the highest unemployment rates.

It was determined relatively early that the absolute numbers criteria did not help to determine explanatory relationships beyond those determined by the percentage criteria. The numbers samples were not carried through the entire analysis since absolute numbers are criteria that can be applied independently; that is, areas can be ranked according to other welfare criteria and then selections from the ranking can be made to satisfy an absolute number criterion. This procedure is reasonable in view of the fact that the welfare measures based on absolute numbers appear to be closely related to population. Furthermore, the numbers criterion may be more appropriate for deciding levels of financial assistance than for determining levels of area distress.

In addition to the unconditional samples, a set of *conditional samples* were selected for analysis. In these conditional analyses, we examined the interaction of pairs of welfare characteristics, examining the extremes of one while holding the other relatively constant. For example, an analysis was performed of unemployment rates among areas with low percentages of low-income families. Roughly put, this could be described as attempting to discriminate between high and low unemployment rates among relatively wealthy areas. In turn, this analysis was compared with another analysis describing the unemployment behavior among relatively poor areas; that is, areas having high percentages of low-income families. Table 2 shows the complete range of models or problems selected for initial analysis.

Table 2.   Descriptions of Samples and Discriminant Analyses Performed[a]

Problem	Set[b]	Characteristic of counties from which selections were made	Criteria used for selection
1	−	Low percent of families with low income[c]	High percent unemployed
1	+	Low percent of families with low income	Low percent unemployed
2	−	High percent of families with low income	High percent unemployed
2	+	High percent of families with low income	Low percent unemployed
3	−	High percent of families with low income	High percent unemployed
3	+	Low percent of families with low income	Low percent unemployed
4	−	High percent unemployed	High percent of families with low income
4	+	High percent unemployed	Low percent of families with low income
5	−	Low percent unemployed	High percent of families with low income
5	+	Low percent unemployed	Low percent of families with low income
6	−	High percent unemployed	High percent of families with low income
6	+	Low percent unemployed	Low percent of families with low income
7	−	Low number of families with low income	High number unemployed
7	+	Low number of families with low income	Low number unemployed
8	−	High number of families with low income	High number unemployed

Table 2. (continued)

Problem	Set[b]	Characteristic of counties from which selections were made	Criteria used for selection
8	+	High number of families with low income	Low number unemployed
9	−	High number of families with low income	High number unemployed
9	+	Low number of families with low income	Low number unemployed
10	−	High number unemployed	High number of families with low income
10	+	High number unemployed	Low number of families with low income
11	−	Low number unemployed	High number of families with low income
11	+	Low number unemployed	Low number of families with low income
12	−	High number unemployed	High number of families with low income
12	+	Low number unemployed	Low number of families with low income
13	−	High median income	High percent unemployed
13	+	High median income	Low percent unemployed
14	−	Low median income	High percent unemployed
14	+	Low median income	Low percent unemployed
15	−	Low median income	High percent unemployed
15	+	High median income	Low percent unemployed
16	−	High percent unemployed	Low median income
16	+	High percent unemployed	High median income
17	−	Low percent unemployed	Low median income
17	+	Low percent unemployed	High median income
18	−	High percent unemployed	Low median income
18	+	Low percent unemployed	High median income
19	−	High median income	High number unemployed
19	+	High median income	Low number unemployed
20	−	Low median income	High number unemployed
20	+	Low median income	Low number unemployed
21	−	Low median income	High number unemployed
21	+	High median income	Low number unemployed
22	−	High number unemployed	Low median income
22	+	High number unemployed	High median income
23	−	Low number unemployed	Low median income
23	+	Low number unemployed	High median income
24	−	High number unemployed	Low median income
24	+	Low number unemployed	High median income
25	−	All counties	High percent of families with low income
25	+	All counties	Low percent of families with low income
26	−	All counties	High number of families with low income
26	+	All counties	Low number of families with low income
27	−	All counties	High median family income
27	+	All counties	Low median family income
28	−	All counties	High percent unemployed
28	+	All counties	Low percent unemployed
29	−	All counties	High number unemployed
29	+	All counties	Low number unemployed

Table 2. (continued)

Prob- lem	Set[b]	Characteristic of counties from which selections were made	Criteria used for selection
30	−	3-way selection:—High percent unemployed, high percent of families with low income, and high number of families with low income[d]	
30	+	3-way selection:—Low percent unemployed, low percent of families with low income, and low number of families with low income[d]	

Source: *1960 Census of Population.*
[a] Sample sizes are as follows:
    Problems 1–24—300 (150 each for + and − samples)
    Problems 25–29—600 (300 each for + and − samples)
    Problem 30—342 (171 each for + and − samples)
[b] Minus and plus designations are arbitrary, plus being the better-off sample in each case.
[c] Low income throughout the table signifies 1959 family income under $2,000.
[d] For a complete description of these samples see text.

Problem 4 in Table 2, for example, contrasts two conditional samples. Both samples are selected from a population of the 600 counties with the highest unemployment rates (characteristic for selection). The distressed area set contains the 150 counties of the 600 that have the highest percent of families with income less than $2,000. The viable or healthy set contains the 150 counties of the 600 that have the lowest percent of families with income less than $2,000.

Problem 30 is a special unconditional problem using the joint criteria where the areas in each of the two samples satisfy three conditions simultaneously. The distressed area sample is made up of 171 counties, all having ranks *less* than 1,142[8] on percent un-

---

8. This number was crudely derived by assuming the ranks on these variables were relatively independent and requiring a sample of approximately 5 percent. It was further arbitrarily assumed for purposes of this sample that the percentiles on all three variables were equally important. The derivation is as follows: let the total number of counties be N; then:

$$Pr\{\text{County } i \text{ selected at random has rank } R_{ni} \leq R_n \text{ on variable } n\} = \frac{R_n}{N} = p_n.$$

Then if the variables are independent:
$Pr\{\text{County } i \text{ selected at random has } R_{1i} \leq R_1, R_{2i} \leq R_2, \text{ and } R_{3i} \leq R_3\} = p_1 p_2 p_3.$
If we assume equal probabilities, i.e.,
$$p_1 = p_2 = p_3 = p,$$
and if we wish to obtain a 5 percent sample we have
$$p^3 = .05,$$
or
$$p = .368,$$
and
$$R_1 = R_2 = R_3 = .368N = 1142$$

employed *and* percentage of families with income less than $2,000 *and* numbers of families with income less than $2,000. The viable area sample is made up of the counties having ranks on these variables *greater* than or equal to 1,142. Because we wanted samples equal in number, we selected sequentially (from 1,142 on numbers of low-income families) until the viable area sample had 171 members. This procedure tended to eliminate counties of extremely small population from the viable area sample, thereby reducing the disparities in average population between the two samples.

In order to emphasize the characteristics of persistency, an attempt was made to explain economic welfare at a particular point in time in terms of relevant explanatory variables that either describe the area at an earlier time or describe physical conditions that are independent of time, such as weather and terrain. Specifically, we attempted to explain 1960 income and unemployment in terms of 1950 (and some 1940) demographic conditions and in terms of physical characteristics of the areas.

Visual inspection of the 187 variables selected for initial analysis shows that many are similar in fundamental concepts.[9] As in the case of the welfare variables, however, there are definitional and measurement differences. The magnitude of these differences can only be concluded from investigation of their differences in explanatory ability. It should be pointed out that slight differences in measurement or in concept may result in great differences in explanatory power.

The analysis of 30 discriminant problems with 187 variables is a task of some magnitude. To reduce the original number of explanatory variables, a simple one-way analysis of variance was employed. For each of the 30 paired sets of problems, the 187 variables were examined to discover if there were significant differences in the levels of the proposed explanatory variables as they related first to the distressed sample and then to the healthy sample in each problem. The analysis of variance was used to eliminate variables that have little or no discriminatory power—that is, no significant difference between their average values for the distressed and for the healthy groups. Variables eliminated initially were those that failed to have important discriminant power for all of the discriminant problems. Some additional explanatory variables were elim-

9. See Appendix.

inated because, while they could discriminate on some problems, they did so for basically irrelevant reasons. Primarily, these were absolute number variables that discriminated only on number problems.

By these procedures, the list of 187 variables was reduced to 78. The list of variables found in the Appendix to this paper indicates which of the original variables were retained. For all 30 problems, simple correlations were then computed for all possible pairs of the 78 explanatory variables and for each explanatory variable with the binary dependent variables as defined by the 30 problem sets. This analysis made it possible to determine in a preliminary and simple fashion the direction of the relationships between the explanatory variables and area economic welfare; that is, it was possible to establish whether the high levels of a given explanatory variable were associated with economic viability or with economic distress.[10] On the basis of these correlation analyses and their relationship to considerations of economic theory the number of explanatory variables was further reduced from 78 to 15.

The Discriminant Functions

Results obtained from 6 of the 15-variable discriminant analyses are shown in Tables 3 and 4. These illustrate the range of results obtained from the various problems as analyses.

It is interesting to note in Table 3 that, while unemployment can be moderately well explained by the 15 variables in the unconditional problem, the same phenomenon becomes difficult to explain with the same variables when restricted to relatively wealthy or to relatively poor areas. Both the conditional and the unconditional income problems in Table 4 show that income can be fairly well explained by the 15 variables in areas of low unemployment and of high unemployment, as well as in general. It should also be noted that the joint criteria problem, with three criteria considered simultaneously, shows a high degree of discrimination, even though one of the joint criteria is percent unemployed.

10. It should not be assumed, however, that a given explanatory variable and income, for example, are linearly related merely because the linear coefficient of correlation is high. The 1,0 assignment produces a deformation of the dependent variable scale. Thus, there is no guarantee that linearity is preserved by the assignment.

Table 3. Results of 15-Variable Discriminant Analysis—Unemployment

Variable	Unconditional % Unemployed	Relatively Wealthy Areas		Relatively Poor Areas		Joint[b]
		Low % low inc.[a] % Unemployed	High med. inc. % Unemployed	High % low inc.[a] % Unemployed	Low Med. inc. % Unemployed	
Percent population increase, 1940–1950	.033	−.126*[c]	−.170*	−.134*	.135*	.034
Percent of population nonwhite, 1950	.001	−.003	.003	.200*	.172*	.046
Percent of population rural farm, 1950	.381**	.170*	.141*	.601**	.640**	[d]
Infant deaths per live birth, 1950	−.096*	−.100*	−.054	−.085	−.078	−.068*
Percent of persons age 14–17 in school, 1950	−.044	−.078	−.071	−.034	−.069	[d]
Percent of persons over 25 who completed high school or more, 1950	.296**	.371**	.423**	.023	.089	.053
Percent of structures dilapidated or lacking plumbing, 1950	−.069	.075	.149	−.004	−.085	−.178*
Percent of occupied dwelling units with refrigerators, 1950	.119*	−.013	.108	.358**	.194*	.402*
Savings deposits per capita, 1950	−.017	−.123*	−.085	.022	.074	.035
Proportion of soil inventory in Classes I and II	.131*	.180*	.147*	.038	−.049	[d]
Annual normal mean temperature	.312**	.188*	.163*	.322*	.345*	−.207**
Annual normal precipitation	−.186*	.106*	.129*	−.312*	−.242*	−.120*
Pupils per teacher, 1964	−.216**	−.115	−.152*	−.092	−.207*	−.034
Annual payroll of local government employees other than teachers per capita, 1962	−.034	.033	.006	−.023	.027	.056*
Terrain variability index	−.140*	−.352**	−.334**	−.046	−.091	−.110*
Total R^2	.606	.396	.375	.384	.368	.867

[a] Percent of families with income less than $2,000.
[b] Comparison of areas having a high percentage of unemployment and a high percentage of low income families versus those with a low percentage of unemployment and a low percentage of low income families. Sparsely populated areas were excluded.
[c] * = t value between 1.96 and 5.
** = t value 5 or over.
[d] In the stepping process, the determinant would have vanished before introducing these variables.

Table 4. Results of 15-Variable Discriminant Analysis—Income

Variable	Unconditional % low income[a]	Low Unemp. Rate % low income[a]	Low Unemp. Rate Med. income	High Unemp. Rate % low income[a]	High Unemp. Rate Med. income	High Unemp. Rate Joint[b]
Percent population increase, 1940–1950	.032*[c]	.056	.035	.067*	.074*	.034
Percent of population nonwhite, 1950	−.024	.017	−.033	−.045	−.014	.046
Percent of population rural farm, 1950	−.175**	−.195*	−.229*	−.121*	−.133*	[d]
Infant deaths per live birth, 1950	−.024	−.002	.035	−.058*	−.061*	−.068*
Percent of persons age 14–17 in school, 1950	.041*	.029	.010	−.061*	[d]	[d]
Percent of persons over 25 who completed high school or more, 1950	.032	.059	−.007	.280**	.291**	.053
Percent of structures dilapidated or lacking plumbing, 1950	−.515**	−.514**	−.542**	−.187*	−.196*	−.178*
Percent of occupied dwelling units with refrigerators, 1950	[d]	−.206*	−.095	.083	.102*	.402*
Savings deposits per capita, 1950	−.048**	.108*	−.003	.035	.008	.035
Proportion of soil inventory in Classes I and II	.019	−.057	[d]	.029	−.011	[d]
Annual normal mean temperature	−.225**	−.152*	−.198*	−.179**	−.191**	−.207**
Annual normal precipitation	−.038*	−.209*	−.088	[d]	−.017	−.120*
Pupils per teacher, 1964	−.013	.198*	.205*	−.010	−.005	−.034
Annual payroll of local government employees other than teachers per capita, 1962	.053*	.076*	.140*	.121	.164**	.056*
Terrain variability index	[d]	.017	.008	[d]	−.038	−.110*
Total R^2	.922	.753	.764	.909	.901	.867

[a] Percent of families with income less than $2,000.

[b] Comparison of areas having a high percentage of unemployment and a high percentage of low-income families versus those with a low percentage of unemployment and a low percentage of low-income families. Sparsely populated areas were excluded.

[c] * = t value between 1.96 and 5.
** = t value 5 or over.

[d] In the stepping process, the determinant would have vanished before introducing these variables.

The purpose of the conditional analyses was primarily to identify special effects in the event that the unconditional analyses did not provide satisfactory discriminations. As the level of discrimination in the unconditional problems was very high, it seemed unnecessary to pursue further the investigation of the conditional problems. Also, those problems referring to the number of unemployed and the number of families with low income, were discarded for the reasons given previously.

As can be seen from Table 4, when using percentage of families with income under $2,000 as the selection criterion, the results were almost the same as those using median income. Thus, only one was retained for further examination, namely, the percentage of families with income below the amount necessary for subsistence. We considered it to be a more direct representation of the state of affliction of an area for income reasons than median income. Furthermore, median income and percent of families with income under $2,000 are, for practical purposes, identical with respect to describing the welfare of the area selected.

With attention centered upon the three discriminant analyses based on percent of families with income under $2,000 (Problem 25), percent unemployed (Problem 28), and the joint income-unemployment problem (Problem 30), two further questions are worth considering. Could the degree of explanation for the discrimination, R^2, be increased by additional variables or possibly by replacement of some variables by others? Could more reasonable models be selected—that is, could more direct causal explanatory variables be substituted?

To answer these questions, alternative forms of the discriminant analyses for the above three problems were attempted, varying the selection of explanatory variables. To begin, the explanatory variables were introduced one at a time and, in effect, a separate discrimination was performed after each such introduction. It was thus possible to follow the behavior of the beta weights for a given variable as additional variables entered the analysis. This procedure offers a fairly good test of the stability of explanation of a given variable as other variables are added. In addition, at each stage of the analysis, the potential contributions of the remainder of the 78 variables to the explanation of the discrimination were calculated, making it possible to determine whether an omitted variable should be included in terms of its contribution to R^2. Whether two or more should be added could not be readily determined because of possible intercorrelation wherein one of two variables might contribute little or no more to R^2 than both together.

Using these procedures, several alternative discriminant functions were examined for each of the three remaining problems. As a result of several such trials, a single candidate for each of the three final problems was selected. Two forms of the equation were retained at this stage in order to determine whether there were any significant long-run income or unemployment conditions that were not taken into account. This was accomplished by contrasting the selected form of the equations for the unconditional income and unemployment models with an alternative form that was identical except that lagged values of the appropriate selection criterion variables (1950 values of percent of low-income families and percent unemployed, respectively) were included. In the case of the joint problem, 1950 income, but not 1950 unemployment, was examined.

The final models emerging from all this experimentation, as well as some important associated data, are presented in Table 5. As before, the variables are listed and beta weights are given. In addition, b-weights and a constant are given which can be applied to the values of the explanatory variables for any county to obtain its discriminant score.[11]

Data columns labeled $\overline{X}_-$ and $\overline{X}_+$ in Table 5 contain the average values for the explanatory variables in the representative distressed and viable samples, respectively. Columns $b\overline{X}_-$ and $b\overline{X}_+$ represent the average contribution of the variables to the discriminant scores within each sample. The last column, the difference, $b\overline{X}_+ - b\overline{X}_-$ represents the average contribution to the partitioning of the two samples and gives some insight into the importance of the variable.

With the exception of the b-weight for annual normal precipitation in the unemployment model, all the b-weights for a given model have the same sign. This was accomplished by suitable redefinition of variables.[12] For example, we can change the sign of the

11. The discriminant score, S_j for county j, based on the values of the n explanatory variables for county j, $X_{1j}, X_{2j}, \ldots, X_{nj}$ can be represented as follows:
$$S_j = C + b_1 X_{1j} + b_2 X_{2j} + \ldots + b_i X_{ij} + \ldots + b_n X_{nj};$$
where
C = the constant for the particular discriminant function,
and
b_i = the b weight for the ith explanatory variable, $(i = 1, \ldots, n)$.

12. For our purposes of ranking areas according to need, the constant term is arbitrary and could, in fact, be ignored. However, to place the scores on a comparable scale with respect to the values of the artificial dependent variable, zero or one, the change is necessary.

Table 5. Final Discriminant Equations

Structural group[a]	Variable description[b]	β weight	b weight	Sample Mean Values of Variables		bX̄_-	bX̄_+	(bX̄_+ − bX̄_-)
				X̄_-	X̄_+			
	Problem 28—Criterion is percent unemployed							
	Constant[c] −4.6877							
1	Proportion of soil inventory land in Classes I and II	0.072	0.1698	0.1551	0.2757	0.0263	0.0468	0.0205
1	Annual normal mean temperature	0.376	0.0244	51.99	54.23	1.2686	1.3232	0.0546
1	Annual normal precipitation[g]	−0.737	−0.0286	36.14	27.36	−1.0336	−0.7825	0.2511
1	April-September normal Precipitation	0.593	0.0453	19.15	18.07	0.8675	0.8186	−0.0489
1	Terrain variability index	0.089	0.0047	19.71	11.74	0.0926	0.0552	−0.0374
2	Infant survival rate, 1950[h]	0.059	1.5228	0.9622	0.9743	1.4652	1.4837	0.0185
2	Percent of structures sound, with plumbing, 1950[d,i]	0.129	0.3341	0.3318	0.4217	0.1109	0.1409	0.0300
4	Percent of population rural farm, 1950[d]	0.318	0.8440	0.3257	0.4518	0.2749	0.3813	0.1064
4	Percent of population between ages of 21 and 65, 1950[d]	0.179	2.0112	0.4901	0.5171	0.9857	1.0400	0.0543
4	Percent of farm operators working off farm more than 100 days, 1950[d]	0.228	0.8121	0.6765	0.8568	0.5494	0.6958	0.1464
3	Percent of persons over 25 who completed high school or more, 1950[d]	0.231	1.0146	0.2357	0.3194	0.2391	0.3241	0.0850

Problem 25—Criterion is percent of families with income under $2,000

Constant[c]   2.2083

1	Annual normal mean temperature	−0.212	−0.0137	61.99	50.82	−0.8493	−0.6962	0.1531
1	Annual normal precipitation	−0.066	−0.0023	47.54	30.48	−0.1093	−0.0701	0.0392
2	Percent of population rural farm, 1950	−0.192	−0.3466	0.6160	0.1232	−0.2135	−0.0427	0.1708
2	Infant Deaths per live birth, 1950	−0.032	−1.0798	0.0363	0.0254	−0.0392	−0.0274	0.0118
2	Percent of structures dilapidated or lacking plumbing, 1950[d]	−0.488	−0.8018	0.8670	0.3030	−0.6952	−0.2429	0.4523
3	Percent of persons age 14-17 not in school, 1950[d e]	−0.039	−0.1879	0.2718	0.1293	−0.0511	−0.0243	0.0268
3	Percent of persons over 25 who completed less than high school, 1950[d f]	−0.074	−0.2398	0.8657	0.5939	−0.2076	−0.1424	0.0652

Table 5 (continued)

Structural group	Variable description[b]	β weight	b weight	Sample Mean Values of Variables		$b\overline{X}_-$	$b\overline{X}_+$	$(b\overline{X}_+ - b\overline{X}_-)$
				$\overline{X}_-$	$\overline{X}_+$			
	Problem 30—Criteria are percent unemployed and number and percent of families with income under $2,000							
	Constant[c] 2.9592							
1	Annual normal mean temperature	−0.283	−0.0205	61.57	52.34	−1.2622	−1.0730	0.1892
1	Annual normal precipitation	−0.113	−0.0041	47.05	29.27	−0.1929	−0.1200	0.0729
1	Terrain variability index	−0.113	−0.0065	14.58	11.46	−0.0948	−0.0745	0.0203
2	Infant deaths per live birth. 1950	−0.121	−4.1104	0.0389	0.0275	−0.1599	−0.1130	0.0469
2	Percent of structures dilapidated or lacking plumbing, 1950[d]	−0.558	−1.3127	0.7899	0.4208	−1.0369	−0.5524	0.4845
3	Percent of persons over 25 who completed less than high school, 1950[d][f]	−0.041	−0.1554	0.8432	0.6227	−0.1310	−0.0968	0.0342

[a]Classifications for partial scores, see text.

  Group 1—Physical variables
  Group 2—Income-related variables
  Group 3—Education variables
  Group 4—Labor market imperfections variables

[b]For complete descriptions and sources see the Appendix.
[c]Adjusted to reflect redefinition of certain variables, see text.
[d]Data labeled percent are expressed as decimal ratios (e.g., 10.2 percent is expressed as .102).
[e]Redefined variable (1 − percent of persons age 14-17 in school, 1950).
[f]Redefined variable (1 − percent of persons over 25 who completed high school or more, 1950).
[g]This variables was not redefined because there is no logical interpretation of its complement.
[h]Redefined variable (1 − percent infant deaths per live birth, 1950).
[i]Redefined variable (1 − percent of structures dilapidated or lacking plumbing, 1950).

b-weight for infant deaths per live birth by defining the variable as infant survival rate, i.e., one *minus* infant deaths per live birth. This procedure does not affect the total score or the absolute value of the b-weight; it only changes the constant term and sign of the b-weight.[13]

The standardization of beta weight and b-weight signs facilitates comparisons. The discriminant score for a county can be analyzed in terms of several broad structural components, or groups of variables. The group to which a variable belongs is indicated in the first column of Table 5. The groups are: 1) Physical, 2) Income-related, 3) Educational, and 4) Labor Market Imperfections. The percent of an area's total variable score (the total score *minus* the constant) that is attributable to a particular structural group can be readily calculated; with the b-weights all the same sign for variables in a group, each variable affects the economic welfare in the same direction, so that the effects of a variable in a group are not cancelled out by other variables with opposite signs within the group.

The structural group of Physical variables (Group 1) can be readily interpreted for the most part. The terrain, or hilliness measure, probably is an important proxy for the quality of transportation facilities, and the soil capability measure represents the availability of good-quality agricultural land.

The Income-related variables (Group 2) represent long-run private and social income. The percent of dilapidated structures is quite probably representative of a fairly long-run low-income history of the inhabitants, at least insofar as housing expenditures have a relatively high priority in the family budget. The percent of the population living in rural farm areas has an income relationship insofar as there must be an income adjustment due to payment of wages in kind. The variable, infant deaths per live birth, reflects the investment in and quality of health facilities and services, such as hospitals and clinics.

The variables in the Educational structural group (Group 3) are self-explanatory, indicating the general level of the area population's educational achievement.

13. One variable, annual normal precipitation, carried a negative coefficient and, since there is no reasonable complement of the variable, no adjustment was made. As a consequence, a few counties in the Pacific Northwest have negative partial scores for the Physical structural group (the selected "normal" for this problem was positive, and the constant was negative).

Finally, the Labor Market Imperfections structural group are made up mainly of proxy measures of this difficult-to-evaluate concept. The percent of the population living in rural farm areas is of importance because farm employees may not report themselves as unemployed when work is scarce on a farm. To the extent that such workers seek work elsewhere, as indicated by, say, the percent of farm operators working off the farm more than 100 days in a year, the need for yet another modification in unemployment estimates is perhaps implied. The percent of the population between the ages of 21 and 65 represents that segment of the population that is most likely to seek work and least likely to retreat from the labor force when the job market shrinks.

A graphical representation of the partitioning effected for the three problems is presented in Figures 1, 2, and 3. Also shown in these figures are the three distributions for the discriminant scores for the entire population of counties. Along the horizontal axis are the scores assigned to the counties, and the vertical axis refers to the percent of counties that have scores within the stated intervals. The lower values of the discriminant scores are associated with greater distress. The figures show that, as expected, there is little or no dichotomization of the population, although the income and

Figure 1. Distribution of the discriminant scores for all counties and for the defining samples when the criterion is percent of families with income under $2000.

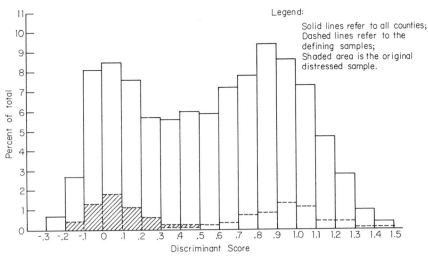

Figure 2. Distributions of the discriminant scores for all counties for the defining samples when the criterion is percent unemployed.

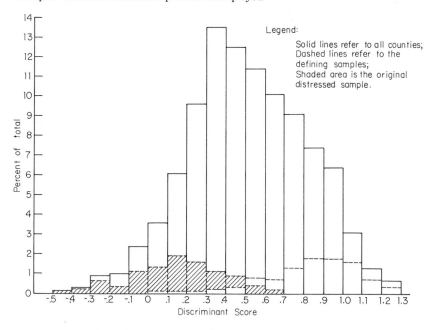

Figure 3. Distributions of the discriminant scores for all counties and for the defining samples when the criteria are percent unemployed plus number and percent of families with income under $2000.

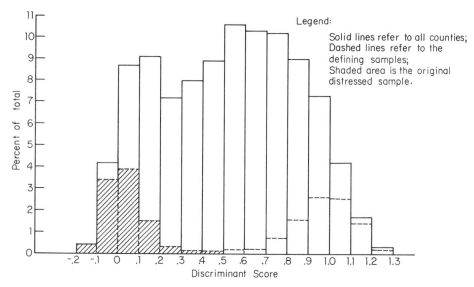

joint criteria discriminant distributions do show some bimodality. Nevertheless, the discriminant functions appear to preserve the general pattern of the area income and unemployment distributions; there is a tendency for the discriminant score distributions to concentrate toward the viable end of the scale.

The original samples in each of the three figures are the smaller distributions indicated by dotted lines. The sample representing the distressed areas (the areas beneath the dotted lines on the low-score end of the scale) has been shaded. In interpreting these results (for example, determining the amount of separation the three discriminant scoring systems achieve for the economically distressed and viable areas), it should be remembered that the statistics used for the criteria may not adequately portray the area welfare conditions being analyzed by the discriminant functions. For example, area unemployment rates as reported for a short time interval generally lack the dimensions of labor force composition, participation, and unemployment duration. [14]

In addition, the discriminant functions attempt to explain 1960 economic welfare in terms of persistent physical variables or in terms of area conditions that existed in 1950. In this way an explanation of long-run economic welfare is sought. Even assuming that such an explanation has been successfully achieved, it must be expected that economic conditions at a given point in time may be at variance with long-run potential performance.

Examination of Figures 1-3 shows that in all cases the paired viable and distressed samples are recognizable as being extreme with respect to each other. In general, it appears that the scores for the pairs of samples for the family income problem and the scores of the pairs of samples for the problem that jointly considers unemployment rates and family income have very little overlap. The scores for the samples for the unemployment rate problem show substantially more overlap and therefore tend to indicate that this economic phenomenon is not so easily delineated on a satisfactory, long-run basis. Again, this may be due in part to the conceptual problems inherent in the gross unemployment rate.

It can also be seen from Figures 1–3 that, for each of the three discriminant functions, there are counties at the low end of the scale that were not in the original representative samples. If most of these

14. Regional and Urban Planning Implementation, Inc., *Area Welfare—Eligibility for Development Assistance* (Cambridge, Mass., May 1965), vol. I, chap. iv.

are not depressed areas, then the functions are doing a poor job. The joint criteria discriminant function, in particular, while achieving a good separation, appears to place a large number of counties at the low end that were not in the sample that defined the relatively distressed areas.

For the purpose of evaluation, the counties with the lowest 300 scores were selected from each discrimination. This number represents approximately one-tenth of all the counties in the United States. [15] The geographic locations of these counties are shown in Figures 4, 5, and 6.

Some interesting comparisons can be made by considering the number of counties that fall into two or more of the sets of 300 depressed counties as determined by the discriminant scores. Tables 6 through 9 list the common counties for the four possible combinations of the sets. The ten counties that appear in all three groups classified as distressed are listed in Table 6. Removing the joint criteria—that is, looking at the intersection of the distressed sets for unemployment rate and family income functions alone (Table 7), adds only one county.

The most striking observations occur in Tables 8 and 9. The joint criteria function has 35 members in its set of distressed areas that are also in the distressed set for the unemployment rate discriminant function (Table 8).[16] This is a relatively small number when

15. In future contexts, counties classified as distressed by one of the functions will refer to this set of 300 as determined by the discriminant analysis.

16. An anomaly is observed in these results that illustrates a problem of interpretation when the variable considered is a percentage and its base is extremely small. For example, Alpine County, California, a very thinly populated area, achieved very low scores in the discriminant analyses based on the percent unemployed criterion and on the joint criteria. Examination of the partial scores for Alpine indicates a substantial departure from the pattern of its surrounding counties in terms of the Income-related group. One variable in the Income-related group, infant deaths per live birth (redefined as infant survival rate in the percent unemployed problem), had a value of nearly 17 percent, or over five times the prevailing rate for California in 1950. The base for this estimate, however, was only six live births, with one infant death! Clearly care must be taken in interpreting such statistics, taken on a one-year basis, for very small counties.

The other explanatory variables selected for the final models do not suffer this "snapshot" risk. Unfortunately, only a one-year record for this variable was available for this study. A priori, we considered it important as it was the only available proxy measure for the general quality of health services and facilities. The results of the analysis proved that it had substantial explanatory power. In any long-term use of the discriminant analysis technique it is desirable to substitute a longer-term record of this variable, so that the small-numbers problems encountered can be eliminated.

Figure 4. 300 counties with lowest scores. Discriminant criterion is percent of families with income under $2000.

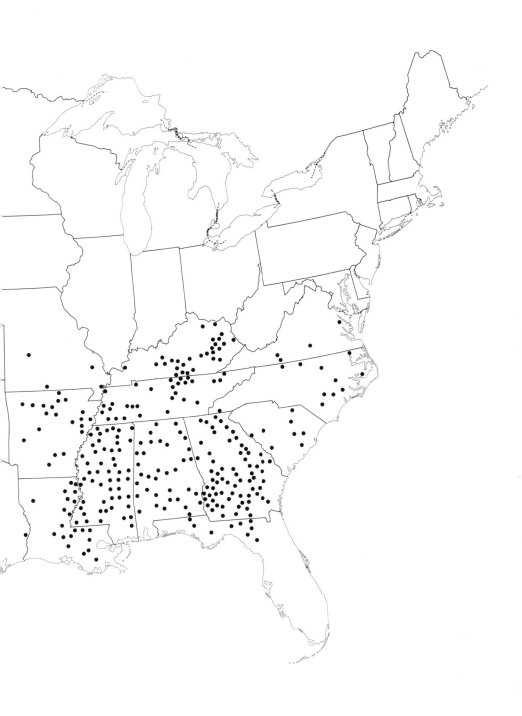

Figure 5. 300 counties with lowest scores. Discriminant criterion is percent unemployed.

Figure 6. 300 counties with lowest scores. Discriminant criteria are percent unemployed plus number and percent of families with income under $2000.

Table 6. Counties Among 300 Lowest Scoring on All Three Bases for Computing Final Discriminant Scores

State	Counties
Alabama	Bibb
Georgia	Gilmer
Kentucky	Clay, Lee, Leslie, Martin
Tennessee	Fentress, Perry, Van Buren, Wayne

Table 7. Counties Among 300 Lowest Scoring on Both Percent of Families Having Income Under $2,000 and Percent Unemployed Criteria

State	Counties
Alabama	Bibb
Georgia	Gilmer
Kentucky	Clay, Lee, Leslie, Martin
Tennessee	Fentress, Perry, Van Buren, Wayne
Texas	Newton

Table 8. Counties Among 300 Lowest Scoring on Both Percent Unemployed and Percent Unemployed and Number and Percent of Families Having Income Under $2,000 Criteria

State	Counties
Alabama	Bibb, St. Clair, Shelby, Walker
California	Alpine
Georgia	Dade, Gilmer
Kentucky	Clay, Harlan, Knott, Lee, Leslie, Letcher, Martin, McCreary, Pike
Louisiana	Grant, Iberville, Sabine, St. John The Baptist
Missouri	Iron
North Carolina	Cherokee
Tennessee	Campbell, Fentress, Marion, Morgan, Perry, Polk, Scott, Sequatchie, Van Buren, Wayne
Virginia	Buchanan, Charles City, Dickenson

compared to the 220 that are in the distressed sets for both the joint criteria and the family income discriminant functions (Table 9). Thus, at the distressed end, at least, the joint criteria function fundamentally discriminates or classifies much like the family income function. In addition to the selection criteria of percent of families with low income and percent unemployed, members of the representative samples for the joint criteria function were selected on the conditions that the counties have high numbers of low-income families and be populous. Comparison with the income function shows that those counties scoring low on the joint criteria function but not included in the representative samples are largely those identified as distressed (even though possibly not populous) by the family income discriminant.

Table 9. Counties Among 300 Lowest Scoring on Both Percent of Families Having Income Under $2,000 and Percent Unemployed and Number and Percent of Families Having Income Under $2,000 Criteria

State	Counties
Alabama	Barbour, Bibb, Blount, Bullock, Butler, Cherokee, Chilton, Choctaw, Clay, Cleburne, Conecuh, Coosa, Crenshaw, De Kalb, Geneva, Greene, Hale, Henry, Jackson, Lawrence, Lowndes, Marengo, Marion, Monroe, Perry Pickens, Randolph, Sumter, Washington, Wilcox, Winston
Arkansas	Cleburne, Cleveland, Lincoln, Montgomery, Newton, Perry, Stone, Van Buren
Florida	Hamilton, Holmes, Jefferson, Lafayette, Liberty, Madison, Suwannee, Washington
Georgia	Appling, Atkinson, Bacon, Baker, Banks, Bleckley, Brantley, Brooks, Burke, Calhoun, Candler, Clay, Coffee, Cook, Crawford, Dawson, Dodge, Dooly, Early, Echols, Emanuel, Forsyth, Gilmer, Glascock, Grady, Heard, Irwin, Jeff Davis, Jenkins, Johnson, Lanier, Lee, Macon, Madison, Marion, Miller, Montgomery, Murray, Oconee, Oglethorpe, Paulding, Pike, Quitman, Randolph, Screven, Stewart, Talbot, Taliaferro, Tattnall, Terrell, Turner, Twiggs, Union, Warren, Washington, Webster, Wheeler, White, Wilcox, Worth
Kentucky	Breathitt, Butler, Clay, Edmonson, Elliott, Jackson, Lee, Leslie, Lewis, Magoffin, Martin, Menifee, Metcalfe, Monroe, Owsley, Wolfe

Table 9. (Continued)

State	Counties
Louisiana	Assumption, Catahoula, Concordia, East Carroll, East Feliciana, Evangeline, Franklin, Lafourche, Madison, Red River, Richland, St. Helena, St. James, St. Landry, St. Martin, Tensas, West Carroll, West Feliciana
Mississippi	Amite, Attala, Benton, Calhoun, Carroll, Choctaw, Clairborne, Clarke, Covington, Franklin, George, Greene, Humphreys, Issaquena, Itawamba, Jasper, Jefferson, Jefferson Davis, Kemper, Lawrence, Leake, Madison, Marshall, Noxubee, Perry, Pontotoc, Quitman, Sharkey, Smith, Sunflower, Tallahatchie, Tishomingo, Tunica, Walthall, Wayne, Wilkinson, Winston, Yalobusha
Missouri	Bollinger, Ozark
North Carolina	Caswell, Clay, Duplin, Greene, Hyde, Jones
South Carolina	Chesterfield, Clarendon, McCormick, Williamsburg
Tennessee	Cannon, Clay, Crockett, Decatur, De Kalb, Fentress, Grainger, Hancock, Hardeman, Henderson, Jackson, Macon, McNairy, Meigs, Moore, Perry, Pickett, Smith, Stewart, Union, Van Buren, Wayne
Texas	Burleson, Lee, Rains, San Jacinto, Wilson, Zapata
Virginia	King and Queen

Thus, two differently defined discriminant functions agree in classifying a large number of areas as economically distressed. Whether or not these counties can also be classified as distressed in terms of conventional single or unidimensional measures, such as low family income, has yet to be determined. Similarly, no evidence has yet been given as to whether there is any agreement between the unemployment discriminant classifications of distressed areas and the classification that would result using conventional unemployment rate statistics. Any evaluation of the three discriminant functions in terms of conventionally reported welfare data must, of course, be qualified by considerations of data inadequacy and long-run analysis requirements, as mentioned previously.

Because of the demonstrated independence of the family income and unemployment rate phenomena, the family income and joint criteria discriminant functions are inadequate measures of area distress based on the unemployment rate. Also, the unemployment function is an inadequate measure of area family income status. We shall, therefore, restrict ourselves to measuring the adequacy of the family income and joint criteria discriminant functions with respect to area family income while measuring the adequacy of the unemployment function only with respect to area unemployment statistics.

To do so, a standard for "distress" must be established. One way of doing this would be to say arbitrarily that a certain percentage of the counties in the United States are distressed from the point of view of percent of families with low income. In this vein, it can be shown that one-third of the counties in the nation had at least 27 percent of their families with incomes below $2,000 annually in 1960. By comparison, 97 percent of the counties classified as distressed by discriminant function are also classified as distressed by the one-third, or 27 percent, criterion. In slightly more formal terms, the probability is 0.97 that a county distressed in the discriminant analyses is also distressed in the reported lower one-third income sense.

Using the same procedure (assuming one-third of the counties are distressed) for the other two discriminant functions, it can be shown that: (1) 72 percent of the counties classified as distressed by the unemployment rate function are distressed in that they have an unemployment rate greater than 5.8 percent, as did one-third of U.S. counties in 1960; and (2) 94 percent of the counties classified as distressed by the joint family income and unemployment rate discriminant function are distressed in that they had more than 27 percent of their families earning less than $2,000 in 1960.

These tests lend credence to the following conclusions: the joint criteria function is very much like the family income discriminant function and performs about as well in the classification of distressed areas. As a result of this similarity, and since both perform well in identifying distressed areas, the existence of long-run distress with respect to family income is convincing. The long-run unemployment rate function, however, yields no such conviction.

It is reasonably easy, in short, to demonstrate that a high unemployment rate in an area is not invariably associated with the more common manifestations or measures of low-income status. Furthermore, persistency of low-income and of unemployment status by areas seems to differ; specifically, low-income seems to be a considerably more persistent phenomenon in a particular areas than high unemployment. As persistence of low-income or unemployment status by geographic areas must underlie any sensible rationalization of area redevelopment as a public policy, these observed differences in the persistency characteristics of low income and unemployment could have important policy implications.

Appendix

Table A-1. Basic Explanatory Variables Available for Analyses

	One of final 78 variables	Notes*	Variable number	Data sources*
GENERAL POPULATION CHARACTERISTICS				
Population, 1940		1	1	1
Population, 1950	×		2	1
Population, 1960			3	2
Population increase, 1940–1950		1	4	1
Population increase, 1950–1960		1	5	2
Percent population increase, 1940–1950	×	2	6	1
Percent population increase, 1950–1960		1,2	7	2
Nonwhite population, 1950		1	8	1
Nonwhite population, 1960		1	9	2
Percent of population nonwhite, 1950	×	2	10	1
Percent of population nonwhite, 1960		2	11	2
Nonwhite population increase, 1950–1960		1	12	1,2
Percent nonwhite population increase, 1950–1960		1,2,25	13	1,2
White population increase, 1950–1960		1	14	1,2
Percent white population increase, 1950–1960		1,2,25	15	1,2
Population per square mile, 1950	×		16	1
Population per square mile, 1960			17	2
Urban population, 1950			18	1
Urban population, 1960		1	19	2
Percent of population urban, 1950	×	1,2	20	1
Percent of population urban, 1960		2	21	2
Percent urban population increase, 1950–1960		1,2,25	22	1,2
Rural nonfarm population, 1950			23	1
Rural nonfarm population, 1960		1	24	2
Percent of population rural nonfarm, 1950		1,2	25	1
Percent of population rural nonfarm, 1960		2	26	2
Percent rural nonfarm population increase, 1950–1960		1,2,25	27	1,2
Rural farm population, 1950			28	1
Rural farm population, 1960		1	29	2
Percent of population rural farm, 1950	×	1,2	30	1
Percent of population rural farm, 1960		2	31	2
Percent rural farm population increase, 1950–1960		1,2,25	32	1,2
Population five years old and over, 1950	×		33	1
Percent of population five years old and over, 1950	×	1,2	34	1
Median age of the population, 1950	×		35	1
Median age of the population, 1960			36	2
Population between ages of 21 and 65, 1950		1,3	37	1
Percent of population between ages of 21 and 65, 1950	×	1,2,3	38	1
Population between ages of 21 and 65, 1960		1	39	2
Percent of population between ages of 21 and 65, 1960		1,2	40	2
Live births, 1950			41	1
Live births per family, 1950	×	1	42	1
Number of infant deaths, 1950			44	1
Number of families, 1950			45	1
Number of families, 1960			46	2
Percent increase in number of families, 1950–1960		1,2	47	1,2

Table A-1. (continued)

	One of final 78 variables	Notes*	Variable number	Data sources*
Average family size, 1950	×	4	48	1
Average family size, 1960		4	49	2
Percent change in average family size, 1950–1960		2,4	50	1,2
Number of males over 14 years old, 1950		8	69	1
EDUCATION STATUS AND EDUCATION ACHIEVEMENT				
Number of persons age 7–13 in school, 1950			57	1
Percent of persons age 7–13 in school, 1950		2,28	58	1
Number of persons age 14–17 in school, 1950			59	1
Percent of persons age 14–17 in school, 1950	×	2,28	60	1
Number of persons over 21 years old who completed less than five grades, 1950	×	7	61	1
Percent of persons over 25 years old who completed less than five grades, 1950	×	2	62	1
Number of persons over 21 who completed high school or more, 1950		7	63	1
Percent of persons over 25 who completed high school or more, 1950	×	2	64	1
Number of persons over 21 who completed less than high school, 1950	×	7	65	1
Percent of persons over 25 who completed less than high school, 1950	×	2	66	1
Median school years completed by persons over 25 years old, 1950	×		67	1
EMPLOYMENT CHARACTERISTICS				
Number of persons over 14 years old in civilian labor force, 1950			68	1
Number of males over 14 years old in civilian labor force, 1950		1,8	70	1
Percent of males over 14 years old in total labor force, 1950	×		71	1
Percent of females over 14 years old in total labor force, 1950	×		72	1
Number of unemployed persons in labor force, 1950	×	1	73	1
Percent of labor force unemployed, 1950	×	1	74	1
Number of persons employed in agriculture, 1950			75	1
Number of persons employed in mining, 1950			76	1
Number of persons employed in manufacturing, 1950			77	1
Number of persons employed in wholesale and retail trade, 1950			78	1
Percent of total employed persons in agriculture, 1950	×	1,2	79	1
Percent of total employed persons in mining, 1950	×	1,2	80	1
Percent of total employed persons in manufacturing, 1950	×	1,2	81	1
Percent of total employed persons in wholesale and retail trade, 1950	×	1,2	82	1
Number of employed persons in agriculture per capita, 1950		1	83	1
Number of employed persons in wholesale and retail trade per capita, 1950		1	84	1

	One of final 78 variables	Notes*	Variable number	Data sources*
EMPLOYMENT CHARACTERISTICS(CONTINUED)				
Number of employed persons, 1950			85	1
Ratio of number of employed persons to number of persons over 14 years old, 1950	×	1	86	1
Relative extent of unionization in state, 1939	×	20,21	178	9
Relative extent of unionization in state, 1953	×	20,21	179	9
CHARACTERISTICS OF THE INCOME DISTRIBUTION				
Median family income, 1950	×	5	51	1
Median income per family member, 1950		5,6	52	1
Number of families with income less than $2000, 1950	×	1,5,6	53	1
Percent of families with income less than $2000, 1950	×	2,5	54	1
Number of families with income $5000 or over, 1950	×	1,5	55	1
Percent of families with income $5000 or over, 1950		2,5	56	1
OTHER MEASURES RELATED TO INCOME				
Infant deaths per live birth, 1950	×	1,26	43	1
Dwelling units per family, 1950		1	87	1
Number of dwelling units in one unit detached structures, 1950	×		88	1
Number of dwelling units in one unit detached structures per family, 1950	×	1	89	1
Number of families per one dwelling unit detached structure, 1950		1	90	1
Percent of structures dilapidated or lacking plumbing, 1950	×	1,2	91	1
Number of dwelling units dilapidated or lacking plumbing per family, 1950		1	92	1
Median number of persons per occupied dwelling unit, 1950			93	1
Number of occupied dwelling units per capita, 1950	×	1	94	1
Median number of persons per room		9	95	1
Percent of dwelling units in structures built in 1940 or later, 1950	×	2	96	1
Number of occupied dwelling units with refrigerators, 1950		1	97	1
Percent of occupied dwelling units with refrigerators, 1950	×	2	98	1
Number of retail stores (excluding food stores and eating and drinking places), 1950		1	99	1
Population per retail store (excluding food stores and eating and drinking places), 1950	×	1	100	1
Sales of retail stores (excluding food stores and eating and drinking places), 1950		1,10	101	1
Sales of retail stores (excluding food stores and eating and drinking places) per capita, 1950	×	1	102	1
E-bond sales, 1950	×	1	120	1
Total bank deposits, 1950		10	121	1

Table A-1. (continued)

	One of final 78 variables	Notes*	Variable number	Data sources*
Savings deposits, 1950		10,12	122	1
First mortgage loans outstanding by savings and loan associations, 1950		10	123	1
E-bond sales per capita, 1950	×	1,10	124	1
Total bank deposits per capita, 1950		1,10	125	1
Savings deposits per capita, 1950	×	1,10	126	1
First mortgage loans of savings and loan associations per capita, 1950	×	1,10	127	1
CHARACTERISTICS OF FARMS				
Total value of farm products sold, 1950		10	103	1
Value of farm products sold per acre harvested, 1950	×	1,10,26	104	1
Value of farm products sold per farm, 1950	×	1,26	105	1
Average number of tractors per farm, 1950	×	1,26	106	1
Tractors on farms, 1950			107	1
Number of farms without horses, tractors, or mules, 1950			108	1
Percent of farms without horses, tractors, or mules, 1950		1,26	109	1
Acres harvested per tractor, 1950	×	1,10,26	110	1
Average number of automobiles per farm	×	11,26	111	1
Average number of trucks per farm	×	11,26	112	1
Number of automobiles on farms, 1950	×		113	1
Number of trucks on farms	×		114	1
Number of farms operated by tenants, 1950		1,2	115	1
Percent of farms operated by tenants, 1950	×	2,26	116	1
Average value of land and buildings per farm, 1950	×		117	1
Number of farm operators working off farm more than 100 days			118	1
Percent of farm operators working off farm more than 100 days	×	1,2,26	119	1
Number of commercial farms, 1959		16	145	3
Number of commercial farms with sales of farm products under $2500		16	146	3
Number of commercial farms with sales of farm products under $5000	×	16	147	3
Number of commercial farms with sales of farm products under $10,000		16	148	3
Number of commercial farms with sales of farm products under $20,000		16	149	3
Number of commercial farms with sales of farm products under $40,000		16	150	3
Percent of commercial farms with sales of farm products under $2500		1,2,26	151	3
Percent of commercial farms with sales of farm products under $5000	×	1,2,26	152	3
Percent of commercial farms with sales of farm products under $10,000		1,2,26	153	3
Percent of commercial farms with sales of farm products under $20,000		1,2,26	154	3
Percent of commercial farms with sales of farm products under $40,000		1,2,26	155	3
Number of farms, 1959			156	3

Table A-1. (continued)

	One of final 78 variables	Notes*	Variable number	Data sources*
CHARACTERISTICS OF FARMS (continued)				
Number of farms with tractors, 1959			157	3
Percent of farms with tractors, 1959		1,2,26	158	3
Percent of farms fully owned by farm operators, 1959		1,2,26	159	3
Percent of farms operated by tenants, 1959		1,2,26	160	3
Percent of farms operated by negroes, 1959		1,2,26	161	3
Percent of farms operated by nonwhites, 1959		1,2,26	162	3
PHYSICAL AND GEOGRAPHIC CHARACTERISTICS				
Proportion of soil inventory land in Class I		13,26	128	4
Proportion of soil inventory land in Classes I and II	×	13,26	129	4
Proportion of soil inventory land in Classes I-III		13,26	130	4
Proportion of soil inventory land in Classes I-IV		13,26	131	4
Annual normal maximum temperature		14	132	5
Annual normal minimum temperature		14	133	5
Annual normal mean temperature	×	14	134	5
Annual heating degree-days		14	135	5
Annual normal precipitation	×	14	136	5
Number of months in which monthly normal mean temperature is less than 32 degrees		14	137	5
April–September average of monthly normal mean temperature		14	138	5
October–March heating degree-days		14	139	5
April–September average of monthly normal precipitation	×	14	140	5
Distance to nearest SMSA of population over 250,000	×	15	141	6
Distance to nearest SMSA of population over 500,000		15	142	6
Distance to nearest SMSA of population over 750,000		15	143	6
Distance to nearest SMSA of population over 1,000,000	×	15	144	6
Terrain variability index	×	23	196	12
MEASURES OF GOVERNMENT AND OTHER PUBLIC ACTIVITIES				
Monthly average earnings of public school teachers, 1962	×		163	7
Number of full-time equivalent public school teachers, 1962			164	7
Pupils per teacher, 1964	×	17,26	165	8
Number of local government employees other than teachers, 1962		1	166	7
Local government employees per capita, 1962		1,18	167	2,7
Local government employees other than teachers per capita, 1960		1,18	168	2,7
Annual payroll of local government employees other than teachers, 1962		18,19	169	7
Annual payroll of local government employees other than teachers per capita, 1962	×	18,19	170	2,7

	One of final 78 variables	Notes*	Variable number	Data sources*
MEASURES OF GOVERNMENT AND OTHER PUBLIC ACTIVITIES (continued)				
Average number of pupils per school, 1950		1,26,27	171	8
Average number of schools per pupil, 1950		1,26,27	172	8
Average number of permanent classrooms per school building, 1964	×	1,26	173	8
Average total number of rooms per school building, 1964		1,26	174	8
Average number of rooms other than permanent classrooms per total rooms, 1964		1,26	175	8
Pupils per room, 1964	×	1,26	176	8
Full-time school employees other than teachers per pupil, 1964		1,26	177	8
Electric power cost (mills per KWH), 1963	×	21	180	10
State property tax exemptions for industry, 1961	×	21,22	181	11
City–county general obligation bonds for industrial development in state, 1961	×	21,22	182	11
City–county revenue bonds for industrial development in state, 1961	×	21,22	183	11
State financial assistance available to industry, 1961	×	21,22	184	11
State chartered private development corporations in state, 1961	×	21,22	185	11
Any of above state incentives to industry available in state, 1961	×	21,22	186	11

*See notes at end of this Appendix.

1. Calculated from data in cited source(s).
2. For convenience in statistical calculations, all data labeled percent were converted to decimal ratios (e.g., a 10 percent increase is expressed as 1.1, a 5 percent decrease as 0.95).
3. Number of persons 21 years old and over was not available for 1950; this was approximated by using number of citizens 21 years old and over.
4. Population divided by number of families.
5. Since the Census was taken in April of cited year, the income data are for the previous calendar year.
6. Median family income times number of families divided by population.
7. Estimated by multiplying number of citizens 21 years old and over by percent of persons 25 years old and over who had completed schooling in the stated range. This assumes that the schooling of persons 21–25 is the same as that for persons 25 and over.
8. Number of males 14 years or over:

Let P = the population 14 years or older,
L = the civilian labor force,
m = the fraction of the population 14 or over that is male,
f = the fraction of the population 14 or over that is female,
k_m = the male labor force participation rate, and
k_f = the female labor force participation rate.

The *County and City Data Book, 1952*, gives P, L, k_m, and k_f for each county. To find the number of males in the population, mP, consider the following:

$$mPk_m + fPk_f = L;$$

[The equation is only true if L is equal to the total labor force, since the participation rates are on a total basis. To the extent the total differs from the civilian labor force, the estimates are in error.]

but
$$f = 1 - m;$$
thus

$$mPk_m + (1 - m)Pk_f = L,$$
$$mPk_m + Pk_f - mPk_f = L,$$

or

$$mP(k_m - k_f) = L - Pk_f,$$

and

$$mP = (L - Pk_f)/(k_m - k_f). \qquad\qquad (k_m - k_f \neq 0).$$

9. Estimated by dividing median number of persons per unit by median number of rooms per unit.

10. Figures stated in thousands in the *County and City Data Books* (e.g., 191,321, stated as 191) have been restored (multiplied by 1000) in our data file and in our statistical results.

11. Autos (trucks, tractors) on farms divided by number of farms.

12. Time deposits in banks plus savings capital of savings and loan associations.

13. Land in the Soil Inventory was classified into one of eight capability classes, with I being the best and VIII the worst. Class I soils have few limitations that restrict their use; Class II soils have some limitations that reduce the choice of plants or require moderate conservation practices; Class III soils have severe limitations that reduce the choice of plants or require special conservation practices, or both; Class IV soils have severe limitations that restrict the choice of plants, require very careful management, or both. Soils in Classes V–VIII are not generally suitable for the production of crops, although the better classes in this group may be suitable for grazing livestock. The stated proportion is the ratio of the acreage and the class or classes denoted to the total inventory acreage.

14. The 1931–1960 30-year records for all weather stations operating throughout the period were used to provide estimates for each weather variable for the 1960 population center of each county. Since few counties had complete station records for all weather variables, county data were estimated by taking a weighted average of the values for the variable in question using data for the five nearest stations reporting these data. Each observation was weighted inversely with the 4th power of distance to the county population center, so that stations at or near the population center would dominate if they reported the variable being estimated.

15. Calculated great-circle distance from 1960 county population center to 1960 population center of the nearest SMSA of stated minimum size. Existence of rivers, mountains, and other natural barriers is not considered.

16. Commercial farms are farms with sales of $2500 or more, plus farms with sales of $50 to $2499 where the farm was the primary occupation of an operator and was the family's major source of income.

17. As reported in the cited survey, collected between 1962 and 1964, primarily in the spring of 1962.

18. Government employment data are for 1962, population data are for 1960.

19. Average monthly payroll for the group, times 12, times number in the group.

20. An index value. Base data are not available.

21. A single figure for the state is included in each county record.

22. County record contains a 1 if incentive exists in the state, otherwise it is 0.

23. This figure represents a weighted average of the contour intervals used in mapping all $7\frac{1}{2}'$ (latitude and longitude) blocks within the county in a standard geological survey map series. Since the contour interval used varies with the hilliness of the area, this provides a rough measure of the relative hilliness of various counties.

24. Published unemployment rate times civilian labor force.

25. A positive value divided by 0 was arbitrarily give the value of 2. If 0 appeared in both numerator and denominator, the variable was given a value of 0.

26. Where the denominator was 0, the state average for the variable was used.

27. Pupils from 1950 Census divided by schools completed in 1950 or earlier and still existing at the time of the *National Inventory of School Facilities and Personnel* (1962–1964).

28. In some counties of small enrollment, data are not published in the cited source. In these cases, state averages were used.

DATA SOURCES

1. County and City Data Book, 1952, U.S. Department of Commerce, Bureau of the Census, Washington, D.C., 1953.

2. County and City Data Book, 1962, U.S. Department of Commerce, Bureau of the Census, Washington, D.C., 1962.

3. Census of Agriculture, 1959, U.S. Department of Commerce, Bureau of the Census, Washington, D.C., 1961.

4. Soil and Water Conservation Needs Inventory, published by most states in cooperation with the Soil Conservation Service, U.S. Department of Agriculture, and special tabulations supplied by the Soil Conservation Service.

5. National Weather Records Center, Weather Bureau, U.S. Department of Commerce.

6. Geography Division, Bureau of the Census, U.S. Department of Commerce.

7. Census of Governments, 1962, Volume III: Compendium of Public Employment, U.S. Department of Commerce, Bureau of the Census, Washington, D.C., 1964.

8. Office of Education, U.S. Department of Health, Education and Welfare, special summaries of unpublished data from the *National Inventory of School Facilities and Personnel,* conducted by the Elementary and Secondary Studies Branch, Office of Education.

9. Victor R. Fuchs, *Changes in the Location of Manufacturing in the United States Since 1929,* Yale University Press, New Haven, 1962.

10. Federal Power Commission data reported in "Utilities and Fuels," *Chemical Week,* July 20, 1963, page 76.

11. "The Bait That States Offer Industry," *Business Week,* December 16, 1961.

12. Derived from mapping contour interval data supplied by the Geological Survey, U.S. Department of the Interior.

Part II *The Impact of Industrial Development*

DANIEL SHIMSHONI

Regional Development
and Science-Based Industry

Within an affluent nation such as the United States there are regions of unusual social and economic backwardness, poorly endowed for agriculture or for economic mining, and with few industries.

At another social and economic extreme are centers of technical industry, such as Los Angeles and San Francisco, the northeast corridor from Boston to Washington, Ann Arbor and Minneapolis. In these "complexes" there is extensive research and development activity, carried on in government, university, and industrial laboratories. The products of a host of large and small technical firms incorporate the most advanced technology. Incomes, educational levels, industrial techniques, and cultural amenities are at the highest levels in the country or, indeed, in the world.

The example of these technical centers suggests that the introduction of science-based industry could advance depressed areas. The arguments for this proposition are somewhat as follows:

(a) For science-based industries, distance from raw materials or from mass consumer markets is no handicap. The raw material input comes from diverse sources and represents a very small part of the high value of the products, which are essentially sophisticated capital goods, research tools, or complicated and unusual weapons components.

(b) These industries are at an early or growth stage, and technical capability is the major input factor. Much of the high value added in manufacture represents the work of scientists and engineers.

(c) The structure of the national economy is changing to give greater weight and a faster relative growth rate to industries and services in which technology is a substantial part of the product cost.[1]

(d) The presence of research-based industry raises the general educational and social level of a region. The training or importation of scientists and technologists may produce a kind of multiplier process. Their presence in the area begins to affect the cultural life, and particularly the schools. Regional universities gain in stature. These cultural advances lead to more amenities in general, which in turn draw or retain talented individuals and their families.

(e) Finally, it is assumed that a failure to develop such industries will impair the region's ability to keep up economically and culturally with the rest of the country; and to lose, as a consequence, its talented people—thus falling irrevocably behind.

On the other hand, an attempt to create a technical industry complex in a backward area may not be the most advantageous way to solve the area's chronic unemployment, nor to get the best return, nationally, on investment in research and development. Some considerations follow:

(a) Short-run and long-run national goals for science may conflict. In allocating R & D funds, government agency decisions are dominated by considerations of the technical advances to

1. Machlup, Fritz, *The Production and Distribution of Knowledge in the United States* (Princeton, N.J.: Princeton University Press, 1962).

be achieved and the best current utilization of funds and people.[2,3]

(b) If resources were available, the philosophy of the scientific establishment, which decides federal grants, would separate rewards for excellence or promise (R & D grants per se) and allocations for institutional or regional development. Because resources are limited, however, "secondary" or "tertiary" institutions, or developing regions, may never reach a "critical mass" of capability.

(c) In backward regions, investments for education and for the learning periods of new technical plants are large, and the results are uncertain. The problems of employment and economic growth for these regions might be better solved, in the short run, by advancing such services as tourism and recreation; or, if near enough to consumer markets, by assembly plants and distribution centers, as in Memphis. (The fact that recreational activity does not usually support a large and learned population may not, on balance, be injurious from a national point of view, except for the hardships involved in what is essentially a population transfer.)

(d) The present so-called "centers of excellence" may well exceed the number of scientists and supporting services which are needed for excellent work, and the returns to scale of increased support for the most advanced regions may be diminishing. On the other hand, these are regions which, while not backward, are still somewhat secondary, but where returns to research investment may be larger. Examples are found in locations in the Middle West which train large numbers of graduate students, but whose universities have not reached the stature of those on the East and West coasts, and whose science-based industry and Federal R & D expenditures are limited.

The strategy alternatives which can arise thus include:

(a) Regional specialization: that is, let the region already highly

2. See, for example, Greenberg, D.S., "National Research Policy: Ambuscade for the Establishment," *Science,* 153 (August 5, 1966), 611.

3. Committee on Science and Astronautics, U.S. House of Representatives, 88th Cong. 2nd sess., *Geographic Distribution of Federal Research and Development Funds,* (Washington D.C.: Government Printing Office, 1964).

developed in education and R & D specialize in such activities; and let other regions specialize as well in the use of their current endowments (for example, nearness to market areas, or scenery, or climate).

(b) A step-wise program to advance backward regions: Here, moderately advanced regions, near but not quite at the top of the intellectual pyramid (such as some of the mid-western states) would receive substantial aid at the advanced scientific level; more backward areas would be moved toward a skilled technical and engineering level, hopefully to advance still further at a later state. Or,

(c) Priority given to enabling the most backward regions to achieve capability in advanced technology and to develop science-based industries.

In an attempt to clarify these issues, an analysis is made of those factors which seem to have influenced the establishment and growth of science-based industry in the United States today.

On the basis of a study by the author of the instrument industry,[4,5] it was supposed that the location of science-based industry could be related to (1) the presence of potential entrepreneurs; (2) the availability of professional manpower; (3) the proximity to demand for products and services, and government demand in particular;

4. Professor John R. Meyer of Harvard gave helpful guidance and criticism. Assistance was freely given by Professor Edward Roberts of M.I.T., who is directing a NASA-sponsored study of companies which originated from M.I.T. (see i and ii below) and by Albert Shapero who is directing a DOD-sponsored study at Stanford Research Institute on the "R & D Industry," (see iii and iv below). Most of the basic data were gathered with the financial support of the Harvard Program on Technology and Society, and the analysis and evaluation for the present paper were carried out under a grant from the Office of Economic Research of the Economic Development Administration in the Department of Commerce. The author is responsible for any errors of fact or of analysis.

(i) P. Teplitz, "Spin-off Enterprises from a Large Government-sponsored Laboratory," unpubl. thesis, Sloan School, M.I.T., Cambridge, Mass., 1965.

(ii) Herbert A. Wainer, "The Spin-off of Technology from Government-sponsored Research Laboratories: Lincoln Laboratory, unpubl. thesis, Sloan School, M.I.T., Cambridge, Mass., 1965.

(iii) Shapero, Howell, and Tombaugh, *An Exploratory Study of the Structure and Dynamics of the R & D Industry*, (Palo Alto, Calif.: Stanford Research Institute, June 1964).

(iv) Shapero, Howell, and Tombaugh, *The Structure and Dynamics of the R & D Industry* (Palo Alto, Calif.: Stanford Research Institute, November 1965).

5. Daniel Shimshoni, "Aspects of Scientific Entrepreneurship," unpubl. thesis, Harvard University, Cambridge, Mass., 1966.

(4) ease of communication; (5) venture capital; and (6) community attitudes and amenities.

It was thought that the characteristics found in the highly developed centers of technical industry might indicate the relation of these factors to location and thus help in policy formation for other areas. Accordingly, attention is directed to the science-based industry in the Boston area and to a lesser extent to San Francisco and the peninsula.

The Nature of a "Complex"

The term *complex* is used to describe a clustering of related firms in one locality, usually a metropolitan area. The common link can be that of role—research, for example—or of belonging to an industry (aerospace, garments). There is interdependence between the firms (suppliers, contractors). Diversity gives continuity of activity since the success of the area does not depend on one large manufacturer, contract, or mine.

The Boston area has a complex of firms developing or using advanced technology.[6] Table 1 shows the distribution of firms in the Chamber of Commerce list by size and the years in which they were founded.

There are probably more small firms proportionately than are shown in the table since the chance of overlooking them is greater than for the large company. Well over half the companies are active in electronics or related fields, and in over half, more than 20 percent of the employees worked in R & D. While many companies were formed recently, the picture is no doubt distorted by the disappearance of many firms founded in previous years.

In Greater Boston, some 35,000 R & D engineers and scientists were employed in companies, with probably several thousand more in the local universities or governmental laboratories—which include Quartermaster Corps Research laboratories, the USAF Cambridge Laboratories, and the NASA Electronics Research Center.

Comparable technical industry complexes are found in Los Angeles and around San Francisco Bay, in Washington-Baltimore,

6. The Greater Boston Chamber of Commerce, *Directory of Electronics Research and Development, Defense and Space Facilities,* January 1965; *A List of Small Business Concerns Interested in Performing Research and Development* (Washington, D.C.: Small Business Administration, 1966).

Table 1. Characteristics of Boston Area Technical Firms

1. Size distribution and R&D

Size group Total no. of employees	No. of firms	Firms with 20% of employees in R&D
0–19	107	88
20–49	75	42
50–99	83	36
100–399	86	31
400–999	28	10
1000	27	6

2. Company formation (where known).

Period of founding	No. of firms replying (BAS)
Pre 1900	7
1901–1913	6
1914–1941	20
1942–1945	7
1946–1950	26
1951–1955	28
1956–1960	54
1961–1965	30
Total	178

and in the New York metropolitan area. These differ from Boston in size and population. Each has several separate clusters, located at considerable intervening distances. The concentric transport design of Boston (Routes 128 and 135 providing semicircular major arteries around the central city), combined with the central location of Harvard and M.I.T., gives that complex an unusual spatial coherence. Other studies of the technical industries show strong tendencies for specific industries to cluster geographically. Spiegelman found, for example, that more than half of the instrument companies were located in 19 counties, largely in metropolitan areas. In the New York area in 1956, 98,000 people were employed in electronics, 260,000 in garment-making, and 160,000 in publishing.

New England seems to concentrate more heavily on development, with production proportionately stronger in New York and the West. The large number of small firms in New England is associated with its specialization in development.

University Attitudes

Technical industry complexes are frequently said to be a direct outcome of university research. There has in fact been a direct relationship between industrial growth and the universities in Palo Alto and in the Boston-Cambridge area, a more tenuous one between CalTech, U.C.L.A., and Los Angeles industry. In Minneapolis and Ann Arbor, industry has a close university relationship; for example, the University of Michigan has set up a research park next to the campus. Enterprise in these localities, however, is small in scope compared to that in Los Angeles, San Francisco, and Boston. Near other large graduate schools, such as midwestern state universities, there is comparatively little technical industry.

After World War I, M.I.T. began to develop a major scientific capability in addition to engineering. With Harvard, it had an important part in the growth of American science. During World War II, the Office of Scientific Research and Development (OSRD) worked through universities to enlist the scientific community in defense research. The Radiation Laboratory at M.I.T., and on a smaller scale the Radio Research Laboratory at Harvard, drew to Cambridge outstanding physicists and electronics engineers from the entire country. At the war's end, these activities largely closed down. Many of the scientists stayed in the area—on faculties, as employees, or eventually as entrepreneurs.

Massachusetts Institute of Technology continued to operate government laboratories: the Instrumentation Laboratory in guidance systems, the Lincoln Laboratory in general air defense programs, and MITRE for systems development. Lincoln Laboratory personnel grew from 258 in 1952 to nearly 2200 at its peak in 1957. In 1958, MITRE was split off from Lincoln and eventually employed 1800.

Professor Roberts' group at M.I.T.[8] is making a systematic study of M.I.T. spin-off companies. Their data show that 80 companies "spun off" from the Instrumentation and Lincoln Laboratories. Of 182 companies questioned in our Boston Survey (BAS), 62 reported that they had originated from a university and 47 from a company or governmental laboratory (see Table 3).

7. Max Hall, ed., *Made in New York*. Case Studies in Metropolitan Manufacturing (Cambridge, Mass.: Harvard University Press, 1959); Robert G. Spiegelman, "A Method for Analyzing the Location Characteristics of Footloose Industries," *Land Economics*, February 1964.
8. See Wainer, "Spin-off of Technology," and Teplitz, "Spin-off Enterprises."

M.I.T. as an institution has been helpful to new company formation in a passive way, often allowing an entrepreneur to continue for some time on a half-time assignment when starting his firm. In several cases (for example, Edgerton, Germeshausen, and Greer), private companies were formed when the Institute divested itself of an R&D program in order to avoid taking on large development project management. Recently, M.I.T. has become more concerned with the possibility that the outside interests of faculty members might be excessive, and has worked against faculty participation in ongoing management as officials of companies.

Only seven of BAS respondent companies reported having spun off from Harvard, compared to 49 from M.I.T. The University does not operate any laboratories for the government, nor does it contract for classified projects. While not unmindful of the benefits of equity participation, members of the Harvard faculty have taken much less interest in extra-curricular corporate activities than their colleagues at M.I.T.

Palo Alto technical industry was fostered in an active way by Stanford.[9] Under the leadership of Frederick Terman, formerly Dean of Electrical Engineering, the University encouraged entrepreneurs, providing every facility and striving for government research grants, hoping to industrialize the area and provide employment opportunities in California for Stanford graduates.

Before the war there was little electronics industry in the Bay area,[10] despite strong university departments. Students went to the East Coast after graduation. The country's talents were concentrated during the war in a few centers, such as the Radiation Laboratory at M.I.T., the Radio Research Laboratory at Harvard, and the Manhattan project.

After the war, Stanford aggressively sought research contracts,[11] permitted summer research salaries, often brought capital and entrepreneurs together, and financed graduate research which could lead to commercial products. Nascent companies helped with laboratory space, part-time appointments, and so on. Paralleling these activities, the unique capabilities of Stanford and companies in the area in the microwave field, and subsequent strength in solid-

9. Interview with F. Terman, July 1965. Terman served during the war at the Harvard Radio Research Laboratory and saw something of the attitudes of the Boston financial community and of science-based industry.
10., 11., *Ibid.*

state devices, in workshop facilities, and in technical capabilities, contributed to the formation of a group of companies which could interact and form a substantial industrial complex. Companies from outside Boston and the San Francisco Bay region have now established branches.

Other research institutions have shown a variety of attitudes. Dr. Alvin Weinberg at Oak Ridge has a policy which does not permit the use of government time or facilities by scientists for private ends. The local business community believes that this inhibits new company formation. Dr. Weinberg sees the question as one of values and principles.[12]

Although small in cost when compared to the large-scale government or corporate investments in R & D which are the basis for many of the innovations exploited by scientific entrepreneurs, the willingness of employers to permit part-time employment and provide laboratory space is important in enabling these individuals to establish their own companies.

Other Regional Characteristics

If the universities were central to the growth of Boston and Northern California industry, though in somewhat different ways, in other regions other factors have been important.

The pre-existence of heavy industry in Pittsburgh and in the Middle West, for example, has probably held back the formation of new scientific companies. The existence of heavy commitments in capital, management, and technology made the leaders and institutions in these communities less sensitive to nascent sciences which were only beginning their growth cycles. This factor might also tend to explain the loss of young Ph.D.'s from the Middle West. New England, on the other hand, was stimulated by the earlier decline of textiles to seek new enterprises.

In New York, according to the New York Metropolitan Area Study, clusters developed through historical circumstances, such as the impact on the garment industry of Jewish and Italian immigration. Gradually, the garment, electronic, and publishing-printing clusters lost their standardized operations to other regions, while activities needing the peculiar external economies of the metropolis

12. Interview with D. Weinberg, March 1965.

increased. These economies, the regions' attraction to skilled and professional people, the breadth of technical services available, and the ease of face-to-face communication are particularly important to creative activities, where uncertainty as to future needs, inputs, markets, and technical changes are dominant factors.[13]

The external economies of Boston and the two California complexes are similar and include amenities and an atmosphere which attract and keep skilled people, highly developed technical services (testing laboratories, data processing, precision manufacture and maintenance, complex component fabrication), and a favorable attitude in the colleges and financial community.

As in the case of New York, many external economies developed from historical circumstances. New England had a skilled labor potential from the days of shipping and textile prominence and from such sources as the machine tool industry. In California, major and unusual state investments in education, together with national migration trends, offered advantages in skilled manpower. The movie industry developed electronic skills, while the CalTech aeronautics laboratory is reported to have trained some of the leading technicians of the instrument industry (IIS).

Given the attractiveness and success of the metropolitan areas, and the immense prestige of New England and California, many hope to emulate them. The following sections consider what is known about capital, personnel, communications, and nearness to market in the Boston area in particular. One thing seems to be certain: once an area has achieved some scope and size, its external economies are aided by growth, and the process is reinforcing. What we do not know, however, is the size and scope of the complex at which the returns to growth begin to diminish.

Scientists, Engineers and Entrepreneurs

Professional work is the principal input of the firm which is developing advanced technology—particularly in the early years of the company when production may be small in relation to development. Firms that hope to grow through new products and processes, how-

13. Hall, *Made in New York,* and discussions with Professor Raymond Vernon of the Harvard School of Business Administration.

ever, will continue to invest a substantial proportion of sales in research and development.

Clearly, the ability of a region to produce or attract scientists and engineers is a major advantage, and inability to do so is an effective barrier to the growth of science-based industry. As an example, a survey of forty-five instrument companies showed that the entrepreneurs' "personal considerations" and the availability of skilled and professional staff entered into the location determination for nearly two-thirds of the firms; proximity of suppliers and markets were considered by one-third, and salary and other costs were considered by very few.[14]

Three kinds of individuals have made the new technical companies possible. The founders, or entrepreneurs, have usually been scientists or engineers in addition to having other necessary qualities. The sum of their decisions to form companies, and where to locate them, determines the initial geographic patterns of technical industry location. A second group are the technical leaders who do not form their own companies, but who may move to join existing firms. Lastly, there are the great bulk of professional employees of various degrees of creativity whose total numbers are important. Like an individual laboratory, a region needs a minimum supply of scientists in order to be technologically effective. A concentration of professional people with a variety of talents in science, engineering, and technical specialities, can make an area both productive and attractive.

The pertinent questions are: Where do entrepreneurs form companies in relation to their previous places of employment or study? How do the patterns of movement of leading technologists compare with those of entrepreneurs? What forms have the concentration and movement of scientists and engineers generally taken? The patterns appear to differ among industries and disciplines.

In the instrument industry study,[15] entrepreneurs were found to form new companies in the community in which they were already working or studying; or, failing this, in their "home towns" or near their undergraduate college. It is not surprising to find that the great majority of firms were founded "locally." Facing many risks,

14. Spiegelman, *Land Economics*, February 1964.
15. Shimshoni, "Aspects of Scientific Entrepreneurship."

company founders try to keep unknown factors to a minimum by starting in an environment which is already known.

The origins of Boston technical firms are summarized in Table 2. Of 109 companies which identified themselves as spin-offs, at least 93 originated in Boston area companies or universities. Data of companies founded by employees of the M.I.T.-organized Lincoln Laboratory and the Instrumentation Laboratory, both in Greater Boston, are shown in Table 3.[16]

Unlike entrepreneurs, prominent scientists and technologists who did not form their own companies moved freely between regions. In the instrument industry they crossed regional boundaries frequently, often moving across the country. An analogy would be the movements of senior university faculty, which tend to be national if not fully international in character. An outstanding scientist or technologist is highly sought after. As an employee he faces fewer unknown risks than the company founder and hence feels freer to move great distances. His employment by a company is often seen as the key to acquiring a new technical capability, and a nationwide search is not unusual.

The great number of engineers and scientists are concentrated in a few regions. In both absolute numbers and in proportion to regional population, there are states—as, for example, in the Midwest and South—with very few scientists, and states, particularly on the North Atlantic and Pacific coasts, with many. Figure 1 shows absolute numbers of scientists and engineers in 1962.[17] In the Boston area, more than 35,000 professionals were reported to be working in R & D in 1965, of whom more than 1,800 had a doctor's degree.[18] (These numbers do not include the universities.)

Relative concentration seems to change slowly in favor of the science-rich areas. In such disciplines as chemistry, which are not peculiarly associated with defense or space, the professional population is becoming more evenly distributed. On the other hand, physics and electronics are slowly becoming more concentrated, apparently in correlation with the location of defense research expenditures. Both effects tend to strengthen the science-rich regions,

16. Wainer, "Spin-off of Technology," and Teplitz, "Spin-off Enterprises."
17. Shimshoni, "Aspects of Scientific Entrepreneurship"; see also *American Science Manpower, 1962*, NSF 64–16 (Washington, D.C.: National Science Foundation, 1964), and Ira Horowitz, "The Regional Distribution of Scientific Talent," *Southern Economic Journal*, January 1965.
18. Horowitz, *ibid.*

Table 2. Origins of Companies by Technical Area[a]

Company origin	Electronic	Communication system, etc.	Computer hardware	Data processing	Metallurgy	Chemicals	Mech. engr.	Process control	Others	Instruments	All companies
MIT	21	9	5	5	9	3	11	5	3	12	(49)
Harvard	3	1				1			3	4	(7)
Another local university						2			1		3
Nonlocal university						1			2		3
Gov't Laboratory	2	1							1	1	3
Another company	17	4	6	2	6	7	9	3	3	10	(44)
TOTAL "spin-offs"	43	15	11	7	15	14	20	8	13	27	109
Formed as subsidiary	1			1	1	4	3	1		2	
Formed independently	19	10	3	5	14	17	12	6	5	8	
Other	1				1		1				
TOTAL "non-spin-offs"	21	10	3	6	16	21	16	7	5	10	78
TOTALS All origins	64	25	14	13	31	35	36	15	18	37	187

[a] A company can be in more than one technical area.

Table 3

	Total estimate spin-offs	Complete data available for	Number locating in Greater Boston area
Lincoln Laboratory	50	45	39
Instrumentation Laboratory	30	27	25

since the nondefense disciplines were not originally strongest on the East and West Coasts.

The intensity of engineering employment has shifted markedly from heavy industry to aerospace and to sophisticated laboratory and production control equipment, and proportionately from production to R & D. These changes have been accompanied by an overall proportional decline in nonagricultural employment (and with it scientists and engineers) in the Midwest, and a proportional increase in the Pacific and Mountain regions. By 1960 it was estimated that a quarter of the engineers in the United States worked in either New York or California.[19]

The net sum of individual movements seems to produce a flow which is highly correlated with general population movements and with federal expenditures on R & D.[20] In any given year the contracts awarded and the purchases made determine the job opportunities for the mass of scientists and engineers. On the other hand, a more precise definition of "opportunity"[21] would also include the level of the various kinds of amenities provided. These decisions, in turn, change regional manpower potentials and thus affect procurement decisions.

The mobility of scientists and engineers begins early in life. They leave home in order to study, particularly for postgraduate courses. They continue to move, due partly to the on-off nature of Department of Defense contract awards and partly to a continuing shortage of scientists, which has led to higher turnover. A peculiar feature of

19. Testimony of Dr. Seymour Wolfbein, *Impact of Defense Spending on Labor Surplus Areas*-1962, p. 43f. Hearing, Select Committee on Small Business, U.S. Senate (Washington, D.C.: Government Printing Office, 1962).

20. Shapero, Howell, and Tombaugh (iii and iv in n. 4 above); also, Horowitz, "Regional Distribution of Scientific Talent."

21. Samuel A. Stouffer, "Intervening Opportunities: A Theory Relating Mobility and Distance," *American Sociological Review*, 5 (December 1940), 845–867, and "Intervening Opportunities and Competing Migrants," *Journal of Regional Science*, 2 (Spring 1960), 1–26.

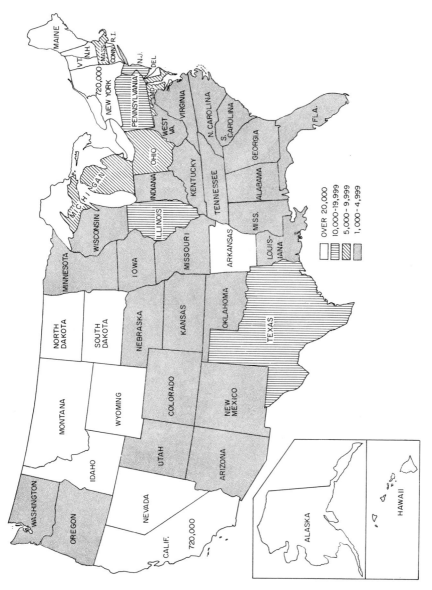

Figure 1.   Distribution of scientists by state. (Source: National Science Foundation: *National* Register of Scientific Personnel, 1962.)

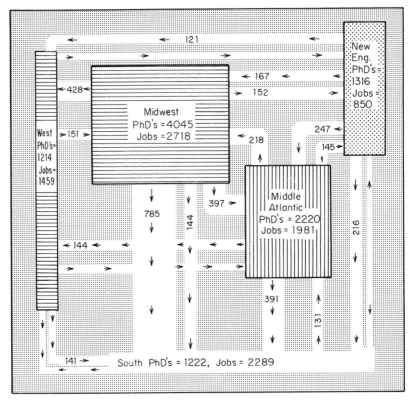

Figure 2. Diagram of interregional flow from doctoral to first postdoctoral job. Relative sizes of regions are shown as of doctorate production. Interregional flows of less than 100 are not specified. (Source: NAS-NRC No. 1293, 1965.)

the movement pattern is regional specialization in education, especially in New England and the Middle West. The Northeast and Middle West are producers of graduates, and the Far West and South are consumers.[22] New England educated two-thirds of its intellectual workers and California only one-fifth.

The newer areas of concentration, the Mountain and Western regions, are making heavy investments in universities, but still lag in proportion to their growing research needs. The South, long depressed, is now also on balance, importing scientists as space and defense programs are moved in, followed by efforts to build stronger universities.

22. Report No. 1293, NAS–NRC, Washington, D.C., 1965. Also, *American Science Manpower, 1956–58*, NSF 61–45 (Washington, D.C.: National Science Foundation, 1961).

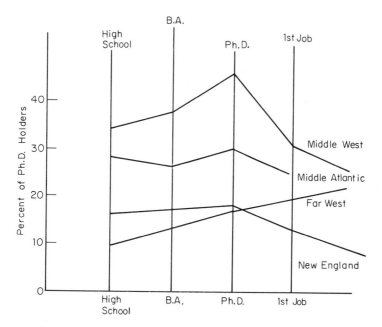

Figure 3. Migration patterns for holders of the Ph.D. degree.

The career patterns and flows (Figures 2 and 3) show that large postgraduate educational facilities will not, in and of themselves, make a region relatively stronger in professional employment. The data go back to 1930[23] and show a fairly consistent pattern. It can be asked why this educational effort has not produced greater proportionate local demand for scientists and engineers, particularly in the Midwest, but in New England as well. It should be said of New England, however, that the region might have been in a far poorer position and have made far less significant advances in science-based industry without its educational concentration.

The human potential of a region would seem to be determined by a number of considerations: the position, at a given time, of its industries in the birth and growth cycle of technologies; by specific local history, such as the concentration of talent in New England during World War II, and by the scope and quality of education; by overall population movement trends (e.g. immigration to New York, and the westward movement in the United States); and by an area's

23. Report No. 1293, NAS–NRC.

attractiveness, which is in turn affected by the diversity of job opportunities, climate, the urban form, and reputation.

Large R & D allocations coupled with educational development investments can give a regional potential for science-based industry. The realization of this potential will depend on whether entrepreneurs, scientists, and engineers consider the region an attractive place to live. Indeed, scientists seem to be attracted to the same areas as the general population.

Government Procurement and Industry Location

Government R & D budgets are heavily concentrated in comparatively few institutions, generally in the areas where science-based industries are clustered. California is especially prominent, often receiving large sums for major systems development. Table 4, which gives Federal R & D spending (obligations) by region in the fiscal year 1964,[24] illustrates this regional concentration. Of all R & D in the United States in 1964 (some $20 billion), $15 billion came from the government. In major universities, such as California and M.I.T., the government supplied some 90 percent of the research budget.

In the scientific "complexes," most subcontracting is to local firms, and these areas also receive many subcontracts from states with less-developed facilities.[25] Government stimulation of R & D and of nonresearch purchases results in greater demand for instruments and other scientific products, thereby increasing the potential markets for small technical firms.[26]

Government supports a large part of the R & D for technical industries. In the instrument industry (defined in a broad sense as by SIC groups 381, 382) the government finances more than half of the research and development (see Table 5).

24. *Obligations for Research and Development and R & D Plant:* Report to the Subcommittee on Science and Astronautics, U. S. House of Representatives, 88th Cong., 2nd sess. (Washington, D.C.: Government Printing Office, September 1964).

25. Shapero, Howell, and Tombaugh (n. 4 above), II, 70. In 1962, Boston prime contractors purchased over 70 percent of their material and services in New England or the Middle Atlantic States, and about 15 percent in the Far West. Similarly, Los Angeles establishments purchased 15 percent in the Northeast and about 70 percent in the Far West.

26. *Research and Development in Industry,* NSF 64–9 (Washington, D.C.: Government Printing office).

Table 4. Federal Research and Development Obligations by Region in 1964

Regions	Obligations ($1000)	Percentage of total
New England	761,344	5.3
Massachusetts	510,303	4.0
Pacific States	5,256,033	36.7
California	4,953,121	34.6
Middle Atlantic States	2,087,762	14.6
New York	1,133,240	7.9
East North Central States	853,483	6.0
Illinois	208,632	1.5
Other regions	5,107,942	35.6

In the instrument industry, the government provided the initial market for one-half of the innovations in electronic and advanced analytical instruments which were studied.[27] The indirect effect of government demand is probably even greater; a region's investment in R & D develops the basic job opportunities for professional people and, as a result, for potential entrepreneurs.

An obvious strategy for a region is to seek government research and development. Although the acquisition of government contracts is not enough in itself, it is appropriate to ask if government contracts are necessary. Boston survey data show that government markets predominate for the smallest companies and recently formed firms, but that some diversification occurs as a company develops. Table 6 summarizes the responses to the question: "Which

Table 5. Financing Instrument R & D (in $ millions)

Year	R & D	Government	Industry
1957	138	80	58
1958	153	93	60
1959	180	116	64
1960	214	139	75
1961	191	109	82

27. Shimshoni, "Aspects of Scientific Entrepreneurship."

Table 6.   Percentage of Firms Having More than 20% of Company
Sales in a Given Market

	Firm's first two years	1965
Government contract R&D	28.4	31.6
Products to government	22.7	33.3
Products *or* R&D, government	46.0	60.5
Commercial R&D	14.7	20
Commercial product sales	54.5	63
Commercial consulting	17	11

market categories formed more than 20 percent of your company's
sales during the first two years of operation and the present (1965)?"

All categories except commercial consulting tended to increase—
that is, more and more firms were active in more and more areas.

Firms were asked what the proportion of government sales was
in their first two years, and in 1965. Their responses are tabulated
in Table 7 and 8.

Over time company markets diversified. Firms which originally
were mainly government suppliers went into more commercial
markets; firms which were almost wholly commercial became more
government-oriented. Consulting, a way in which such firms often
start, becomes less important as time goes by than product sales.

Government markets are shown to be very important as a start,
as shown by the high proportion of companies which had more than
one-third—or even two-thirds—of their sales to government in their
first two years. Table 9 shows little consistent effect of company size.
Of small companies with zero to 19 employees, 65 percent had more
than one-third of government or prime contractor business in their
first two years.

Table 7.   Frequency Distribution by Fractions of Total Sales to
Government by Industry

Proportion of govt. sales	Firms							
	Electronics		Instruments		Chemicals, mat'ls, etc.		All firms responding	
	Orig.	1965	Orig.	1965	Orig.	1965	Orig.	1965
0–1/3	50.8	41.5	46.0	44.4	72.7	69.7	52.3	42.5
1/3–2/3	10.2	23.1	6.2	25.0	9.1	9.1	12.0	27.1
2/3–3/3	39.0	35.4	46.9	30.6	18.2	21.2	35.7	30.4

Table 8.   Percentage of Firms with Sales to Government Exceeding One-third of Total Sales by Industry

			Firms				
Electronics		Instruments		Chemicals, mat'ls, etc.		All firms responding	
Orig.	1965	Orig.	1965	Orig.	1965	Orig.	1965
50	58	49	55	27	30	37.7	57.5

The government thus appears as the predominant customer for science-based industries, particularly in their early years. In chemistry and metallurgy the role of government is less than in electronics and other aerospace-related fields.

There are limits to the use of this large purchasing power as a policy instrument to develop backward areas. Aside from funds explicitly intended to underwrite regional growth, most allocations will depend on capability—that is, having outstanding leaders and capable associates on a significant scale. The analysis of such factors as the availability of technical services and technicians, attractiveness to professional people, a diversity of market and employment, and communications, shows that the growth of a complex is not only arduous but takes time, and is the result of a fortunate interaction of historical trends, events, and initiative.

Table 9.   Relationship of Firm Size to Size of Government Contracts for 186 Boston Area Firms in 1965

Size distribution by employment	$0-\frac{1}{3}$	$\frac{1}{3}-\frac{2}{3}$	$\frac{2}{3}-1$	Total number of firms
0–19	16 (38.4%)	15 (32.6%)	15 (32.6%)	46 (100%)
20–49	19 (46.3%)	11 (26.8%)	11 (26.8%)	41 (100%)
59–99	19 (43.2%)	13 (29.5%)	12 (27.3%)	44 (100%)
100–399	13 (37.1%)	8 (22.9%)	14 (40.0%)	35 (100%)
400–999	4 (44.4%)	2 (22.2%)	3 (33.3%)	35 (100%)
≥ 1000	8 (72.7%)	2 (18.2%)	1 (9.1%)	11 (100%)

Communications

A technical company depends for its existence on communications. The kinds of intelligence include:

(a) An early awareness of trends in market needs and their implications.

(b) An early awareness of trends in the state of the art and their implications.

(c) Technical information for the solution of problems and for decision.

(d) Transfer in depth, i.e., the acquiring of an independent mastery of technology.

(e) Market information for solution to problems and decisions.

(f) Getting information to customers—and selling.

Occasionally a new technology is transferred in depth; that is, a firm acquires the ability to continue to develop a technology on its own. Frequently, development is a joint effort with a customer. In the instrument industry it appears that transfer in depth takes place mainly through the movement of individuals, whether to form their own companies or to join existing firms. In a great many cases new products and processes came to the market largely through individual mobility.

On-going communication is understood only imperfectly. The existence of large clusters of companies in such areas as Boston, and the reports of the New York Metropolitan study, suggest that on-going communication is substantially verbal and informal and that concentration thus provides important economies.

Data on the value to firms of this communications network are few and contradictory. Many firms, perhaps because of the uniqueness of their products, successfully serve markets and are related to distant technical centers in the United States and throughout the world. The literature may be a more important resource than is generally believed, further reducing the sensitivity to distance. On the other hand, in a score of conversations, technical leaders mentioned the effects of serendipity, the unexpected communication which comes from chance meetings made possible by proximity.

It was not possible to compare systematically the relative costs of information among regions and the relative profitability and growth of similar firms in these different locations. Instead, tech-

Table 10. Principal Market Sources for 141 Boston Area Firms

Market Area	Universities		Government laboratories		Companies	
	No. of firms	%[a]	No. of firms	%	No. of firms	%
New England	24	17	22	16	60	42
New York area	8	6	19	13	48	34
Midwest and South	7	5	18	13	31	22
Far West	8	6	15	11	27	20
Other U.S.	3	2	12	9	7	5
"All" U.S.	32	23	41	29	67	48
Foreign	20	15	21	15	38	27
Total firms answering	59	42	81	58	139	99

[a]Percentage of 141 firms replying to query on location of markets.

nical firms in the Boston area were asked what they regarded as their principal market and technical centers (for example, New England), and what kinds of sources of information they most frequently used (as, for example, consultants, technical literature, and so on). Firms in the Boston Area Survey were asked the following questions:

(a) Where are the principal centers in your technical field?

(b) Where are your principal market centers?

The replies, summarized in Tables 10 and 11, were tabulated by the kind of industry, the size of the firms, the origin of the company,

Table 11. Company Origin and Source of Technical Knowledge for 142 Boston Area Firms

Source of technical knowledge	Spin-off from local university	Spin-off from nonlocal university	Company spin-off	Independent company
Local university	13		5	10
Any university	15	1	6	11
Consultants	11	1	13	24
New employees	13	1	9	13
Local sources	23	1	21	34
Nonlocal sources	4	1	2	9
Total no. of companies in sample	33	3	36	70

(whether university or company spin-off), and whether or not government R&D represented more than 20 percent of sales.

The results of the survey did not generally conform to expectations. It was anticipated that virtually all Boston area firms would list institutions in the region among the principal market and technical centers. Yet, despite the high technical level of New England, a significant proportion (about one-half of the companies) did *not* list any New England institution as being a principal market or technical center. Of the kinds of institutions mentioned, "other firms" were named most often. Indeed, replies citing companies in the New York area, or in "all of the U.S.," exceeded those citing New England universities as "technical centers," and "companies in the Far West[11] were cited more often than "New England government laboratories." Market centers were seen to be even more dispersed than technical centers,[28] with a substantial emphasis on markets in "all of the U.S." and on foreign markets.

As for the kinds of sources, the predominant source of market knowledge, as might be expected, is the customer (69%), or, put another way, the salesman (60%). Similarly, market surveys are extensively made, but "outside" or consulting groups are in disfavor (60% cited them as least frequently used). Thirty-four percent said that technical literature is a principal source of market knowledge.

The sources of technical information "most frequently used" were technical literature (cited by 77%), customers (by 54%), professional and social contacts in the area (by 35%), and local university faculty and services (by 22%), while universities were also "least frequently used" (local, by 44%; and from other areas, by 55%).

The reported extensive use of literature was unexpected. Technical literature might not have been expected to be as important as less formal means in rapidly advancing technologies. If, however, replies citing "customers" as a source of technical information are combined with those citing "personal and professional contacts" and "consultants," the frequency with which interpersonal and written technical sources are used is about equal; however, interpersonal contacts predominate in the area of marketing.

Small firms or those with fewer total R&D employees might be expected to rely more on technical literature, since it would have a

28. See page   above regarding the location of subcontracting.

Table 12.   Use of Literature versus Number of R & D Employees

	R & D employees					
	0–5	6–15	16–30	31–50	51–100	> 100
Firms listing literature as a principal source	36	46	17	8	2	4
Total number of firms responding	44	51	26	12	4	5

narrower background of expertise. This does not seem to be the case, as shown in Table 12.

The survey provided no clear evidence of the effect of company size on its use of local vs. nonlocal sources. Companies which originated as spin-offs from local firms or universities would be expected to use local sources more because of previous acquaintance and the probability that they would engage in parallel kinds of work. This turned out to be the case. As shown in Table 11, there is a significantly higher use of local university resources by spin-offs from local universities—40 percent vs. 14 percent reported by non-spin-off companies.

Companies engaged in newer technologies could be expected to make more frequent use of local technical sources and markets because of a possible lack of written data, a faster rate of change in the art, and the consequent greater imprecision of formal technical intercourse and the need for strong customer–manufacturer interaction. On the other hand, because of their scarcity, newer technologies might be expected to find a more widespread market. The kind of technology, however, does not seem to be consistently related to the information sources used.

Firms doing much government contract R & D might be expected to make greater use of consultants as well as of nonlocal sources. Their client will pay for the expense involved perhaps more readily than a private firm, and the technology may be more advanced, requiring greater effort in problem-solving. Table 13 shows that firms heavily engaged in government R & D make much more extensive use of universities and consultants, but no other consistent pattern is apparent.

A great many firms in a developed industrial complex rely on local sources of information, but a significant number do not. A

Table 13. Frequency with Which Firms Mentioned Sources of Technical and Market Knowledge, by Importance of Government R & D Activity

| | Government R & D as Proportion of Company Sales | | | | |
| | Percentage of firms mentioning source | | Number of firms mentioning source | | |
	Govt. R&D greater than 20% of firm's sales	Govt. R&D less than 20% of firm's sales	Govt. R&D greater than 20% of firm's sales	Govt. R&D less than 20% of firm's sales	All Firms
TECHNICAL SOURCES					
Local and other universities	37%	19%	15	19	34
Consultants	44	31	18	32	50
New employees	29	24	12	24	36
"Local" sources (1, 3a, 4a, 9)	61	54	25	55	80
"Nonlocal" sources	15	10	6	10	16
TOTAL			41	102	143
MARKET SOURCES					
Universities or consultants	13%	12%	6	13	19
Market survey by staff or outside organization	51	46	24	49	73
New employees	4	9	2	10	12
TOTAL FIRMS INTERVIEWED			41[a]	102[a]	143[a]

[a]The number of technical sources and market sources do not need to equal number of firms involved because of multiple responses.

given technology often tends to be developed at about the same rate in several firms and locations, and a specialist firm, if it is above the smallest size, will often be entirely independent of nearby sources of information.

A further impression, reinforced by interviews with the instrument industry, is that such industrial complexes as Boston are not, as often believed, heavily dependent on local university-centered technical communities for current information. Firms do not confine their discourse to local universities; they were found to consult a great deal with professors from out-of-town as well as from local universities. The role of the university on the local scene may be much more that of the creator and collector of leadership and entrepreneurial talent and attracter of other institutions, such as the radiation laboratory.

Possibly the contradictions of the findings relating to the importance of easy face-to-face communication may be explained by the positions held by those interviewed in the survey or by those who answered the questionnaires, or by the growing importance of travel and telephone. Those interviewed or responding to questionnaires were mostly company executives or technical leaders. These people travel more extensively than others in their firms, go to more conferences, and see more out-of-town or foreign visitors, making distant centers more visible and useful to them. Meetings of Bostonians as often as not take place on airplanes and at airports.

On the other hand, it appears that firms rely more on universities for basic research and information about visionary developments and major innovations than these replies suggest. Further study of the way in which technical information is exchanged is warranted.

Capital Availability as a Local Characteristic

The finding of venture capital for a new scientific enterprise, based on sound technology, has not generally been seen as a problem. It has been generally assumed that the tax laws would encourage individuals to invest at a speculative stage of new enterprise. The investment community is thought to be looking constantly for unusual individuals and special opportunities, so that the scarcity is one of ideas rather than money.

Although there is considerable truth in these views, the difficulties are far greater than is commonly supposed. Interviews of industry personnel gave the impression that the difficulty of obtaining venture capital may be a serious obstacle in some regions or cities. Leaders in the national capital market and technical venture capital firms, such as AR & D, or Rockefeller Brothers[29] have been primarily interested in firms with proven records of sales and profits and are not, as a result, a significant factor in new enterprise formation.

Each stage of growth demands a different capital source. Before there is a proven market, sales record, or even a product, the founders tend to use personal or family funds, or those of acquaintances. Later, receivable financing, payment delays, and a host of intricate methods are used by resourceful treasurers. When growth has started and the need for funds begins to accelerate, outside investors, usually found through the financial community, become important sources.

Evidence for the financial difficulties of new enterprises is scanty and was not gathered systematically. In talks with a cross section of Boston area firms, the problem was introduced voluntarily by a large proportion of small companies and by one or two larger firms which were in a period of rapid growth. Several new entrepreneurs asked us for help. Others were found to be negotiating for mergers as a possible solution to capital problems. Nearly one-half of the Lincoln Laboratory spin-offs studied by Wainer reported that they were hindered by lack of capital.[30] The total impression is that even in the highly developed technical complex, such as the Greater Boston area, there are difficulties in securing venture capital.

Shapero[31] and Deutermann[32] collected evidence of regional differences in the availability of venture capital. Stanford Research Institute cites Tucson, St. Louis, and Denver as examples of areas where the local financial community lacks experience in evaluating science-based industry. Boston financiers, on the other hand, are said to be "at home with science," as they are strange to other fields.

29. For example, see Victor J. Danilov, "Venture Sources of Capital," *Industrial Research,* (October 1966).

30. Wainer, "Spin-off of Technology," pp. 85f.

31. Shapero, Howell, and Tombaugh (n. 4 above).

32. Elizabeth P. Deutermann, "Seeding Science-Based Industry," *Business Review, Federal Bank of Philadelphia,* (May 1966).

As a leading Boston banker said, "I have never made a loan to support wheat, oil, cattle, or minerals."[33]

Boston companies believe commercial banks to be helpful, particularly in bringing the technical entrepreneur into "a strong communication network in financial circles." A bank can also be helpful by understanding the potentials of technologies and appreciating the value of contracts which a technical firm may have. By giving a company leeway at a crucial time, a bank can allow a firm to establish favorable customer and supplier relations. At the same time, Boston financial circles have comparatively little difficulty, in their turn, in getting expert technical evaluations. Philadelphia area companies reported a far less helpful attitude and far less concrete help from local banks.

People apparently invest in things which they understand and on which they can get reports readily, and so the capital market for the new small firm is basically local, while established firms use a more national market. Indeed, local patriotism often has a positive effect in unexpected localities.

Summary

There is a recognizable pattern in the way in which the leading centers of scientific industry, or "complexes," have grown: Technical leaders and potential entrepreneurs were attracted to these areas by universities or by scientific enterprises of unusual scope, such as the Radiation Laboratory at M.I.T. in World War II.

Large government expenditure for R&D and for weapons and space systems has been necessary for the establishment of these institutions and for the formation of many firms. Once firms are well established, the government is less essential as a customer, but is still preponderant.

Government expenditure, however, is not enough; nor can it be obtained unless a region has technical leadership and skills. People having these capabilities are attracted to and held in a region by the kinds of amenities which attract the general population (such as climate, the characteristics of urban areas, education and rec-

33. Gordon Baty, *Initial Financing of the New Research-Based Enterprise in New England.* Research Report to the Federal Reserve Bank of Boston, November 25, 1964. See also, interview with Arthur F. Snyder, Vice-President, New England Merchants Bank, July 1966.

reation). Other strong external economies for the technical firms include investment in education and technical services. Once sufficient scale and diversity are reached, economies of communication and marketing develop.

The choice of policy alternatives will depend to some extent on whether the interests of the nation as a whole or that of residents of a specific underdeveloped region are given primary weight.

The best strategy for a region seeking technical growth would seem to be to invest heavily in its general educational system, in higher education, and in other basic contributions to cultural life, and at the same time to seek federal help in advancing the quality of the local universities, and federal procurement of R & D. The universities are of major importance in this regard—not as the hub of the network of technical communication in the area, but as a force in attracting and keeping leaders, as a contributor to the surrounding culture, as an attraction for government investment, and as an instructor of entrepreneurs.

ROGER E. BOLTON

Defense Spending and Policies for Labor-Surplus Areas*

The regional impact of national defense spending concerns some professional economists, most politicians, and occasionally the man in the street. Some find it inherently interesting to know the effects of specialization in defense industries or operations on the rate and the character of growth in various regions. More importantly, national defense demand is something we would hope to *replace* with other kinds of resource demand when the international situation

*I have benefited from comments by John Meyer, John Kain, Karen Polenske, William Chartener, Will Steger, Henry Bruton, Gordon Winston, and faculty members and students who participated in seminars at Harvard, Dartmouth, and Western Michigan. I also benefited from my fellow-members of the Independent Study Board on the Regional Effects of Federal Procurement and Related Policies (whose report is cited later). I am solely responsible for the contents of the paper, however.

Parts of this paper rely heavily on my earlier paper, "Statistics of Regional and Industrial Defense Impact," read at the December 1967 meetings of the American Statistical Association, and published in the Association's *1967 Proceedings of the Business and Economic Statistics Section*, (Washington, D.C., 1968, pp. 200–207).

would allow it. Naturally, then, we tend to worry about how the regional impact of defense compares to the regional impact of whatever other private and public demands we would like to substitute.

Difficulties arise in estimating the regional distribution of defense production, or the net effects on various regions of hypothetical changes in the composition of final demand. Some of the difficulties are statistical, namely, the lack of necessary data of good quality. Others are analytical. Because the ultimate impact of defense demand is determined by interindustry and interregional trading patterns, a good analytical model of those patterns is needed to provide an accurate representation of reality without overstraining the data.

In this paper I shall discuss the policy considerations which are raised by the inevitable unevenness of the regional impact of defense expenditures and within this framework present the appropriate background for a discussion of the statistical and analytical difficulties. I shall conclude with a brief review of the problems in generating the kinds of data which the policy discussion suggests are desirable.

Several important questions will not be discussed. One relates to the effect of defense business on the *potential* output of a region and whether initial defense business triggers the growth of technologically related nondefense industry because of external economies. For example, difficult chicken-or-egg problems occur in evaluating the interaction between the nature and quality of higher education in an area experiencing rapid growth in some kinds of defense production. Second is the non-economic character of culture and society in areas which specialize greatly in defense. For example, are local politics affected by a felt need to exert lobbying pressure for continued defense business? Is participation in social and cultural activity affected by the nature of military families? These undoubtedly interesting questions should be properly left to the sociologist.

Why Regional Effects Are Important

Although the answer may seem obvious, it is useful to ask why the regional effects of economic trends and policies are important.[1] The ultimate goal of economic policy is the welfare of persons; and

1. See my statement in U.S. Congress, Joint Economic Committee, Hearings, 90th Cong., 1st sess., *Economic Effect of Vietnam Spending*, 1967, I, 153–157.

therefore it should be concerned with the effect on people. Except for the political fact that congressmen and senators represent specific regions, why are regional groupings of people important? Why should the enlightened economic policy-maker care about the regional tag on a person?

The lack of easy mobility of people between regions is of course the reason. This lack of mobility is one of the structural features which make it impossible to achieve full employment and price stability merely by balancing aggregate supply and demand on the national level. If mobility were easy, when international political developments called for an increase or decrease in defense spending the changes could be offset by general monetary and fiscal policy, and it would not matter if the regional distribution of demand changed in the process. That distribution would be an incidental result of the composition of output chosen on consumer and investment demand and public expenditure criteria. In regions where demand declined, temporary unemployment would occur, and in regions where demand increased, there would be labor shortages and inflation. Two kinds of regional adjustments would then reduce both the inflation and unemployment. Labor would leave the declining area for the expanding one, and, if the declining area were suitable for the production of some items in demand in the new situation, firms would move operations into them to escape higher wages and labor shortages.

In the competitive model, these adjustments occur because relative prices change and resources move in response to them. The movement of specific capital goods out of declining regions is usually very difficult in a purely technical sense. The owners of inflexible capital goods in a declining region may have to accept lower quasi-rents to keep them employed, or abandon them if the alternative is negative quasi-rents. From an allocation point of view flexible prices will produce the following correct results: if quasi-rents fall below fixed costs, but remain positive, the capital goods will remain in service; however, if the quasi-rents fall below zero, the capital goods will be abandoned. Both alternatives are socially appropriate, and while their owners will be disappointed and hurt, this is the natural risk investors take and is widely tolerated even without the compensation that the rest of the population could pay and still benefit.[2]

2. William Fellner, "Influence of Market Structure on Technological Progress," *Quarterly Journal of Economics, 55* (1951), 556–577.

Labor may also be immobile, not so much because of technical fixity or high transportation costs but psychological factors, which are often summed up in the word "roots," and rational economic behavior, as will be described in a moment. In the competitive model, the failure to move forces the same adjustment on labor as on the owners of capital—that is, lower return.

It is possible, however, that some resources remaining in the region will not be employed even if their market prices fall to zero. In the real world production functions do not necessarily exhibit enough substitutability to insure full employment even at a zero price. If we are talking about production in a narrowly defined geographical area, the requirement that it take place in that area inevitably limits substitution. The area may have characteristics which make it unsuitable for any production unless *minimum* quantities of new factors are brought in from outside. These characteristics may be distance from other areas, climate, terrain, or skill-mix of labor force. The new factors from outside may be skilled labor or new capital for transportation, or other factors needed to overcome the characteristics. This requirement for minimum quantities of other factors is the definition of complementarity. The new resources may have a high opportunity cost, and even if the price of resident factors is zero, the productivity of the combined dose may be lower than the opportunity costs.

Naturally, this is more likely to occur the more narrowly defined a region is, and the more it had specialized, before its decline, in products very unlike other products in the economy. In the extreme, a region may have been particularly suited for some defense activity but totally unfit for anything else. This is suggested by certain kinds of installations which not only have very specific requirements, but also are best located where they will not interfere with civilian life, that is, in empty areas where nothing else is done. A less extreme example is provided by any depressed area with a labor force left unbalanced by selective emigration.

The point can also be made by assuming that production possibilities are described by a linear programming model, in which the production of each commodity by each method at each place is a "process." Each process is characterized by fixed proportions, but there are so many processes that there really is much substitutability. Nevertheless, not all processes need to be operated at positive levels, and it may be that none of the processes applying to a given area is run at a positive level.

Therefore, some persistent unemployment may actually be an efficient result. The competitive model notwithstanding, the minimum, socially efficient unemployment of labor and capital is unfortunately augmented by unemployment caused by downward rigidity of resource prices. As experience in depressed areas indicates, prices and wages do not fall far enough, and unemployment persists, even though global efficiency would be improved if these resources were used.[3] This condition need not be present in all prices to induce the above effect; for if factors are complementary in production, the failure of some factor prices to fall will affect the demand for the rest located in the region. Capital remains idle, despite the fact that its use has a short-run marginal cost lower in real terms than the long-run marginal cost of output in other areas where full employment already exists. Again, if the wage does not decline enough, labor will not be employed, although its value of marginal product is substantial even after accounting for certain difficulties of producing in the given area. The unemployment of labor is regarded as a more serious result of rigidity than that of business capital. There is a more sympathetic view toward labor, especially if the owners of capital are absentee or impersonal (corporate) ones. While physical capital may wear out relatively quickly, men may not wear out so quickly. This means that the equity problem and the social waste represented by idleness are greater. Although the owners of capital may be knowledgeable and have incomes so high we can ignore equity problems, the situation may be different for labor in both respects.

This should make clearer why the regional effects of changes in the level and composition of defense demand are important. Immobility can cause persistent unemployment in some areas, and persistent inflation in others after such changes occur. Persons do suffer, and there is waste. Thus even those policy-makers who are interested solely in national goals must consider the regional effects. Others with more parochial interests consider the additional political implications of changing regional fortunes, plus the fact that even when mobility does occur, it is the result of pressuring many individuals who undoubtedly would have preferred not to have gone to the trouble.

3. George Borts and Jerome Stein, *Economic Growth in a Free Market* (New York: Columbia University Press, 1964), pp. 193–205.

The Causes of Immobility

Even with optimum information, immobility is to be expected from the usual models of economic behavior. Lack of incentive to move from labor-surplus areas is not necessarily the result of laziness or other features of "peculiar" preference functions. Involuntary movement is not the optimum solution to the adjustment problem, even from a strict efficiency point of view. This means we need not rely on equity arguments to justify subsidies to industry in declining areas. Naturally, equity arguments are powerful and in fact sufficient because efficiency can never be the only goal of economic policy; from standard welfare economics theory we know that nothing makes an "efficient" point preferable to an inefficient one if practical choice is restricted only to some of the theoretically possible points. But even efficiency can be improved by subsidies.

Given the downward rigidity of wages and prices, people in the declining area face two options: move to another area where money incomes are higher, or stay in their present area where money incomes are lower due to unemployment. Either choice is logical. While the people who remain in the area, un- or underemployed, have low money income, the variable costs of living in the region are also low. Real income may therefore remain higher than if they moved. The existence of two kinds of capital goods makes this possible: the tangible capital of residences, and the intangible capital which Rothenberg called "capital in specific neighborhood adjustment" in his study of urban renewal programs:

> . . . social capital [is] developed by living in, and becoming adjusted to and part of a neighborhood. Housing location is a crucial part of one's whole pattern of living. It determines the direction in which substantial energies are expended—to learn about the various nonhousing consumption opportunities that are available, and to develop a configuration of social interaction, extending from particular specialized relationships through deep friendships. These investments in knowledge and decision-making about consumption and social interaction are largely lost when a family moves out of a neighborhood.[4]

For some time after a region suffers from loss of demand, both these kinds of capital remain serviceable. The maintenance costs may be very low for each kind, making the variable costs of living

---

4. Jerome Rothenberg, *Economic Evaluation of Urban Renewal* (Washington, D.C.: The Brookings Institution, 1967), p. 147.

in the present community low, especially when compared to the marginal costs of establishing residence elsewhere, which include (adjusted to annual flows) moving costs and the capital costs of housing and of creating new neighborhood adjustment capital.[5] In other words, the failure of money wages to decline forces persistent unemployment in the declining region, but the fact that real living costs are partly independent of current prices keeps the cost of remaining very low.

Some people, primarily those who leave the stagnant area quickly, find the psychic costs of creating new neighborhood adjustment capital lower than others.[6] Thus the services of existing neighborhood adjustment capital will weigh more heavily in the utility functions of some, just as most goods do not have the same value for all persons. If the quantity of these services is considered just as appropriate an argument in utility functions as the quantities of other goods and services, then economizing on adjustment capital is an important social as well as private goal. If choice is limited to the two options described, the correct choice on social grounds is the correct one on private grounds. The higher private marginal costs for moving into an expanding area represent higher social marginal costs; the gains from exploiting existing durable neighborhood adjustment capital are social as well as private gains.

One cannot protest this conclusion without challenging a social welfare function within which individual utility functions "count." One could protest the conclusion on the same grounds as are used to condemn the consumption of cigarettes, the consumption of narcotics, or the consumption of the services of intangible private capital invested in "adjustment patterns" of racial discrimination. In those cases private goods enter into individual utility functions, but many consider them socially harmful. In the first case, the justification is a failure to recognize self-harm; in the second, the same failure plus external effects harmful to others; and in the third, harmful external effects alone. Condemnation of immobility, in this sense, would not be based on the economic grounds used to condemn market failures. Although persons may easily disagree on

5. If a person moving into an expanding area had owned his own residence previously, but suffers disadvantages in obtaining credit in the new area, the capital costs of maintaining the same standard of housing consumption will be all the greater, because higher interest rates will be paid or because credit cannot be obtained at all for purchase of a residence.

6. Rothenberg, *Economic Evaluation of Urban Renewal*, p. 147.

what community standards relating to ambition and mobility ought to be, neighborhood adjustment capital does not involve patently irrational preferences or harmful externalities. Immobility is more a matter of the general style of life in our economy, not merely a market imperfection. The persistent unemployment resulting from wage rigidity is a market failure, but the failure to move cannot be called a market failure.

The Role of Subsidized Employment

If the individual's choice included a third option, employment at going wage rates, it would be preferred and might be the best solution for the economy generally, even if a subsidy is required to insure employment. It is preferable to unemployment because some socially useful output can be produced at low or zero opportunity cost. It may also be preferable to reemployment in expanding regions if the marginal costs of new capital goods, including social overhead and housing, is high and if a high value is put on the services the existing neighborhood adjustment capital provides in the declining area. If subsidized employment is superior to migration, employment subsidies are a better policy than such subsidies to relocation as moving allowances, compensation for losses in the value of homes, and so on. Relocation assistance may leave the migrating family no better or no worse off than before, but it does not economize on the various kinds of social capital, including neighborhood adjustment capital, in the way employment in the old area does.

"Subsidy" can refer to several different policies. Conscious efforts in government procurement policy may guide orders into areas with surplus labor by giving "preference" to firms that either would produce there or buy inputs from there, by limiting competition to such firms in the first place, or by defraying outright some of the money costs government vendors incur there, so that they can profitably underbid other firms. The deviations from competitive procurement policy now legally allowed are sharply limited, for no regional preference may cause a higher price to be paid.[7] Another

---

7. U.S. Department of Commerce, *Report of the Independent Study Board on the Regional Effects of Government Procurement and Related Policies* (Washington, D.C.: U.S. Government Printing Office, 1967), pp. 5–10.

possibility would disregard some market prices in favor of estimated opportunity costs (shadow prices) when making cost-benefit evaluations of public investment projects. A third and theoretically superior alternative insures that the prices of all products, not just those bought by the government, reflect opportunity costs. In other words, any firm, producing to government order or not, would receive reimbursement for its money costs that exceed shadow prices. Naturally, any of these policies can be used regardless of the extent of unemployed resources, even in prosperous areas.

The wise use of subsidies will increase real output, although a procurement agency's money costs may be higher. The money expenditures of the whole government may or may not be higher, for lower welfare payments offset higher procurement costs and increased taxes will result when higher incomes are produced. These budgetary offsets, rather than the real output advantages, are often used by laymen justifying these subsidies. While the entire population benefits, the subsidies will also change the distribution of income. One can identify three components of this change for the population whose resources are not subsidized: (1) the effects of lower goods prices in areas where employment is full because resources with low opportunity costs have been used; (2) the increase in taxes because subsidy must be paid; and (3) the decrease in taxes required to finance a given quantity of public goods, which is possible because the subsidized persons increase their tax payments. The net effect of these depends on the productivity of the newly employed resources, which determines the subsidy to be paid, and on the tax rate levied on the increased incomes of the resources.[8]

However, opportunity costs do not remain low forever. The crucial question is how long would resources remain unemployed in the absence of subsidized employment. If the subsidies continue, how

---

8. I am ignoring any political and administrative difficulties the government may have in raising the taxes to pay the subsidies. This is acceptable in the present context. In the underdeveloped country context, where subsidies based on shadow prices are widely debated, these difficulties are more important. If the effective constraint is a purely financial one rather than the total quantity of resources, increased subsidies may force a reduction in public investment, which may significantly offset the improvements in static efficiency from subsidies. I am also ignoring efficiency effects of excess burden caused by increasing taxes to pay subsidies, which also might be more important in an underdeveloped country, especially if it relies heavily on a few taxes. See Peter Eckstein, *Accounting Prices as a Tool of Development Planning*, Center for Research on Economic Development, University of Michigan, February, 1968 (mimeo).

much of the output can be counted as benefits without opportunity costs? *Some* of the resources employed in subsidized production would clearly have found alternative employment elsewhere, and more and more resources have opportunities the longer the program continues.[9] In the absence of subsidies, some families will move.[10] The relative weight of existing neighborhood adjustment capital declines the longer the family foregoes other consumer goods, and residences wear out; eventually capital costs must be incurred to maintain the housing standard whether or not the family moves. Once subsidized employment lasts beyond the time when emigration would have occurred, labor is not being employed in locations where it is most productive. The danger of subsidized employment programs is that they will delay movement when eventual movement is socially efficient.[11]

For example, assume that without subsidized employment families would move away after two years of unemployment because the costs of resettling elsewhere would then no longer outweigh the income advantages. If employment for this family's labor is maintained over the two years, and then the family immediately moves to a new area and is employed there, the net benefits of the program are large; but if the subsidy retards mobility, there is some loss in the third and every succeeding year until movement does take place. This loss is the difference between the productivity of the worker in the new area and in the old. This is a problem which makes it necessary to use subsidies very carefully. Even if movement is ultimately desirable, subsidized employment may possibly postpone costs of producing new capital as long as existing assets are good, and postponing costs is socially worthwhile if the discount rate is positive; but subsidies may likewise postpone the benefits

9. In the context of post-disarmament policy, this point is discussed in "Defense Spending: Burden or Prop," *Defense and Disarmament,* Roger Bolton, ed. (Englewood Cliffs, N.J.: Prentice-Hall, 1966).

10. See Frederick W. Bell, "An Econometric Forecasting Model for a Region," *Journal of Regional Science,* 7 (Winter 1967), 113–114, and references cited there.

11. Borts and Stein, *Economic Growth in a Free Market,* p. 200. McKean notes: "'Moderate' amounts of unemployment, although it may sound callous to say so, are often more valuable than alternative uses of the resources. The 'idle' are often seeking information that has more value, both to them and in terms of Pareto optimality, than would the jobs at hand. And the fact of unemployment sometimes produces information of value—that a location or occupation should have fewer resources devoted to it." Roland N. McKean, "The Use of Shadow Prices," *Problems in Public Expenditure Analysis,* Samuel Chase, ed. (Washington, D.C.: The Brookings Institution, 1968), p. 43.

of changes in demand and technology. One of the greatest challenges to the effective use of subsidized employment programs is to use genuinely unemployed resources without establishing habits which inhibit long-run flexibility.

Cost-Benefit Analysis

The structure of cost-benefit analysis for subsidized employment, a blanket phrase covering many possibilities, should now be apparent. Much depends on how one values the importance of neighborhood adjustment patterns as durable social capital; how far unemployed resources will be used if activity is subsidized; how productive the resources can be in the declining area; and the social discount rate. Unless they increase aggregate demand, regional subsidies cannot cope with widespread unemployment throughout the nation because they will merely shift output and employment from one region to another without increasing the national totals. G. S. Tolley has also pointed out that real output will not be increased to the extent that the subsidized project draws upon a kind of labor (e.g., an age or skill group) which is in excess supply in many regions.[12] Furthermore, production in labor-surplus areas will not automatically use idle resources, and Tolley mentions the complications this introduces. If the project uses resources which, having been employed elsewhere, migrate into the region in response to the subsidy, their opportunity costs are not zero. (Tolley suggests "back-migration" of persons who left the area earlier). Analytically, this is not different from a delay in out-migration from the area that would occur. Additionally, subsidies are less effective if the in-migrants cause new capital to be built in a declining area which has no real long-term future. If the area has been depressed for some time, past selective out-migration has likely left it with an unbalanced labor force; and if some people must in-migrate, they will desire new capital, private and social, when existing facilities are not satisfactory.

Tolley notes that opportunity costs are high for high-wage professional men and for unattached single women—groups which are quite mobile. He suggests real employment gains will be greater

12. G. S. Tolley, "The Impacts of Water Investments in Depressed Areas," *Water Research*, Allen V. Kneese and Stephen C. Smith, eds. (Baltimore: Johns Hopkins Press, 1966), pp. 458–462.

if the project employs married women and young women who have not yet left the home, both groups being less mobile, but that there are opportunity costs of services in the home which are relevant to cost-benefit analysis. Consequently, such women may be employed at an opportunity cost lower than the market wage rate but not zero. Finally, he notes that for other workers one must examine separately specific age and skill groups to determine what would happen in the absence of subsidies.[13]

Haveman and Krutilla suggest practical approaches to adjusting cost-benefit ratios to allow for correct opportunity costs.[14] They consider adjustments required by excess supplies of labor and capital in the whole nation during the 1957-1964 period, rather than unemployment limited to regional pockets. Regarding the applicability of the method to the regional allocation of spending, however they refer to some preliminary work on more refined models. Although their empirical estimates are only for public water investment, similar results could be calculated for any public investment or private spending induced by tax reductions, if the basic data are available.

Haveman and Krutilla estimate the direct and indirect effects of final expenditure for water resource investment, but not induced consumption, on *industries* and *occupations*, using recent information on what inputs are needed in water project construction, on the national input–output matrix, and on an industry–occupation matrix. The other crucial variable is the proportion of the resources employed which are actually idle. Here Haveman and Krutilla use hypothetical response functions for labor and capital which assume a positive relationship between the rate of unemployment in an occupational group and the probability that idle labor will be used, a positive relationship between the excess capacity rate in an industry and the probability that idle capital will be used. Alternative results are presented for linear and various nonlinear response functions. The estimates of adjusted cost-benefit ratios are significantly lower than the ones based on money costs, 15 percent or more below.

13. *Ibid.*
14. Robert Haveman and John Krutilla, "Unemployment, Excess Capacity, and Benefit-Cost Investment Criteria," *Review of Economics and Statistics*, 49 (August 1967), 382–392; and "Unemployment, Excess Capacity, and Benefit-Cost Investment Criteria: Some Supplementary Estimates," *Review of Economics and Statistics*, 49 (November 1967), 654–655.

The analysis offers an intriguing attempt to fill what is often an empty theoretical box. For extension to regional allocations a more sophisticated input–output model will be required to allow for interregional trade and measurement of induced effects on local industries. On the supply side, the labor response functions will differ from national ones, because the *duration* of unemployment will become important. The relationship between the probability of drawing on idle labor and the duration of unemployment may not be monotonic, however. For example, assume in Case A the unemployment rate is .10 in many regions; in Case B, it has been .10 in one region for a short time, but is much lower elsewhere; in Case C, the rate has been .10 in one region for a long time and is much lower elsewhere. Then if the regional allocation of given expenditures is shifted toward the region, real output gains will probably be greater in Case B than in Case A. But they may be lower in C than in B, because of the effect of previous selective outmigration mentioned earlier.

Extensive empirical analysis may show that resources which are immobile are also very unproductive. Perhaps the only laborers really in excess supply are unskilled ones. An area's inherent advantages of location, transportation access, climate, natural resources, culture, and the other "amenities" important to professional and managerial personnel may fall far short of requirements under new technologies and demands. Then income maintenance provides a better solution than subsidies, which waste the resources that must complement the ones genuinely in excess supply. Some areas might best decline and eventually die so long as the *people* in them are not in undue distress.[15]

While this possibility must be faced up to, there are two other factors which can favor subsidies. First, the market not only does

---

15. U.S. Congress, *Economic Effect of Vietnam Spending,* pp. 154–173; Bolton, "Defense Spending: Burden or Prop?" pp. 47–48. The conclusion that income maintenance is preferable may be modified if the social welfare function considers the incomes of individuals *and* the means by which a desired distribution is reached. For example, equity may be best improved in a way which preserves individual dignity and self-respect by offering work, even if it wastes complementary resources, instead of flat relief grants (the infamous dole); and the ultimate subsidizers may actually prefer to pay taxes hidden in excessive product prices than ones explicitly levied. See Arthur Maass, "Benefit-Cost Analysis: Its Relevance to Public Investment Decisions," in Kneese and Smith, eds., *Water Research,* pp. 317–318, and Stephen Marglin, "Objectives of Water-Resource Development: A General Statement," *Design of Water-Resource Systems,* Arthur Maass *et al.* (Cambridge, Massachusetts: Harvard University Press, 1962), pp. 63–67, and McKean, "The Use of Shadow Prices" (above, n. 11).

not produce equilibrium prices for unemployed resources, but also possibly undervalues the productivity of resources employed in the area, because of external economies or the uncertainty that efficient scales of operation can be achieved in new industries. If so, there are what we may call "reincarnation" arguments, which are analogous to "infant industry" arguments. One must be skeptical here, since the depressed area has already had a historical trial run.[16] Nevertheless, future changes in technology and demand may cause the pendulum to swing back, and subsidies would then turn out to make that resurgence less expensive. Second, external diseconomies frequently result from continued growth in expanding areas with discrepancies between private and social costs which unduly penalize declining areas and favor expanding ones. Baumol, for example, suggested that the cost of externalities will rise more rapidly than population, perhaps as roughly the *square* of the size of the population.[17] There may be incomplete, or at least delayed, internalization of these costs to residents of the expanding area through budgetary changes. Other countries have felt the need to interfere with natural market forces on location patterns and to adopt explicit planning.

In its report to Congress, an "Independent Study Board" discussed reconsideration of recognizing true opportunity costs in federal procurement, as well as location of installations.[18] The report mentioned the following possible policies: (1) bidding credit to firms hiring long-term unemployed; (2) expanded set-aside programs, which would limit competition on some contracts to labor-surplus firms; (3) conscious geographical direction of procurement of standard items, perhaps by 100 percent set-asides for certain products; (4) a bid-assistance scheme, which would directly reimburse vendors who produce in labor surplus areas, so that procurement agencies would not bear the higher money costs in their own budgets. The Board merely mentioned these and recommended none for immediate use. One general problem applies to all of the schemes: if only a few pockets of excess unemployment exist, money costs might be even higher than necessary to achieve the preferred regional allocation due to lack of vigorous competition in bidding.

16. Borts and Stein, *Economic Growth in a Free Market*, 194–196.
17. W. J. Baumol, "Macroeconomics of Unbalanced Growth: The Anatomy of Urban Crisis," *American Economic Review*, 57 (June 1967), 423–424.
18. U.S. Department of Commerce, *Report of the Independent Study Board*, pp. 24–30.

Defense Expenditure

All of the above is relevant to a study of defense expenditure, because shifts in defense may produce the structural adjustment problems and use of policies discussed above. One may go further and ask if a subsidy can be extended by tinkering with the regional allocation of defense spending itself. Is defense equipment so technologically advanced and research-oriented that it would be out of the question to guide it toward declining or depressed areas? Even if not, does it make sense to take an area in trouble and to try to rehabilitate it, even temporarily, with a kind of demand which is volatile in the first place?

On the first question, if in the future the problem is caused by a shift in defense spending, some labor-surplus areas may have adequate technical capacity, because they were producing for defense previously and may be well suited to produce whatever defense needs remain, assuming opportunity costs are considered. Even in some other context, the needs of the defense establishment are enormous and diverse, and the military buys large quantities of mundane items, "off the shelf" and similar to items widely used in the civilian economy. The regional differences in the money costs of producing these items may be rather small. Even when final items are highly specialized, there is flexibility regarding where the separate components are manufactured, especially those produced in the intermediate stages. For example, little choice is necessary to determine where the steel and aluminum for a missile are produced, or where the missile if finally assembled, but more options are available on where intermediate fabrication and assembly takes place. The regional allocation of these stages can be influenced by provisions for subcontracting.

On the second question, the defense contract may have advantages in implementing a subsidy because it calls for a definite quantity of goods to be procured and thus can be clearly limited in size and duration at the outset. These characteristics make it suitable, for the government must have the freedom to "turn off" a subsidy when it is no longer warranted. Also, reasons for altering the regional allocation of defense spending may include the socially desirable results obtained by avoiding over-concentration of it in certain regions, even if they offer the lowest real cost. Over-specialization presents dangers, and allowing areas to exploit their advantages for defense industry fully may not be wise. Of course, over-specialization in anything can be dangerous, but defense is highly volatile by its nature. It is also subject to political pressures, which may have unfortunate effects on our political decisions. If a decline in spending is contemplated, economic readjustment problems are anticipated. The resulting fears of unemployment may lead to political pressure against the decisions to reduce spending, although a reduction is desirable in the international situation. The significance of this is unmeasurable, but the pressure can be seen in the furor and lobbying over several base-closing episodes.

Although the likelihood of political pressures in procurement is a point in favor of avoiding extreme specialization, it unfortunately limits the usefulness of defense spending as a means of subsidizing depressed areas, because any political factors which result in the expenditure rigidities offset the advantages of specified quantity and duration mentioned above.

Estimating the Regional Impacts of Defense

The previous discussion should indicate why we need to know the ultimate impacts of changes in the defense budget; however, the great interdependence between specialized parts of the economy creates difficulties in precisely indicating these impacts. The final delivery of any good or service is the end of a long chain of production, parts of which are completed in many different regions. To trace the impact of a defense order, one must know the inter-industry and interregional trading patterns involved. Assumptions about them are crucial in any study of the impact of defense demand; and even estimates of national aggregate impact are somewhat dependent on them, for the aggregate effects depend on how much production occurs where there is excess capacity.

Identification of the direct effects emanating from all parts of a defense item does not complete the analysis. Multiplier and induced investment effects remain to be determined. Some studies are confined to tracing through the chain of defense production and do not consider the multiplier process. This may be justified under the assumption that while production chain defense items may be quite different from the one for nondefense items, the multiplier process is nearly the same whether the exogenous stimulus is defense or not. If true, this facilitates the assessment of the fate of a particular region under different hypothetical national development. But the assumption is not completely valid; for example, the consumption habits of armed forces families are different from the habits of other families.[19] Thus, the multiplier is not the same in every region, a fact which must be considered when regions are compared with each other. And if investment is endogenous, the multiplier depends on the composition of exogenous demand, because that will determine if new demands can be satisfied by switching existing capital from one use to another.

To describe the raw data, defense spending should be divided into three parts: payrolls of military personnel; payrolls of civilian employees of the armed services; and procurement, meaning all other purchases from the private sector, including research and development, services, operating and maintenance supplies, construction, and so forth.[20]

Military Payrolls

Three facts about military personnel are relevant when considering regional measures of military payrolls: (1) they are often stationed far from their permanent homes; (2) their cash wages are below the alternative wages they would earn in the civilian sector, but they receive considerable income in kind (food and clothing); and (3) they have part of their pay deducted and alloted to dependents.

These facts raise problems for compilers of data, given the exogenous-endogenous classification used by analysts who use regional data. One possibility is to report all income, cash and in kind, before allotments are deducted, as military payrolls in the area where the serviceman is stationed. This requires that one ignore the fact that other areas provide the source of the food and clothing and are the recipients of allotment expenditures. The justification might be that military expenditure on food and clothing merely substitutes for induced private consumption and that expenditure by dependents is obviously induced consumption. Since official data on the

19. As shown in the Survey of Consumer Expenditures, 1960–61. See U.S. Bureau of Labor Statistics, Report No. 237–293, *Consumer Expenditures and Income, Total United States Urban and Rural*, 1960–61 (Washington, D.C.: U.S. Government Printing Office, 1965).

20. This division is not the same as the federal *Budget*, where some procurement and some civilian payrolls are grouped together in "Operations and Maintenance," and the "Procurement" title excludes research and development and construction.

regional distribution of nondefense wages do not pretend to trace through any part of the multiplier process, this should not be done for military wages either. One could argue that if the compilers of data adjust military wages for leakages, and if analysts use those wages in models which assume certain standard patterns of leakage, the result would be an overadjustment for leakage—thus underestimating the ultimate demand effect in states where military installations are located.

The other possibility is to assign the cash wages to the area of duty station, but to allocate food and clothing expenditure and the allotments to more appropriate areas. This could be justified on the assumption that the regional distribution of this induced demand is so different from the average, given the conditions of military life. Military food and clothing are perhaps much different from the kind civilians buy, and the regional distribution of consumption of local services is much different if allotments are sent to dependents who live elsewhere.

A major source of data on military payrolls is the Commerce Department's series on personal income by state, which shows military payrolls as a separate source of income in each state.[21] These data include the value of in-kind income in the state of duty station, and the allotments in the state where the dependent lives. This is appropriate for the purpose of the data, which is to measure personal income where received. It is also appropriate for impact measure if the allotment process greatly affects the regional pattern of activity while in-kind income does not. This does seem plausible, since so much of a person's consumption produces ultimate demand in the area where he lives, but the problem of consistency with nonmilitary wages remains. The personal income data do not reflect adjustments to allow for nonmilitary workers sending regular amounts to their dependents when they are working away from home. Construction workers may do a lot of this, for example. That the adjustment should be made for military personnel and not for others is not clear. Many people not in the military spend money

---

21. These data are published annually in an issue of the *Survey of Current Business* (U.S. Government Printing Office, monthly), usually in August. A detailed description of how the state distribution is estimated is in U.S. Office of Business Economics, *Personal Income by State since 1929, a Supplement to the Survey of Current Business* (Washington D.C.: U.S. Government Printing Office, 1956), pp. 95–97, 100–101.

outside the state where they live. Nevertheless, in the income data these people are treated differently from servicemen. This may be significant because construction has been the major kind of defense spending in some states in recent years.

Civilian Payrolls

Civilian employees fill a variety of jobs, ranging from the highest Pentagon officials down to contract administrators, shipyard and arsenal workers, scientists, and secretaries in installations all over the country. The Commerce Department has made available data on payrolls by state, although these figures are not separated out from total federal payrolls in the published data on personal income by state. Recent Censuses and Surveys of Manufactures have included data on workers in federal manufacturing-type installations, but these are far less detailed than data available for employees in the private sector.[22]

Procurement[23]

The ideal data would include the value added by defense work in every business establishment, so the figures could be grouped into industries and regions as detailed as desired. These ideal data do not exist. Instead, two kinds of regularly published official data are available. The first enumerate the value of prime contracts classified by state and by defense item; for example, the dollar value of contracts for ships in Connecticut or for combat vehicles in Indiana for a particular year is known. The second show the operations of certain large manufacturing plants which are known to specialize in defense products.

Both kinds of data are useful to indicate the pattern of some defense demand, especially the last stages of assembly; however, they cannot reveal the total impact because they do not show the incidence of earlier stages. To estimate this, the analyst must know general interindustrial and interregional trading patterns and must then assume that the patterns for defense production are similar

22. For data sources, see Bolton, "Statistics on Industrial and Regional Impact," p. 203.
23. For a much more detailed discussion and exact citations to data sources, see *ibid.*, pp. 203–206.

or else differ predictably. Presently, this combination of assumptions cannot give very precise estimates of the regional distribution, and the error of the estimates cannot be expressed in the usual probability terms of statistical inference.

Before commenting on this further, some difficulties in using the prime contract statistics even for the location of final assembly work must be noted. As the final stages are quite important, being more specialized than the earlier ones and thus presenting more potential readjustment problems in case of large shifts in the level or composition of defense spending, increased knowledge of the distribution of contracts would be valuable and one suspects it could be obtained with considerably less expenditure than required to improve the estimates of the location of earlier stages. One difficulty is that a large volume of small contracts, which may include supplies procured locally by bases, is not classified by item and state at all. Thus the lack of information makes it hard to estimate the dependence of areas with bases on procurement. A random sample of small contracts would be useful. Other difficulties arise in classification. The item classification is not similar to the industrial classification usually employed in analysis, and it is not consistently applied. For example, government-furnished electronics equipment is classified under electronics and the state where the equipment is produced; electronics subsystems bought by an aircraft maker are classified under aircraft in the state where the aircraft firm is located.

Input-Output Studies

Since interindustry and interregional flows are important in determining the ultimate regional impact of defense spending, input-output models are major tools in estimating the impact. A recent important effort along this line is the study by Leontief and others.[24]

This study estimates for industries and regions the net change in employment which would result if defense spending were reduced and replaced by a combination of other final demands. The estimates assume that defense purchases fall by 20 percent, with all industries suffering the same percentage reduction in the value of their final

24. Wassily Leontief, *et al.*, "The Economic Impact—Industrial and Regional—of an Arms Cut," *Review of Economics and Statistics*, 47 (August 1965), 217–241.

deliveries to defense, and that consumption, private investment, nondefense government purchases, and net exports increase by enough to maintain employment in the entire nation at the previous level. Since the model is closed with respect to consumption, this means that the average propensity to consume each product, assumed equal to the marginal propensity, is increased by the same percentage.

Some industries are classified as "national" and others as "local." National industries are those for which the supply and use are balanced only on the national level; local industries are those for which all the production in a region is used within that region. The household sector is a local industry, selling factor services to other industries and buying consumer goods from them.

Concerning the allocation of defense value added to regions, the study makes no use of the prime contract data, described earlier, as evidence of the regional distribution. It merely assumes defense production in a national industry is regionally distributed in the same way as the industry's total production. In other words, it assumes that the combined direct and indirect production for defense is the same proportion of a national industry's total production in every region. However, both the prime contract data and other data from Census of Manufactures surveys[25] suggest that this is not true. Even in industries which are generally very dependent on defense, like aerospace, dependence varies from region to region, a conclusion which could be deduced by anyone with the casual knowledge that different *firms* in the same industry cater to defense demands to different degrees and that these firms are dominant in different regions (for example, General Electric and United Aircraft in aircraft engines, Lockheed and Boeing in airframes, and so on).

In this connection, as in many input-output studies, the aggregation is high. Other data show that the industrial mix *within* such broad categories is not stable over time. For example, "aircraft" includes both airframes and engines. Their relative importance changes over time, and the regional distributions of the two are quite different.[26]

25. U.S. Bureau of the Census, *Current Industrial Reports, Series MA-175 (65)-2, Shipments of Defense-Oriented Industries: 1965* (Washington, D.C.: The Bureau, 1967).

26. Research Analysis Corporation, *Economic Impact Analysis: A Military Procurement Final-Demand Vector* (McLean, Virginia: RAC, 1967), pp. 19-34.

For local industries, the final shipments to the defense customers are assumed to have the same regional distribution as Department of Defense payrolls. This is a reasonable assumption, given the nature of local industries (public utilities, trade, finance, services, and so forth). All intermediate shipments by local industries in a region are assumed to meet direct or indirect requirements of national industries located in the region. The share of local industry's intermediate shipments attributed to defense depends on the share of the region's national industries assumed to be for defense. For example, estimated defense dependence of the local industry "maintenance construction" in region X is high if X has many military installations or if X is dominated by such defense-dependent national industries as aircraft and ordnance.

Military personnel payrolls are assumed to be final deliveries from the local household industry to defense demand. They apparently exclude in-kind income and include allotments.

The relationship between local and national industries is similar to the one in a regional base model; however, the same industries are in the exogenous sector in all regions. They do not vary as they would with a location coefficient selection method, for example. The model departs greatly from the regional base notion in other important respects as well. It retains the usual classification of final demand in input-output studies, which is in the spirit of simple Keynesian income models for the nation as a whole: consumption is endogenous, but investment, government spending, and exports are exogenous. These demands are exogenous both for the nation as a whole and for each region, because a region's share in them is assumed to be absolutely independent of its share in national defense and in consumption. In the hypothetical situation which the study analyzes, the regional distribution of investment demand is the same before the arms cut as after. This contrasts sharply with the regional base approach, which would recognize some parts of these demands as endogenous. Specifically, the independence between a region's share in total investment, or state and local government spending, and its share of defense demand and consumption is unjustifiable. The final estimates are incongruous in showing areas like California having large net declines in employment and yet having the same share as before in the national totals for investment and state and local government purchases—indeed, having absolute increases in these two, since the national totals for them have increased. Naturally, this incomplete closing of the model is necessitated by the lack of hypotheses on investment and state and local government demand, in which theorists show as much confidence as they do in hypotheses on consumption behavior. The result of this inadequate allowance for induced effects is almost certainly an underestimate of the structural problems which would actually result in the hypothetical situation studied.

Conclusion

There is enough merit in a policy of subsidies to induce production in declining regions to justify much more study than it has received so far in this country. The present blanket prohibition against paying any price differential to favor a region in government procurement seems too severe. The prohibition is perhaps explained by earlier fears that government policy would not be adequate to keep unemployment confined to a few pockets of the economy, so that preferences would merely shuffle employment from regions with high unemployment to ones with still higher unemployment. Now, however, aggregate demand policy seems enlightened enough so that preferences would really mean an increase in the utilization of resources.

As usual, one can safely call for more research; but we need particular kinds of research. In the specific context of defense spending we have progressed quite far in describing the broad impacts on regions and industries. Models of such broad impacts can be improved still further. But we also need research on how rather narrowly defined regions would fare in hypothetical situations. Some research should be focused on the metropolitan areas most likely to face major readjustment in the event of a defense reduction. Previous work has already shown unambiguously where some of these areas are. The net impact on them of changes in demand must be forecast, as well as the extent to which prompt mobility and relative price adjustments will alleviate unemployment. Given the resulting estimate of the severity of the remaining readjustment problems, it is important to ascertain what industries can reasonably be subsidized in the areas. As suggested earlier, there are clear guidelines for this determination, relating to the need for complementary factors from outside and to the mobility which will eventually result if no subsidy is given.

Research into these problems must naturally take some policy objectives as given. In turn, the predictions of the results may suggest how the goals should be changed. In this respect, there are three questions to which more explicit answers should be articulated:

—What patterns of alternative resource use will be encouraged by federal budgetary and monetary policy in the event of a marked fall in defense needs? While there are political difficulties in any advance commitment to details, there are also some advantages in it.

—Do the external diseconomies created by continued growth in the expanding metropolitan areas justify concerted efforts to reduce whatever incentives for migration into them already exist? Is enhancing the attractiveness of less crowded, declining areas a legitimate part of such efforts?

—What value do we place on geographical mobility? I have argued above that this is a social question, that it involves value judgments, and that the answer is not automatically given by traditional economic theory. Although it often *assumes* mobility, that theory does not really supply a justification for keeping pressure on for mobility, or even for subsidizing mobility, because it leaves wide open the question of how big a weight should be placed on the predilection of many for immobility.

WILLIAM H. MIERNYK*

Local Labor Market Effects of New Plant Locations

The Objectives of Regional Development Policy

Regional development programs in the United States have two specific objectives: (a) to provide jobs for the unemployed in designated labor-surplus areas, both urban and rural, and (b) to increase the per capita income of residents of designated rural areas. These objectives are to be accomplished either by direct public investment

*The author wishes to acknowledge helpful comments on an earlier draft by members of the Seminar on Regional Economics at Harvard University, and in particular by Professor Raymond McKay of West Virginia University. It is important to add that no one but the author should be held accountable for the final results.

or by investment in social overhead capital.[1] Viewed more broadly, regional development is part of the general effort by the federal government to reduce the *national* unemployment rate. It includes various training and manpower programs, administered by the U.S. Department of Labor or the Office of Economic Opportunity, whose unifying feature is their focus on the *structural* component of unemployment. One of the assumptions behind these programs is that direct intervention in the labor market will reduce unemployment without generating upward pressure on wages or prices.

Both in this country and abroad, public investment funds have been channeled to areas of high and persistent unemployment by means of favorable loans to private establishments. This involves the implicit assumption that such investment in new or expanded plant facilities will reduce local unemployment, because it is expected that workers will be recruited from the ranks of the unemployed. It is also assumed that new secondary jobs will be created, in the local trade and service sectors, for example, so that total employment in the area will increase by some multiple of the number of direct new jobs. If these assumptions are realized, the local unemployment rate will fall as workers are shifted from an unemployed to an employed status.

In a development context these assumptions seem plausible, but in formulating programs of direct public investment, policy-makers have given relatively little thought to the operation of local labor markets or to the characteristics of the unemployed in labor-surplus areas. Partly because of this, some of the early expectations of what direct public investment in depressed areas might accomplish were exaggerated. Although some of the criticism of the federal government's first efforts at area redevelopment was politically motivated, the critics were able to muster statistical support for their attacks by pointing to the gaps between projected and realized changes in employment and unemployment in the areas where loans and grants had been made.

The early projections of new employment that public investment

1. For the purposes of this paper the distinction between direct public investment (DPI) and social overhead investment (SOI) is not significant. This is not to say, however, that the two approaches are equivalent. Direct public investment is one way of subsidizing employment in a region, and if the subsidy is made large enough it is almost certain to add to the number of jobs in that region. Investment in social overhead capital, such as water, sewer, or highway systems, is a somewhat riskier proposition. It is made on the assumption that public investment, which is not directly concerned with the creation of long-run job opportunities in the region, will stimulate job-creating private investment.

was expected to generate in depressed areas were high because they were based on an unrealistic estimate of the average regional employment multiplier. In the absence of better information, a multiplier of 1.6 was used. This figure had been employed by the U.S. Chamber of Commerce in some of its promotional literature. But in many depressed areas, trade and service establishments were operating below capacity when new plants were located in them and were able to handle an increase in the demand for their services without significant changes in employment. Also, some estimates of the impact of new plants on local unemployment missed the mark because the Area Redevelopment Administration (ARA) assumed that these plants would be staffed almost entirely from the ranks of the *locally* unemployed. This assumption ignored possible changes in labor force participation rates and the possibility of the movement of workers into and out of local labor markets either on a commuting or on a permanent basis.

Under Title II of the Economic Development Act of 1965 the Secretary of Commerce is authorized to make loans to private establishments that will locate in eligible areas, provided that relocation from another area is not involved. The Act also states that loans will be made only if the project is "reasonably calculated to provide more than a temporary alleviation of unemployment or underemployment within the redevelopment area."[2] Before a loan is granted, the applicant must submit an estimate of the number of jobs the project is expected to provide initially and the estimated potential employment when the project reaches full capacity. In general, estimates of direct employment at the plant level have not been far from realized levels. It has been more difficult, however, to make advance estimates of the effects on local *unemployment*. Some newly hired workers have been migrants into the area, and some projects have attracted a substantial number of new entrants to the labor force. As a consequence, the local labor force and local employment have expanded without a corresponding reduction in unemployment.[3]

2. *Public Works and Economic Development Act of 1965*, 89th Congress (August 26, 1965), p. 5.

3. There is a growing literature on movements into and out of the labor force under changing economic conditions. See, for example, T. Dernberg and K. Strand, "Cyclical Variation in Civilian Labor Force Participation," *Review of Economics and Statistics*, November 1964, pp. 378–391; A. J. Tella, "The Relation of Labor Force to Employment," *Industrial and Labor Relations Review*, April 1964, pp. 454–469, and Tella, "Labor Force Sensitivity to Employment by Age, Sex," *Industrial Relations*, February 1965, pp. 69–83.

The effects of new plant locations on local employment and unemployment will be examined in this paper. To provide general background, and at least rough bench marks, I will first consider plants attracted to their locations by market forces alone. These are manufacturing establishments which located in predominately rural areas without subsidy. This part of the paper considers the hiring practices of employers attracted to surplus labor locations. In the first group of cases to be discussed, hiring practices can only be deduced by comparing the characteristics of employees in the new plants with random samples of local labor forces. Another case considered in this section provides more specific information because it permits a comparison of the characteristics of employed workers with those of rejected applicants.[4] Following this, the characteristics of workers employed by a sample of new plants established as the result of ARA loans will be considered. Unfortunately, because of lack of data, the characteristics of employed workers in these plants cannot be compared with those of rejected applicants. General comparisons of the effects of market-induced and subsidized plant locations on local labor markets are possible, however.

Market-Induced Plant Locations

The labor market operates more sluggishly than most product markets, but it does exhibit the general tendencies suggested by economic theory. Labor surpluses in some areas will attract investment, and inadequate job opportunities will induce a certain amount of out-migration from such areas.[5] Employers who locate plants in areas of above-average unemployment are not interested, however, in hiring a random sample of the locally unemployed. Like their counterparts elsewhere, these employers have specific hiring standards, and these standards generally favor younger workers and those whose educational attainment is relatively

4. Much of this section is based on William H. Miernyk and Robert D. Britt, *Empirical Labor Market Studies—A Summary and Synthesis*, Report to the Area Redevelopment Administration, U.S. Department of Commerce, August 1965 (mimeo.).

5. For a general discussion of this point see Lowell E. Gallaway, "Labor Mobility, Resource Allocation, and Structural Unemployment," *American Economic Review*, 53 (September 1963), 694–716.

Table 1. Age and Education of Employees in Rural Manufacturing Plants

	Employees		Area Sample		
	Number	Percent	Number	Percent	t
AGE					
Under 25	139	17	49	3	3.5
25 to 34	292	35	266	17	5.0
35 and over	396	48	1,278	80	−11.4
Total	827	100	1,593	100	
YEARS OF SCHOOL					
8 or less	283	34	742	46	−3.53
9 to 12	421	51	651	41	1.27[a]
13 or more	123	15	201	13	.50[a]
Total	827	100	1,594	100	

Source: Sheridan T. Mailtand and Reed E. Friend, *Rural Industrialization, A Summary of Five Studies*, Agriculture Information Bulletin No. 252, Economic Research Service, U.S. Department of Agriculture (November 1961).
[a]Difference not significant at the 1 percent level.

high. This is illustrated by Table 1, which summarizes the age and educational characteristics of the employees of five small manufacturing plants located in rural areas between 1948 and 1957.[6]

The studies upon which Table 1 is based are among the few that compare the characteristics of newly hired employees with random samples of the local labor force. The summary of these studies shows quite clearly that, in terms of age distribution, the new employees were not a representative sample.

It appears that there had been substantial out-migration of young people from the areas under study because only 3 percent of those in the combined area samples were under 25; at the same time, 17 percent of the newly hired workers were in this age group. Seventeen percent of those in the local samples were in the prime working age group of 25 to 34, but 35 percent of the new employees were in this age bracket. Finally, 80 percent of the members of the local labor force in the area samples were 35 or over, but only 48 percent of the new employees were in this age group.

Regarding education, 46 percent of the local sample workers had completed eight or fewer years of school, but only 34 percent of those

6. The states involved are Iowa, Louisiana, Mississippi, and Utah.

hired were in this category of educational attainment. At higher levels, however, the new employees represent a random sample of the combined local labor forces. Since young workers and those with relatively high educational attainment tend to be more mobile than older workers with low educational attainment, it is possible that some of the new employees in these cases were in-migrants or new entrants to the labor force. Employers locating new plants in labor-surplus areas can afford to be selective in their hiring practices. An analysis of 13 cases of market-induced plant locations reveals that the number of applicants ranged from six to thirty times the number of accepted employees.[7]

A more direct comparison can be made on the basis of a study conducted by Gerald Somers in 1957. Somers surveyed the characteristics of workers hired by the Kaiser Aluminum and Chemical Corporation when it located a plant at Ravenswood, West Virginia. These characteristics were then compared with those of a random sample of unaccepted applicants.[8] About 25,000 workers had applied for jobs at the Ravenswood plant when hiring commenced in the summer of 1957, and 894 had been hired at the time Somers conducted his study.

The company followed a prescribed set of hiring standards. The minimum age was 18 years and the maximum, 65. Preference was given to applicants between the ages of 25 and 35, and the company hoped that more than half of the initial work force would be in this age group. Specific educational requirements were not set, but preference was given to high school graduates for hourly-rated and clerical jobs. Most of the professional and technical occupations required college or university training. Preference was also given to workers with a history of "reasonable job stability," and the company had planned "to give distinct preference to applicants whose commuting time from the plant did not exceed 30 minutes."[9] All else being equal, the company planned to hire local residents in preference to those applying from outside the area. Table 2, which gives the distribution of employees and rejected applicants by age, education, and address on application form, shows that the company was able to come relatively close to its hiring speci-

7. Miernyk and Britt, "Empirical Labor Market Studies," p. 53.
8. Gerald Somers, "Labor Recruitment in a Depressed Rural Area," *Monthly Labor Review*, October 1958, pp. 1113–1120.
9. *Ibid.* p. 1114.

Table 2. Percentage Distributions by Age, Education, and Address on Application, of Employees and Rejected Applicants, Ravenswood Plant of Kaiser Corporation summer 1957

	Employees	Rejected applicants
AGE		
Under 20 years	6	9
20–24 years	20	16
25–34 years	48	39
35–44 years	22	25
45–64 years	4	11
EDUCATION[a]		
Elementary school	4	23
High school	49	48
College or university	30	10
Elementary + trade school	1	2
High + trade school	12	15
College + trade school	4	5
ADDRESS ON APPLICATION FORM		
Ravenswood area	48	37
Other W. Va. location	17	43
Contiguous state	13	16
Noncontiguous state	22	4
	N = 894	N = 522

Source: Gerald Somers, "Labor Recruitment in a Depressed Rural Area," *Monthly Labor Review,* October 1958, pp. 1114, 1117.
[a]This classification shows those who began but did not necessarily complete education at each of the specified levels.

fications. In terms of age, the differences between employees and rejected applicants are not large, but there is a slight bias toward workers under 35. Only a small number of workers with an elementary school education or less were hired, although almost one-fourth of those who applied had not gone beyond elementary school.[10] It is interesting to note that hiring standards apparently favored workers with some high school over those with a combination of high school plus trade school. It is also significant that 10 percent of the rejected applicants had completed some college or university work. Some of these applicants may have failed to show the history of job stability that the company expected.

10. Detailed distributions by broad occupational classification are given by Somers in the original article.

The company was able to obtain almost half of its initial work force from within the prescribed commuting area. The rather large proportion of employees from noncontiguous states included a number of Kaiser workers transferred from other locations to the new Ravenswood plant rather than "new hires" as such. In spite of the rural character of Ravenswood and the surrounding area at the time the plant was opened, only 2 percent of the clerical and blue-collar workers had been employed in agriculture during the seven years preceding their Kaiser jobs. Almost 40 percent had worked on a farm at some time, however. More than two-thirds of all employees in these groups came from nonmanufacturing jobs, and most of the hourly-rated employees had held a higher skill classification on their previous jobs.

The initial work force of a large new plant, such as the Ravenswood plant of the Kaiser company, will not be representative of the work force at a later date when the plant is operating on a routine production schedule. This is because many of the workers initially hired for hourly-rated jobs will enter training programs and eventually be in supervisory positions. In the Ravenswood plant, for example, about 27 percent of the workers initially hired were classified as professional, managerial, or supervisory employees, while operatives represented only 18 percent of the total. Also, in screening applicants the personnel office "gave preference to applicants with previous managerial experience or potentiality."[11] A follow-up to the Somers study would undoubtedly show an increase in the proportion of operatives and a decline in the proportion of new hires in the occupational classifications that require relatively high levels of educational attainment. In such a case as this, however, with a backlog of more than 24,000 applicants, the company probably did not have to modify its age and educational standards significantly in subsequent hiring.

Subsidized Plant Locations—
Direct Investment under the Area Redevelopment Act

The Area Redevelopment Act, predecessor to the current Economic Development Act, was the first piece of social legislation enacted by the Kennedy Administration. One of the major pro-

11. *Ibid.*

grams under ARA consisted of direct investment in areas of sub-stantial labor surplus. This section summarizes the results of a survey of 33 new plants that were induced to locate in eligible areas by ARA loans.[12] The survey was conducted about two years after the Act had been passed and included only those establish-ments in full operation at that time. A sample of 50 establishments was initially selected, but 17 were not included in the survey. More than half of these were eliminated because they did not meet the criteria for inclusion. Some were not new plants or new branches of established firms; others were still in the construction stage and had not started to hire production workers; and the rest declined to participate in the study. The 33 participating establishments, however, represented a good cross section of ARA-supported proj-ects in 1963 in terms of industrial classification, size of establish-ment, and area designation.[13] Since the establishments selected had already entered the operating phase at the time of the survey, it may be assumed that the characteristics of their employees were not significantly affected by the transfer of managerial staff or the hiring of trainees.

Between 1950 and 1960 population had declined in about 60 per-cent of the areas studied, and there had been net in-migration in only 13 percent of them. Either the unemployment rate was above or median family income was well below the national average in all of the areas. In about two-thirds of the areas the median age of male members of the population was higher than the national aver-age, but there was no significant age difference between females in the study areas and in the nation. It is difficult to compare levels of educational attainment in the survey areas and in the nation without going into extensive detail. In 97 percent of the areas studied, the proportion of males 25 years old and older who had

12. ARA loans were not limited to new establishments. Such loans were also made to eligible establishments for expansion purposes or "to save existing jobs". Only *new* establishments were included in the survey discussed in this paper, however. The complete results of the survey are given in William H. Miernyk and Robert D. Britt, *Labor Mobility, The Transfer of Skills, and Area Redevelopment*, Report to the Area Redevelopment Administration, U.S. Department of Commerce, April 1965 (mimeographed).

13. The ARA classified eligible areas as: (i) 5 (a) areas with 15,000 or more workers in the labor force, designated on the basis of unemployment histories, (ii) 5 (b) areas which were primarily designated on the basis of family income, and (iii) 5 (b) 5 areas with fewer than 15,000 in the labor force, designated on the basis of unemployment histories. All three types of areas were covered by the survey.

completed high school was below the national average. The average labor force participation rate in the combined areas was 51.5 percent compared with the national average of 55.3 percent at that time.

Most of the sample establishments were relatively small. Eighteen establishments, slightly more than half of the sample, had 35 employees or less at the time of the survey; ten establishments, or almost one-third of the sample, employed between 36 and 100 workers; and only five (15 percent) reported employment of 101 or more workers. Almost two-thirds of the sample establishments (61 percent) were located in the Northeast and the Great Lakes regions, and only about one-fifth were located in Appalachia or the Southeast.[14] All but four of the sample establishments were engaged in manufacturing, and the manufacturing plants covered a fairly wide range of industries.

Worker Characteristics

Establishments participating in this survey had a combined work force of 2,140 at the time of the study, and of these 1,262, or 59 percent, submitted usable returns to a mailed questionnaire. Slightly more than half of the respondents (51.3 percent) were female, and about one-third of all respondents were under 25 years of age. Eighty-two percent were under 45. The median ages of managers, craftsmen, foremen, and service workers ranged from 36 to 41 years, while the median ages of clerical and sales workers, operatives, and laborers were under 30. The median number of years of school completed, 12.1, was relatively high, and more than 52 percent of the respondents had finished high school. Ten percent had attended college. Less than half (43.6 percent) of all respondents were married breadwinners. An additional 32 percent were married but were claimed as dependents by their spouses. Most of the remainder were unmarried and claimed no dependents.

14. The distribution of sample establishments was representative of the geographical distribution of ARA-supported activities at the time of the study, but the regions included were clearly not representative of the most seriously depressed areas of the nation. This is because a precondition to an ARA loan was an acceptable Overall Economic Development Plan. Such plans were submitted shortly after the Act was passed by industrial development groups in the older industrial regions of the nation, and they were the first to be declared eligible for loans. Because of this many of the initial ARA loans went to relatively small depressed areas in relatively prosperous regions.

Employment and Labor Force Status at Time of Hire

Almost half of the respondents to the survey were unemployed at the time they were hired by one of the new plants.[15] Slightly more than 30 percent of the male respondents were employed full-time when they found their present jobs, and an additional 12 percent had part-time jobs. Only a small proportion of the females (16 percent) had full-time jobs before their present employment and 9 percent had part-time jobs.[16] More than 36 percent of the female respondents were not members of the labor force prior to their present employment. This indicates rather clearly that a substantial number of secondary workers was pulled into the active labor force by the location of new plants in the survey areas. This is typical of cases where new plants employ a substantial proportion of females. In a study of three small labor market areas Richard Wilcock found that between 37 and 59 percent of employees hired by new plants were not in the labor force at the time they applied for their jobs.[17] Almost two-thirds of the respondents were classified as operatives at the time of the survey, and more than 28 percent of these (mostly female) were new entrants to the labor force. It should also be noted that 42 percent of the operatives were unemployed before they found their present jobs. The details of the unemployment and labor force status of all respondents, in terms of sex and occupation, are given in Table 3.

Fifty-five percent of the respondents indicated that they had experienced unemployment during the five years preceding the survey. Sixteen percent of these did not indicate the duration of their unemployment, but 47 percent reported that they had been out of

15. The standard definition of "unemployment" was used. To be counted as unemployed the respondent had to be an active member of the labor force without a job, and actively searching for work at the time he found his present employment.

16. This is in sharp contrast to the findings of Somers in his Kaiser Aluminum study. He found that 86 percent of the Kaiser employees were working at the time they applied for a job at the Ravenswood plant, and only 20 percent of the successful applicants had been unemployed at any time during the three years preceding their job at the plant. Somers, *Monthly Labor Review*, October 1958, p. 1117. In 12 other cases where new plants were located in surplus labor areas without loans or other forms of subsidy between 40 and 57 percent of the sampled workers had a job just prior to joining the new plant (Miernyk and Britt, *Empirical Labor Market Studies*, p. 60).

17. See Richard C. Wilcock, "New Firms and the Labor Supply in Small Communities," *Current Economic Comment*, November 1954, pp. 3–15. For further details on movement into and out of the labor force see Miernyk and Britt, *Empirical Labor Market Studies*, p. 60.

Table 3. Employment and Labor Force Status at Time of Hire

	Status not reported		Employed full-time		Employed part-time or part-year		Unemployed		Not in labor force		Total	
	No.	%	No.	%	No.	%	No.	%	No.	%	No.	%
SEX												
Male	8	1.3	188	30.6	75	12.2	298	48.5	46	7.4	615	100.0
Female	4	0.6	105	16.2	61	9.4	243	37.6	234	36.2	647	100.0
CURRENT OCCUPATION												
Professional and technical	1	3.6	9	32.1	2	7.2	13	46.4	3	10.7	28	100.0
Managerial	—	—	15	78.9	2	10.6	1	5.3	1	5.3	19	100.0
Clerical and sales	—	—	25	30.1	12	14.4	37	44.6	9	10.8	83	100.0
Craftsmen and foremen	—	—	71	44.1	13	8.1	67	41.6	10	6.2	161	100.0
Operatives	7	0.8	148	17.8	90	10.8	351	42.1	237	28.5	833	100.0
Service	2	3.4	12	20.3	6	10.2	31	52.5	8	13.6	59	100.0
Laborers	2	2.5	13	16.5	11	13.9	41	51.9	12	15.2	79	100.0
Total	12	1.0	293	23.2	136	10.8	541	42.9	280	22.2	1,262	100.0

Source: William H. Miernyk and Robert D. Britt, *Labor Mobility, The Transfer of Skills, and Area Redevelopment*, Report Submitted to Area Redevelopment Administration, U.S. Department of Commerce, April 21, 1965 (mimeo.).

work for 20 weeks or less. An additional 22 percent had been jobless at some time for 21 to 52 weeks, and 15 percent had been out of work for 53 weeks or more. Although a substantial proportion of the new employees had experienced some unemployment before finding their present jobs, only a minority would fit the category of "hardcore unemployed." Most of those who had been unemployed for 21 weeks or more were either operatives or laborers.

There was a substantial amount of movement into and out of the labor force during the five years preceding the survey. As might be expected, most of the males (67 percent) had been in the labor force continuously, but 22 percent had dropped out at least one time during the preceding five years. These proportions were almost reversed when the female respondents were considered. Sixty-three percent of the women in the survey had been out of the labor force at least one time while only 20 percent had been continuously attached to the labor force during the preceding five years. Those respondents who dropped out of the labor force tended to stay out for some time. Eighty-six percent of the male respondents and 92 percent of the females who had been out of the labor force remained out for more than two years.

The lower part of Table 3 shows the distribution of respondents by occupation and labor force status at time of hire. The largest number of unemployed were operatives at the time of the survey, and these were preponderantly male. Most of the new entrants to the labor force were also classified as operatives at the time of the survey, and these were predominantly female. Operatives accounted for two-thirds of all respondents.

Respondents with a prior history of employment had been fairly mobile during the five years preceding the survey. The average male respondent had changed jobs 2.1 times, occupations 1.7 times, and industry of attachment 1.9 times. The female respondents were somewhat less mobile, changing jobs 1.8 times and occupational or industrial attachment 1.5 times. The occupational mobility of sample workers is illustrated in part by the shift between last and present jobs summarized in Table 4. The rows of this table give the distribution of jobs last held, and the columns show the jobs held at the time of the survey. The ratios given in the last row of Table 4 show the relative occupational shifts. A ratio greater than one indicates an increase in current occupations, and a ratio less than one represents a decline.

Table 4. Occupational Shifts between Last and Present Jobs

Occupations on last job	Current Occupations															
	Professional and technical		Managers		Clerical and sales		Craftsmen and foremen		Operatives		Service workers		Laborers		Total	
	No.	%	No.	%	No.	%	No.	%	No.	%	No.	%	No.	%	No.	%
Professional and technical	8	33.3	—	—	3	4.1	2	1.3	4	.7	—	—	—	—	17	1.8
Managers	1	4.2	12	63.2	7	9.6	14	9.3	22	3.7	3	6.2	3	4.6	62	6.4
Clerical and sales	3	12.5	3	15.8	37	50.7	10	6.6	77	13.1	2	4.2	4	6.2	136	14.1
Craftsmen and foremen	—	—	3	15.8	4	5.5	72	47.7	17	2.9	2	4.2	1	1.5	99	10.2
Operatives	6	25.0	1	5.3	14	19.2	45	29.8	289	49.3	10	20.8	15	23.1	380	39.3
Service workers	3	12.5	—	—	3	4.1	3	2.0	94	16.0	20	41.7	5	7.7	128	13.2
Laborers	3	12.5	—	—	4	5.5	5	3.3	62	10.6	10	20.8	32	49.2	116	12.0
Previous occupation not reported	—	—	—	—	1	1.4	—	—	22	3.7	1	2.1	5	7.7	29	3.0
Total	24	100.0	19	100.0	73	100.0	151	100.0	587	100.0	48	100.0	65	100.0	967	100.0
No other job during last 5 years	4		—		10		10		245		11		14		295	
Ratio of occupation in current job to last job held	1.41		.31		.54		1.53		1.54		.38		.56			

Source: See Table 3.

Except for the managerial, clerical, and sales categories, more than half of the jobs in the new plants were held by persons who had made a change in occupation since their last employment. There was an increase in the proportion of professional or technical workers, craftsmen or foremen, and operatives, and a decline in the other occupational categories given in Table 4. These shifts represent a significant upgrading in skill classification and also a pronounced shift from nonmanufacturing to manufacturing jobs. Almost 58 percent of the respondents with previous employment records had been employed in nonmanufacturing activities prior to their current jobs, but about 92 percent of all respondents were in manufacturing at the time of the survey.

A substantial decline in the proportion of managers between preceeding last and present jobs is shown in Table 4. Part of this decline is due to the fact that plant managers and superintendents were excluded from the survey, although department heads and others of lesser managerial rank were included. Because of the small size of the average establishment in the survey the number of such managerial positions was limited. To some extent, however, Table 4 accurately indicates a shift from managerial to nonmanagerial occupations. A number of farm owners and small businessmen had found employment in the sample establishments, but about one-third of them continued to maintain an interest in their farms or businesses, with other members of the family handling day-to-day operations. Most of these indicated that they had sought employment in the new firms because their farms or businesses failed to provide sufficient income to meet family needs.

The upgrading of skills would suggest a corresponding increase in earnings, which generally occurred. About 44 percent of all respondents with a prior history of employment reported higher earnings on their current jobs. An additional 29 percent reported that their earnings were about the same, while only 16 percent reported lower earnings. The remaining 11 percent failed to reply to this question. On a priori grounds, one would expect more improvement in earnings among the workers who had been employed when they applied for their present jobs than among those who were unemployed, and this was the case. About 53 percent of the workers who had been employed full-time before moving to their present jobs reported higher earnings, but this was true of only 37 percent of those who had been unemployed. Also, 12 percent of the employed

Table 5. Earnings on Current and Last Job by Employment and Labor Force Experience

Duration of Unemployment; Total for Preceding Five Years

Current rates compared with rates on last job	No response		No unemployment reported		Unemployment Indicated, duration not given		One to 20 weeks		21 to 52 weeks		53 weeks or more		Total	
	No.	%	No.	%	No.	%	No.	%	No.	%	No.	%	No.	%
Earnings not reported	10	100.0	39	10.6	32	47.8	15	5.3	5	3.4	6	6.3	107	11.
Earnings higher on current job	—	—	187	51.0	16	23.9	131	46.5	58	40.0	34	35.4	426	44.1
Earnings about the same	—	—	108	29.4	13	19.4	84	29.8	39	26.9	33	34.4	277	28.6
Earnings lower on current job	—	—	33	9.0	6	8.9	52	18.4	43	29.7	23	23.9	57	16.2
Total	10	100.0	367	100.0	67	100.0	282	100.0	145	100.0	96	100.0	967	100.0

Labor Force Status at Time of Hire

	Status not reported		Employed full-time		Employed part-time or part-year		Unemployed		Not in labor force		Total	
	No.	%	No.	%	No.	%	No.	%	No.	%	No.	%
Earnings not reported	4	33.3	26	8.9	20	14.7	49	11.3	8	8.7	107	11.1
Earnings higher on current job	5	41.7	154	52.6	60	44.1	163	37.5	44	47.8	426	44.1
Earnings about the same	2	16.7	78	26.6	42	31.0	128	29.5	27	29.3	277	28.6
Earnings lower on current job	1	8.3	35	11.9	14	10.2	94	21.7	13	14.2	157	16.2
Total	12	100.0	293	100.0	136	100.0	434	100.0	92	100.0	967	100.0

Source: See Table 3.

workers reported lower earnings on their current jobs. This was true of almost 22 percent of those who had been unemployed. Further details on comparative earnings are given in Table 5.

There are a number of reasons why employed workers might accept a reduction in earnings. Some might be willing to sacrifice a certain amount of income in order to minimize commuting time; others might accept a lower-paying job if it offers greater opportunity for advancement than their present employment. Unemployed workers do not have this option, and those past the age of 45, in particular, must frequently accept lower earnings if they are to return to an employed status.[18]

A substantial majority (94 percent) of all respondents lived within 50 miles of their present places of employment at the time they applied for their jobs. Almost all of those in the semiskilled and unskilled categories lived within 50 miles of their present jobs at the time they applied. One-fourth of the professional and technical employees, one-third of those in managerial positions, and 15 percent of the craftsmen and foremen lived outside this radius at the time of application. Some no doubt were transferred to their present jobs when the new plants were opened.

If the local labor market area is defined as a circle with a radius of 20 miles, more than two-thirds of the workers who were employed at the time they applied for their present jobs lived in this area. The details by age and education are given in Table 6. One would expect a relatively large proportion of older workers to come from the local areas. This was particularly true for workers past the age of 45, as indicated in the upper part of Table 6. Eighty-one percent of the workers under 20 also came from the local areas.

Empirical labor market studies have generally shown a positive correlation between education and geographic mobility. The lower part of Table 6 shows some tendency in this direction but nothing particularly startling. Almost as large a proportion of workers with an eighth-grade education or less had worked elsewhere in the states involved as those who had completed high school. The differences are larger when out-of-state employment is considered. Only 9 percent of the workers with 11 years or less of education reported that their last job had been outside the state of their

18. For a detailed discussion of the drop in earnings among reemployed workers displaced by plant shutdowns see Miernyk and Britt, *Empirical Labor Market Studies,* pp. 30–44.

Table 6. Location of Last Job by Age and Education

1. AGE

Location of Last Job	Age not reported		Under 20		20 to 24		25 to 34		35 to 44		45 to 54		55 and over		Total	
	No.	%	No.	%	No.	%	No.	%	No.	%	No.	%	No.	%	No.	%
No response	—	—	—	—	9	4.1	33	7.5	14	6.9	8	5.8	3	5.7	56	5.8
Local area	3	72.7	43	81.1	140	63.6	182	61.9	136	67.0	101	73.2	29	54.7	634	65.7
Rest of state	3	27.3	5	9.4	49	22.3	53	18.0	32	15.8	14	10.1	14	26.4	170	17.5
Outside of state	—	—	5	9.4	22	10.0	37	12.6	21	10.4	15	10.8	7	13.1	107	11.0
Total	6	100.0	53	100.0	220	100.0	294	100.0	203	100.0	138	100.0	53	100.0	967	100.0

2. EDUCATION

Location of Last Job	Years not reported		0 to 8 years		9 to 11 years		12 years		Attended college		Total	
	No.	%	No.	%	No.	%	No.	%	No.	%	No.	%
No response	—	—	21	9.9	15	6.1	18	4.6	2	1.8	56	5.8
Local area	1	50.0	140	65.7	157	63.8	268	68.2	68	60.2	634	65.7
Rest of state	—	—	32	15.0	51	20.7	66	16.8	21	18.6	170	17.5
Outside of state	1	50.0	20	9.2	23	9.3	41	10.4	22	19.5	107	11.1
Total	2	100.0	213	100.0	246	100.0	393	100.0	113	100.0	967	100.0

Source: See Table 3.

residence at the time of the survey. This was true of more than 19 percent of the workers who had attended college.

Although respondents with a prior history of employment exhibited some geographic mobility, the obvious employment impacts of the new plants were largely limited to the local labor market areas. Perhaps even more important, most of the workers who were unemployed at the time they found their present jobs, as well as the new entrants to the labor force, came from the local labor market areas. From a geographic point of view it is clear that the ARA-supported plants had their greatest employment impact on the communities in which the new plants were located. It is also evident, however, that the opening of these plants had more direct impact on local employment than on unemployment, because most of the workers who staffed these plants had transferred from other jobs or had entered (or re-entered) the labor force when the new plants began hiring. Also the new plants were somewhat selective in their hiring, because they tended to favor young applicants whose educational attainment was about equal to the national average.

Unfortunately, the results of the survey are limited to the *direct* effects of the location of new plants on labor surplus areas. It is safe to assume that the employed workers who shifted to the new plants created job openings for others, but no information is available on the workers who filled the vacated jobs. If the vacated jobs were filled from the ranks of the unemployed, the impact on local unemployment would be greater than that suggested by the direct changes discussed here. Actually, the average unemployment rate for a constant sample of ARA areas (those whose boundaries remained unchanged) fell more rapidly than the national average between 1961 and 1963.[19] It is impossible, however, to estimate how much of this improvement was due to direct investment in redevelopment areas and how much was induced by general improvement in the national economy.

As noted earlier, ARA officials used an estimated local employment multiplier of 1.6 in projecting local changes in employment. Some recent evidence indicates that this was too high. Max Jordan

19. In 1961 the unemployment rate for the constant sample of areas was 63 percent above the national average, and in 1963 it was only 32 percent above this average. See The *First Three Years of the Area Redevelopment Program*, U.S. Department of Commerce, Area Redevelopment Administration, September 1, 1964, p. 39.

has analyzed the *local* and *total* employment effects of the location of a garment factory in a rural area in Arkansas.[20] He estimated the number of jobs that had been generated by the shirt plant during its first year of stabilized employment, and on the basis of his estimate the garment factory had a *local* employment multiplier of 1.1. Jordan also estimated the direct and indirect employment impacts on suppliers outside the area and computed a total employment multiplier of 1.56.[21] Jordan's estimates are based on an ingenious combination of plant data and information provided by the Census of Manufactures. A series of studies of this kind could provide similar estimates of employment multipliers under a variety of labor market conditions.

One shortcoming of cross-sectional studies of the effects on local labor markets of new plant locations is that they fail to show labor force changes over time. A recent study by John Petersen and Earl Wright showed that as one local labor market became increasingly tight, a growing proportion of new hires consisted of new entrants to the labor force and of in-migrants.[22] Although the evidence remains scanty, it suggests that employers need not alter their hiring standards even if local unemployment drops. As long as there is a substantial amount of unemployment, some workers will be recruited from the unemployed. Petersen and Wright found, for example, that about 20 percent of the employees hired by new plants in northwest Arkansas in 1966 were unemployed when they found their new jobs. However, housewives and others who may not have been in the labor force tended to be given preference, if they met the age and educational requirements of employers.

The persistence of high levels of localized unemployment at a time when the national labor market has become relatively tight underscores what labor economists have known for years—that the local labor market does not respond as perfectly to changing market forces as do product markets. For one thing, the local labor supply

20. Max F. Jordan, *Rural Industrialization in the Ozarks: Case Study of a Shirt Plant at Gassville, Arkansas*, Economic Research Service, U.S. Department of Agriculture, Agricultural Economic Report Number 123 (November 1967).

21. *Ibid.*, p. 11. The methods of estimating intra-area and total employment are given on pp. 17–23.

22. John M. Petersen and Earl Wright, *Dynamics of Small Area Labor Supply; A Case Study* (Little Rock, Arkansas: Industrial Research and Extension Center, University of Arkansas, September 1967), p. 40.

Table 7. Percentage Distribution, by Labor Force Status, of New Hires in Market-Induced and Subsidized Plants

Case	Employed %	Unemployed %	Not in labor force %	Total (Number)
Michigan Motor Vehicle Parts (1955)[a]	51	35	14	466
Ravenswood Aluminum (1957)[b]	86	11	3	894
Mt. Airy Appliances (1957)[c]	45	8	47	435
Total, market-induced	67	16	17	1,775
ARA survey	35	43	22	1,262

Sources: [a]James Blum, "Sources of Workers for a new Establishment," *Labor Market and Employment Security* (May 1961). [b]Estimated from Gerald Somers, *Monthly Labor Review*, October 1958, pp. 1113-1120. [c]*Staffing a New Plant in a Small Labor Market Area,* North Carolina Employment Security Commission, Bureau of Research and Statistics, May 1960 (mimeo.).

is anything but homogeneous. Because the American labor force is a fluid one, with secondary workers moving in and out as job opportunities and family needs change, employers are rarely required to make major alterations in hiring standards. Also, local labor markets are even more fluid than the national market because of in- and out-migration.

A Comparison of the Local Labor Market Effects of Market-induced and Subsidized Plant Locations

Before turning to some general conclusions and the policy implications of the ARA survey, it will be useful to compare the effects on local labor markets of cases in which plants were located on the basis of market considerations with those where the locations were influenced by ARA loans. In addition to the Kaiser Aluminum case discussed earlier, roughly comparable data are available for a motor vehicle parts plant located in Michigan in 1955 and an appliance factory located in Mount Airy, North Carolina, in 1957.[23] A summary comparison is given in Table 7.

The three market-induced examples vary considerably, but there

23. For further details on these cases see Miernyk and Britt *Empirical Labor Market Studies*, pp. 52–86.

are substantial differences between these cases when they are combined and those included in the ARA survey. It is evident that the ARA plants had a greater impact on local *unemployment* than the other three cases in Table 7. The aluminum and appliance plants, in particular, had an almost negligible impact on local unemployment during their initial staffing phases. Slightly more than one-third of the workers in the vehicle parts plant were unemployed at the time they found their jobs, but this is still substantially less than the average of 43 percent in the plants covered by the ARA survey.

The aluminum plant and the vehicle parts plant had little impact on labor force participation rates, at least during the initial hiring phase. About one-fifth of all employees in the ARA plants were not in the labor force at the time they found their jobs. This is a substantially higher proportion than was found in the motor vehicle parts and aluminum plants, but considerably lower than the proportion of new entrants to the labor force hired by the appliance factory. All three of the market-induced cases show significantly larger proportions of employed workers among their new hires than the ARA cases, and only two-thirds of those classified as employed in the ARA cases had full-time jobs when they applied for their new positions.

The comparisons in Table 7 must be interpreted cautiously. The composition of hires changes as a plant moves from the phase of initial staffing and training to stabilized production. Selection standards are probably higher at the beginning than during later phases when there is a greater need for routine workers. In spite of this qualification, one can conclude that the ARA-supported plants had a larger impact on local unemployment than those whose locations were determined by market considerations.

From a research point of view there is need for further study of the dynamics of local labor markets. It would be helpful, for example, to know more about the cumulative employment impacts of new plants over time. Studies of the type made by Petersen and Wright would shed some light on the changing composition of labor supply in areas of industrial growth. Additional studies of the kind conducted by Jordan would provide estimates of local and total employment multipliers. The latter could be used to estimate the costs and benefits associated with subsidized plant locations.

Policy Implications

What are the policy implications of this brief survey of the employment effects of subsidized plant locations? In spite of a lack of knowledge about the long-run consequences of direct investment in surplus labor areas some tentative conclusions can be ventured. The ARA survey suggests that plants which are induced to locate in depressed areas by favorable loans hire a larger proportion of unemployed workers than those which are located on the basis of market considerations. One of the major objectives of the Area Redevelopment Act was the reduction of localized unemployment, and its loan provisions were making an important contribution to this objective. It was precisely the subsidy features of ARA, however, which evoked the strongest criticism from its detractors. Partly because of this criticism, emphasis under the Economic Development Act has shifted from business loans to grants and loans for the construction of public works facilities. Of the first billion dollars spent by EDA, for example, approximately 10 percent was used to make a total of 135 loans for the construction or expansion of industrial and commercial facilities, and almost 45 percent went for the construction of public works.[24]

The study of subsidized plant locations reported here sheds no new light on the issue of direct investment versus investment in social overhead capital. The ARA survey showed that direct investment does have an impact on localized unemployment, but less is known about the employment and unemployment effects of investment in social overhead capital. Investment in public works facilities has attracted new industries to some depressed areas. The Ozark garment factory studied by Jordan, for example, was able to locate at Gassville, Arkansas, only after small ARA grants and loans permitted the community to develop a water system that was needed before the factory could locate in that area. This factory was followed a few years later by a large pharmaceutical manufacturing plant and a second garment factory.[25] Unfortunately, systematic information about the extent to which other investments of this kind have stimulated growth in depressed areas is lacking. A series of studies comparing the long-run effects on em-

24. *Economic Development*, U.S. Department of Commerce, Economic Development Administration, Volume 4 (December 1967), p. 1.
25. Jordan, *Rural Industrialization in the Ozarks*, p. 2.

ployment and unemployment of the two major types of investment made by the Economic Development Administration would provide useful guidelines for the future allocation of regional development funds.

It might also be necessary to re-examine one of the basic principles of the Economic Development Act, namely, that loans can be made to employers in redevelopment areas only if a relocation is not involved. The British have long recognized that if market forces alone are permitted to determine plant locations there will be areas of serious industrial congestion, with tight labor markets, and at the same time there will be areas of substantial labor surplus. As a consequence, they have initiated a series of programs since the end of World War II designed to encourage the *relocation* of establishments from congested areas to labor-surplus areas, largely by requiring Board of Trade approval for the location of new industrial plants.[26] This approach has resulted in some relocation of industry, and hence of manufacturing employment; but in spite of the Board's efforts, the tendency toward increasing concentration in some areas and persistent unemployment in other areas has not been eliminated. In an effort to speed up the relocation of industry, the British have recently instituted a Regional Employment Premium which grants a direct subsidy, amounting to about 7 percent of the total wage bill, to *all* manufacturing employers in development areas.[27]

It would be unreasonable to expect Congress to sanction this much interference with the location of American industry, but at a minimum the restrictive provision against relocation could be eliminated from the Economic Development Act. Workers displaced by the shutdown of establishments in tight labor market areas would have a better chance of finding new employment locally than those in areas that have had a labor surplus for years or even decades. Although one can only speculate about the outcome, it is not unreasonable to expect that elimination of the relocation barrier,

26. See William H. Miernyk, "British and American Approaches to Structural Unemployment," in *Industrial and Labor Relations Review*, October 1958, pp. 3–10; and "Experience Under the British local Employment Acts of 1960 and 1963," *ibid*, October 1966, pp. 30–49.

27. For a concise and lucid discussion of this subsidy, together with a critique of the financing provisions of the British regional development program, see T. Wilson, "Finance for Regional Industrial Development," *The Three Banks Review*, September 1967, pp. 3–23.

coupled with an expansion of investment in labor surplus areas, would have a measurable impact on the national unemployment rate.

The evidence presented in this paper strongly suggests that even a stepped-up program of investment in labor surplus areas will not reduce local unemployment to its purely frictional component. Employers will continue to maintain hiring standards even if they locate facilities in areas of substantial unemployment. Given the flexible nature of the American labor force, the supply of qualified workers will continue to adjust to changes in demand at the local labor market level. If a serious effort is to be made to eliminate residual unemployment it will no doubt be necessary to adopt one of the recommendations of the National Commission on Technology, Automation and Economic Progress: "We recommend a program of public service employment providing, in effect, that the Government be an employer of last resort, providing work for the 'hard-core unemployed' in useful community enterprises."[28]

28. *Technology and the American Economy*, Report of the National Commission on Technology, Automation, and Economic Progress (Washington, D.C.: Government Printing Office, 1966), I, 110.

Part III *Regional Growth and Capital Flows*

GEORGE H. BORTS

Growth and Capital Movements Among United States Regions in the Postwar Period

Neoclassical growth models of the type introduced by T. W. Swan[1] and Robert Solow[2] may be adapted for the analysis of external borrowing and lending in regions or countries. Although savings are identically equal to investment in the closed, full-employment versions of these models, they may diverge in an open economy. Such divergence constitutes the flow of borrowing or lending.

The use of an explicit growth model permits the derivation of time-path solutions for the level of investment, the level of savings,

* The author is a Professor of Economics at Brown University and was a guest scholar at the Brookings Institution when work on the paper was completed. Financial support was provided by the National Science Foundation, under grant No. GS-825. An earlier draft was read at the December 1967 Meetings of the American Economic Association.

1. Trevor W. Swan, "Economic Growth and Capital Accumulation", *Economic Record*, 32 (1956), 334-361.

2. Robert M. Solow, "A Contribution to the Theory of Economic Growth," *Quarterly Journal of Economics*, 70 (February 1956), 65-94.

the flow of external borrowing or lending, and the flow of income payments on external borrowing or lending. The latter flow is sometimes defined as the net factor income.

If we assume a large national (world) economy containing a small region (country) and a perfect national (world) capital market, this framework permits us to describe the long-run flow of capital that will occur between borrowing or lending regions. In addition, it permits the analysis of changes in key behavioral parameters and the description of the system as it is shifted from one long-run equilibrium time path to another. In this respect the analysis is similar but superior to the method of comparative statics where we analyze the effect of parameter changes in moving the system from one comparative static equilibrium point to another. Here the movement is from one time path to another.

The analysis may also be used for prescriptive purposes, if we assume that the capital market is not perfect or that for some reason firms in the borrowing region, or country, are prevented from paying market rates of interest to external lenders. In this case we may treat the borrowing region as a potential recipient of aid (either domestic or foreign) in the form of a capital transfer. The analysis may then be used to project the aid requirements and the likely time paths of borrowing and repayment of aid.[3]

In this paper two growth models will be presented and used to derive time-path solutions for investment, the balance of payments on current account, and the net factor income. These solutions will be calculated as ratios to Gross Regional (National) Product under the assumption that the region's economy is advancing on its long-run steady-state growth path. The solutions themselves are functions of parameters such as the interest rate, the marginal propensity to save, the growth rate, and the capital coefficient. The solutions will be estimated numerically by substituting numerical estimates for the parameters, and will then be compared with actual behavior for the 48 states in 1953. A description of the data follows in a later section of this paper. The statistical comparisons are quite promising and indicate that the growth models have a good deal of potential use in this area.

3. For a discussion of aid projections using the Harrod-Domar model rather than neoclassical growth models, see Hollis B. Chenery and Alan M. Strout, "Foreign Assistance and Economic Development," *American Economic Review*, 56 (September 1966), 679–733; and Ronald I. McKinnon, "Foreign Exchange Constraints in Economic Development and Efficient Aid Allocation," *The Economic Journal*, 74 (June 1964), 388–409.

Borrowing, Lending, and Net Factor Income

Borrowing and lending among regions may be analyzed in the same fashion as among countries. The transfer of resources is accomplished when the lender or grantor experiences a surplus in its current account balance of payments, offset by a deficit in its capital or transfer account. The movement of resources may be financed through private or governmental channels, through short-or long-term instruments of debt, or through equities. Excluding grants and gifts, transfers of capital are ultimately followed by a reverse flow of income representing interest and dividends, and by repayment, when debt instruments fall due at maturity. The function of borrowing and lending among regions is to equalize the rates of return among competing investment opportunities. Capital will flow from areas of high savings and low investment to areas of low savings and high investment. To the extent that investment levels are related to rates of growth, this means that capital also will flow from slowly to rapidly growing regions.

Capital movements into a region are the sum of net private and net governmental borrowings. The net private borrowings consist of the difference between private investment and savings; the net government borrowings consist of the governmental deficits. Each type of borrowing generates a return flow of income payments representing interest and dividends. A region that has been a net borrower will show in its current account balance a negative item representing the payment of income to foreign owners or lenders of domestically employed capital. Conversely, a net lender will show a positive item representing the receipt of income.

Flows of current borrowing and of current income on past amounts borrowed represent considerable quantitative importance in the balance of payments of U.S. regions. The following tabulations are made from J. Thomas Romans' data on savings and on the current account balance of various states and from my estimates of net income on *private* external borrowing.[4]

(a) In 1953, 30 states were net borrowers on current account, such borrowings accounting for an average of 34 percent of the sum of gross state savings and borrowings. In 1953, 18 states were net

4. J. Thomas Romans, *Capital Exports and Growth Among U.S. Regions* (Middletown, Conn.: Wesleyan University Press, 1965), and George H. Borts, "The Estimation of Produced Income by State and Region," in C. L. Schultze and L. Weiner, eds., *The Behavior of Income Shares,* Studies in Income and Wealth, vol. XXVII (New York: National Bureau of Economic Research, 1964).

lenders on current account, such lending amounting to an average of 39 percent of gross state savings.

(b) Net income on external borrowing or lending exceeded the whole current account balance in absolute value in 10 states and exceeded one-half the current account balance in 26 states.

(c) Net income on external borrowing or lending varied from +21 percent to −11 percent of received state income, measured on a national income basis.

The reverse flow of interest and dividends—that is, the net factor income—reflects the past values of the current account balance of payments. If we assume that all lending had taken place at a particular and unchanged rate of interest, we could write the following definition:

(i) $$D_t = r \sum_{\tau=0} B_\tau$$

where B_τ represents the value of the current account balance of payments at time τ, which runs from the beginning of history up to time t; and D_t represents the total flow of income received from external lending at time t. Consequently $\dot{D}_t$, the change in D_t, from one period to the next, depends on the value of the balance of payments at time t.

(ii) $$\dot{D}_t = rB_t$$

We may also examine the net factor income through the definitions of the region's produced and received income. Anticipating a model to be presented later, Z will represent the region's received income (Gross National Product) and XP the produced income (Gross Domestic Product). Then we have

(iii) $$Z = XP + D$$

Using the dot to represent the time derivative, this implies,

(iv) $$\dot{Z} = (\dot{X}P) + \dot{D} = (\dot{X}P) + rB$$

We know from the definitions of national product that B, the current account balance, equals net lending or borrowing, the sum of savings plus taxes minus investment plus government spending. Government borrowing will be ignored in the rest of the discussion.[5] The balance of payments on current account B will be treated as equal to the excess of private savings over private investment.

(v) $$\dot{Z} = (X\dot{P}) + r[S - I]$$

Savings will be treated as a function of the level of received income, and investment as a function of the change in produced income. With the aid of appropriate assumptions generating the time path of produced income, it is possible to analyze the investing and borrowing behavior of regions within a dynamic framework. Solutions are obtained for the time paths of savings, investment, the current account balance of payments, and the flow of net income on past lending.

The following section presents a simple growth model and the time-path solutions for the dependent variables. The qualitative implications of the analysis are that, other things unchanged, a region will increase its lending if its savings propensity rises, if its growth rate declines, and if its capital-output requirements decline. In addition, a region will respond to higher interest rates by lending more or borrowing less. Improvement in the terms of trade also will induce borrowing. This latter result is specialized to the present formulation of the model, however, and only occurs when capital goods cannot be produced at home.

1. The Simple Model

Definition of Variables

Z Received income (Gross National Product)
XP Produced income (Gross Domestic Product)
X Physical output
P The national price of X
L Labor
K Units of accumulated capital
D Flow of income on external investment or borrowing (Net Factor Income)

5. There are two reasons for ignoring government borrowing in this model. First, the data used to measure state income payments on external borrowing relate only to private borrowing. Second, data are available which measure state interest payments on state and federal governmental debt, but they would have to be used with caution because federal fiscal operations in a state do not generate interest payments on federal debt commensurate with the federal deficit or surplus in that state.

r National interest rate
Xc Consumption of X
Xe Export of X
M Flow of imported capital goods
P_k The nation's price of capital goods
S Money value of savings
B Balance of payments on current account
I Money value of investment
C Money value of consumption

Definition of Coefficients

α Savings ratio
a Elasticity of output with respect to capital
A Technology index
ρ Rate of growth of output price
λ Rate of growth of labor force

The following conditions are assumed: the economy produces a single commodity, X, which employs labor, L, and an indestructible capital good, K; the capital good is imported at an exogenously determined price that may grow over time; and the commodity X may be exported or consumed at home. In this formulation the external demand for X is infinitely elastic at a price that may grow over time. Alternative formulations of the demand function for exports of X will be discussed later. A Cobb-Douglas production function subject to constant returns to scale describes the production of X. It also is assumed (a) that the economy is at full employment, in competitive equilibrium with regard to the use of labor and capital, and that the labor force grows at some exogenously determined rate; (b) that borrowing or lending occurs at an interest rate which is determined in the national capital market; and (c) that savings are a fixed ratio to Gross Regional Product. Note, however, that the model provides no aggregate or nationwide constraint on the supply of capital. This negates the possibility of examining interactions between one regional economy and another.

The regional economy grows through time in a physical sense because of the growth of the labor supply, shifts in the production function due to technological change, and the accumulation of an imported capital good. As a matter of analytic convenience, considerations of the import of consumer goods or intermediate goods have been omitted, although they could be incorporated. The economy's output also grows in money value relative to other regions' output because of growth of P, the price of output.

The equations and definitions containing the above assumptions are shown below.[6]

Relationships in the Simple Model

(1)	$X = A(t)L^{1-a}K^a$	Production function for X
(2)	$X = Xc + Xe$	Use of X
(3)	$L = L_0 e^{\lambda t}$	Full and growing employment
(4)	$M = \dot{K}$	Capital goods imported at
(5)	$P_k = \overline{P}_k$	Constant price
(6)	$P = P_0 e^{\rho t}$	P is exogenous, grows at ρ percent
(7)	$rKP_k = aXP$	Competitive equilibrium
(8)	$r = \overline{r}$	Exogenous interest rate
(9)	$S = \alpha Z$	Savings function
(10)	$I \equiv \dot{K}P_k$	Definition of investment
(11)	$Z \equiv XP + D$	GNP, GDP, net factor income
(12)	$D \equiv r\Sigma B$	Net factor income defined
(13)	$B \equiv XeP - MP_k + D$	Current account balance of payments
(14)	$Z \equiv C + S$	Income identity
(15)	$C \equiv XcP$	No importation of consumer goods

These assumptions permit the derivation of the following investment function from equation (7):

$$\text{(vi)} \qquad I = \dot{K}P_k = \frac{a}{r}\dot{\overline{XP}}$$

Assume that XP (domestic product) grows through time at the rate of k, the sum of $\lambda, \rho/(1 - a)$, and any effects stemming from changes in the technology index of the production function $A(t)$. Also assume that $\dot{A}/A$ is constant over time.

$$XP = X_0 P_0 e^{kt}$$

Substituting in (vi),

$$\text{(vii)} \qquad I = \underline{\frac{akX_0 P_0 e^{kt}}{r}}$$

6. A simpler version of this model was developed by Philip A. Neher, *A Neoclassical Theory of International Capital Movements*, unpublished PH.D. dissertation, Brown University, 1966.

Savings and investment functions can be substituted in equation (v) to obtain time path solutions for the major dependent variables Z, D, B, and I,

(viii) $$\dot{Z} = (1 - a)kXP + r\alpha Z$$

which also may be written

$$\dot{Z} - r\alpha Z = (1 - a)kX_0 P_0 e^{kt}$$

This differential equation may be solved to yield the following:

(ix) $$Z_t = \frac{(1 - a)kX_0 P_0 e^{kt}}{k - \alpha r} + (\text{constant})e^{\alpha rt}$$

which also may be written

$$Z/XP = \frac{(1 - a)k}{k - \alpha r} + \frac{\text{constant}}{X_0 P_0} e^{(\alpha r - k)t}$$

The second term will decay if $k > \alpha r$, and the result will be a positive, steady-state value for the ratio of received to produced income. This steady-state value may be used to derive solutions for the following ratios:

(a) Net factor income to GNP $\equiv D/Z$
(b) Balance of payments on current account to GNP $\equiv B/Z$
(c) Investment to GNP $= I/Z$

(x) $$D/Z = \frac{\alpha r - ak}{k(1 - a)}$$

$$B/Z = \frac{\alpha r - ak}{r(1 - a)}$$

$$I/Z = \frac{a(k - \alpha r)}{r(1 - a)}$$

B/Z measures the steady-state share of a region's gross product devoted to lending or borrowing from other regions. Lending will increase as a proportion of income when α, the savings ratio, and r, the interest rate, increase. It will decrease when there is a rise in a, the share paid to capital in the production function, and in k, the growth rate of domestic product.

Two constraints on the values of the parameters are suggested by the requirements that the solutions be stable and that the share of domestic product exported lie between zero and unity. The stability condition for the model is $k > \alpha r$. This is not a stringent condition to meet, since it requires only that a positive fraction of GNP be invested. This result may be seen from the previously derived expression for I/Z. The constraint on the share of domestic product exported is more stringent.

$$\text{(xi)} \qquad \frac{XeP}{XP} = 1 - \frac{XcP}{XP} = 1 - \frac{(1 - \alpha)(1 - a)k}{k - \alpha r}$$

The condition that this ratio is less than unity implies that $k > 0$, the produced income must grow over time. This has already been assumed. The export ratio must also be positive and this implies that

$$\text{(xii)} \qquad k > \alpha r/[a + \alpha(1 - a)].$$

Since the bracketed term is less than unity, this condition is more restrictive than the stability condition. It should also be noted that condition (xii) implies an upper bound to the ratio of net factor income to GNP. In fact this ratio could not *exceed* the savings ratio for a lending country or region.

$$\text{(xiii)} \qquad \alpha > D/Z$$

Statistical Tests of the Model

We might construct estimates of D/Z, B/Z, and I/Z for each state by substituting into each solution estimated values of the parameters a, r, k, and α. For this simple model, I have not constructed estimates of B/Z or I/Z. B/Z is very likely dominated by government spending and taxing, both of which would be exogenous. Although I/Z could be constructed, it is a net investment concept because it excludes depreciation. The available data show only gross investment by state. In the more sophisticated model presented next, gross investment is predicted. All of the tests on the simple model were performed on D/Z, the ratio of net factor income to received income.

There is a small body of data on U.S. regions that can be used to test the simple model. In a paper written in 1960, this author estimated state-produced and received income for the continental United States for the years 1929 and 1953.[7] These estimates were

7. Borts, "Estimation of Produced Income" (n. 4. above).

constructed so that the difference between produced and received concepts would equal the net earnings of interest and profit on net private borrowings and lending by each state. Thus we have observations on D, Z, and XP. The estimates of produced income were partitioned into labor and capital shares, resulting in estimates of a for each state. The exact value of k, the growth of produced income, is unknown because we have only the 1929 and 1953 observations on produced income. More recent and more frequent data are available, however, for received income. Accordingly, the growth rates of received personal income in the states are used to measure k on the assumption that received and produced income would closely parallel each other. k is then measured by the growth rate of received personal income between 1940 and 1950. The savings ratio α was derived from work done by Romans, who has estimated the value of net savings in the states for 1953. It is assumed that the ratio of savings to income for 1953 is a constant that is different for each state. Data are unavailable on r, the interest yield on external borrowing and lending; thus it is assumed to be the same for all states, and its value has been approximated to provide a reasonable distribution of estimated borrowers and lenders. In view of the linear dependence of D/Z on r, this procedure will not be erroneous if r is truly exogenous and equal for all regions. More will be said about this below.

Using the above estimates, hypothetical ratios of D/Z have been constructed for each state. When the hypothetical and actual ratios are compared, a correlation coefficient of $r = +.64$ is obtained between actual and hypothetical estimates of D/Z. This correlation coefficient is most encouraging in view of the errors attending the construction of the data and in view of the other influences on private savings and investment that such simple models obviously ignore.

Although for 1953 there are no reliable data on r, the borrowing or lending rate in different states, there are data for later dates. Recently, E. Bruce Fredrickson wrote a paper analyzing data on mortgage interest rates as they were compiled by the Federal Home Loan Bank Board.[8] The interest rates in this paper were compiled for the year 1963, were tabulated by state, and were used to measure

8. E. Bruce Fredrikson, "The Geographic Structure of Residential Mortgage Yields," unpubl. manuscript, Syracuse University, Syracuse, N.Y.

r. As expected, they do show some regional variation. When these interest rates are used in the estimate of D/Z, they have virtually no effect on the predictive accuracy of the computed ratio. The correlation between actual and predicted ratios is then $+.61$, instead of $+.64$, as above, presumably because of some correlation between the level of interest rates and the growth rate. There are a number of reasons why data on interest rates as they were in 1963 might not be useful to explain behavior in 1953. Consequently in further developments of the model, interest rates are assumed to be the same in each region.

2. A More Sophisticated Model

It is possible to expand and articulate the preceding model to explain a wider range of phenomena. The changes are simple to incorporate and are discussed below.

(a) Depreciation as an element influencing the level of savings and investment in the region was ignored in the simple model. A preliminary glance at the concept might lead one to believe that depreciation plays no role because it is netted out of the difference between gross savings and gross investment. This is a mistake. First, depreciation as an element of gross savings is some fraction of the capital owned by the region's residents, while depreciation as an element of gross investment is some fraction of the capital employed in the region. Consequently, the two items do not cancel each other. Second, depreciation may enter the savings function in a manner which does not allow netting out against the depreciation which is part of investment. For example, we may write gross savings as the sum of net savings and depreciation, where net savings is some constant fraction of net national product. Thus,

(i) $\qquad S - \text{depreciation} = \alpha(Z - \text{depreciation}),$
(ii) $\qquad S = \alpha(Z - \text{depreciation}) + \text{depreciation},$

where S is now gross savings, and Z is now gross product, so that

(iii) $\qquad S = \alpha Z + (1 - \alpha)\ \text{depreciation}.$

Consequently, the depreciation in gross savings will not net out against that in gross investment.

Estimating the depreciation rate in each state is possible, assuming one wishes to take account of its variations. The estimation procedure makes use of data available on depreciation and income paid to capital. First, note that the production function of the simple model is reinterpreted to refer to a relation between gross output X, labor L, and capital net of depreciation K. Next rewrite equation (7) of the model, which is the equilibrium condition for the use of capital:

$$(7') \qquad (r + \beta)KP_k = bXP,$$

where β is the rate of depreciation, and b the share of Gross Domestic Product paid to capital, includes net profit plus depreciation.

Total depreciation received by the region equals the sum of depreciation on domestically employed capital plus depreciation on externally owned capital.

$$(iv) \qquad \text{Total received depreciation} = \frac{\beta bXP}{r + \beta} + \frac{\beta b'X'P'}{r + \beta},$$

where the second term $b'X'P'/(r + \beta)$ represents the gross income paid to external capital owned by the region's residents. Note the assumption that both β, the depreciation rate, and r, the profit rate, are the same on both types of capital. Moreover, total received income to capital net of depreciation, equals

$$(v) \qquad \frac{rbXP}{r + \beta} + \frac{rb'X'P'}{r + \beta}.$$

β/r may then be calculated for each state from the ratio of equations (iv) to (v). The data on total received depreciation are available in Romans' study. The data on total income to capital net of depreciation come from my study of produced and received income, and consist of the received net entrepreneurial income shown in that paper.[9]

Once we admit the existence of depreciation, it becomes necessary to include it in the definition of net factor income. State gross product is measured as the sum of state Gross Domestic Product and gross income on external lending.

Z = Gross Domestic Product + Net Income on External Lending (D) + Depreciation on Externally Owned Capital

Although the depreciation on externally owned capital is unknown, it may also be estimated from the above procedure.

9. Borts, "Estimation of Produced Income" (n. 4 above).

(vi) Depreciation on externally owned capital $= (\beta b' X' P')/(r + \beta)$

(vii) Net income to externally owned capital $D = (r b' X' P')/(r + \beta)$

Thus depreciation on externally owned capital equals $\beta D / r$, and the definition of Gross State Product may be written as follows:

$$(11') \qquad Z = XP + D\left[\frac{r + \beta}{r}\right],$$

where XP is now equal to State Gross Domestic Product.

(b) In the simple model it was assumed that savings were not influenced by taxation. Some error may be introduced if, as likely, savings depend upon disposable income. We know from Romans' work that tax collections by state, local, and federal government do vary as a percent of Gross Product from one state to another. Consequently in this model, I have assumed that net savings are a fraction of net disposable income, where taxes are assumed to be a given fraction of Gross Product, τ. The Gross Savings function is therefore written:

$$S = \alpha(Z - \text{taxes} - \text{depreciation}) + \text{depreciation}$$

$$(9') \qquad S = \alpha(1 - \tau)\, Z + (1 - \alpha)\ \text{depreciation}$$

where the coefficients α and τ are different for each state.

(c) Originally it was assumed that the price of imported capital goods was fixed and unchanged. This was not true during the decade 1940–1950, for which k, the growth of domestic product, was measured. In the simple model there were no difficulties introduced by ignoring this price change. Now it must be taken into account, in order to satisfy the stability conditions of this version of the model,

$$(5') \qquad\qquad P_k = \overline{P}_k e^{\gamma t}.$$

It is not possible to estimate a different value of γ for each state. Robert A. Gordon estimated that it equalled between 5.5 and 6.5 percent per year nationally.[10] The investment function must be rewritten to take into account the new assumptions about β and γ. Originally, the investment function was

$$I = \dot{K}P_k = \left(\frac{akX_0 P_0}{r}\right)e^{kt}.$$

10. Robert A. Gordon, "Differential Changes in the Prices of Consumers and Capital Goods," *American Economic Review*, 51 (Dec. 1961), 937–957.

Gross investment may be derived as follows: Gross Investment = $\dot{K}P_k$ + depreciation on employed capital. Each term may be derived in turn. Differentiate equation (7') to obtain

(viii)
$$\dot{K}P_k + K\dot{P}_k = \frac{b(\overline{\dot{XP}})}{r + \beta},$$

from which

net investment $= \dot{K}P_k = \dfrac{bXP(k - \gamma)}{r + \beta}.$

In addition, depreciation on employed capital equals $\beta bXP/(r + \beta)$, so that

(ix)   Gross investment $= \dfrac{bXP}{r + \beta}(\beta + k - \gamma).$

(d) The solution to the new model may be outlined. Differentiate the definition of Gross State Product

(x)
$$\dot{Z} = kXP + \dot{D}\left(\frac{r + \beta}{r}\right).$$

Note that $\dot{D} = r$ [Gross Savings $-$ Gross Investment]. The net lending or borrowing occasioned by governmental deficits or surpluses is agained ignored. Therefore

(xi) $\dot{Z} = kXP + (r + \beta)$
                    [Gross Savings $-$ Gross Investment].

Substitute the following Gross Savings Function

(9') $S = \alpha(1 - \tau)Z + (1 - \alpha)$ depreciation

Note that depreciation equals the sum of
  a. depreciation on domestically employed capital, which is

$$\frac{\beta bXP}{\beta + r}, \text{ and}$$

  b. depreciation on externally owned capital, which is

$$\frac{\beta D}{r} \text{ or } \frac{\beta}{r + \beta}(Z - XP).$$

Thus the Gross Savings Function is

(xii) $S = Z\left[\alpha(1 - \tau) + \dfrac{\beta(1 - \alpha)}{r + \beta}\right] - \dfrac{XP(1 - \alpha)}{\beta + r}\left[\beta(1 - b)\right],$

while the Gross Investment Function is written above in (ix). When these functions are substituted in (xi), the following differential equation is obtained:

(xiii) $\dot{Z} - N_1Z = N_2X_0P_0e^{kt}$, which has the solution

(xiv)
$$Z_t = \frac{N_2X_0P_0e^{kt}}{k - N_1} + ce^{N_1t}$$

The coefficients of the equation are

$$N_1 = \alpha(1 - \tau)(r + \beta) + \beta(1 - \alpha),$$
$$N_2 = k - b(k - \gamma) - \beta[1 - \alpha(1 - b)].$$

This solution reduces to that of the simple model when τ and $\beta = 0$. Provided that $k > N_1$ and that $N_2 > 0$, there will be a stable, positive solution for the ratio of the State Gross Product to State Gross Domestic Product and stable solutions for the ratios D/Z and I/Z, where I is now Gross Investment.

(xv)
$$D/Z = \frac{r}{r + \beta} \frac{[N_2 + N_1 - k]}{N_2}.$$

(xvi)
$$I/Z = \frac{b(\beta + k - \gamma)}{r + \beta} \cdot \frac{k - N_1}{N_2}.$$

This model therefore provides constructive estimates of two ratios: D/Z, the ratio of net income on external investment to Gross State Product; and I/Z, the share of gross product which consists of gross investment. In each case there is enough information to measure all parameters except r and γ. As noted earlier, γ is assumed equal to 6 percent and is the same for each state, while a common r was chosen to provide a reasonable distribution of borrowers and lenders. In the 1940-1950 period, the r chosen was in the range of 15–20 percent before taxes on investment returns.

The statistical comparisons between hypothetical and actual ratios of D/Z and I/Z are again quite promising. Although a good deal of extra variation is introduced into the estimates by considering taxes and depreciation, the correlation coefficients between actual and hypothetical ratios are as high as before. For D/Z, the correlation between actual and hypothetical ratios is $r = +.64$. For I/Z, the correlation between actual and hypothetical ratios is $r = +.67$. Thus the more sophisticated growth model can explain a wider range of phenomena with no sacrifice of closeness of fit between hypothetical and actual ratios of the dependent variable.

It will be useful to evaluate the effect of individual parameters of the model on the behavior of individual states. The chief parameters are α, k, a, τ, and β; they take on different values for each state and are used to provide hypothetical estimates of D/Z and I/Z. The purpose of this evaluation is to identify the major forces acting on borrowing and lending behavior. For example, if only one parameter varied with the dependent variable, a much simpler analysis would be equally useful. The comparison is carried out in Table 1 where the states are split into a group of 27 debtors and 21 creditors. The identification is made from the sign of D, the income on external borrowing or lending. The columns of the table identify the number of states with parameter values above and below the mean for the 48 states. Thus the first column indicates that 17 debtor states had net savings ratios below the mean and 10 had net savings ratios above the mean. On the other hand, 11 creditor states had net savings ratios above the mean and 10 below the mean. In view of the fact that an increase in the savings ratio induces a region to lend more or borrow less, the above comparisons suggest that actual variation of the savings ratio had a significant but small effect on the debtor-creditor relations.

Above the letter identifying the parameter is a plus or minus sign indicating the a priori sign of the partial derivative of lending with respect to the parameter. Private lending is expected to increase with an increase in α or β; it is expected to decrease if there is an increase in k, a, or τ. These expectations are confirmed in all but one case by the cross-classification presented in Table 1. Each classification may be summarized by subtracting the number of deviations from the mean with incorrect signs from the deviations

Table 1.   Effects of Individual Parameters on State Debtor Position

	+ α(savings ratio) above mean	− k(growth rate) above mean	− a(capital coefficient) above mean	− τ(tax rate) above mean	+ β(depreci-ation rate) above mean
27 debtor states	10	21	14	7	8
21 creditor states	11	6	4	18	16
	below mean	below mean	below mean	below mean	below mean
27 debtor states	17	6	13	20	19
21 creditor states	10	15	17	3	5

with correct signs. A correct deviation is one which accords with the a priori sign of the partial derivative of lending with respect to the parameter. Thus the 17 debtor states with α below the mean and the 11 creditors with α above the mean are correct deviations.

Parameters	Correct deviations minus incorrect deviations
α savings ratio	8
k growth rate	24
a capital coefficient	14
τ tax rate	−28
β depreciation rate	22

With the exception of τ, all of the parameters have the expected effect on actual behavior. The most important parameters are k and β, with a and α having smaller influence. Note that τ has the wrong effect, indicating that it might generate a coefficient with an incorrect sign in a multiple regression analysis. The reason is clearly that creditor states tend to be high-income states, and, for a number of reasons, such states pay a higher share of income in taxes. The incorrect sign of τ in the above analysis may not indicate incorrect specification of the savings function as much as it points up the pitfalls in using gross or first-order comparisons.

There are two methods of analyzing more precisely the effects of the parameters on borrowing and lending behavior. The first is to test the sensitivity of the estimates to independent variation in each parameter. The second is a multiple regression analysis that relates actual behavior to a linear combination of the parameters. Each of these methods has been carried out and will be described.

Sensitivity Analysis

From the above analysis of the gross relations between parameter values and actual lending behavior, one might conclude that the chief explanatory variables are k, the growth rate of received income, and β, the depreciation rate. The sensitivity analysis to be presented below suggests that the actual variations in β were too small to have a meaningful effect on lending. Moreover, it appears that variations in α the savings ratio, and a the capital share, had a considerable effect on lending behavior. The analysis was performed in the following manner. All but one parameter was held constant at its mean level, and the remaining parameter varied through its high to low range. The range of variation for each parameter was estimated visually and was chosen to represent limits beyond which two or three observations might still be made. The mean level of each parameter, the range through which it was allowed to vary, and its actual standard deviation is shown in Table 2. The variation of the constructed value of D/Z from an assumed mean of zero is also shown. The constructed values of D/Z were most sensitive to the actual range of variation of: k, the growth rate of income; α, the savings ratio; and, a the share of product paid to capital.

Table 2. Sensitivity of State Debtor Position to Parameter Variation

Parameter	Variation in parameters about mean			Variations in estimated D/Z about assumed zero mean
	Mean	Extremes	Standard deviation	
α	0.1083	0.1800-0.0600	0.0355	+0.1272 to −0.1504
k	0.1114	0.1300-0.0900	0.0142	−0.1005 to +0.1956
a	0.4169	0.5000-0.3600	0.0583	−0.0987 to +0.0548
τ	0.1046	0.2400-0.1700	0.0262	−0.0159 to +0.0158
β	0.0476	0.0540-0.0350	0.0069	+0.0008 to −0.0015

The actual ranges of variation of τ and β were too small to have much influence on the constructed estimates. This undoubtedly explains why the introduction of τ into the model failed to raise its explanatory power in a purely statistical sense. This analysis also indicates that while the depreciation ratio may have some effect on the theoretical levels of lending, in practice they can be ignored. Although depreciation does not net out the difference between gross saving and gross investment, the remainder is apparently of small quantitative importance.

Regression Analysis

A regression plane was also used, treating the five parameters as independent explanatory variables and using the *actual* ratio

D/Z as the dependent variable. In the following notation the letter b refers to the appropriate regression coefficient.

(xvii) $D/Z = b_0 + b_1 k + b_2 \alpha + b_3 a + b_4 \beta + b_5 \tau.$

When the coefficients were estimated, the tax rate coefficient had the wrong sign, indicating, as before, the dominance of a correlation between creditor position, high income, and share of income devoted to taxes. Consequently, this variable was dropped from the multiple regression, and the following coefficients were obtained with the standard errors shown in parentheses:

$$\begin{aligned}
\text{constant: } b_0 \quad &0.0561 \ (0.0389) \\
k: \ b_1 - \ &0.9178 \ (0.5112) \\
\alpha: \ b_2 + \ &0.6769 \ (0.1633) \\
a: \ b_3 - \ &0.1975 \ (0.1170) \\
\beta: \ b_4 + \ &1.1394 \ (0.9565)
\end{aligned}$$

The multiple correlation coefficient is $+.705$.

Each coefficient has the correct a priori sign, and the coefficient of α exceeds twice its standard error, while the other coefficients approximately exceed 1.5 times their standard error. When the less significant independent variables are dropped from the regression, we obtain two independent explanatory variables whose coefficients exceed twice their standard error. These are k and α.

$$\begin{aligned}
\text{constant: } b_0 \quad &0.0885 \ (0.0398) \\
k: \ b_1 - \ &1.514 \ \ (0.4116) \\
\alpha: \ b_2 + \ &0.7304 \ (0.1643)
\end{aligned}$$

The multiple correlation coefficient is $+.672$.

The most important explanatory variables in this regression framework are k, the growth rate, and α, the savings ratio. The savings ratio apparently reasserts its importance in the multiple regression framework because of its large variance, which was missed in the gross analysis presented earlier. Moreover, the depreciation rate β loses its explanatory power in the multiple regression because of its small variance and its high correlation with the savings ratio.

A measure of the independent contribution of each variable to the explanation of D/Z may be obtained by multiplication of the respective regression coefficients by the ratio of standard deviations. Thus we have $b_1 \sigma_k / \sigma_{D/Z}$), etc. These constructed coefficients are identical to regression coefficients that would be obtained if each variable were measured in units of its own standard deviation, so that each had a unit variance. The resulting coefficients may be regarded as measures of the independent influence of each explanatory variable, since they summarize the effect of the regression coefficient and the recorded variation of the independent variable. They of course leave out the effect of any interactions among explanatory variables. The resulting coefficients are shown below for the case of four explanatory variables. For the sake of notation $\sigma_{D/Z}$ is written as σ_1.

$$k: b_1 \cdot \sigma_k/\sigma_1 = -.2483$$
$$\alpha: b_2 \cdot \sigma_\alpha/\sigma_1 = +.4577$$
$$a: b_3 \cdot \sigma_a/\sigma_1 = -.2193$$
$$\beta: b_4 \cdot \sigma_\beta/\sigma_1 = +.1497$$

Clearly the two most important variables are k and a. Even if β had a significant coefficient, it has much less influence in explaining variations in D/Z.

Thus, the chief influences on the debt position of the states in 1953 appear to be the savings ratio and the rate of growth of income in the preceding decade.

An examination of the residuals from the regression is instructive for the possibilities of improving the analysis. There are two possible reasons why the actual value of D/Z would exceed its predicted value. First is the possibility of errors in measuring D, which is the net factor income, derived as the difference between received and produced income in each state. When the statistical procedures underlying the measurement of produced and received income were first published, they attracted criticism on the grounds that the underlying data were not adequate to the task. In addition it was suggested that the allocation methods were subject to some error and might in fact result in an understatement of produced income in heavily industrialized areas. Such an understatement yields an overstatement of net factor income.

Another possible source of error in estimating D/Z arises from the shortfall of a correctly measured produced income from its long-run growth path. The growth, k, was measured for the period 1940-1950, while the data on D/Z pertain to 1953. Any downward departure from the growth path yields a lower than expected level of produced income, and consequently a higher than predicted value of net factor income.

With these considerations in mind, the residuals from the regression should be examined for any noticeable patterns. The residuals appear to have a geographic pattern with positive residuals occurring in all states in New England and in the Far West and Mountain areas.[11] Negative residuals appear in the middle western and plains states.[12] In view of the fact that the residuals are not associated with degree of dependence on manufacturing industry, attention should be drawn to the possibilities that produced income deviated from the trend in the areas marked by residual patterns. One could speculate that cyclical disturbances played some role in producing the patterns. Produced incomes in New England and in western states producing forest products were adversely affected by business conditions after 1949. This suggests that produced incomes in these areas were below their long-run normal patterns. In addition, the industrialized Midwest enjoyed an income boom during the Korean War which may have placed their produced incomes above the long-run normal paths. Cyclical departures from a trend of the kind described might account for the regional pattern of residuals.

3. Assumptions Underlying the Model

In this section I shall analyze some of the simplifying assumptions of the model, and suggest alternatives to them.

a. INFLUENCES ON THE RATE OF GROWTH OF INCOME

It will be valuable to examine in detail the components of k, the rate of growth of produced income.

$$(i) \qquad XP = (X_0 P_0)e^{kt}.$$

We know more about k than is contained in the above expression. Since this is a neoclassical growth model, k represents the rate of growth along an equilibrium time path. The growth rate of physical output may be explicitly derived from the definition of the production function. Recall that ρ is the rate of growth of P.

11. Far Western and Mountain states with positive residuals include California, Arizona, Colorado, Idaho, Montana, Oregon, and Washington.
12. Middle Western and Plains states with negative residuals include Illinois, Indiana, Michigan, Ohio, Wisconsin, Iowa, Kansas, Minnesota, Nebraska, and South Dakota.

(xvii) $$k - \rho = \dot{X}/X = \frac{\dot{A}}{A} + (1 - b)\lambda + b\dot{K}/K,$$

where A is an assumed neutral technological shift, and λ the growth rate of population.

We may substitute for the last term in (xvii), which is the rate of growth of the capital stock net of depreciation:

$$\text{Net investment} = bXP\ (k - \gamma)/(r + \beta).$$

Substituting, we have

(xix) $$k - \rho = \frac{\dot{A}/A}{1 - b} + \lambda + \frac{b(\rho - \gamma)}{1 - b}.$$

The rate of growth of physical output depends not only on technological change and the growth of the labor force but also on improvement in the terms of trade between output and imported capital goods. If capital goods were produced at home and not imported, there would be no terms-of-trade effect. Indeed, it would be possible to generate a model in which capital goods were produced at home exclusively, and changes in the terms of trade would not affect the growth of output. The level of investment and the debtor-creditor position of the state would then depend on the growth of output in physical terms, not in money terms. Unfortunately, since the growth of real output by state is not known, data are not available to test this alternative specification.

B.   THE DEMAND FOR A REGION'S EXPORTS

Another assumption requiring clarification is the rate of growth of output prices. Each state is assumed to produce one good whose price is determined in the national market, implying that the national demand for that good has infinite price elasticity.

Alternative assumptions concerning the nature of the demand function for exports lead to a number of interesting theoretical hypotheses, which unfortunately are not testable with the regional data available. They are nevertheless sufficiently important to explore, because the method of obtaining time path solutions is somewhat different from those presented earlier and because of the significant economic content of such solutions. The assumptions will be explored within the framework of the first model, in which taxes and depreciation are ignored.

The implications of the assumption that P, the price of output, is a function of the volume of exports from the region will be explored. Assume a demand function of the form

(6') $$XeP = uP^\delta U^\epsilon,$$

where u is a constant term, $(\delta - 1)$ is the price elasticity of demand for exports, U is the National Income of the country, and ϵ is the income elasticity of national demand. This equation would replace equation (6) of the original model. In addition, the time path of U.S. national income must be specified and will assumed to grow at a constant rate σ, resulting in the additional equation

(16) $$U_t = U_0 e^{\sigma t}$$

and the demand equation may be written:

(11') $$XeP = c_1 P^\delta e^{\epsilon \sigma t}, \text{ where } c_1 = uU_0^\epsilon$$

Solution of the original model now proceeds as follows: Write the original income definition, and take its time derivative

$$Z \equiv XP + D$$

$$\dot{Z} = (\dot{XP}) + \dot{D} = (\dot{XP}) + r[S - I] = \dot{\overline{XP}} + r\alpha Z - a\dot{\overline{XP}}$$

(i) $$\dot{Z} = r\alpha Z + (1 - a)\dot{\overline{XP}}$$

Note that the time path XP is no longer accepted as given since it will depend on the path of exports. A second equation in Z is, however, derived from the output identity

$$XcP \equiv XP - XeP.$$

(ii) $$(1 - \alpha)Z = XP - XeP$$

When equation (ii) is substituted in (i), the result is

(iii) $$N_1(\dot{XP}) - N_2 XP = (\dot{XeP}) - N_2(XeP),$$

where $$N_1 = 1 - (1 - a)(1 - \alpha),$$

$$N_2 = \alpha r.$$

Some characteristics of the solution, which will be derived below, may be perceived from equation (iii). A condition of steady-state equilibrium requires that produced income, XP, and exports, XeP, grow at the same rate through time (k), and maintain a constant ratio, E, where $E = Xe/X$. When these assumptions are substituted in (iii), the result is

(iv) $$(kN_1 - N_2)XP = E\, XP(k - N_2);$$

so that

(v) $$E = \frac{kN_1 - N_2}{k - N_2} = 1 - \frac{k(1-a)(1-\alpha)}{k - \alpha r}.$$

This is the same solution obtained for the simple model, and the implications of the requirement that the ratio E lie between zero and unity have already been noted.

The actual solution to equation (iii) is obtained by substituting expressions for XP and XeP as functions of P, and solving for the resulting differential equation in P.

XeP has already been specified as a function of P.

(vi) $$XeP = c_1 P^\delta e^{\epsilon\sigma t}$$

Taking the time derivative of all variables,

(vii) $\dot{XeP} = (c_1 P^\delta)[\epsilon\sigma + \delta P^*]e^{\epsilon\sigma t}$, where P^* denotes $\dot{P}/P$.

In addition XP is expressed as a function of P, by writing

$$XP = \frac{X}{L}PL_0 e^{\lambda t},$$

and noting that

$$X/L = (c_2)e^{ht}P^{a/1-a},$$

where

$$c_2 = \left(\frac{rP_k}{a}\right)^{a/a-1} \text{ and } h = \frac{\dot{A}/A}{1-a}.$$

The equation for X/L is derived from the production function and from the equilibrium conditions for the use of capital, so that

(viii) $$XP = c_3 P^{1/1-a}e^{St},$$

where $S = h + \lambda$, and $c_3 = c_2 L_0$.

Take the time derivative,

(ix) $$\dot{XP} = c_3 P^{1/1-a}[S + P^*/(1-a)]e^{St}$$

Substitute equations (vi), (vii), (viii), and (ix) into (iii):

(x) $c_3 e^{St}P^{1/1-a}[N_1(S + P^*/(1-a)) - N_2] = c_1 e^{\epsilon\sigma t}P^\delta[\epsilon\sigma + \delta P^* - N_2].$

Now assume that $P = P_0 e^{\rho t}$, where $P^* = \rho$, and substitute

$$P_0^{1/1-a} c_3 e^{[S + \rho/1 - a]t}[N_1(S + \rho/(1-a) - N_2]$$
$$= c_1 e^{[\epsilon\sigma + \delta\rho]t}[\epsilon\sigma + \delta\rho - N_2]P_0^{\delta}$$

A steady-state solution will be obtained when $S + \rho/(1-a) = \epsilon\sigma + \delta\rho$, or

(xi)
$$\rho = \frac{\epsilon\sigma - S}{(1/1 - a) - \delta}.$$

Note that the growth rate of produced income is $k = S + \rho/(1-a)$. Assuming that the price elasticity of demand is negative ($\delta < 1$), the rate of change of price will vary positively with the difference between the rate of growth of export demand ($\epsilon\sigma$) due to growth of U.S. income and the rate of growth of regional output (S) due to the growth of the region's labor supply and the growth of technology. From the above a solution for P_0 may be obtained:

(xii)
$$P_0^f = \frac{c_3}{c_1} \frac{N_1 k - N_2}{k - N_2},$$

where $k = S + \rho/(1-a) = \epsilon\sigma + \delta\rho$ and $f \equiv \delta - 1/(1-a)$.

Stability conditions for the above solutions may be derived by examining departures from the assumed trend of P_t. A price that departs from the trend line is assumed. For example, let $Q = P/Pe$, where Pe denotes the trend line, $Pe = P_0 e^{\rho t}$, and P is a price which may be above or below it. Then $Q^* = P^* - \rho$; that is, the proportionate growth of Q equals the proportionate growth of P minus the proportionate growth of the trend line. We may, therefore, re-examine equation (x) to see whether a price other than that on the trend line will move to the trend line. Substituting $P = PeQ$ and $P^* = Q^* + \rho$, we have

(xiii)
$$c_3 e^{kt} P_0^{1/1-a} Q^{1/1-a}[N_1(k + Q^*/(1-a) - N_2]$$
$$= c_1 e^{kt} P_0^{\delta} Q^{\delta}[k + \delta Q^* - N_2].$$

Define $V = Q^f$, where f was defined earlier. Making all necessary substitutions,

(xiv)
$$V^* = \frac{(V - 1)fc_3(kN_1 - N_2)}{[(c_3 N_1)/(1-a)] - c_1 P_0^f \delta V}.$$

The system will be stable if $dV^*/dV < 0$, and this will occur when

$$\delta < 1/(1-a)$$

and

$$\delta < \frac{N_1}{1-a}\frac{(k-N_2)}{N_1k-N_2} = \frac{N_1}{1-a} \cdot \frac{1}{E} = [a/(1-a)+\alpha]\frac{1}{E}.$$

E is the equilibrium share of domestic product exported. Clearly, the stability constraint on δ is not very strong and, in fact, δ could exceed unity and the system remain stable. Thus stability is consistent with very small values of price elasticity of demand for exports, or even with some positive slope to the demand curve.[13] The above formulation provides useful hypotheses about the determination of ρ and k, respectively, the growth rate of output price and the growth rate of domestic product. Output price and domestic product now depend upon the price elasticity of U.S. demand (δ-1), the income elasticity (ϵ), and the growth rate of U.S. income (σ). These factors are additional to the growth of population and technology. In the absence of better regional data, it is not possible to employ these more powerful hypotheses, and we must be content that this formulation is consistent with the statistical procedures actually employed in the earlier sections. Such hypotheses would be extremely useful in evaluating growth patterns among different countries.

C.   THE COMPOSITION OF REGIONAL OUTPUT

Under certain circumstances it would be useful to expand the model to include more than one output sector. A multisector approach would be needed if one wanted to depict improvements over time in the allocation of labor and to explain the movement of labor from low to high productivity sectors. This approach was followed by Stein and myself in earlier work.[14]

A second use for a multisector model is to analyze observable changes over time in the export sector's share of gross domestic product. If, for example, the focus of development is capital investment in an import-competing industry, the export share may decline from one steady-state level to a lower level.

13. There is a second set of stability constraints on δ which are not shown. These imply positively sloped demand curves, exclude negatively sloped demand curves, and ordinarily are not considered reasonable.

14. George H. Borts and Jerome L. Stein, *Economic Growth in a Free Market* (New York: Columbia University Press, 1964).

We have assumed that full employment exists in each region. This condition insures that the rate of growth of physical output is independent of the demand conditions for output, with the exception of the terms of trade effect noted earlier.

How would one treat the growth of state output in those periods when full employment is not reached? If unemployment persists in one or more states for a period of time, the assumptions of the model are inappropriate.

One way to introduce unemployment with these models is to use the multisector approach described above, where labor is less efficiently allocated in one sector relative to the other. This introduces the concept of underemployment, rather than unemployment attributed to a deficiency of aggregate demand. This may be the correct way to proceed when the unemployment is not nation-wide.

In order to handle the deficiency of aggregate demand directly it would be necessary to relate output to the demand for exports. This requires the use of the negatively sloped rather than infinitely elastic demand for exports. Each state would then face a different export demand function, growing at a different rate through time. Unemployment would be introduced through assumptions about institutional wage-setting which kept the demand for labor below the supply.

E. MIGRATION

An assumption which raises considerable question is the constant exogenous rate of growth of the labor force. Evidence from other investigations shows that migration between regions is influenced by differences in income levels and unemployment rates.[15] This suggests the possibility of a second relation between the rate of growth of the labor supply and the rate of growth of output. The first relation is the production function.

Consequently, specific assumptions about labor migration may be introduced and still preserve the steady-state moving equilibrium of the regional economy. The simplest assumption to make is that the number of migrants per 1000 of population is a function of

15. Ira S. Lowry, *Migration and Metropolitan Growth: Two Analytic Models* (Los Angeles: University of California Press, 1966).

the wage ratio between one region and the rest of the country. Additionally, one might assume that if the wages were equal between regions, then migration would be zero, or some other constant rate reflecting tastes and other noneconomic information. A second feature of such a migration function would be upper and lower limits on the migration rates as a function of the wage ratio. Such limits are necessary in order to obtain manageable solutions. Useful migration functions would have the graphical properties shown in Figure 1.

Perhaps the simplest approximation to such a function is

$$M = \frac{a + bu}{c + du},$$

where u is the wage ratio and M is migration per thousand. The asymptotic values of migration per thousand are then a/c when $u = 0$, and b/d when u goes to infinity. Such a function might be estimated, perhaps in simpler form, from statistical data. This migration function then makes it possible to specify a new labor supply function of the following type:

$$L^* \equiv \left(\frac{1}{L}\right)\left(\frac{L}{dt}\right) = n + \frac{a + bu}{c + du},$$

Figure 1.   Graphic properties of useful migration functions.

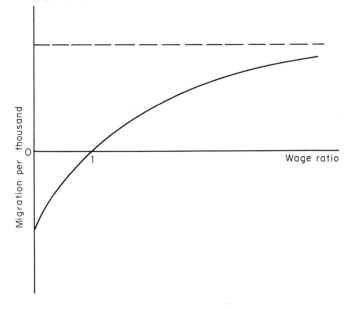

where n is a natural rate of population growth in the absence of migration. The asymptotic value of L^* would be determined by substituting for u a function of time, such as $u = u_0 e^{\phi t}$. As seen in earlier presentations of the model, ϕ is exogenous because the region's wage rate is determined by export prices, interest rates, and capital goods prices. Two possible *asymptotic* solutions for the growth of labor supply are:

$$L^* = n + a/c \text{ when } u \to 0;$$
$$L^* = n + b/d \text{ when } u \to \infty.$$

As an alternative, one may regard the wage ratio as constant over time and solve the migration function with that value of u; that is,

$$L^* = n + \frac{a + b\bar{u}}{c + d\bar{u}}$$

It is not clear which is the best procedure to follow in light of the fact that the model does not really explain how wage differentials might be eliminated over time. Nevertheless, any one of these methods of solution permits us to derive steady-state solutions for the borrowing and lending patterns of each region and permits us to incorporate migration behavior.

MAHLON R. STRASZHEIM

An Introduction and Overview of Regional

Money Capital Markets

I. Introduction

There have been few attempts to measure or analyze the regional structure of money capital markets and interregional capital flows. The belief seems widespread that capital markets in the United States are so extensively developed and so close to "perfect" on a nationwide basis that regional variation in interest rates (for otherwise comparable lending opportunities) is empirically insignificant. The most significant restraint on interregional capital mobility is information costs. For a wide range of savers and borrowers, it is most economical to deposit or obtain funds from lending institutions located nearby. However, several factors facilitate interregional capital flows: the existence of secondary markets in a number of important credit instruments, methods to pool and share lending and borrowing opportunities regionally, and the extensive participation of "local" lending institutions and financial intermediaries in national money markets.

Accordingly, regional growth models have focused generally on factors other than capital market imperfections as the cause of regional differences in the level or growth of income. These include differences in the level or rate of labor migration, technological change, agricultural displacement, public investment, and structure of demand,[1] all of which result in regional differences in capital productivity. Differences in income levels and savings rates create regional differences in the volume of savings. In a perfect capital market, interregional capital flows arise in response to these regional differences in the demand and supply of funds.

Whether long-term regional growth models should be based on the assumption of a perfect capital market or whether there is some more direct causal role for the capital market in regional growth has not been critically examined. Whether or not capital markets exhibit significant regional compartmentalization, and if so, the extent to which this inhibits growth in particular regions, remain unanswered questions. Changes over time in the structure of capital markets and the role of interregional capital movements have not been analyzed. There is considerable disagreement over both the interrelationships between financial and real activity and the fundamental causes of change in national income, prices, and employment on a national level. Introducing a regional dimension greatly complicates the analysis of these interrelations and makes their measurement extremely difficult.

II. Structure of Capital Markets and Measurement of Regional Compartmentalization

A "perfect" capital market exists if financial loans of comparable maturity and risk yield the same rate of return in all regions, not including a premium or "location rent" to cover the cost of transmitting information and funds to and from borrowers and lenders. If such transmission costs are significant, borrowers located "remote" from sources of funds will pay more. Failure of either bor-

1. G. H. Borts and J. L. Stein, "Regional Growth and Maturity in the United States: A Study of Regional Structural Change," in *Regional Analysis*, ed. L. Needleman, (Penguin 1968), pp. 159–197: George H. Borts, "Growth and Capital Movements among U.S. Regions in the Postwar Period," this volume, pp. 189–217.

rowers or financial intermediaries to respond to regional differences in market rates will result in regional compartmentalization. Market power exercised by borrowers or lenders will also produce regional imperfections.

The capital markets include a wide range of financial intermediaries and a complex set of secondary market mechanisms which facilitate interregional capital transactions. References to "the capital market" or "rate of interest" are a very considerable oversimplification. Many different types of financial institutions channel savings into investment. Characteristics of borrowers differ widely, and hence borrowing needs can be most efficiently served by a variety of lending institutions. For example, large corporate borrowers rely on different sources of credit from those available to households or to state and municipal governments. Similarly, there are differences in the characteristics of savings flows of businesses and households; therefore, different kinds of lending institutions can best serve the different investment interests of particular groups.

The result is much specialization in the processes of financial intermediation. Most financial intermediaries serve only a subset of all borrowers and lenders, obtaining funds from particular sources and making loans to particular classes of borrowers. Some financial intermediaries operate almost solely in "local" markets, while others operate solely in "national" markets. In some cases, this arises from legal restrictions on the sources and uses of funds by financial intermediaries. In other cases, the explanation lies in the relative costs to certain kinds of borrowers or lenders of participating in various submarkets of the capital market. Information costs are one important determinant of the range of a financial institution's activity; for example, local lending institutions will have certain advantages in servicing home mortgage and consumer credit financing. The size of the transaction is also important; larger transactions are typically made in national markets.

Thus, in order to accommodate the particular needs of potential borrowers or lenders, an increasing number and variety of financial institutions have been established. Many new debt instruments have been created with varying maturity, risk, negotiability, and marketability. New secondary markets for certain credit instruments have arisen. The demise of some forms of debt instruments and credit institutions whose functions are served in new ways has also occurred. A relative decline in the share of assets held by commercial banks and thrift institutions has occurred over several decades as other financial intermediaries have grown.[2] Most dramatic is the rise in life insurance companies, private and public pension funds, and finance companies. In many instances new lending institutions have arisen as a means of meeting specific credit or investment needs; good examples are private and public pension funds.

The reaction of financial intermediaries to lending opportunities is the basic mechanism for reducing regional compartmentalization. There is a variety of secondary market mechanisms by which funds flows occur between classes of borrowers and lenders. Large funds flows among lending institutions occur through trading in credit instruments. The most important of these are corporate bonds and government securities. Financial institutions also directly borrow and lend funds in the national money markets on their own account, in response to differing relative rates of return nationally vis-à-vis "local" lending opportunities. Both processes tend to equalize rate of return in all markets.

Much analysis of these interrelationships between borrowers and lenders has been done using aggregate flow of funds accounts. The structure and changes over time in interest rates among different types and maturities of credit instruments and in the secondary markets in which they are traded have also been extensively studied. However, the complexity of capital markets and the considerable variation in the extent to which actors on both the borrowing and lending side participate in "local" versus national markets make "regional" limits on capital markets very difficult to define. Data deficiencies complicate the examination of regional compartmentalization. Delineating the character of financial transactions requires several dimensions—risk, time duration of the transaction, and negotiability of the resultant credit instrument. There are insufficient data on interest rates for particular kinds of transactions in different regions to measure regional differences directly. Non-price rationing also exists in some parts of the capital market, though it seems unlikely that it varies significantly regionally.

2. Raymond W. Goldsmith, *The Flow of Capital Funds in the Postwar Economy* (National Bureau of Economic Research, 1965), p. 39.

Tracing interregional flows of funds in a large, well-developed economy with complex capital markets is equally difficult. Flow of funds accounts and their relationship to income and product accounts have only recently been developed.[3] While considerable detail is available on capital markets and the processes of intermediation on a national basis, the flow-of-funds accounts have not yet been developed regionally.[4] Some pressure exists for extending these accounts to regions, but there are both conceptual and practical problems in doing this.[5] There is some question whether funds flows could be traced among even broad classes of institutions on a state or "region" basis. Thus, it is essentially impossible, given current data, to relate the nature of money capital market structures and the behavior of financial intermediaries to real expenditure decisions, either over the course of the business cycle or as an influence on long-run growth patterns.

Since flow-of-funds accounts or data on interest rates on financial transactions on a regional basis are unavailable, it is necessary to infer the significance of regional differences by less direct means. The discussion below surmises the nature of regional differences on the basis of the behavioral patterns of borrowers and lenders in the various segments of the capital markets. By examining the behavior of different classes of borrowers and lenders and the nature of secondary markets in which credit instruments are traded, one can

3. The income and product and flow-of-funds accounts are one of the most useful tools for broad analysis of income levels and financial markets. The national income and product accounts relating income, investment, and savings are familar. The flow-of-funds accounts is a simple extension of these accounts to incorporate changes in financial claims. A double entry set of accounts is employed, with each actor having both "uses" and "sources" of funds. The essential accounting relationship is that gross savings = real investment and financial investment. Each item is broken into component parts, with financial investment composed of all uses and sources of funds—changes in bank deposits, credit instruments, pension funds payments, and so on.

4. Romans developed income and product accounts for states. He observed that New England and the Middle Eastern states are large net savers, with this savings absorbed elsewhere. Looking at changes over the period 1929–1959, he observed that the change in financial investment is negatively correlated with real growth. This suggests that the wealthy states are net savers, exporting capital and hence contributing to growth in areas with lower incomes. Romans does not explain how this process of financial intermediation occurs on a regional basis—J. Thomas Romans, *Capital Exports and Growth Among U.S. Regions* (Middletown, Conn.: Wesleyan University Press, 1965).

5. Richard Ruggles and Nancy D. Ruggles, "Regional Breakdown of National Economic Accounts," *Design of Regional Accounts* (Baltimore, Md.: The Johns Hopkins Press, 1961), pp. 121–142; Charles L. Leven, "Regional Income and Product Accounts: Construction and Application," *ibid.*, pp. 148–195.

deduce the broad outlines of regional capital market compartmentalization. The following overview denotes which actors on both the borrowing and lending side are likely to pay particular attention to conditions in regional or local markets, as opposed to interest rates in national markets. Behavioral models of both the borrowing and lending side are necessary to make these regional differences in the "capital market" explicit and to analyze the causes of regional compartmentalization. A major aim of this paper is to indicate where further research delineating the regional dimension would be most productive.

III. An Outline of the Extent of Compartmentalization

Examination of aggregate flow of funds accounts reveals that several fairly well defined segments of the capital market can be identified, with particular borrowers and lenders operating within each segment (see Table 1). Some of these submarkets are national markets in which only the largest borrowers and lenders participate. In other instances the submarket is essentially a local market made up of small borrowers and lenders. As "local" lending institutions perceive changes occurring in various secondary markets, changing credit conditions in the national money markets are gradually transmitted throughout the capital market.

The discussion below of regional compartmentalization considers borrowers first, then lenders, though at times these are heavily intermingled. Any taxonomic scheme necessarily ignores to some extent the many shades of market compartmentalization. In this paper, borrowing has been divided into three classes: household, business (corporate non-farm, unincorporated business, and farm), and government. The discussion of borrowers attempts to indicate which borrowers are limited to "local" funds sources.

The discussion of financial intermediaries focuses on the extent to which lenders react to both local and national rates of return. Much of the story on regional differences lies on the lending side, especially in the actions of commercial banks and thrift institutions. Financial intermediaries are grouped into four classes. Three of these represent rather distinct submarkets: first, thrift institutions, which dominate the home mortgage markets; second, large institutional lenders of many kinds who are mostly involved in national capital markets (in corporate and government bonds, corporate

Table 1. Sources and Uses of Funds, Private Sector 1965 (in $ billion)

	Households	Farm and noncorporate nonfinancial business	Corporate nonfinancial business
Gross savings	105.1	15.0	55.3
Gross investment	107.8	15.0	54.6
Consumer durables	66.1		
Business planning & equipment	4.2		51.3
1—4 family residential constr.	{19.5	{17.9	{3.9
Other residential construction			
Change in inventories		2.3	6.8
Net financial investment (Uses, &, Sources of funds,—)	18.1	−5.1	−7.3
Demand deposits	7.2		−1.9
Time and savings accounts	26.4		3.9
Life insurance reserves	4.8		
Pension fund reserves	10.9		
Credit market instruments			
U.S. Govt. securities	2.6		−2.1
State and local obligations	2.2		.7
Corporate & for bonds	−.1		−5.4
Corporate stocks	−1.5		0
1—4 family mortgages	−15.8	{−5.4	3.1
Other mortgages	−1.1		−3.2
Consumer credit	−9.4		1.2
Bank loans n.e.c.	−1.3	−3.0	−9.3
Other loans	−.8	−2.1	−1.3
Security credit	−.8		
Trade debt (net)		−1.4	6.4
Equity in noncorp. business		5.8	
Misc. financial transactions		3.8	−3.2

Source: *Federal Reserve Bulletin*, May 1967, pp. 850-860.)
NOTE: This table is based on flow of funds accounts by sector. Columns do not add up. The balancing account "Discrepancy" not included here.

equity, and commercial mortgages); and third, consumer finance companies. The fourth group, commercial banks, is active in all these submarkets.

PRIVATE DOMESTIC BORROWING FOR CAPITAL EXPENDITURE

(1) *Households:* Households' capital financing can be divided into mortgages and consumer credit. Both markets exhibit considerable regional heterogeneity. The market for mortgages on

1-4 family homes, largely a local market on the borrowing side, is dominated by savings and loan associations, which finance 45 percent of home mortgages. Commercial banks, life insurance companies, and mutual savings banks share equally the remainder. Interest rates in the mortgage market exhibit significant regional differences, though these are declining over time. The range between lowest and highest average yields in eighteen large SMSA's in 1965 was 86 basis points, with the average interest rate in most cities lying between 5.5 and 6.0 percent.[6] Interest rates probably vary a good deal more in smaller cities and for non-urban residential mortgages, but there are no systematic data on the terms of such mortgages.

No evidence is available on the regional variation in the price of consumer credit. Most consumer credit is installment credit, of which automobile financing is a significant portion. Commercial banks dominate the supply side; other participants are sales finance companies, consumer loan companies, and department stores.

(2) *Business:* Non-farm, corporate, external capital financing takes the form of equity issue, bond issue, bank borrowing, commercial mortgages, and direct borrowing from other corporations (trade credit[7]). About two-thirds of corporate external financing is borrowing on long term, and includes bonds, stocks, mortgages and, to a limited extent, bank borrowing. Since 1966, the share of funds obtained by bank borrowing has declined; equity and corporate bond issue now comprise about two-thirds of the total. Equity and bond financing is conducted in markets largely national in character. Insurance companies and private and public pension funds are the major source of funds for corporate bonds.

Short-term corporate financing is normally done by bank borrowing and trade credit. The credit standing of large companies is likely to be widely known. Whereas it is easier for most borrowers to present their cases for a loan locally and most convenient for banks to review the credit worthiness of local borrowers, the cost of researching loans is less than proportional to size, so that large

6. Federal Home Loan Bank Board, *Savings and Loan Fact Book*, 1966.
7. Relatively little is known about trade credit. In the aggregate, net funds flows due to trade credit are small. Trade credit is so closely related to the merchandising processes of particular commodities that it does not appear to exhibit important characteristics of other financial markets. There are some significant differences among sizes of firms, smaller firms being more dependent on their suppliers for their financing.

loans can be obtained in a much wider geographic market. In addition, large firms are usually served by larger banks, whose activities are more closely tied together by the many national markets in which they participate. Thus, as the size of the loan increases, the greater are the alternative sources of funds (both bank and non-bank sources), and hence the less likely that there will be regional differences in rates.

Unincorporated business also is financed by borrowing at commercial banks. It is not economical for small firms borrowing small amounts to register and float bond or stock issues very frequently. Moreover, smaller businesses cannot economically search as widely for bank loans as larger corporations.

Farm capital financing is probably the least institutionalized sector of the capital market. About 40 percent of farm financing is obtained from private individuals, merchants and other non-institutional lenders. Of the remainder, life insurance companies and federal land banks dominate farm mortgage lending (55 percent of total farm debt); while commercial banks and federal intermediate credit banks handle the non-real-estate portion of farm financing. Life insurance companies usually lend to the larger farmers. The federal bank system essentially involves twelve district banks selling securities in the national capital markets, the proceeds of which are lent locally via local "land banks" and "intermediate credit" banks. This action by the federal government greatly reduces regional variation in interest rates which otherwise would be severe, since farmers would be forced to rely on small, local commercial banks.[8] Still, regional variation in credit availability is probably considerable.

Thus, the source of regional variation for business financing is largely the dependence of some borrowers, largely small businesses and farmers, on small, local commercial banks. However, small bank loans represent only a small share of total business financing. Regional variation in business loan rates is not nearly as pronounced as that in residential mortgages. Examination of this regional variation is hampered by the differences in type and size of loans and by the unavailability of data for small geographic regions. The Federal Reserve System's quarterly series on short-term bus-

8. N. N. Bonsher, J. D. Dane, and R. Einzig, "Flows of Funds among Regions of the U.S.," *Journal of Finance*, March 1958.

iness loans represents a reasonably homogeneous sample. Average business loans rates in New York City, seven northern and eastern cities, and eleven southern and western cities differ on the order of 20–75 basis points, the larger spread existing for smaller loans. There is also a cyclical pattern in business loan rates; interest rate differentials narrow substantially during periods of tight credit. This pattern is very evident in the last three such periods, 1957, 1959, and 1965-66. Reductions in the differential are most dramatic in the class of largest loans, amounts over $200,000.[9] Large borrowers and banks which make up the market for large loans are active participants in federal funds, dealer loans, commercial paper, certificates of deposit and Eurodollars, all of which are highly interrelated money market instruments closely tied together by the New York money market. It is through the money market that changes in credit conditions are transmitted to the major banks and the means by which tight credit reduces regional variation.

Explanation of interest rate differences on loans requires a disaggregated examination of the loan market by region. Most of the empirical analysis of regional variation in loan rates has been cross-sectional in nature. Such cross section studies reveal the long-run forces which determine regional interest rate differences. These studies reveal that much of the variation in loan rates in different cities can be explained by bank size, loan size, income growth, and concentration in the banking market.[10]

(3) *Government*: The federal government is borrowing and lending in an essentially perfect nationwide market. In the case of the market for state and local government securities, there would appear to be many shades of compartmentalization. These securities are almost always serial bonds used to finance longterm capital requirements. Many issues are placed once and are not actively traded thereafter. Among larger issues, however, the secondary market is more active. The underwriting process and the secondary market for large offerings is such that there are probably no significant regional differences in rates because of imperfections on the supply side. Participants on the lending side are largely com-

9. *Federal Reserve Bulletin*, various issues.
10. Paul A. Meyer, "Price Discrimination, Regional Loan Rates, and the Structure of the Banking Industry," *Journal of Finance*, March 1967, pp. 37–48; A. Phillips, "Evidence on Concentration in Banking Markets and Interest Rates," *Fed. Res. Bulletin*, June 1967, pp. 916–926.

mercial banks, high-income individuals, and casualty life insurance companies—all much influenced by the tax-free status of such issues. All participants are somewhat sensitive to aggregate credit conditions; hence, their participation in state and local government securities markets tends to mirror aggregate credit conditions. As in the other credit issues of large size, this is essentially a national market, with interest rate differences reflecting differences in maturity and risk rather than regional imperfections on the lending side.

FINANCIAL SECTOR

(1) *Commercial Banks*: The role of commercial banks as financial intermediaries in the capital market is very wide since they are active in funding almost all of the major types of credit needs. Banks typically participate in local and national markets. Their investment decisions are quite sensitive to national credit market conditions, and hence they are an important means by which credit changes are quickly disseminated throughout the capital markets.

There are large differences in the demand and supply of funds in local or regional markets, which are potentially the source of large differences in interest rates. Regional differences in the demand for bank loans arise from differences in the economic composition of regions and differences in growth rates of particular sectors. The size of the bank and the size of borrowing transactions are most critical in determining the extent to which bank transactions reflect purely "local" market conditions. Smaller borrowers generally must borrow in "local" markets, and, similarly, smaller banks tend to be more insulated from conditions in the national capital market. In contrast, larger banks, borrowers, and depositors often find it more economical to participate in a range of national money and capital markets; hence they have more options available.[11]

Owing to market responses on the lending side, there are only slight regional differences in loan rates. Correspondent banking relationships, which entail the use of interbank balances between smaller correspondent banks and bigger city banks, are one factor

11. Mahlon R. Straszheim, "The Regional Dimension to Commercial Bank Markets and Counter-Cyclical Monetary Policy," Program on Regional and Urban Economics, Harvard University, Discussion Paper No. 50, July 1969.

reducing regional differences.[12] Arrangements among smaller banks to share in making new loans, either by pooling their funds to make loans or by "buying" a share of a loan placed by a larger bank, also tend to lessen regional differences. Finally, and probably of most significance, is the relative ease with which banks can participate in the national money markets—borrowing or lending excess funds through transactions in government securities and federal funds, and through loans and repurchase with government securities dealers. Thus, whereas bank loans are not sufficiently homogeneous to permit the development of an extensive secondary market, banks' access to national money markets as a means of adjusting their investment portfolios serves the same function. These adjustments tend to mitigate or reduce any potential regional compartmentalization in bank loan markets.

That these forces are operative over the long run is clear, certainly for banks making medium and larger size loans. The trend toward lessening loan rate differences was noted. Banks' management of their assets also seems to exhibit less covariation regionally over time.[13] Whereas banks in the South held large volumes of excess reserves in the early postwar period, they have gradually evolved to a tighter liquidity position and have become more sophisticated in managing their portfolios. Participation in national money markets is becoming more widespread geographically, gradually extending to smaller banks, which, for example, are becoming increasingly active in the federal funds market via their big city correspondents.[14]

The recent development of bank competition for time deposits is yet another force working against regional compartmentalization. Commercial banks, especially the smaller ones, have traditionally obtained deposits "locally." The regional distributions of demand deposits by class of bank for Federal Reserve Districts, states, or SMSA's are closely related to the regional distribution of income.[15] Until quite recently, the regional distribution of time and

12. U.S. Congress, House. "A Report on the Correspondent Banking System," Subcommittee on Domestic Finance, Committee on Banking and Currency, 88th Cong., 2nd sess., December 10, 1964.

13. Straszheim, "Regional Dimension to Commercial Bank Markets . . . " (n. 11 above).

14. Nevins D. Baxter, "Country Banks and the Federal Funds Market, *Business Review*, Federal Reserve Bank of Philadelphia, April 1966, p. 7.

15. Straszheim, "Regional Dimension to Commercial Bank Markets . . . ," pp. 5-6.

savings deposits (at both commercial banks and thrift institutions) were also quite closely related to income. However, the advent of bank competition for time deposits and the recent development of the market for negotiable time certificates of deposits are reshaping this distribution of time deposits. Certificates of deposit were largely a local instrument used in the West and Southwest and made up a relatively insignificant share of total funds flows to commercial banks until February 1961, when banks in the New York money market began to issue them in large numbers. New York City banks have raised large amounts of deposits by this means, and now larger banks all over the country are in a competitive struggle for deposits from corporate treasurers and other large depositors. This competition for CD's is another important means of facilitating interregional funds flows.

(2) *Savings Institutions*: Savings institutions essentially borrow and lend locally, investing predominantly in 1–4 family home mortgages. About 80 percent of savings and loan associations belong to the Federal Home Loan Bank Board System, which prescribes limits on minimum down payments, maximum maturity, and maximum rates offered to depositors. Such rates are permitted by law to vary regionally, and they do. While restrictions defining permissible S & L lending vary among states, limits on what kinds of loans can be made tend to be fairly strict, usually permitting only the financing of single family housing. Permission to finance apartments and undeveloped land has been granted in some states recently, but this relaxation of previous restrictions has been very modest to date. There are also geographic limits on loans typically 50 miles from the home office. (This was extended in 1964 to 100 miles for federal associations. Geographical restrictions on state chartered S & L's have also gradually been relaxed by some states.)

While mortgage placement is done essentially locally, there are several means by which interregional funds flows accommodate differential regional demands for mortgage financing. Since March 1, 1957, associations insured by the Federal Savings and Loan Insurance Company have been allowed to acquire participation in conventional mortgage loans held by other institutions. As of 1965, participation loans of $6 billion have been transacted (S & L's hold $110 billion of mortgages), with the sales in large part by S & L's in the San Francisco district and acquisition by S & L's in the New York, Chicago, San Francisco, and Greenboro districts.[16] This facilitates interregional transfers of funds, though as yet the transfers have been modest.

Interregional funds flows also occur through lending done by the Federal Home Loan Bank Board (FHLBB). The FHLBB holds the deposits of its member S & L associations, and makes loans to them. The FHLBB's role, as initially conceived in the 1930's, was to serve as a secondary reserve for S & L's, but in recent years its ability to facilitate interregional funds flows has assumed increasing importance. It achieves these interregional transfers by borrowing in the national capital market and by borrowing and lending to member S & L's at different interest rates. The rates paid by each FHLBB district bank to its member S & L's vary regionally (in 1965, from 3.5 to 4 percent), whereas the rates at which the FHLBB banks lend to member S & L's vary much less (12 basis points at the end of 1965). The geographic variation in S & L borrowing is becoming more pronounced, with San Francisco district S & L's the predominant borrowers.[17]

Mutual savings banks are the other important class of thrift institution investing in mortgages. MSB's are state-chartered deposit institutions, located largely in the Northeast, with a broad choice of investment vehicle. However, rate competition with other deposit institutions to attract funds has led MSB's to specialize largely in mortgage financing. MSB's have requested federal charters to extend the geographic limits of their lending opportunities, and increasingly they are joining the FHLBB System in order to obtain participation in out-of-state mortgages.

Finally, certain government actions have facilitated interregional transfers. Government guarantees of FHA and VA home mortgages have created a "standardized" mortgage which can be traded in a secondary market. There is little or no secondary market in conventional mortgages. The secondary market for FHA and VA guaranteed mortgages has been greatly aided by the Federal National Mortgage Association (FNMA). Its original purposes were to provide some degree of liquidity to mortgage holders and to aid in implementing certain special public housing programs. Its recent actions in the secondary market have taken on a direct regional

16. Savings and Loan Fact Book, 1966, p. 90.
17. *Ibid.*, p. 120.

dimension; during the 1965-1967 period, FNMA was acquiring proportionally more mortgages from the Far West than anywhere else. Thrift institutions in the West were more severely hurt in this period by deposit withdrawals than thrift institutions elsewhere.

(3) *Insurance Companies, Private Pension Funds, and Trusts:* These non-deposit financial intermediaries all participate primarily in national markets—in corporate stocks and bonds, in large business mortgages, and in state and local government securities. The one exception is life insurance companies which have historically invested about 20% of their funds in home mortgages. Since 1966, however, life insurance companies have altered their investment strategy, reducing their commitment in home mortgages in both absolute dollar terms and as a percentage of their portfolio. Much of these funds are now being placed in corporate stock. Non-life insurance companies invest in stocks, in bonds, and in federal, state, and local government securities. In the case of private pension funds, about two-thirds of their funds are now invested in corporate stocks, with most of the remainder in corporate bonds. Private trust accounts are largely invested in corporate stocks, bonds, and tax-exempt and federal securities. Private trust management is constrained by the concept of "prudence" in their administration. There is no significant "regional" story to be related here; any preferences (independent of risk, maturity and price) these institutions may have for borrowers in particular regions are very small.

(4) *Consumer Finance Companies:* Consumer finance companies finance themselves by issuing long-term bonds and commercial paper, and by borrowing at commercial banks. Their customer rates tend to reflect these capital costs. There are no systematic data available on rates regionally.

IV. The Regional Effect of Short-Run Changes in Credit Conditions

Differential regional effects on economic activity arising from the capital markets are likely to be most pronounced during short periods of rapid change in aggregate credit conditions. Given regional differences in the demands and supplies of funds and in the mix of financial and nonfinancial intermediaries in each region, changes in the national money markets may have significant regional impacts.

Borrowers who are limited to certain classes of lending institutions in particular regions may find themselves disadvantaged if changes in funds flows reduce the supply of funds available to those lenders. The effects of changing aggregate credit conditions on funds flows among lending institutions are now familiar. As noted, since household borrowers are limited to local sources of funds for both mortgages and consumer credit, the geographic bounds of regional submarkets and the limits to regional price differences are essentially determined on the lending side. Changes in monetary policy may well have significant differential regional effects in the short-run for both mortgages and consumer credit.

For example, tight credit generally results in fairly dramatic cutbacks in funds flows to thrift institutions. At the same time, the construction sector is usually of relatively greater significance in fast-growing areas. To the extent that there are not offsetting funds inflows into other sectors, tight credit may place most of its pressure on fast-growing regions. The extent to which tight credit has a "localized" effect depends on whether funds flows among financial institutions are more or less prone to cross-regional boundaries during periods of tight credit.

Borrowing terms for consumer credit also may be influenced differently across regions in the short run. Funds for lending are generally significantly reduced when credit becomes tight. The extent of any differential regional impact in the market for consumer credit as a result of tight money depends on the response of potential lenders to changes in national and local credit market conditions. For example, sales finance companies attempt to act as a buffer to their customers during periods of credit stringency, selling commercial paper and drawing upon lines of credit at commercial banks. However, these attempts by sales finance companies to absorb short-run differences in funds inflows due to cyclical changes in credit conditions are not sufficient to avoid the need to ration lending during tight credit periods. During such periods, commercial banks will also be limiting their own lending to consumers. Since different areas will have a different mix of lending intermediaries, regional differences in the effects of aggregate credit market conditions on consumer borrowing will depend on which of these two sorts of financial intermediation are most successful in countering aggregate monetary pressures.

There may also be a significant regional dimension to short-run changes in aggregate credit conditions in those portions of the capital market more closely related to the national money markets. Commercial banks, for example, react to both *local* sources and demands for funds and *national* money market conditions. The portfolio management problem of commercial banks largely arises as a result of cyclical loan demand, which varies more than the supply of funds. Portfolio adjustments on the supply side—in government securities, dealer loans, discounting, or federal funds— are all in national markets, while loan demand may have some peculiar regional dimensions. Periods of tight money are those in which "local" funds flows, lending opportunities, and interest rates are likely to be changing the most relative to national capital market conditions. Differences in local credit market conditions among regions require different portfolio adjustments. Behavioral responses themselves also may differ regionally.

The Federal Reserve System influences the money supply and the structure of interest rates principally by buying and selling government securities. These operations in the national money markets may produce regional differences in commercial bank deposits and hence in their ability to make loans. Rising money market rates attract funds from areas where business loan rates and profits generally are lower. Also, bank depositors in the large financial centers appear to be most responsive to opportunities in the government securities markets, and therefore changes in credit conditions are likely to be felt first in the money market centers. The growth in time deposits and the market for time certificates of deposit (CD's) during the 1960's provides an additional source of differential regional effects of tight money. The predominant role played by the large money market banks and large corporate depositors in the growth of that market makes these banks most vulnerable to a sudden loss of deposits due to sharp changes in market interest rates.

An examination of changes in bank portfolios by states during the tight money periods of 1957 and 1966 reveals that there are distinct regional differences associated with tight money.[18] In 1957 bank asset declines were inversely correlated with the pre-

18. Straszheim, "Regional Dimension to Commercial Bank Markets . . . ,"

vailing growth rate in loans; hence, tight credit had most of its effects in the slower-growing states. Banks in the southern and Plains states sustained the largest percentage reductions in bank assets, and those in the Far West the least.

A different pattern prevailed in 1966, largely reflecting the new role of CD's in the money markets. As interest rates rose in 1966, first a large savings funds flow from thrift institutions to commercial banks occurred. As market interest rates continued to rise—to a point above the prevailing rate ceiling on commercial bank time deposits, depositors let CD's expire and reinvested in direct credit instruments. As a result, time and savings deposit growth at commercial banks in 1966 was half the growth rate of the previous year, and commercial banks lost about $3 billion of CD's in the second half, about 18 percent of the total volume of CD's outstanding.

There was no regional pattern in the flow of funds out of savings and loan and mutual savings banks. Commercial banks in the large money market centers, however, were especially hurt by the runoff of CD's during the summer of 1966. Banks in the large money market centers enjoyed the least deposit growth, while banks in the southern states and plains states sustained the highest deposit growth. These differences in the changes in time deposits at commercial banks by region are largely due to the regional pattern of deposit changes at state banks. State banks in the South lost fewer time deposits than banks in the rest of the country; their depositors were apparently less prone to switch funds to direct credit instruments as interest rate rose. This suggests depositers in the South have less contact with the national money markets, probably reflecting both the non-urban character and lower income levels of much of the region. Conversely, the plains states sustained their deposit growth largely by attracting very large increases in certificates of deposit relative to banks in the rest of the nation. In summary, the CD market was a significant determinant of the regional distribution of commercial bank time deposits holdings in 1966.

While there are distinct regional patterns in change in bank assets during tight credit, banks' actions in the national money markets tend to mitigate considerably, although they do not completely offset, pressures which can arise in particular "regional" loan markets. Large differences regionally in changes in bank assets are translated into relatively small differences in bank lending as a result of banks' portfolio adjustments. Banks which sustained the largest asset declines were also making the largest portfolio changes to attempt to accommodate loan demand, reducing the percentage of assets held in government securities, bank reserves, and interbank balances.

The nature of bank portfolio adjustments has changed over the postwar period. During the 1950's the adjustment of reserves and interbank deposits was most critical, since the banking system accumulated a large percentage of their total assets in reserves in the postwar period. Changes in interbank deposits were an especially significant part of portfolio adjustments in the fifties, especially in the South where such balances were quite high (e.g., 10 percent of total bank assets). A reduction in interbank balances for all banks of 1½ percent occurred during the first six months of 1957, with the reductions by states positively correlated with the decline in bank assets. This process of "economizing" on interbank balances depends on the character of local correspondent banking relationships and on whether branching is allowed. Government securities holdings were also significant during the 1950's. These securities were gradually sold off, especially during periods of tight credit. The age distribution of government securities held by banks varied considerably, indicating considerable variance in bankers' strategies for dealing in the securities market.

By the middle 1960's, bank holdings of government securities and interbank balances had significantly declined. The important mechanisms which now produce regional impacts involve the market for time deposits and regional differences in bank competition for CD's. The growing importance of time deposits to commercial banks (from one-fourth of total bank deposits a decade ago to over one-half now), indicates that the market for time deposits is increasingly becoming a central focal point in the pursuit of monetary policy. The disintermediation process in periods of tight money is likely to exhibit a significant regional pattern.

The market mechanisms which will be important in the future may be different still. The most recent development in the money markets that has regional implications is the emergence of the commercial paper market and the Eurodollar market[19] as sources of short-term borrowing. By purchasing Eurodollars, usually on a

19. Eurodollars are dollars on deposit in European banks arising from checks held in Europe payable by U.S. banks.

thirty-to ninety-day loan basis, New York banks add to their reserves at the expense of other U.S. banks. During 1966, the major New York money market banks acquired about $1 billion of Eurodollars. During the tight credit period of early 1969, such borrowing from Europe was extensive—the major banks paid interest rates of over 10 percent and obtained several billion dollars of short-term funds.

Analyzing the complete implications of cyclical changes in credit conditions on regional capital markets and economic activity is a demanding task. Regional changes in the money and capital markets are likely to be subtle and complex. Analysis will require a funds-flow model with considerable disaggregation in the definition of actors and regions. Such analysis also needs to focus on time periods which will seem very "short-run" by standards familar to regional economists. Developing such a data base seems almost infeasible, in no small part because relatively perfect capital markets foster interregional transfers which cannot easily be traced. It seems very doubtful if the differential regional impacts of rapid changes in aggregate credit conditions can be adequately described and modeled to be included as a significant variable in the formulation of monetary policy.

V. A Recapitalation of the Regional Dimension

Financial markets have become increasingly complex over the last two decades. Regional differences are slight and can be identified only by an examination with a reasonably high level of disaggregation, which focuses on *particular* needs in the capital market, types of credit instruments, and behavioral patterns of the various actors on both the demand and supply sides.

The trend in the development of financial markets is away from regional or spatial compartmentalization and toward national homogeneity. The number of financial markets which are primarily national in character continues to increase, as does the proportion of the total flow of investment funds which they represent. Institutional restrictions on interregional transfers (for example, geographic limits on thrift institutions' opportunities to finance mortgages) are continually being relaxed. This removal of artificial regional barriers arises largely in response to competition from other classes of lending institutions, which are responding in turn to regional differences in lending opportunities. Commercial banks play a major role in reducing regional compartmentalization, actively shifting the composition of their investments in a large variety of markets in response to changes in relative rates of return. Finally, the use of government securities by most actors in the credit market to maintain a reserve or liquidity position and the good access most actors have to the now very well developed government securities market tend to create homogeneity in the capital market.

Despite sketchy data, the extent of current regional capital market imperfection can be approximated. Corporate stocks and bonds and government securities are all traded in national markets, with essentially equal access. Large commercial mortgages fall in much the same category. Significant regional differences exist in the markets for 1–4 family mortgages, consumer credit, and bank business loans of smaller denomination. As noted, the interest rate differentials range up to 3/4 percent on 1–4 family home mortgages among about a dozen broad regions of the United States. The differences for smaller and medium-size commercial bank loans range up to 50–75 basis points across regions of such size. For consumer credit the differences may be higher. These three components of the capital market comprised about 45 percent of total external credit financing in 1965, and about 17 percent of total real investment.[20] Thus, a relatively small portion of the total capital market, about one-sixth, is subject to significant regional variation, exhibiting regional differences in price on the order of 10 percent.

There are, of course, many instances in which small geographic regions or particular borrowers must pay much larger differentials. A general survey such as this does not observe the extremes in the capital market. The home mortgage market appears to exhibit the largest extremes, but as legal restrictions on MSB and S & L associations lending are rescinded, this market is likely to exhibit less regional compartmentalization.

Whether these differences deserve further attention depends to a considerable extent on research objectives. For analyzing regional

20. Direct lending makes up only about 40 percent of total savings, a considerable portion of real investment financed internally. The household sector finances about 80 percent of residential housing investment by mortgage credit (some of the rest is financed by bank loans). Only about 10–15 percent of the investment in consumer durables appears as an addition to consumer debt each year. Business finances only about 40 percent of its investment through external means, the rest generated by capital consumption and retained earnings.

growth patterns over the long run and for constructing economic models that use states or broader regions as their geographic unit, regional differences in the price of capital are indeed small. As a good first approximation, the assumption of perfect capital markets employed in modeling long-run regional growth is probably reasonable. More critical variables in analyzing long-run regional growth appear to be labor migration, the rate of technological change, and the level of public investment and provision of public services—the very variables upon which regional economic theory has concentrated.[21] Particular attention should be directed at differences between black and white wages and interregional migration.[22] Compared to these variables, regional capital market differences appear slight.

21. Borts and Stein "Regional Growth and Maturity in the United States" (n. 1 above); Koichi Mera, "Regional Production Functions and Redistribution Policies: The Case of Japan, Program on Regional and Urban Economics, Harvard University, Discussion Paper No. 45, April 1969.

22. Victor R. Fuchs, "Differentials in Hourly Earnings by Region and City Size, 1959," National Bureau of Economic Research, 1967, Occasional Paper No. 101.

Guide:
Part IV
Special Problems of Southern Development

JOHN F. KAIN AND JOSEPH J. PERSKY

The North's Stake in Southern Rural Poverty

Even the most casual investigation of poverty in the United States soon reveals that it is disproportionately a condition of rural areas, of the Negro, and of the South. The high incidence of poverty in the South may be partially "explained" by the area's large Negro and rural populations, but a differential remains even after controlling for these factors.

These propositions are supported by data from the 1960 Census of Population on the number of households with incomes below the "poverty line" of $3,000 per year.[1] In 1960, 9.6 million U.S. families

1. This is an operational definition of poverty used by the Council of Economic Advisors. This often-used, and even more frequently criticized, definition of poverty is imperfect, as is any single definition. Still, findings do not differ markedly from those based on other measures. There may be concern about using 1960 Census data in a discussion of poverty today. However, since persistence appears to be a characteristic of poverty, the general picture would be modified little by using more recent statistics.

were living in poverty. Four and a half million of these families lived in the South, and approximately 1.5 million of southern poor families were Negro. The majority of poor southern families lived in rural areas (Appendix Table A1). The geographic distribution of poor unrelated individuals (those having incomes below $1,500 per year) has a similar pattern.

These numbers take on national significance when expressed as percentages of either all poor families or all poor unrelated individuals in the country. (Appendix Table A2). Thus, in 1960, 46 percent of all U.S. poor families and 32 percent of all poor unrelated individuals lived in the South. By comparison, the South contained only 30 percent of all families and 27 percent of all unrelated individuals (Appendix Table A3). Similarly, though only 12 percent of all U.S. families lived in the rural sections of the South, 26 percent of all poor families lived there.

The pervasiveness of southern rural poverty is shown in Table 1, which depicts the incidence of poverty by race and residence. While the incidence of poverty is very high among all residents of the rural South, its incidence among rural Negroes is shockingly so: 78 percent.[2] This is exactly twice the incidence (39 percent) for southern rural whites. The incidence of poverty among urban Negro and white families in the South (that is, those living in communities of more than 2,500 population), although significantly lower than among rural families, is still very high: 53 and 18 percent respectively.

Census statistics for the entire South disguise the very high poverty levels of some areas and thus tend to understate the magnitude of the problem and its implications for the North. This is particularly the case since these areas have very close migration links to the metropolitan North. The census region referred to as the South is made up of a very diverse group of states. These states differ markedly in their level of income, in their proportion of Negroes, and in other important characteristics. Although much of the data used in the remainder of this paper is perforce based on census definitions, it is worthwhile, wherever possible, to make a more meaningful division of the southern states. This is a problem

2. These statistics and many others used in this paper are for nonwhite rather than Negroes. However, Negroes make up the overwhelming preponderance of nonwhites both in the South and in northern metropolitan areas. Thus the text uses the term Negro rather than nonwhite.

Table 1. Incidence of Poverty Among Families and Unrelated Individuals by Residence and Race, 1960

	South			Rest of U.S.			Entire U.S.		
	Nonwhite	White	All	Nonwhite	White	All	Nonwhite	White	All
Urban	18	53	25	12	29	14	14	40	16
Rural farm	52	86	58	38	53	39	44	84	47
Rural nonfarm	35	75	41	20	44	21	26	70	29
All rural	39	78	46	25	45	25	30	74	33
All families	27	63	33	16	30	16	19	48	21
Unrelated individuals	52	68	56	45	45	45	47	56	48

Source: U.S. Bureau of the Census. *U.S. Census of Population*: 1960. vol. I: *Characteristics of the Population*. Part I, United States Summary (Washington, D.C.: Government Printing Office, 1964).

that has caused considerable confusion, so some caution in exposition is in order.

The U.S. Census divides the South longitudinally into the South Atlantic, East South Central, and West South Central divisions.[3] While the use of these divisions by the census is an established fact, they fail to adequately represent the economic and social basis of the subregions of the South. In the first place, several states can be put aside as exceptions to the "southern pattern" of economic development. Maryland, Delaware, and the District of Columbia clearly fall into this category. It also seems reasonable to separate Florida from the rest of the South because of its peculiarities as a vacation and retirement center, its unique agricultural activities, and its rapid rates of growth. With somewhat less confidence, we can add Texas and Oklahoma to this "heterogeneous" group. These states, while having definite southern characteristics, also possess decidedly western elements (for example, petroleum and open lands) that differentiate them from the rest of the region.[4]

Of the remaining states, a sharp division can be made between

3. These divisions consist of the following states: South Atlantic: Maryland, Delaware, District of Columbia, Virginia, West Virginia, North Carolina, South Carolina, Georgia, and Florida; East South Central: Kentucky, Tennessee, Alabama, and Mississippi; West South Central: Arkansas, Louisiana, Oklahoma, and Texas.
4. In *Essays in Southern Economic Development* ed. by Melvin Greenhut and W. Tate Whitman, (Chapel Hill: University of North Carolina Press, 1964) at least three definitions of the South are used by various contributors. All of these exclude Maryland, Delaware, and the District of Columbia. Other states excluded by one definition or another are Oklahoma, Texas, and Florida.

those of the "Core" or Deep South (South Carolina, Georgia, Alabama, Mississippi, Arkansas, and Louisiana), and those of the "Appalachian" or Border South (Virginia, West Virginia, North Carolina, Kentucky, and Tennessee).[5] The primary distinction being drawn here is between states with high and low proportions of Negroes in the population. Table 2 shows this very clearly: 31.3 percent of the Core South and 16.6 percent of the Appalachian South are Negroes. In this respect, the excluded states are more similar to the Appalachian states.

While the summary industrial statistics given in Table 2 for the Core and Appalachian regions seem similar, the numbers actually mask the rapid changes that have been taking place. In particular, the Core South has dramatically reduced its dependence on agriculture since World War II. The demise of the South's cash crop, cotton, brought about by the introduction of synthetic fibers and the greater efficiency of California and Texas cotton producers, has left many whites and Negroes without a source of income. In the Appalachian states, agriculture has been historically less important. Moreover, Appalachia's cash agricultural crop has been tobacco, which, unlike cotton, still requires much field labor. As a result, manufacturing and nonagricultural sources of employment have come closer to offsetting agricultural declines in Appalachia than they have in the Core South.[6] Changes in agriculture have especially affected Negroes in the Core South who, even more than northern Negroes, are usually the last hired. Changes in agriculture have not been so crucial in the Appalachian region, where declines in nonagricultural industries, such as coal in West Virginia and textiles in North Carolina, have been a more significant source of employment decline.

Dividing the South into Heterogeneous, Appalachian, and Core South subregions pinpoints the concentration of poverty in a way

5. The terminology used here was originated by Edgar S. Dunn, Jr., in his *Recent Southern Economic Development, As Revealed by the Changing Structure of Employment* (Gainsville: University of Florida Monographs: Social Sciences, No. 14, 1962). However, Dunn holds West Virginia out of the Appalachian region and Louisiana out of the Core South as special cases.

6. *Ibid.* In analyzing employment changes due to the industrial mix of the two sectors, Dunn finds that fast growth sectors made up almost 50 percent of the Appalachian agricultural losses between 1939 and 1958, but only about 28 percent of the Core South agricultural losses (p. 17). Note that these figures do not take into account any of the "competition effect" which also favors the Appalachian South.

Table 2. Selected Characteristics of the Southern Subregions, 1960

	Population (millions)	Percent Negro	Percent employment in agriculture	Percent employment in mfg.	1950-1960 Net Migration (thousands)
Appalachia	*16.989	16.6	13.2	31.9	−1434.3
Core	*16.813	31.3	11.8	23.7	−1719.3
Heterogeneous	*21.170	15.2	7.1	16.3	+1737.9
South	*54.973	20.6	9.6	21.4	−1415.7
South Atlantic	*25.972	22.5	8.0	23.6	+ 634.8
East South Central	*12.050	22.4	13.2	23.8	−1463.8
West South Central	*16.951	16.3	9.6	16.1	− 586.8

Source: U.S. Bureau of the Census. *U.S. Census of Population: 1960.* vol. I: *Characteristics of the Population.* Part I, *United States Summary* (Washington, D.C.: Government Printing Office, 1964).

the census longitudinal division does not (Table 3). The concentration of Negro rural poverty in the Core South and white rural poverty in the Appalachian South have important consequences for the metropolitan North.

Southern Poverty and the Metropolitan North

The statistics on southern poverty presented above are ample reason for concern. Certainly a society as wealthy as the United States can afford to guarantee the well-being of the disadvantaged, wherever they may live. Humanitarian grounds alone would justify programs designed to eradicate southern, and particularly rural southern, poverty. But we will argue that it is also in the narrow self-interest of the wealthy metropolitan North to be concerned about southern poverty and its persistent causes.

The roots of southern poverty are deeply embedded in racial discrimination and a historical underinvestment in both human and physical capital. To the extent that the metropolitan North is closely linked to the rural South by migration, these factors become pressing problems for that region too. And to the extent that the southern migrant, ill-prepared for urban life, becomes a problem of northern cities, the improvement of the rural South is in the North's self-interest. Moreover, if southern poverty leads to an underinvestment in human capital, the consequences may be more strongly felt in the industrialized North than in the rural South.

Table 3. Incidence of Poverty Among Families and Unrelated Individuals by Southern Subregion and Race, 1960

	Core			Appalachia			Heterogeneous		
	White	Nonwhite (%)	All	White	Nonwhite (%)	All	White	Nonwhite (%)	All
A. FAMILIES									
Total <3000	29	72	40	30	63	35	23	49	26
Urban <3000	18	66	31	18	54	24	16	44	19
Rural nonfarm <3000	36	81	47	36	69	40	31	68	36
Rural farm <3000	55	89	65	55	84	59	45	77	47
B. UNRELATED INDIVIDUALS									
Tot. <1500	57	85	63	55	69	58	49	59	51
Urban <1500	52	74	59	49	67	53	36	57	39
Rural nonfarm <1500	64	83	70	62	72	64	59	70	61
Rural Farm <1500	74	91	81	75	87	78	62	78	64

Source: U.S. Bureau of Census, *U.S. Census of Population: 1960. General Social and Economic Characteristics, Alabama, Arkansas, Delaware, District of Columbia, Florida, Georgia, Kentucky, Louisiana, Maryland, Mississippi, North Carolina, Oklahoma, South Carolina, Tennessee, Texas, Virginia, West Virginia* (Washington, D.C.: Government Printing Office, 1961), Table 65.

Our contention is that the migration streams originating in the rural South form the crucial link in a system of poverty: a system nurtured by the inability and unwillingness of rural communities to adequately prepare their children for the complexities of modern life, a system brought to fruition in overcrowded cities.

This argument is not only true for the poor southern Negro migrant now living in the northern black ghetto. A similar causal chain also explains a great deal of metropolitan white poverty. The Appalachian South plays a role in white urban poverty (especially in the North Central region) similar to that which the Core South plays vis-à-vis the black metropolitan ghetto. Although the southern white does not come up against the same obstacles of discrimination as the southern Negro, he does suffer from similar, though less extreme, educational and vocational handicaps. Clearly the magnitude of both Negro and white migration is a measure of the self-interest northern cities have in the rural South. In the next section we will analyze how migration connects the rural South to the rest of the nation and discuss the implications of these migration streams for the nation's metropolitan areas.

SOUTHERN MIGRATION

High levels of southern out-migration are a people's reaction to a historically underdeveloped region with a "population problem." Declining labor requirements in agriculture have constantly threatened to produce a labor surplus in southern rural areas and have encouraged high levels of out-migration. These changes have not, however, caused a great reduction in the rural southern population, which has shown only small declines. One reason for this has been the growth of a rural manufacturing sector; another, the high birth rates in rural areas.

The continued existence of a hard-pressed southern rural population creates serious problems for metropolitan areas, the natural destination of rural America's surplus population. Indeed, the South's most consistent export has been its people.[7] Starting with the decade 1910-1920 (with the opportunities opened up by World

7. As Eli Ginzberg and Douglas W. Bray put it: "One of the major products of the South is babies. One of its major exports to other parts of the country is young adults" (*The Uneducated* [New York: Columbia University Press, 1953], p. 189).

War I), the South has never failed to run a net migration deficit of less than 1 million. This deficit reached a high of 2¼ million for the decade 1940-1950.[8] These migration streams have become increasingly Negro as new opportunities in the rural and urban South have gone primarily to whites. In light of this magnitude and persistency, the direction of these population streams becomes important. Where have the people gone?

The answer to this question depends on the migrant's characteristics and his place of origin. Available data sources are especially poor in maintaining these distinctions. The 1960 census contains a lifetime migration series that gives state of birth by state of 1960 residence for whites and nonwhites. The same series gives the region of birth for the residents of the large (greater than 250,000) population Standard Metropolitan Statistical Areas (SMSA's). The census also provides five-year migration estimates by state of residence in 1955 and place of residence in 1960. These tabulations, which include several other characteristics of the migrant as of 1960, are based on a 25 percent sample which is notorious for non-reporting. Finally, a special set of reports by the Department of Commerce provides estimates of net migration in regions, divisions, states, and SMSA's by age, sex, and race for the 1950-1960 period.[9]

The implications of the lifetime migration figures must be drawn carefully, since (perhaps understandably) the census does not obtain information on whether the migrant was born in a rural area, a small town, or in a metropolitan area. Moreover, problems emerge from the census definition of regions of the country. As discussed above, the longitudinal division of the South fails to isolate meaningful subregions; therefore, the Core-Appalachian distinction should be kept in mind as an overlay on the census regions. Nevertheless, the peculiarities of the data have a saving grace in that population flows for Negroes run on North–South lines. These are

8. Simon Kuznets, *Population Redistribution and Economic Growth, United States 1870-1950*, (Philadelphia: American Philosophical Society, 1964), III, 251.

9. These three basic sources are: (1) U.S. Bureau of the Census. *U.S. Census of Population: 1960 Subject Reports. State of Birth,* Final Report PC(2)–2A (Washington, D.C.: U.S. Government Printing Office, 1963). (2) U.S. Bureau of the Census, *U.S. Census of Population: 1960. Subject Reports. Mobility for States and State Economic Areas,* Final Report PC(2)–2B (Washington, D.C.: U.S. Government Printing Office. 1963). (3) Gladys K. Bowles and James D. Tarver, *Net Migration of the Population, 1950-1960, by Age, Sex and Color* (Economic Research Service, U.S. Department of Agriculture, 1965).

clearly discernible with the current census division of the South, once it is understood that the majority of Negro migrants was born in the Core South.

With respect to points of destination, much of the following discussion is based on a disaggregation of the divisional in-migration into large metropolitan areas (SMSA's greater than 1,000,000), medium-sized SMSA's (250,000–1,000,000), and the remainder of the division. These categories are dictated as much by the availability of data as by analytical justifications.

The answer to the question, "Where have the migrants gone?" varies sharply with the race of the migrant. Thus, the typical, rural Negro migrant tends to move to large (greater than a million in population) metropolitan areas outside of the South. The white movement is more diffused and has a marked orientation toward medium-sized (between 250,000 and 1,000,000) SMSA's in the North and metropolitan areas of the South itself. Though southern-born whites and Negroes living in large northern SMSA's in 1960 numbered about 2 1/2 million (2.61 and 2.47 respectively), only .42 million southern-born Negroes lived in medium-sized metropolitan areas as compared to 1.42 million southern-born whites. Moreover, large and medium sized SMSA's were the destination of only 60 percent of the whites leaving the South as against 89 percent of the Negroes. With respect to movements within the South, only .86 million Negroes left their state of birth to move to medium-sized southern SMSA's as compared to 2.86 million whites.

The five-year migration series (1955-1960) suggests no recent alteration of the basic pattern. Twenty-five percent of the white out-migrants from the South moved to rural areas in the North and West, as compared to 8 percent of the Negro out-migrants. Within the South, southern SMSA's were the destination of 72 percent of all southern whites moving to urban areas, but only 55 percent of all southern Negroes. Moreover, there is evidence that Negroes moving North move in stages—first to a southern city, then to a northern one.[10] If this is so, the differences between Negro and white migrations are even larger than indicated. It is also important to note that these figures include considerable interurban mi-

10. An interesting example of "chain" migration is given in Melvin Lurie and Elton Rayack, "Racial Differences in Migration and Job Search: A Case Study," *Southern Economic Journal*, July 1966.

gration. If the rural-urban stream could be isolated, it is likely that the pattern would be even sharper, with rural Negroes much less reluctant to move North than their white neighbors.

Some idea of the impact of out-migration on the rural South can be gained by examining the 1950-1960 net migration figures. Table 4 gives net migration from southern counties by race and extent of urbanization. The pattern of internal migration can easily be inferred from these figures—Negroes are quicker than whites to leave all areas and slower to move to the highly urban counties within the South. The magnitude of southern rural out-migration also becomes clear: *almost 2,000,000 southerners (net) left counties having less than 30 percent urban population.* At the same time highly urbanized areas were attracting in-migrants from both the white South and North.

The system of southern migration is even more specific than indicated. This is clearly brought out by an analysis of the fraction of lifetime out-migrants (individuals born in the division now living elsewhere) from the three southern divisions who are now living in various parts of the country. (Appendix Tables A4, A5, A6). Fifty-eight percent of the Negroes born in the South Atlantic division and now living elsewhere, live in the four northeastern SMSA's greater than a million (Buffalo, New York, Philadelphia, and Pittsburgh). Similarly, about 40 percent of the Negro lifetime migrants from the East South Central division have moved to the five East North Central SMSA's greater than a million (Chicago, Detroit, Cincinnati, Cleveland, and Milwaukee). Finally, about 36 percent of the same group from the West South Central division live in the four

Table 4. Net Migration from Southern Counties, 1950-1960, by Extent of Urbanization

Type of County	White		Negro		Total	
	Number (in thousands)	Rate	Number (in thousands)	Rate	Number (in thousands)	Rate
All rural	− 812.6[a]	−15.5	−421.8	−24.7	−1,234.4	−17.8
1-29% urban	−1,113.2	−13.5	−745.7	−25.1	−1,858.9	−16.6
30-49% urban	− 371.3	− 4.3	−476.5	−17.9	847.9	− 7.6
50-69% urban	274.5	+ 4.6	− 71.6	− 5.9	202.8	+ 2.8
70% or more	2,065.3	+13.2	257.4	+ 5.8	2,322.6	+11.5

Source: Gladys K. Bowles and James D. Tarver, *Net Migration of the Population 1950-1960*, vol. II: *Analytical Groupings of Counties* (Economic Research Service, U.S. Department of Agriculture, 1965), pp. 147-149.

[a] Minus sign indicates net loss through migration.

Table 5. Lifetime Migration From the South

Region of destination	Core South Negro	Core South White	Appalachia Negro	Appalachia White	Heterogeneous Negro	Heterogeneous White	Total South Negro	Total South White
	Subregion of Birth							
Northeast	572	169	461	381	135	357	1169	908
North Central	1094	585	311	1838	90	564	1495	2987
West	312	698	40	533	217	1561	569	2792
TOTALS (Non-South)	1978	1452	812	2752	442	2482	3233	6687

Source: Compiled from *U.S. Census, Special Reports: State of Birth*, 1960.

Pacific SMSA's greater than a million (Los Angeles, San Diego, San Francisco, and Seattle). Thus, not only have Negroes from the South and by inference from the *Core* South moved to large metropolitan areas, they have moved along clearcut lines to their destinations, forming at least three major streams, one up the Eastern Seaboard, another up the Mississippi River to Ohio and Michigan, and one westward to California.

The pattern is more diffused for whites. While whites from the three divisions also tend to move along these streams, there is a much greater willingness on their part to cross longitudinal lines and to go to smaller places. A breakdown by Core–Appalachian South is particularly useful here. The number of lifetime migrants by race from these areas to each non-South region is presented in Table 5. White migrants to the Northeast and North Central regions were predominantly from the Appalachian states (57 percent) while the West got a majority of its white migrants from the Heterogeneous South. Negro migration to the non-South originated largely from the Core area. The importance of these distinctions depends on the educational and economic opportunities (or lack of opportunities) available to these specific groups in their home regions. These matters will be discussed in more detail below.

Both northern and southern urban areas have had to cope with vast numbers of poorly prepared rural migrants. The percentage of the population living in various urban areas of the North but born in the South is given in Table 6. The figures for Negroes vary from 12 percent of those in the central cities of large metropolitan areas in the East North Central division to 1 percent of those in the cen-

Table 6. Percent of Southern-born Population Living in Non-Southern Metropolitan Areas

| | New England | | Middle Atlantic | | | East North Central | | |
	Medium SMSA	Large SMSA	Medium SMSA	Large SMSA	Center city of large SMSA's	Medium	Large	Center city of large SMSA's
White	1.61	1.51	1.86	2.00	—	9.38	5.66	—
Negro	1.37	1.04	1.21	4.18	7.45	3.86	6.49	12.01
Total	2.98	2.55	3.07	6.18	—	13.24	12.15	—

| | West North Central | | Mountain | | Pacific | | |
	Medium SMSA	Large SMSA	Medium SMSA	Large SMSA	Medium	Large	Center city of large SMSA's
White	5.77	4.76	10.72	—	10.81	9.21	—
Negro	1.53	3.61	1.39	—	1.53	3.50	9.42
Total	7.20	8.37	12.11	—	12.34	12.71	—

Source: Compiled from U.S. *Census, Special Reports: State of Birth*, 1960.

tral cities of medium-sized metropolitan areas in the Middle Atlantic region. (The central city figures given for Negroes are based on the reasonable assumption that all Negro migrants from the South settled in the central cities of these metropolitan areas.) By comparison, white southern migrants formed a disproportionate share of the population of medium-sized SMSA's in the East North Central and Pacific divisions. White southern migrants comprised 9.4 percent and 10.8 percent respectively of the 1960 population of these areas; southern Negro migrants comprised only 3.9 and 1.5 percent respectively. A further breakdown of the migrant group into those born in the South Atlantic, East South Central, and West South Central divisions would accentuate these patterns of Negro and white migration.

Large as these figures are, they seriously understate the impact of southern migration. Since many migrants leave before forming families, the numbers do not reflect the cumulative effect of migration on the "second generation." What is needed is a measure of "southern households" in particular areas. Moreover, such a figure would be useful in measuring the effect of southern migration on the labor force of the northern and western cities. Estimates of the southern-born fraction of the working-age population (20-65 years) in the various areas are given in Table 7.[11] The percentages increase substantially over those for the total population—16 percent of the working-age population of the largest East North Central cities and 12 percent of the largest Pacific cities were southern-born Negroes. At the same time, the percentage of southern-born whites in the medium-sized SMSA's increases everywhere, with those on the Pacific Coast showing the greatest gains.

The important conclusion to be drawn is that rural out-migration from specific areas in the South becomes in-migration for specific areas outside (and in the case of white migrants, inside) the South. Thus, the link between the rural Negro Core South and the large northern metropolis is a very strong one. Negro migration reduces substantially the pressure on the southern economy (urban and

Table 7. Percentage of Southern-born Migrants 20-65 Years of Age Living in Specific Areas Outside South

	New England		Middle Atlantic			East	North	Central
	Medium SMSA	Large SMSA	Medium SMSA	Large SMSA	Center city of large SMSA's	Medium	Large	Center city of large SMSA's
White	1.90	1.78	2.20	2.23	—	11.68	6.91	—
Negro	1.95	1.47	1.71	5.67	9.78	5.49	8.92	16.02
Total	3.85	3.25	3.91	7.90	—	17.17	15.83	—

	West North Central		Mountain		Pacific		
	Medium SMSA	Large SMSA	Medium SMSA	Large SMSA	Medium	Large	Center city of large SMSA's
White	7.66	6.76	14.18	—	14.32	11.32	—
Negro	2.21	5.06	2.01	—	2.21	4.78	12.34
Total	9.87	11.22	16.19	—	16.53	16.10	—

Source: Compiled from U.S. Census, Special Reports: State of Birth, 1960.

11. The estimation process involved computing the nonwhite and white population of individual SMSA's between the ages of 20 and 65 and the percentage of all non-white and white lifetime migrants from each division (S. Atlantic, E.S. Central, and W.S. Central) falling into this age group. The product of these two numbers for each SMSA and racial group divided by the SMSA 1960 population in each group gives the estimated percentage of 20–65-year-olds in the SMSA coming from the specific division by race. These numbers were then aggregated to compile Table 7.

rural)—pressure produced by high rural Negro birthrates and limited economic opportunity. The southern economy is similarly unable to provide for large numbers of whites, especially in the Appalachian region. Important evidence supporting the behavioral model implied by this interpretation of southern out-migration is presented in a paper by the authors entitled "Migration, Employment and Race in the Deep South."[12] Moreover, an unpublished regression analysis by the authors of the choice of destination of five-year migrants from the Core South indicated that, whereas Negroes were most attracted to large centers of population, whites were more drawn to areas of rapid employment expansion and seemed more reluctant to leave the South.

Education of the Southern Migrant

We have already suggested that the southern migrant's lack of education is an important determinant of the low income he is likely to receive in the North. The question now becomes why the southerner, and in particular the southern migrant, is so poorly prepared for the labor market. Several studies indicate that an individual's income is strongly dependent on his educational background.[13] It is implicit in most discussions of poverty that a lack of education is a major restraint to a decent standard of living. But formal education is by no means the only form of investment in human resources. On-the-job training, experiences in the home, and other kinds of experience may be of great value. Still, virtually no information concerning these factors is available. Granted that other types of training and experience should not be overlooked, it is difficult to deny the importance of a minimum amount of formal education. If anything, the need for minimal skills in reading, writing, and mathematics seems to be increasing. To the extent that poverty is a product of poor education, it is not difficult to understand why the rural South is poor. This same link between poor southern education and low income may well explain much of the poverty among rural southern migrants living in northern metropolitan areas.

While southerners in general receive a poorer education than

---

12. *Southern Economic Journal*, January, 1970.
13. H. S. Houthakker, "Education and Income," *Review of Economics and Statistics*, February 1959.

individuals in the rest of the country, the situation for southern Negroes is substantially worse. This is due in large part to decades of systematic discrimination in the provision of public education, the concentration of Negroes in small towns and rural areas, and low levels of income. Data on the fraction of persons twenty-five and over who have completed fewer than five years of school by region of 1960 residence and by race are presented in Table 8. Five years of good schooling is close to the minimum level of educational preparation needed to perform most tasks in an industrialized society. There is every indication that five years of education in a southern, and particularly a southern Negro, school represents substantially less than five years of good schooling. The most striking finding in Table 8 is the large difference in the proportion of whites and non-whites who have had at least five years of formal education. In 1960, 24 percent of the Negroes and 7 percent of the whites in the United States failed to meet this minimum standard. In the South, especially the Core South, the proportions are still larger: 39 percent of the Negroes and 11 percent of the whites. Outside of the South, the percentages of Negroes and whites with less than five years of school are only about half as large. If these data were compiled by region of birth rather than by region of residence, the discrepancies might be even greater. There is no doubt that a large portion of the poorly educated Negroes living in the North and West received their few years of education in the South.

Information about the quality of formal education is neither

Table 8. Percentage of Persons 25 Years and Over Completing Less than 5 Years of School, by Region and Race, 1960

	White	Nonwhite	All
United States	6.7	23.5	8.3
Northeast	6.6	12.9	7.0
North Central	4.8	14.0	5.4
West	4.8	16.0	5.6
South	10.0	31.8	14.0
Core	10.6	39.2	18.3
Appalachia	11.6	29.3	14.2
Heterogeneous	8.5	23.1	10.6

Source: U.S. Office of Education, *Digest of Educational Statistics, 1965 Edition,* Bulletin 1965, No. 4 (Washington, D.C.: Government Printing Office, 1965), p. 129.

plentiful nor systematic. The fragmentary data indicate, however, that the products of southern, particularly southern Negro, schools are markedly inferior to those of the North. The inadequacies of southern schools first became widely recognized during World War II as a result of the draft. For the entire United States approximately 4 percent of all selective service registrants failed to pass a standardized intelligence test that led to their rejection for military service.[14] Rejection rates for the southern states, and particularly for southern Negroes (given in Table 9), were much higher than for the rest of the nation and population. The rejection rate for southern whites (4.9 percent) was somewhat higher than the national average and almost twice the rejection rate of all whites. For all Negroes the rejection rate was 15 percent; for southern Negroes it was 18 percent. An even more interesting pattern appears for the subregions of the South. Negro rejection rates within the South were highest for the Core South. Rejection rates for southern whites were lower for Core South whites than for whites in Appalachia. This is a pattern that will reappear throughout this discussion of southern education.

The Core South has provided a relatively high level of education for its white population at the expense of its Negro population. By comparison, the Appalachian South seems to have provided somewhat better educational opportunities for its Negroes and poorer educational opportunities for its whites (as compared to whites in the Core South). These differences in education available to Negroes

Table 9. Rejection Rates Per Thousand Registrants for Mental Deficiency by Region and Race

	White Rate per 1000	Nonwhite Rate per 1000
United States	25	152
South	49	184
Core South	46	227
Appalachia	59	166
Heterogeneous South	41	118
Rest of United States	14	51

Source: Eli Ginzberg and Douglas W. Bray, *The Uneducated* (New York: Columbia University Press, 1953), pp. 42-53.

14. Eli Ginzberg and Douglas W. Bray, *The Uneducated*, p. 42.

and whites in the subregions of the South are of particular importance given the marked difference in their migration patterns. The North receives both poorly educated Negroes from the Core South *and* poorly educated whites from the Appalachian South.

Equality of Educational Opportunity, popularly referred to as the *Coleman Report*, confirms the inadequacy of southern education.[15] By the twelfth grade, Negro students in the metropolitan South had an average verbal ability 4.2 grades below white students in the metropolitan Northeast. The verbal ability of scores of Negroes in the nonmetropolitan South was even worse: 5.2 grades behind. By comparison, southern whites did much better. Those in the metropolitan South were less than one year behind (0.9), and those in the nonmetropolitan South, 1.5 years behind northeast whites. If achievement scores were available for the three southern subregions, they would almost certainly show important differences in educational performance between southern Negroes and whites in these subregions. The Core and Appalachian South differ significantly in their expenditures on white and Negro education and in the quality of schooling provided these groups.

While the scores presented in the *Coleman Report* indicate that both southern whites and Negroes test somewhat below their counterparts in other parts of the country, the most striking finding is that Negroes have a low level of educational achievement regardless of their region of residence. Twelfth-grade Negroes in the metropolitan Northeast and Midwest average 3.3 grades behind metropolitan northeast whites in verbal ability. Though this is nearly a grade better than the performance of Negroes in the metropolitan South and nearly two grades better than Negroes in the nonmetropolitan South, it is not a record the metropolitan North can be proud of.

In part, these low levels of Negro achievement in the metropolitan North and West are caused by the same factors that cause them in the South. These include discrimination in the provision of education and low levels of student motivation. However, the low achievement levels of northern Negroes are also due indirectly to the decades of underinvestment in southern Negro education and directly to the fact that many Negroes currently enrolled in northern schools obtained their early years of education in the South.

15. James S. Coleman, *et al.*, *Equality of Educational Opportunity*, U.S. Office of Education (Washington, D.C.: Government Printing Office, 1966).

This not only affects the migrant child's achievement in the North, but also disrupts the operation of these already hard-pressed schools by forcing on them the additional task of compensating for the early years of education in inferior southern schools.

These low achievement levels of both whites and Negroes educated in the South, and particularly of Negroes educated in the Core South, are not difficult to understand when the educational expenditures by southern states are compared to those of other parts of the country. Data on average current expenditures per pupil (based on average daily attendance), expressed in dollars and as a percentage of the U.S. average by region for the years 1964-65, 1955-56, 1945-46, and 1929-30, are presented in Table 10. For the entire South, the level increased from 64 percent of the U.S. average in 1929-30 to 78 percent in 1955-56 and decreased to 76 percent in 1965-66. Per pupil expenditures in the Core South were consistently below this level for the entire period, being only 44 percent of the U.S. average in 1929-30 and 65 percent of the U.S. average in 1964-65.[16]

Dismal as these statistics may be, the actual situation may be even worse. These figures are based on average daily attendance, and ratios of average enrollment to average attendance are higher in the South. Moreover, dropout rates are higher in the South than in other parts of the country. Therefore a smaller percentage of the school-age population is attending school at any given time in the South than in the North.

At the same time, per pupil expenditures for current outlays may exaggerate the difference between the quality of schools in the North and the South because of differences in the cost of inputs. It may be possible to produce a given quality of education for less in the South than in the North. Teachers' salaries, the largest component of current expenditures, are considerably lower in the South.[17] Although differences in teachers' salaries may explain much of the differential in per capita expenditures in a numerical

16. U.S. Office of Education, *Statistical Summary of Education: 1955–56*, pp. 64–65, and *Digest of Educational Statistics*, 1965 ed., pp. 8 and 9 (Washington, D.C.: Government Printing Office, 1959).

17. For example, the average annual salary of instructional staff in full-time public elementary schools in 1961–62 was $6,770 in Connecticut, $6,941 in New York, and $6,300 in Illinois. By comparison, it was only $3,685 in Arkansas, $3,637 in Mississippi, and $3,865 in South Carolina. Instructional staff in these comparisons includes supervisors, principals, classroom teachers, and other instructional staff (U.S. Office of Education, *Digest of Educational Statistics*, 1965 ed., p. 38).

Table 10. Current Expenditures Per Pupil in Average Daily Attendence in Public Elementary and Secondary Schools and Ratio of U.S. Average by Region

| | Dollars | | | | Percent of U.S. Average | | | |
	1964-65	1955-56	1945-46	1929-30	1964-65	1955-56	1945-46	1929-30
United States	484	294	136	87	100	100	100	100
Northeast[a]	539	322	161	101	111.4	109.5	118.4	116.1
North Central	481	304	148	96	99.4	103.4	108.8	110.3
West	508	318	156	106	105.0	108.2	114.7	121.8
South	369	230	97	56	76.2	78.2	71.3	64.4
Core	316	195	70	38	65.3	66.3	51.5	43.7
Appalachia	331	191	88	50	68.4	65.0	64.7	57.5
Heterogeneous	452	297	131	80	93.4	101.0	96.3	92.0

Sources: U.S. Office of Education, *Statistical Summary of Education: 1955-56(1959)*, p. 110; and *Digest of Educational Statistics* (1965 ed.), p. 66 (both published by Government Printing Office, Washington, D.C.).
[a] Per pupil expenditures for regions are simple unweighted averages of state per pupil expenditures.

sense, they do not by any means invalidate the comparison. There is considerable evidence that teachers in southern schools have had fewer years of education than teachers in northern schools and that the quality of each year of education has been less.

As serious as these large discrepancies in per pupil expenditures may appear, they still understate the inadequacies of the southern educational system from the viewpoint of the metropolitan North. Migration from the South to the North is highly selective. Southerners migrating to the North are likely to be Negro and are drawn disproportionately from states where the overall level of per pupil expenditures is low. Moreover, there is abundant evidence of systematic discrimination against Negroes in the provision of public education in the South. While such discriminatory practices may have decreased in recent years, it still appears that less is spent on the Negro child's education than on the white's; consequently the southern Negro receives an extremely poor education.

Prior to 1954, when school segregation was ruled unconstitutional by the Supreme Court, seventeen states and the District of Columbia maintained separate school systems for Negro and white children. Thus, fairly systematic and reasonably accurate information on per pupil expenditures for Negro and white school children exists before 1954. Data on per pupil expenditures for whites and Negroes in a number of the southern states operating segregated school systems are given in Table 11. In all years the data indicate that southern states (with the single exception of Oklahoma) spent significantly less per pupil on Negro students. (The statistics for 1953-54 are for total expenditures for instruction per pupil in average daily attendance, while those for all other years are current expenditures.) The high figures for Oklahoma indicate that a segregated system of education is expensive when the minority population is small and dispersed (the state had only 36,000 Negro pupils in 1953-54). It is perhaps not surprising that Mississippi, Arkansas, Georgia, and Alabama seem to be the most deficient in their efforts to educate their Negro populations. On the positive side, the narrowing of the difference between white and Negro per pupil expenditures between 1945-46 and 1951-52 may represent some attempt to improve the level of educational opportunity available to southern Negroes. This apparent improvement should be viewed with some caution since increased federal pressure over the

Table 11. Current Dollar Expenditures Per Pupil in Average Daily Attendance for White and Negro Public Elementary Schools

State	1945-46		1947-48		1949-50		1951-52		1953-54[a]	
	White	Negro	White	Negro	White	Negro	White	Negro	White	Negro
Alabama	$ 85	38	123	75	130	93	172	108	112	105
Arkansas	74	35	103	60	124	73	138	77	99	72
Delaware	158	25	—	—	—	—	—	—	—	—
Florida	135	62	177	113	196	137	221	160	176	161
Georgia	83	31	127	59	145	80	190	115	—	—
Kentucky	90	98	—	—	—	—	—	—	—	—
Louisiana	136	44	—	—	—	—	—	—	—	—
Maryland	130	111	201	165	217	199	254	201	165	122
Mississippi	75	15	115	24	123	33	147	32	98	43
Missouri	138	133	—	—	—	—	—	—	—	—
North Carolina	86	70	114	96	148	123	186	150	132	125
Oklahoma	111	118	143	168	—	—	—	—	162	166
South Carolina	100	40	146	68	155	80	196	98	—	—
Tennessee	80	56	—	—	—	—	—	—	—	—
Texas	123	91	—	—	—	—	—	—	—	—
Virginia	96	77	—	—	—	—	—	—	—	—
West Virginia	101	111	—	—	—	—	—	—	—	—
District of Columbia	190	149	—	—	290	221	345	261	240	187

Source: U.S. Department of Health, Education, and Welfare. *Biennial Survey of Education in the United States. 1945-46, 1947-48, 1949-50, 1951-52, 1953-54*, chap. I: *Statistical Summary of Education* (Washington, D. C.: Government Printing Office).
[a] Total Expenditures for instruction per pupil in average daily attendance.

period may have caused southern school officials to be less candid in 1952.

In part, the differences in per pupil expenditures for Negro and white schools may reflect differences in the degree of urbanization of the two populations. Per pupil expenditures are generally higher in more urbanized areas.[18] But the differential degree of urbanization of Negroes and whites can explain only a part of the expenditure gap. More importantly, it can explain very little of the even larger difference that existed in earlier periods.[19]

CAUSES OF UNDERINVESTMENT IN EDUCATION

The determinants of the level of educational expenditure by state and local government are many and complexly interrelated. They include community mores and attitudes toward education, the proportion of children attending private and parochial schools, the ratio of school-age children to the economically active population, the degree of urbanization, and the cost of providing a given quality of education. Yet there can be no doubt that the most important explanation of the low level of expenditure by southern states is the level of per capita income.

In Figure 1, average current expenditures per pupil in average daily attendance for all fifty states are plotted against state per capita income. This clearly indicates a strong positive relationship between per capita income and per pupil current expenditures for education. Low levels of educational expenditures appear to be both a cause and an effect of low income. With relatively few exceptions, the states of the Core and Appalachian South spend less on education per pupil and have the lowest incomes. For example, in 1965 Mississippi spent the smallest amount per student—$317—

18. For example, a 1955–56 survey for thirty-eight states indicated that for these states per pupil expenditures in rural counties were $237 per pupil in average daily attendance as compared to $305 for cities of 25,000–99,999 population and $333 for cities of over 100,000 population. Rural counties in the South spend an average of $174 per pupil as compared to $203 spent by the smaller cities and $222 by the larger (U.S. Office of Education, *Statistics of Local School Systems: 1955–56, Rural Counties* [Washington, D.C.: Government Printing Office, 1959], p. 55).

19. See the earlier and longer version of John F. Kain and Joseph J. Persky, "The North's Stake in Southern Rural Poverty" in *Rural Poverty in the United States*, a report by the President's National Advisory Commission on Rural Poverty (Washington, D.C.: U.S. Government Printing Office, 1968), pp. 288–306, for a discussion of these differences in earlier periods.

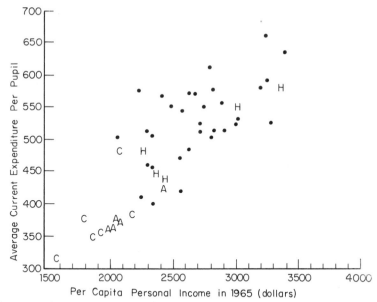

Figure 1. Average Current Expenditure Per Pupil in 1965 Versus Per Capita Disposable Income in 1965 by State.

C. Core South   • Non-South
A. Appalachia South
H. Heterogeneous South

Source: U.S. Bureau of the Census, *Statistical Abstract of the United States: 1966* (87th Ed.) Washington, D.C., 1966. pg. 104 and 330.

and had the lowest per capita income $1,566. South Carolina, Alabama, and Arkansas did not exceed Mississippi's per pupil expenditure rate by much, and all had per capita incomes below $2,000 per year. In the Core South, only Louisiana had a level of per pupil expenditures above $450 per year. The problems faced by low-income southern states in financing education are aggravated by their having relatively large school-age populations in relation to their economically active populations.

If the educational effort of the South is compared to its per capita income levels, its performance is much more credible. For the United States as a whole, direct expenditures of state and local government for education amounted to 5.2 percent of per capita income.[20] All six Core states, all five Appalachian states, and all Heterogeneous states except Delaware and Maryland exceeded this percentage. State and local education expenditures (unweighted average) were 5.7 percent of the per capita incomes of the six Core South states, 5.6 percent of those of the Appalachian South, and 5.2 percent of those of the Heterogeneous South. Unfortunately, this effort by southern states buys fewer educational inputs because their per capita income levels are so low. The average per capita expenditure for education by state and local governments throughout the entire United States was $127. By comparison, that for the Core South was $93, for the Appalachian South, $108, and for the Heterogeneous South, $127 per capita. North Carolina made the greatest effort of any southern state in 1963—spending fully 7.3 percent of its per capita income on education, a level exceeded by only four of the fifty states. However, fourteen states exceeded North Carolina's per capita expenditures on education—$149 per year— because they had higher levels of per capita incomes.

The Shed

The urgency for action to discourage migration from the rural South to the metropolitan North or to alleviate its adverse consequences depends on whether the trends outlined above will continue into the future. The central question then becomes whether or not the rural southern population, white and Negro, will produce a high excess population in the future. The answer depends principally on the age composition and fertility of the region's population and the rate of growth of employment opportunities.

A critical statistic is the number of males entering the rural labor force. Table 12 gives an estimate of male entrants by race and region for the 1960's, based on the assumption of no net migration. Of particular interest are the large number of Negro entrants in the Core South—331,000, and the even larger number of white entrants in the Appalachian South, 808,000. Despite the high level of out-migration experienced by rural areas during the decade 1950-1960, the estimates of Negro and white male entrants for the 1960-1970

20. U.S. Office of Education, *Digest of Educational Statistics*, 1965 ed., Bulletin 1965, No. 4 (Washington, D.C.: Government Printing Office, 1965), p. 137.

Table 12. Entrants to the Male Rural Labor Force (in thousands)

Area	1950-1960		1960-1970	
	Negro	White	Negro	White
South	593	1820	571.4	1837.6
Core South	NA[a]	NA	331.2	571.2
Appalachian	NA	NA	159.6	807.5
Heterogeneous	NA	NA	80.5	458.8

Source: Gladys K. Bowles, Calvin L. Beale, and Benjamin S. Bradshaw, *Potential Supply and Replacement of Rural Males of Labor Force Age, 1960-1970,* Economic Research Service, U.S. Department of Agriculture (Washington, D.C., 1966).
[a]Not available.

period show no appreciable decline. One reason for this is the high birth rates of southern rural areas.[21]

Perspective on the entrants into the rural labor force of the 1970's can be obtained by comparing the 1950 and 1960 rural population under ten years of age. Thus, there has been only a slight decrease in the cohort group that will be responsible for the bulk of Negro migration in the seventies. Similarly, there were 2.0 million white southern males under ten years of age in 1960, as compared to 2.2 million in 1950.

While no figures are available on rural out-migration in the sixties, there are figures for the entire South. Most striking is the rate of Negro net migration. Between 1960 and 1966, 600,000 nonwhites (net) left the South, at an average rate of 0.9 percent per annum.[22] This annual rate is roughly two-thirds of the average migration rate of the 1950's. If, as in the previous decade, metropolitan

21. Thus, in 1950 (the last year in which an entrant to the 1960–1970 labor force could be born) rural Appalachia had uniformly higher white birth rates than the rest of the country, while Core states had Negro birth rates above the national Negro rate and far above national white rates. In 1965, Appalachian and Core South birth rates were still among the highest in the country. According to the Public Health Service's *Vital Statistics of the United States*, 1950, vol. 2 (Washington, D.C.: Government Printing Office, 1953), the national white birth rate for 1950 was 22.7 births per 1000 population. The rural white birth rate for Appalachian states varied between 21.7 for North Carolina (the only state below the national rate) and 25.4 for Kentucky. The rural Negro birth rate for Core South states varied from the 30.3 of Arkansas to the 38.4 of Mississippi.

22. U.S. Bureau of the Census, *Current Population Reports Series* p-20, No. 156, "Mobility of the Population of the United States: March 1965 to March 1966" (Washington, D.C.; Government Printing Office, 1966). These figures are based on data from the Current Population Survey, and must be considered only rough estimates.

areas of the South had some small net in-migration of Negroes (a likely assumption for the sixties) it follows that at least 600,000 Negroes left the nonmetropolitan areas of the South. The native white population showed a net out-migration during this period of about 100,000. This figure, however, is not highly informative since many whites moved into the South and since their metropolitan-nonmetropolitan distribution cannot be so easily hypothesized as that of Negro migrants.

Given that the above figures are only crude estimates of the trends in rural out-migration from the South, they still emphasize that no sudden change in the extent of that movement is imminent. This is especially true for the Negro population. The origins of the current problem can be seen by combining the predicted number of entrants for the 1960's with the Department of Agriculture's replacement ratios, which measure the number of entrants to the rural labor force per 100 departures through death or retirement, assuming no net migration.[23] The ratio for southern rural Negroes rose from 230 for the 1950's to 250 for the 1960's. This meant that 60 percent of the potential rural Negro entrants to the labor force would not find jobs unless the number of rural jobs expanded *or* unless these individuals migrated out of rural areas. In actual numbers, this estimate implies that 343,000 rural male Negroes would not find jobs in the 1960's as compared to 335,000 in the 1950's.[24] The situation for white males was only slightly better. The potential white surplus went from 872,000 to 854,000 between the 1950's and 1960's. Since the pace of technological change in agriculture has been constantly accelerating in the Core South, there is little doubt that these estimates form a lower bound. Moreover, this discussion does not take into account any pull effects of metropolitan areas, but only relates to rural surplus.

The general conclusions are clear: 1) Migration in the sixties was of the same order as that of the fifties. 2) There can be no significant decline in the absolute number of potential out-migrants from the rural South until the 1980's.

23. Gladys K. Bowles, Calvin L. Beale, and Benjamin S. Bradshaw, *Potential Supply and Replacement of Rural Males of Labor Force Age, 1960–70* (Washington, D.C.: Economic Research Service, U.S. Department of Agriculture, 1966).

24. These figures are based on multiplying the number of entrants by the fraction of surplus labor implied by the replacement ratio.

Conclusions and Policy Implications

The metropolitan North has a major stake in the future of the rural southern population. The rural South is impoverished. This alone would justify the North's concern, but we contend that there is an even stronger reason for a commitment on the part of the rest of the country to increase the economic opportunities of the southern population. The fortunes of the metropolitan North are closely linked to those of the rural South through migration. The biggest cities of the North and West attract large numbers of rural Negroes from the Core South. Smaller northern and western areas draw disproportionately large numbers of Appalachian whites. Ironically, of the entire southern population it is these two groups that are relatively the worst prepared to cope with the complexities of the industrial metropolitan North. The educational achievement of both groups is inferior to that of the majority of the southern population from which they come. Negroes of the Core South are especially disadvantaged in this respect. In analyzing the distribution of poverty in the North Central region of the country, we found that a substantial fraction of the metropolitan North's poor were born and educated in the South. This result applies to both North Central Negroes and whites. Finally, we have found no evidence to support the widely held view that rural southern migration to the North will soon abate. The base populations are just too large.

The need for public action is obvious. What form this action should take is not so easily determined. We have identified two potential migrant groups of particular interest to the metropolitan North: the Negroes of the Core South and the whites of the Appalachian South. While many programs might be tailored to deal with the problems faced by the migrant, these must perforce take the form of correcting mistakes made in the past. Therefore, a strong argument can be made for programs that are aimed at these two populations, not after they have arrived in the metropolis, but while they are still in the rural South.

The first and most obvious recommendation that can be made is to strengthen decisively the education received by southern rural children, white and Negro. Admittedly, it would be difficult to attract talented teachers to depressed rural areas, but the difficulties are not necessarily greater than attracting teachers, social workers, and policemen to the urban ghetto. Increased expenditures for education in the rural South *now* may substantially reduce the need for future expenditures for education, police, and welfare in the city. Education is particularly important for the rural Negro, who needs all the aid he can obtain to work against the edge of discrimination. This implied distribution of federal funds is further justified since areas of high out-migration are (perhaps understandably) more reluctant than other areas to maintain and expand their educational systems.[25] At the same time, there can be no compromise with the southern tradition of "noneducation" for its Negro population. It is important to recognize that those very states which uphold this tradition most rigorously are exporting the greatest number of Negro migrants. In a real sense it is the southern establishment that has no right to interfere in the North's business and not vice versa.

A second policy supported by these conclusions is a renewed effort to equalize employment opportunities for Negroes in the South as part of an overall national program. This is particularly important for the Core South, an area where past gains have gone almost exclusively to whites. Even a redistribution of poverty between whites and Negroes might be a net gain to society, considering the cumulative nature of metropolitan ghetto poverty as compared to less constricting white poverty. It seems more reasonable, however, to combine attempts to reduce discrimination in employment with a wider program to increase southern nonagricultural employment and incomes. Indeed, the politics and economics of the South may make equal opportunity feasible only if there is a substantial expansion of the economy.

The question then becomes how to determine the most efficient (in both a human and economic sense) place for economic expansion. The major alternatives include: rural industrialization in the South, metropolitan expansion in the South, and migrant-oriented job creation in the North. From previous research, we would be reluctant to support major efforts to expand the employment oppor-

25. Burton A. Weisbrod's Monograph, *External Benefits of Public Education* (Princeton, N.J.: Princeton University, Industrial Relations Section, 1964), presents an interesting discussion of this point, including a quantitative analysis of the impact of out-migration on school expenditures. He finds a high negative correlation between these two variables.

tunities of southern migrants in the metropolitan North, at least to the exclusion of even larger efforts in the South.[26]

It takes little specialized knowledge to recognize that the major problem facing the large metropolitan areas of the North is assimilating their Negro population. Continued growth of northern ghettos will impose heavy costs on society and move us further from the solution of society's most pressing problem. A major reason for aggressively expanding employment opportunities in the South is to permit a much larger attack on the problems of discrimination and poverty in the ghettos of the metropolitan North. Without a simultaneous effort to expand employment opportunities for disadvantaged southerners, efforts to alleviate poverty in the ghettos of the metropolitan North could prove counterproductive. A delicate equilibrium exists between the poverty areas of the North and the South. Unless efforts to improve conditions in the metropolitan North are accompanied by efforts to expand opportunity in the South, the final consequences of programs aimed at employing the migrant in the metropolitan North may be an acceleration of already uncomfortably large flows of ill-prepared southern migrants. Consequently, the levels of unemployment, poverty, and distress might remain unchanged while the monumental problems of assimilation increase.

In analyzing the remaining alternatives, rural industrialization and metropolitan expansion in the South, we had to consider the historic development of southern manufacturing and other nonagricultural industries. Industrialization in the South has generally differed from the northern pattern of concentration in large metropolitan areas. From the first "bring the mills to the fields" movement of Reconstruction, the rural areas and small towns of the South have accounted for substantial proportions of southern manufacturing activity. Standard Metropolitan Statistical Areas have more than half the manufacturing employment in only one state of the Core South, Louisiana, and in only two of the Appalachian South, Kentucky and West Virginia. By contrast, all of the Heterogeneous states have a majority of their manufacturing employment in metropolitan areas. The implications of this dispersion of industry are of fundamental importance to the south-

26. John F. Kain and Joseph J. Persky, "Alternatives to the Gilded Ghetto," *The Public Interest,* No. 1 (Winter 1969), pp. 75–76.

ern economy. In an extensive analysis of wage differentials in the United States, Victor Fuchs found that quality-adjusted wages are significantly lower for rural areas and small towns than for the entire South.[27] It is to be expected that these low wages and the remaining vast numbers of unskilled workers will continue to attract large numbers of firms that use disproportionate amounts of low-cost, low-skilled labor. The benefits to the South of this continued development should not be minimized. These low-wage industries can serve both as a training ground for rural labor and as a substantial source of income for the region's population.

At the same time, the rapid expansion of southern metropolitan areas suggests that policies designed to foster southern economic development should not ignore the region's growing metropolitan areas.[28] This rapid growth of employment in southern metropolitan areas, like that of the metropolitan North, must be due to factors which increase the productivity of at least some firms at these locations and allow them to pay higher wages. These factors include economies of scale, agglomeration economies, and the access of a large local market. Victor Fuch's data suggest that the expansion of employment in southern metropolitan areas is much less attributable to low wages than that in the rural South, even though quality-adjusted wage levels in southern metropolitan areas remain slightly lower than those of the North.[29]

To a significant degree, southern growth potential may be tied to the development of metropolitan areas. From the viewpoint of the rural South, growth in these cities is no less desirable than rural growth. Expansion of economic opportunities, no matter where it occurs in the South, must of necessity benefit the rural population. The basic remedy is to take up the slack in a surplus population. (The exact point at which tension is applied is not crucial.) If jobs

27. Victor R. Fuchs, "Differentials in Hourly Earnings by Region and City Size, 1959" (Occasional Paper No. 101, National Bureau of Economic Research, 1967).
28. The metropolitan South has been one of the most rapidly growing parts of the country. All U.S. metropolitan areas grew by 55 percent between 1940 and 1960, as compared to a growth in population of the entire United States of only 35 percent. By comparison, southern metropolitan areas grew by 84 percent between 1940 and 1960; (35 percent between 1940 and 1950 and 36 percent between 1950 and 1960). Only the expanding metropolitan areas of the western United States grew at more rapid rates (48 percent between 1950 and 1960). U.S. Bureau of the Census, *U.S. Census of Population: 1960. Selected Area Reports.* Standard Metropolitan Statistical Areas Final Report PC(3)-ID (Washington, D.C.: Government Printing Office, pp. 1–257.
29. Fuchs, "Differentials in Hourly Earnings," (see n. 27 above), p. 19.

are more efficiently created in metropolitan areas, this course of action should be pursued.

Our objective thus becomes one of general southern development and the need to bring that region more in line with national levels of per capita income. This is the basic solution to the problems produced by rural southern out-migration. It is particularly important to guarantee that an expansion of the southern economy will benefit the Negro population. To a certain extent this process may be automatic. General prosperity and the resulting tightness of labor markets are perhaps the strongest forces working for the integration of the Negro into the southern economy. Some evidence of this pattern is visible already in certain parts of the South. Donald D. Osburn concluded from a study of Negro employment in the Carolina textile industry that the Negro labor force has made substantial gains since 1960 and that these gains are due to the abandonment of that industry's "exclusionary hiring practices as whites were attracted to higher paying industries and its need for labor grew." While the Negro is often hired for dead-end jobs, "under tight labor market conditions, employers have more incentive to hire and train Negro job applicants and to upgrade Negro employees."[30]

Clearly, the benefits of general prosperity for poor rural Negroes and whites will be magnified to the extent that educational programs prepare them for these increased and improved opportunities. The gains Negroes will derive from stronger measures against discrimination are even more obvious. Enforcement of equal opportunity laws for government contractors and subcontractors in the South is already increasing the openings for Negroes in southern industry, and these efforts should be stepped up. Broader legislation is also desirable. The task of obtaining and enforcing such measures is substantially eased by a climate of general improvement. Economic expansion and the enforcement of equal opportunity are highly complementary.

An important perspective that derives from this discussion is the need to approach the serious problems of southern rural areas from the vantage point of a larger regional and national system. This is distinctly different from the current approach to depressed areas,

30. Donald D. Osburn, *Negro Employment in the Textile Industries of North and South Carolina*, Office of Research and Reports, Equal Employment Opportunity Commission, Washington, 1966.

which concentrates only on the worst or most distressed areas.[31] A more neutral policy aimed at developing the South in general is required. For example, with respect to capital subsidies to industry, the best approach might be to allow the entrepreneur to locate anywhere he chooses within the South rather than attempt to bribe him into what may well be an inefficient location in a severely distressed rural area. The important point is that economic development in a city or metropolitan area 50 or even 200 miles away can be both advantageous to the rural poor and consistent with national economic trends. The goal is not so much to keep the rural southerner rural as to provide him with an opportunity to earn a decent income in a decent environment. Where the rural South and metropolitan North have failed at this task, the metropolitan South may well be able to succeed.

31. For example, the enabling legislation of the Economic Development Administration of the Department of Commerce limits its development to distressed areas. The Agency has administratively decided, moreover, that the worst counties must be taken first. R. M. Rauner, "Regional and Area Planning: The E.D.A. Experience," paper presented at the Institute of Management Science, Annual Meeting, Cambridge, Massachusetts, April 1967.

Appendix

Table A-1. Number of Families with Incomes below $3,000 and Unrelated Individuals with Incomes below $1,500 by Residence and Race, 1960

Families	South White	South Nonwhite	Rest of U.S. White	Rest of U.S. Nonwhite	Entire U.S. White	Entire U.S. Nonwhite	Total
Urban	1,230	764	2,720	513	3,950	1,277	5,227
Rural farm	606	223	729	11	1,335	234	1,569
Rural Non-farm	1,176	470	1,153	53	2,329	524	2,853
Total	3,013	1,458	4,602	577	7,615	2,035	9,650
Unrelated individuals	1,456	559	3,892	416	5,347	976	6,323

Source: U.S. Bureau of the Census. *U.S. Census of Population: 1960*. vol. I: *Characteristics of the Population*. Part I *United States Summary* (Washington, D.C.: Government Printing Office, 1964).

Table A-2. Families with Incomes below $3,000 and Unrelated Individuals with Incomes below $1,500 as a Percentage of All Poor Families and Unrelated Individuals by Race and Residence, 1960

Families	South White (%)	South Nonwhite (%)	Rest of U.S. White (%)	Rest of U.S. Nonwhite (%)	Entire U.S. White (%)	Entire U.S. Nonwhite (%)	Total
Urban	12.7	7.9	28.2	5.3	40.9	13.2	54.1
Rural farm	6.3	2.3	7.6	0.1	13.8	2.4	16.2
Rural nonfarm	12.2	4.9	11.9	0.5	24.1	5.4	29.5
Total	31.2	15.1	47.7	6.0	78.9	21	100
Unrelated individuals	23.0	8.8	61.5	6.6	84.6	15.4	100.0

Source: U.S. Bureau of the Census. *U.S. Census of Population: 1960*. vol. I: *Characteristics of the Population*. Part I, *United States Summary* (Washington, D.C.: Government Printing Office, 1964).

Table A-3. Families and Unrelated Individuals by Residence and Race as a Percentage of All U.S. Families and Unrelated Individuals, 1960

	South		Rest of U.S.		Entire U.S.		
	White	Nonwhite	White	Nonwhite	White	Nonwhite	Total
Families	(%)		(%)		(%)		
Urban	14.8	3.2	48.9	4.0	63.6	7.2	70.8
Rural farm	2.6	0.6	4.2	0	6.8	0.6	7.4
Rural nonfarm	7.5	1.4	12.7	0.3	20.2	1.7	21.9
Total	24.9	5.2	65.8	4.3	90.5	9.5	100
Unrelated individuals	21.1	6.2	65.6	7.1	86.7	13.3	100

Source: U.S. Bureau of the Census. *U.S. Census of Population: 1960*. vol. I: *Characteristics of the Population*. Part I, *United States Summary* (Washington, D.C.: Government Printing Office, 1964).

Table A-4. Distribution of Migrants from the South Atlantic[a]

	White	Cumulative	Negro	Cumulative
North East Cities > 1 million	13.5	—	58.3	—
East North Central > 1 million	9.3	22.8	14.4	72.7
North East + E.N.C. 250–1,000,000	11.0	33.8	9.6	82.3
Remainder N.E. + E.N.C.	~19.0	52.8	~ 7.7	90.0
W.N.C. + Mountain	8.2	61.0	1.2	91.2
Pacific Cities > 1,000,000	8.9	69.9	2.6	93.8
Remainder Pacific	~ 6.0	76.3	~ 1	94.8
E.S.C. + W.S.C. cities > 250	~ 9.3	85.6	2.7	97.5
Remainder E.S.C. + W.S.C.	~14.4	100	2.5	100

[a]Tables A-4, A-5, and A-6 give the percentage of out-migrants from each of the three census subregions in the South who now live in various regions of the country.

The regions are selectively broken down so as to indicate the differential migration of whites and Negroes to cities of various sizes. Moreover, a cumulative percentage is given to emphasize the magnitude of these differences. The abbreviations used are:

N.E. Northeast
E.N.C. East North Central
W.N.C. West North Central

S.A. South Atlantic
E.S.C. East South Central
W.S.C. West South Central

Table A-5. Distribution of Migrants from the East South Central[a]

	White	Cumulative	Negro	Cumulative
E.N.C. Cities > 1 million	13.4	—	40.6	—
N.E. Cities > 1 million	2.2	15.6	7.8	48.4
W.N.C. Cities > 1 million	1.9	17.5	6.8	55.2
E.N.C. Cities 250–1 million	7.2	24.7	8.4	63.6
N.E. + W.N.C. Cities 250–1 million	1.0	25.7	1.6	65.2
Remainder E.N.C.	~17.4	43.1	~ 8.9	74.1
Remainder N.E. + W.N.C.	~ 3.0	46.1	~ 0.9	75.0
Mountain	3.1	49.2	0.8	75.8
Pacific Cities > 1 million	5.5	54.7	5.9	81.7
Remainder Pacific	4.2	58.9	1.4	83.1
W.S.C. Cities > 250	6.2	65.1	2.8	85.9
Remainder W.S.C.	9.6	74.7	5.0	90.9
S.A. Cities > 1 million	3.9	78.6	1.4	92.3
S.A. Cities 250–1 million	6.7	85.3	2.1	94.4
Remainder S.A.	~14.7	100	~ 5.7	100

[a] See footnote to Table A-4.

Table A-6. Distribution of Lifetime Migrants from the West South Central Division[a]

	White	Cumulative	Negro	Cumulative
Pacific Cities > 1,000,000	20.6	—	36.3	—
E.N.C. Cities > 1,000,000	4.0	24.6	19.1	55.4
W.N.C. Cities > 1,000,000	3.7	28.3	8.1	63.5
Pacific Cities 250–1,000,000	9.8	37.1	5.4	68.9
Remainder Pacific	13.0	50.1	3.4	72.3
E.N.C. + W.N.C. Cities 250–1,000,000	3.6	53.7	4.9	77.2
Remainder E.N.C. + W.N.C.	~12.7	66.4	~ 5.4	82.6
Northeast	4.1	70.5	4.4	87.0
Mountain	15.4	85.9	6.2	93.2
East South Central	6.3	92.2	4.0	97.2
S.A. Cities > 250	3.9	96.1	1.5	98.7
Remainder S.A.	3.9	100	1.2	100

[a] See footnote to Table A-4.

Table A-7. Per Capita White and Negro Expenditures for Teachers' Salaries in Southern States by County Groups, 1911-12

County groups: Percentage of Negroes in the population	Entire South[a]		Core South		Rest of South	
	White	Negro	White	Negro	White	Negro
Counties under 10%	$ 7.96	$7.23	$ 6.98	$3.48	$ 8.16	$8.07
Counties 10 to 25%	9.55	5.55	7.24	2.63	10.11	6.33
Counties 25 to 50%	11.11	3.19	11.60	2.43	10.63	3.90
Counties 50 to 75%	12.53	1.77	12.88	1.65	11.48	2.20
Counties 75 to 100%	22.22	1.78	22.63	1.75	17.59	2.25
All counties	10.06	2.89	10.87	1.96	9.62	4.31

Source: U.S. Department of Interior, Bureau of Education, *Negro Education*, vol. II, Bulletin, 1916, no. 39 (Washington, D.C.: Government Printing Office, 1917), pp. 11, 27, 335, 471.

[a]1,055 counties where per capita expenditures by race were available.

STANLEY L. ENGERMAN*

Some Economic Factors in Southern Backwardness in the Nineteenth Century

The question of southern backwardness has long been of great interest and importance. Since the Civil War, at least, southern per capita income has been markedly below that of other regions. The many discussions of the "Negro Problem" and of the "poor whites" have served to emphasize this lower level of income. The determination of the causes of this backwardness has been a major issue to the historian and the regional economist. It is of particular interest to the latter because if the cause can be attributed to the

*An earlier version of this paper was presented at the Eighth Annual Meeting of the Purdue Seminar on Quantitative Methods in Economic History. I wish to thank Richard Easterlin for helpful comments at several points, as well as for permission to use his worksheets. Since this paper was completed, several of the arguments have been expanded and additional calculations made using different sources of data (See Robert W. Fogel and Stanley L. Engerman, "The Relative Efficiency of Slavery: A Comparison of Northern and Southern Agriculture in 1860," *Explorations in Economic History*, 8 [Spring 1971], 353–367). While these calculations do change several of the quantitative measures there were no major changes in general conclusions.

operation of normal economic forces it would have strong implications for the analysis of the regional diffusion of national growth.[1] To the historian this issue is connected with the study of the antebellum South's "peculiar institution" and the continued existence of the racial problem through Reconstruction, the New South, and the present.

One of the questions that has been discussed recently by economic historians is the pace of economic development in the slave South.[2] This is an important issue because it has often been argued that the South was a stagnant economy on the eve of the Civil War, with a low level of income and little potential for future growth. This situation is attributed to the system of plantation agriculture based upon a slave labor force. Thus the beginnings of southern backwardness could be blamed directly upon its social system. It will be argued below that this version is not consistent with data currently available. These data suggest that it was during the Civil War and in its immediate aftermath that marked southern backwardness first appeared.[3]

Because of the interest in examining the Southern economy before and immediately after the Civil War, there will be only a brief summary of the 1880–1960 period in the first section of this paper. The second section will discuss comparative regional growth rates between 1840 and 1880. The third and fourth will examine aspects of the southern economy in the nineteenth century.

I. 1880–1960

For detailed estimates of regional income before 1929 we are in debt to the statistical reconstructions of Richard Easterlin.[4] Since

1. For a discussion of hypotheses concerning regional diffusion with empirical tests drawn from many countries, see Jeffrey G. Williamson, "Regional Inequality and the Process of National Development: A Description of the Patterns," *Economic Development and Cultural Change*, 13 (July 1965), pt. II.

2. For a discussion of the controversy about the profitability of slavery, a topic which will not be entered into directly in this paper, see Robert W. Fogel and Stanley L. Engerman, "The Economics of Slavery," in Robert W. Fogel and Stanley L. Engerman, eds., *The Reinterpretation of American Economic History* (New York: Harper & Row, 1971), pp. 311–341.

3. Implicit in this statement is that the transition from a slave system could have been accomplished, and with less cost, without the Civil War. While the possibility of a smooth transition does beg the historical question, it is meant to logically distinguish the economic effects under the slave system from the economic and social costs paid to end it.

4. See Richard A. Easterlin, "State Income Estimates," in Everett S. Lee, et al.,

Easterlin has analyzed the basic trends in regional income relatives, it will be necessary only to summarize his findings briefly and to note some implications.

Table 1, taken from Easterlin[5] and brought up to 1960, presents the basic per capita income relatives since 1880, based upon income-originating with each region.[6] The pattern is one of convergence in regional levels of per capita income between 1880 and 1960. Between 1880 and 1900 the major force for convergence was the declining position of the new frontier areas of the West relative to the rest of the country. This decline continued through 1920. In the first two decades of the twentieth century there was a sharp rise in the southern income position. This southern movement was reversed between 1920 and 1930, but in the next three decades there was continued convergence due to the improved relative income position of the South and the relative declines in the older northeastern states. Despite differences in behavior there have been infrequent changes in the relative rankings of regions by income levels. Among the sub-regions, only the Mountain States have crossed from one side of the national average to the other.

The South had a constant per capita income relative between 1880 and 1900 (implying a growth rate of per capita income equal to the national rate), with convergence upon the national average in the twentieth century in all periods except for the decade of the

Population Redistribution and Economic Growth, United States, 1870–1950, vol. I, *Methodological Considerations and Reference Tables* (Philadelphia: American Philosophical Society, 1957), pp. 703–759; Richard A. Easterlin, "Regional Growth of Income: Long-Term Tendencies, 1880–1950," in Simon Kuznets, et al., *Population Redistribution and Economic Growth, United States, 1870–1950,* vol. II, *Analyses of Economic Change* (Philadelphia: American Philosophical Society, 1960), pp. 141–203; Richard A. Easterlin, "Interregional Differences in Per Capita Income, Population, and Total Income, 1840–1950," in Conference on Research in Income and Wealth, *Trends in the American Economy in the Nineteenth Century,* Studies in Income and Wealth Volume Twenty-Four (Princeton, N.J.: Princeton University Press, 1960), pp. 73–140; and Richard A. Easterlin, "Regional Income Trends, 1840–1950," in Seymour Harris, ed., *American Economic History* (New York: McGraw-Hill, 1961), pp. 525–547,

5. Easterlin, "Regional Income Trends, 1840–1950," p. 528.
6. When estimating regional incomes on the basis of income-originating, the net output of each region is valued in prices of that region. The same commodity could be valued at different prices in different regions. This measure does not provide a basis for comparing physical productivities or regional living standards. Some problem of interpretation exists in the comparison of regional income trends when regional price levels are changing relative to each other. Converging per capita income-originating need not imply an equivalent convergence in physical output or in regional living standards.

Table 1. Personal Income per Capita in Each Region as Percentage of United States Average, 1880–1960[a]

Regions	1880	1900	1920	1930	1940	1950	1960
United States	100	100	100	100	100	100	100
Northeast	141	137	132	138	124	115	114
New England	141	134	124	129	121	109	109
Middle Atlantic	141	139	134	140	124	116	115
North Central	98	103	100	101	103	106	102
East North Central	102	106	108	111	112	112	106
West North Central	90	97	87	82	84	94	93
South	51	51	62	55	65	73	77
South Atlantic	45	45	59	56	69	74	78
East South Central	51	49	52	48	55	62	67
West South Central	60	61	72	61	70	80	82
West	190	163	122	115	125	114	114
Mountain	168	139	100	83	92	96	97
Pacific	204	163	135	130	138	121	120

Source: For 1880–1950, Richard Easterlin, "Regional Income Trends, 1840–1950," in Seymour Harris, ed., *American Economic History* (New York: McGraw-Hill, 1961), p. 528. 1960 relatives were computed from income in the years 1959 through 1962, divided by 1960 population—Regional Economics Division Staff, "Total and Per Capita Personal Income, 1965-Record High in All States and Regions," *Survey of Current Business*, 46 (April 1966), 7–13.

[a]The regions are as follows:
New England: Connecticut, Maine, Massachusetts, New Hampshire, Rhode Island, Vermont
Middle Atlantic: Delaware, Maryland, New Jersey, New York, Pennsylvania
East North Central: Illinois, Indiana, Michigan, Ohio, Wisconsin
West North Central: Iowa, Kansas, Minnesota, Missouri, Nebraska, North Dakota, South Dakota
South Atlantic: Florida, Georgia, North Carolina, South Carolina, Virginia, West Virginia
East South Central: Alabama, Kentucky, Mississippi, Tennessee
West South Central: Arkansas, Louisiana, Oklahoma (except 1880), Texas
Mountain: Arizona, Colorado, Idaho, Montana, Nevada, New Mexico, Utah, Wyoming
Pacific: California, Oregon, Washington

1920's. This pattern is found in each of the three subregions within the South. Despite the steady convergence, however, it was not until around 1950 that the southern relative returned to antebellum levels. It has taken almost a century for the South to regain the relative standing it held on the eve of the Civil War. Since there has been little change in the southern share of population in the years after 1880, converging per capita income has meant an increased share of total national income in the South. The South Atlantic region regained its antebellum relative by 1940 and the East South Central states by 1960, but the West South Central region is still considerably below its relative standing of a century ago.[7] Within the South there was some relative shift in population from the East South Central to the West South Central before 1920, but since then the population shares of the subregions have changed very little.

In explaining the patterns of regional income change it is useful to distinguish between those factors which led to increased income within a region and those which gave rise to regional differences in income change. Within each region the major contributions to growth have been intrasectoral. In explaining regional patterns of convergence and divergence, however, changes in economic structure have been important. In this sense convergence in per capita income has reflected convergence in economic structure. As Easterlin has pointed out, there has been considerably less convergence within each income category than there has been in the simple measure of economic structure which distinguishes agriculture from all other sectors.[8] While all the components of income described by Easterlin have converged, the convergence in the ratio of non-agricultural labor force to total labor force has been particularly marked. The difference in the timing of the shift out of agriculture can explain most differences in relative per capita income trends.

The implications of this type of structural change have been analyzed by George Borts and Jerome Stein[9] for the United States, as well as in the recent work by Edward Denison[10] contrasting the postwar United States with Western Europe. They suggest that a large labor force share in agriculture represents an inefficient allocation of labor, which can be eliminated by transferring labor to more modern sectors. Once this transferal has occurred, the potential for rapid growth relative to other areas has been reduced and growth rates slow down to those within the modern sectors. A crude calculation can show the tremendous impact of these labor

7. Easterlin, "Regional Income Trends, 1840–1950," p. 528.

8. Easterlin, "Regional Growth of Income: Long-Term Tendencies, 1880–1950," and "Interregional Differences in Per Capita Income, Population, and Total Income, 1840–1950."

9. George H. Borts and Jerome L. Stein, *Economic Growth in a Free Market* (New York: Columbia University Press, 1964), chap. 2

10. Edward F. Denison, assisted by Jean-Pierre Poullier, *Why Growth Rates Differ: Postwar Experience in Nine Western Countries* (Washington, D.C.: The Brookings Institution, 1967), chap. 16.

force shifts on measured income levels and comparative growth rates. Easterlin's computed service income per worker in agriculture in 1880 was 36.7 percent of that in nonagriculture. From 1880 to 1950 service income per worker in agriculture increased at about 1.9 percent per annum.[11] At this rate of increase it would have taken fifty-three years for agricultural output per worker to equal the 1880 level of output per worker in the nonagricultural sectors.

While the effectiveness of this shift out of agriculture is clear, there remain some disquieting aspects in the use of these income measures to evaluate the impact of structural change at any moment of time. These comparisons usually ignore differences in the quality of labor, as well as in the quality and quantity of physical capital each laborer has to work with, and it is probable that the use of average productivities do not truly reflect the marginal productivities we are interested in measuring.[12] It is necessary to note this because one of the key points in arguing for southern backwardness in the antebellum period has been that slavery blocked the movement to higher productivity industrial sectors. This is generally supported by average productivity comparisons of the type described. Though these differentials appear large, it is not obvious that a simple reallocation of labor would have automatically raised income levels and growth rates. This has been clearly indicated by recent experience in less developed economies, where government-sponsored efforts at structural transformation have frequently not had the anticipated effects.

II. 1840–1880

A. 1840–1860

The analysis of regional incomes in the antebellum nineteenth century must begin with Easterlin's data. Before his systematic presentation of available census material, statements of the South's relative income position were generally based upon various proxies such as share of manufacturing output or percentage of population in urban areas which did not truly reflect the more complete set of

11. Easterlin, "Regional Growth of Income: Long-Term Tendencies, 1880–1950," p. 187. In 1950 the relative service income in agriculture was 73 percent of that in nonagriculture.
12. These factors are taken account of in Denison's analysis.

estimates. It is true that sufficient information existed in the Census of 1840 and in subsequent ones to criticize the notion of a low-income economy, as had been done by Ezra Seaman[13] and George Tucker.[14] This material generally has been ignored, however, and in the literature a picture has emerged of a South poor and backward relative to the North, a region which was economically stagnant. Easterlin's data for 1840 and 1860 have put us in a better position to evaluate such a portrayal.

In making comparisons it is unfortunate that we have these data for a period of only twenty years. There are no available estimates before 1840, so we are unable to examine growth rates over the early years of the nineteenth century. We do know that there was a large shift in the rural-urban population distribution in the North, and that such a movement has frequently been associated with the development of nonagricultural sectors. Yet any backward extrapolation of the 1840 sectoral regional income relatives will be hazardous, since this period saw the rise of the cotton kingdom and the development of a market-oriented agriculture in the Midwest.[15] For this reason statements about the economic performance of the antebellum economy are limited to years after 1840.

Easterlin's published 1840–1860 estimates show a slight decline in the overall southern per capita income position vis-à-vis the rest of the nation. The decline is from 76 percent of the national average to 72 percent of the national average.[16] The implication is that between the chosen terminal years (whose representativeness may, of course, be questioned), the South was growing almost as rapidly as were the northern states. Given the small reduction, four percentage points, it seems difficult to use these estimates to

---

13. Ezra C. Seaman, *Essays on the Progress of Nations, in Civilization, Productive Industry, Wealth and Population* (New York: Charles Scribner, 1852), pp. 463, 620.

14. George Tucker, *Progress of the United States in Population and Wealth in Fifty Years: With an Appendix Containing an Abstract of the Census of 1850* (1855) (New York: Augustus M. Kelley, 1964), pp. 195–201.

15. Stanley Lebergott presents data on farm laborer wages for selected years. There is convergence in farm laborer wages between 1818 and 1850, the outcome of a decline in southern relatives, and a rise in those for the North Central states. Common laborer earnings converge between 1832 and 1850, with both the South and North Central increasing with respect to the national average. The increase for the former region was slight. Between 1850 and 1860 there is marked convergence of both classes of wages in the South upon the national average. Stanley Lebergott, *Manpower in Economic Growth: The American Record Since 1800* (New York: McGraw-Hill, 1964), pp. 539, 541.

16. Easterlin, "Regional Income Trends, 1840–1950," p. 528.

argue that the southern economy was undergoing noticeable re-tardation before the war or that the system was on the way to im-minent collapse. Given the usual margins of error it would seem better to have argued that there was no clear evidence for any marked change in the southern income position relative to that of the North.

This minor decline in the southern relative has one computational aspect which has misled some users. Because of the difficulty of preparing consistent estimates of income-originating for those states in 1860 which had not belonged to the union in 1840, Easter-lin's per capita relatives for both years exclude Texas. Allowance was made for Texas, however, as well as for the other new states, in the national total for 1860. Thus the comparisons are of a South ex-cluding Texas with a nation including Texas. There are two ways to modify these estimates. First, the comparison can be made for only those states which were included in both 1840 and 1860. In this case the southern per capita income relative falls slightly, from 76 to 75—hardly enough to be the base for a stagnationist argument. Second, an 1840 estimate for Texas can be derived on the grounds that Texas was an important part of the southern economy and should not be ignored.[17] This method was used in the prepara-tion of Table 2. This inclusion raises the southern relative for 1860 above its 1840 level, from 77 to 80. Again it is clear that the margins are such that the estimates cannot be used to forcibly argue that the South was converging upon the national average. The moderate course would seem to be that it is hard, on the basis of these data, to establish a relative movement in either direction for the ante-bellum South.[18]

There are two points to note in Table 2. First, each subregion of the South was growing more slowly than the national average. In the absence of migration within the South its relative income position would have declined. This pattern has been used to argue

17. To bias downward the southern growth rate, it was assumed that per capita income in Texas was the same in 1840 as it was in 1860. See Stanley L. Engerman, "The Effects of Slavery Upon the Southern Economy: A Review of the Recent Debate," *Explorations in Entrepreneurial History, Second Series,* 4 (Winter 1967), 71–97.

18. The growth rates of income per capita of the total population, derived from Table 2, are 1.3 percent for the North and 1.65 percent for the South. The low north-ern rate is due to the fact that the measured effect of mobility from the Northeast to the North Central states is to cause a reduction in per capita income. Therefore the overall northern rate is below that of the two major regions, 1.7 percent for the North-east and 1.6 percent for the North Central states.

Table 2. Per Capita Income By Region, 1840 and 1860 (in 1860 prices)[a]

	Total Population		Free Population[b]	
	1840	1860	1840	1860
National Average	$ 96	$128	$109	$144
North:	109	141	110	142
Northeast	129	181	130	183
North Central	65	89	66	90
South:	74	103	105	150
South Atlantic	66	84	96	124
East South Central	69	89	92	124
West South Central	151	184	238	274

[a]The national totals are from Robert E. Gallman, "Gross National Product in the United States, 1834-1909," in Conference on Research in Income and Wealth, *Output, Employment, and Productivity in the United States After 1800,* Studies in Income and Wealth Volume Thirty (New York and London: Columbia University Press, 1966), p. 26. The regional relatives were derived from worksheets underlying, Easterlin, "Regional Income Trends, 1840-1950," pp. 528, 535. The national average excludes the Mountain and Pacific states in 1860.

[b]The "maintenance cost" per slave used in these calculations was $20. It should be noted that while a higher maintenance cost would reduce the relative per capita income of free southerners in 1860, it would raise the rate of growth of their income between 1840 and 1860.

Calculations of growth rates of commodity output between 1840 and 1860, based upon allocating Gallman's estimates, present a more favorable picture for the North. These are on the basis of uniform national prices applied to output in each region. See Robert E. Gallman, "Commodity Output, 1839– 1899," in Conference on Research in Income and Wealth, *Trends in the American Economy in the Nineteenth Century,* Studies in Income and Wealth Volume Twenty-Four (Princeton, N.J.: Princeton University Press, 1960), pp. 13– 67.

	Allocation in 1879 Prices	Allocation in Current Prices
South	1.0%	1.3%
North	1.5	1.3
Northeast	1.8	1.5
North Central	1.1	1.3

Calculations were also made substituting the Towne-Rasmussen agricultural output series for Gallman's. See Marvin W. Towne and Wayne D. Rasmussen, "Farm Gross Product and Gross Investment in the Nineteenth Century," in Conference on Research in Income and Wealth, *Trends in the American Economy in the Nineteenth Century,* Studies in Income and Wealth Volume Twenty-Four (Princeton, N.J.: Princeton University Press, 1960), pp. 255– 312. Growth rates were computed using alternative antebellum years as the price base. These estimates show higher relative southern growth rates for commodity output than those derived from the Gallman series, and generally yield southern growth rates in excess of northern. Also, a different measure of regional income in 1860 was derived, and was more favorable to the South than those computed on the basis of Easterlin's relatives.

the need for continuous expansion as the basis of the viability of the slave system, as well as to suggest a different type of southern political behavior than would have occurred if each area within the South maintained a stable position. This is a traditional historical argument. Given the possibilities for capital creation by land improvement, the southerners had a choice between fertilizing soil in older areas to maintain productivity and moving to clear new lands. Of these two alternative investments, it is clear that at the relative prices of the period the second yielded a higher private return. The presence of cheap new lands caused a drain of capital and labor from the Old South (the South Atlantic states). Thus, retardation in older regions in the presence of possibilities for migration need not represent a basis to argue for similar retardation if mobility were precluded and more investment occurred in the Old South. Nevertheless, about 73 percent of southern per capita income growth was intraregional, the shift among regions explaining only 27 percent of the increase.[19] Even if mobility were precluded, the southern growth rate could have been about five-sixths of the national rate. Thus an extreme version of the expansionist thesis cannot be supported on the basis of these estimates.[20]

The second issue concerns alternative treatments of the slave population within the national income framework. The appropriate ethical concept would seem to be to regard the slaves as well as the whites as ultimate consumers. Yet it can be argued, from the point of view of the whites, that slaves were more appropriately to be regarded as intermediate goods producing outputs for the free population. The ownership of slaves provided an increased per capita income for the free population in two ways. It permitted the owners to expropriate the maximum amount possible between average product and subsistence, particularly important in a time when land availability meant that average and marginal product of labor were close to equal. The excess of the marginal product over subsistence, which would be paid to free labor, was kept by the slave owner. Ownership of slaves also permitted a greater labor participation rate than would have occurred if the work-leisure decision were

19. This was calculated by weighting the subregional growth rates by shares of southern population in 1840.

20. It would have to be shown that there would have been rapidly diminishing returns in the older areas without migration and that there would have been no shifts in agricultural output mix or industrial structure.

voluntary.[21] Using a rather low subsistence estimate of $20 per slave for both 1840 and 1860 means that free southern income per capita grew at 1.8 percent and that the average income of the free southerner was above that of the northerner. A perhaps more accurate subsistence figure of $30 would reduce the southern level while leaving it above the northern, but raise the free southern growth rate to 1.9 percent.[22] Thus, the average free southerner's income was five-sixths that of the average northerner residing in the industrialized Northeast. Clearly the slave system placed southern whites in a favorable income position in 1860.

B. 1860–1880

The marked impact of the Civil War upon the southern income position can be clearly seen in the Easterlin estimates.[23] The 1880 southern per capita income relative was 51, only 70 percent of the unadjusted 1860 relative. The decline in per capita income during the war period was so sharp that it was not until about 1890 that the South regained its 1860 level. There were income declines in all three southern subregions, with a particularly sharp decline in the

21. Lebergott's method of estimating the labor force yields calculations showing a participation rate (labor force to population) for the South about 24 percent higher than in the northern states. This is because both female and male slaves over 10 years of age were considered to have had participation rate equal to that of males over 15. See Stanley Lebergott, "Labor Force and Employment, 1800–1960," in Conference on Research in Income and Wealth, *Output, Employment and Productivity in the United States After 1800*, Studies in Income and Wealth Volume Thirty (New York and London: Columbia University Press, 1966), pp. 117–204.

White rates for males under 15 were lower, and white females in agriculture were apparently excluded from the labor force count. Therefore the comparisons in Table 4 may understate the relative position of the South. Freeing the slaves meant a sharp reduction in measured participation rates for the South. However, the welfare implications, as well as the possible existence of any divergence between measured and "true" reductions, are unclear.

22. For subsistence estimates see Alfred H. Conrad and John R. Meyer, "The Economics of Slavery in the Ante-Bellum South," *Journal of Political Economy*, 66 (April 1958), p. 104, and Easterlin, "Interregional Differences in Per Capita Income, Population, and Total Income, 1840–1950," p. 92.

23. All remarks in the next two paragraphs about income positions are based upon the application of Easterlin's regional relatives to Gallman's Gross National Product estimates. The 1880 estimate was the average for the decade 1874–1883. See Easterlin, "Regional Income Trends, 1840–1950," p. 528; and Robert E. Gallman, "Gross National Product in the United States, 1834–1909," in Conference on Research in Income and Wealth, *Output, Employment, and Productivity in the United States After 1800,* Studies in Income and Wealth Volume Thirty (New York and London: Columbia University Press, 1966), pp. 3–76.

richer West South Central states. Indeed, it is probable that, unlike the other two areas, the West South Central states had a lower per capita income in 1880 than in 1840. The magnitude of this decline is striking, combining the relative decline found in frontier areas and the loss of New Orleans' status as a major commercial center, with the general disruption faced by the South. The decline in the older South Atlantic states was sharper than that in the East South Central states. The latter group includes Kentucky and Tennessee, states in which the impact of the war and the end of the slave system had a smaller impact.

Growth was particularly rapid in the North Central states in the 1860–1880 interval. In the Northeast, per capita income grew at 1.3 percent while in the North Central states the growth rate was 3.1 percent, raising the per capita income of that region from two-thirds of the national average in 1860 to approximate equality in 1880.[24]

In order to separate the war decade from the recovery period, I have prepared estimates of commodity output (agriculture plus manufacturing) for 1860, 1870, and 1880[25] based upon Gallman's estimates.[26] Regional allocations were made on the basis of census material. Separate estimates were made for allocations in current prices (the deflator being the price index referring to total commodity output) and in prices of 1879. The choice of variant has some effect upon the discussion by decades since there were sharp relative price changes for key commodities. The current price allocation allows for a terms-of-trade effect among regions, based upon changing relative commodity prices, while the use of the prices for any one year alone excludes this effect. (The interpolating procedure does not allow for changes in relative prices of given commodities vis-à-vis the national average, so does not truly pick up changing terms of trade.) However, since wheat and cotton, the two com-

24. The calculated growth rates for commodity output (Variant B) between 1860 and 1880 are 1.6 percent for the Northeast and 2.2 percent for the North Central states.

25. In an earlier paper I prepared estimates, in 1879 prices, for the Confederacy and all other states. These differ from the estimates in Table 3 in the definition of the South (Table 3 includes Kentucky, which accounted for over 10 percent of southern population in 1870) and included mining in commodity output. The earlier estimates had a sharper drop and a more rapid rise than the estimates in Table 3. See Stanley L. Engerman, "The Economic Impact of the Civil War," *Explorations in Entrepreneurial History, Second Series,* 3 (Spring 1966), 176–199.

26. Gallman, "Commodity Output, 1839–1899," Appendix.

Table 3.   Commodity Output per Capita (1879 prices)[a]

| | VARIANT A (Allocation in 1879 prices) | | | VARIANT B (Allocation in Current Prices) | | |
	Northeast	North Central	South	Northeast	North Central	South
1860	$ 78	$ 64	$77	$ 76	$ 65	$78
1870	78	78	50	78	74	55
1880	105	102	62	105	102	62

[a]See text for description. These are useful only for estimation of growth rates, differences in the ratio of labor force in commodity output to total labor force precluding cross-section comparisons.

modities whose price changes have the most impact on regional incomes, were each concentrated within one region the current price allocation is of interest.[27] Nevertheless the overall 1860-1880 pattern is not affected by the choice between these variants.

Table 3 shows that for both series there is a sharp southern decline between 1860 and 1870, 35 percent in Variant A and 30 percent in Variant B, with some growth in the decade of the 1870's.[28] From 1870 to 1880, the Variant A increase is 2.2 percent per annum, while for Variant B it is only 1.2 percent. The difference is attributable to the sharp rise in the price of cotton and tobacco relative to other agricultural prices in 1870, reflecting the scarcity of these commodities in the immediate postwar period. In the 1870's the impact of the rapid expansion of cotton output was mitigated by the fall in its relative price from the scarcity levels of the early postwar period. By either measure southern per capita output in 1880

27. In 1870, over 67 percent of wheat output was produced in the North Central States and 100 percent of the cotton was grown in the South.

28. Substituting the Towne-Rasmussen agricultural output series for Gallman's reduces the southern decline between 1860 and 1870 to about 20 percent for both variants. The difference is largely attributable to the former series showing cotton output increasing slightly in the decade, while the Gallman series has a decline of 44 percent. This discrepancy reflects the Towne-Rasmussen use of the USDA series and Gallman's use of the census estimate. The figure used by Towne-Rasmussen for 1870 is about one-third greater than both the 1869 and 1871 estimates. See U.S. Bureau of the Census, *Historical Statistics of the United States, Colonial Times to 1957* (Washington, D.C.: Government Printing Office 1960), p. 302.

Similarly, the higher 1880 agricultural output derived from Towne-Rasmussen yields a higher per capita output for the South in 1880 than does Gallman's, but it is still at least 10 percent below the 1860 level. Thus the general pattern remains unchanged, with output per capita in the South declining between 1860 and 1870 and then increasing at about 1 percent per annum between 1870 and 1880. For the other regions the general pattern described in the text holds, with some increase in the North Central growth rate in each decade, but with a higher growth rate in the 1870's than the 1860's.

was about 80 percent of the 1860 level, and the 1870–80 growth rate was below that of the two northern regions.[29]

Growth in the North in the 1860's was slow by historical standards.[30] This point was forcibly noted by Thomas Cochran in his analysis of statistical data relating to the Civil War period.[31] There were differences in the behavior of the Northeast and that of the North Central states. For the former there was virtually no growth. In the North Central states growth was at a higher rate than in the Northeast, but at a rate below that of the 1870's. Variant A shows more rapid growth in the 1860's and a smaller expansion in the 1870's than does Variant B, due in large part to the sharply lower relative price of wheat in 1870.

Growth during the 1870's was quite rapid in the northern states. Using Variant B, per capita output expanded at an annual rate of 3.3 percent in the North Central states and at 3.0 percent in the Northeast.[32] These northern rates were unusually high by prior and subsequent experience. However, for the entire 20-year period the northern growth rate was not out of line with historical experience. The high growth rates of the 1870's (and early 1880's) may be considered as a "catching-up" for the North from its poor record in the Civil War years. After 1885 growth rates of per capita income in the North slowed down, and since then the South has been growing more rapidly than the North.

The pronounced impact of the Civil War decline and the lack of any immediate "catching-up" suggests that discussions of southern backwardness should emphasize adjustments during the war and Reconstruction. The major explanation for the South's lower level

29. See note 28 above for an alternative estimate.

30. The reason for this slow growth can be seen in Gallman's commodity output estimates. The constant dollar value of manufacturing output increased only 26 percent in this decade, while total commodity output per capita actually declined. See Gallman, "Commodity Output, 1839–1899," p. 16. The Northeast's share of agricultural output declined slightly, so that the reduction in the southern share was fully offset by the increased share for the North Central states. Indeed the high North Central growth rate between 1860 and 1880 is largely attributable to expanding agricultural output, with a high export share. For further discussion see Engerman, "The Economic Impact of the Civil War."

31. Thomas C. Cochran, "Did the Civil War Retard Industrialization?," *Mississippi Valley Historical Review*, 47 (September 1961), 197–210.

32. In variant A the Northeast rate is the same, but the North Central rate falls to 2.7 percent. Substituting the Towne-Rasmussen agricultural series would raise the North Central rates, but the pattern vis-à-vis the Northeast would be the same.

of income was neither slow antebellum growth nor a stagnant post-1870 economy. Rather it was the sharp decline in the war and the slower recovery (than the North) before 1880. Unlike the experience of Germany and Japan after World War II, there was no period of accelerated growth in the aftermath of the war. It is this absence of a "southern miracle" akin to the German and Japanese "miracles" that it is necessary to explain.

III. The South in 1860

It is useful to distinguish among three hypotheses when discussing the antebellum South. The first is that the South was poor and stagnant on the eve of the Civil War. This is a position placed in grave doubt by the data discussed in Section II. The level of southern per capita income for the total population in 1860 was high relative to that of the rest of the world at that time, and no doubt higher than that of much of the world today. Antebellum per capita income in the South possibly exceeded that in France, and it could have been about the third richest "nation," after England and the northern United States.[33] Similarly, its growth rate from 1840 to 1860, and possibly before, would rank high in any comparative listing of growth rates for developing areas.

A second hypothesis is that, although the South was growing, it did not grow as rapidly as it could have under some alternative socio-economic system. It is argued that the South was growing at a rate below some maximum, and it is implied that its short-fall from such a maximum was larger than the North's. It is possible to describe circumstances under which the southern growth rate (though not necessarily its welfare) could have been higher, but it is not obvious either that growth in the absence of slavery would necessarily have been at this rate or that the South was further below this level than the North.[34] This latter point is of interest since many of the reasons proposed to account for southern backwardness relative to its potential have also been applied to the North; for

33. For levels in 1840 see Gallman, "Gross National Product in the United States, 1834–1909," p. 5.

34. Putting aside its distributional effects, slavery, if profitable, would have increased society's investable surplus, though not necessarily its investment.

example, wasteful agricultural techniques, poorly constructed (as well as unlinked) railroads, and conspicuous consumption by the wealthy wasting investable funds. Another aspect of this argument is that the South's social system prevented the desirable shift out of agriculture into industry and the movement of population from rural to urban areas. It is therefore necessary to establish whether or not the South's comparative advantage lay in agriculture before 1860, and if specialization in agriculture would have been desirable under any other form of social organization.[35]

A third hypothesis argues that, whatever had been true up to 1860, the southern economy necessarily would have been retarded in subsequent years. The point made is that the South was locked into agriculture (more particularly cotton) by the slave system, and that it lacked the capacity to make the necessary adjustments to expected future changes in economic conditions. It is this question which is hardest to answer, since it implies detailed examination of the response patterns of southern entrepreneurs. There are many indications that within the plantation system responses were economically rational, but this evidence does not disprove the fact that the system itself could have been inefficient. I shall make several North-South comparisons for the antebellum period, suggesting approaches to some of the questions posed by the second hypothesis.

EFFICIENCY IN AGRICULTURE

It has often been argued that southern agriculture was inefficient. Not only was plantation labor considered less productive than an equal quantity of yeoman labor would have been, but the system was held to have forced many whites into low productivity subsistence farming. Data on outputs and inputs can be used to derive measures of comparative efficiency (defined as measured output per unit of input) for the North and the South in 1860 to evaluate this argument.[36] Unfortunately, the crucial information on the

35. Lacking national independence meant that the South was limited in its ability to force structural change. For example, the use of tariffs to encourage southern manufactures was precluded since the South belonged to a large free trade area. While it is by no means clear that such encouragements would represent economic efficiency, secession could at least have permitted this "modernization" of the economy to be attempted.

36. Output and labor force estimates were calculated by regionally allocating the Gallman and the Lebergott estimates, respectively. See Gallman, "Commodity

output elasticities with respect to the inputs is not known. For this reason several estimates for hypothetical elasticities which should bracket plausible values are presented in Table 4. In these estimates slaves, comprising two-thirds of the southern agricultural labor force, are included in the labor force. Table 4 indicates that relative southern agricultural efficiency was not markedly below, if it was at all below, that of northern agriculture. The southern agricultural laborer had less land and other productive factors to work with than did the northern laborer. The data in Table 5 suggest that these factor proportions were not due to southern inability to save and invest, while Table 4 is consistent with the argument that the choice represented a response to cost differentials.

Qualifications can be made in Table 4 which would raise the measured efficiency of southern agriculture in 1860. Labor inputs have been measured as number of bodies. Yet the regions have labor forces with differing age–sex proportions, as well as differing amounts of education. The southern labor force included more females and children than the northern. Not only was the slave presumably an ill-educated worker, but the southern white farmer was considered backward as well. Thus, the effective input per unit of labor may be still less in the South, raising its relative output per unit of total input.[37]

INDUSTRIALIZATION AND CAPITAL FORMATION

It has been argued that even if southern agriculture was efficient, the overall southern economy was not because of its failure to industrialize. This comparison is directed particularly at the northeastern states. This argument can be examined with efficiency comparisons of the type performed above for agriculture. The relative output per unit of input in commodity output (agriculture plus

---

Output, 1839–1899," Appendix, and Lebergott, "Labor Force and Employment, 1800–1960." The land and capital values are from U.S. Census, Ninth (1870), vol. III, *Wealth and Industry* (Washington, D.C.: Government Printing Office, 1872), p. 86.

The assumptions underlying the analysis are that each region's output can be described by a Cobb-Douglas production function, with output elasticities the same in both regions. Nonlabor service inputs are considered proportional to stock values.

37. It can be argued that bodies provide the better measure of labor input, at least as far as males are concerned, since it is necessary to explain the low level of education in the South. The relative efficiencies in Table 4 do raise questions about the relationship between diffused education and labor productivity in the early stages of agricultural development.

Table 4. Southern versus Northern Agriculture in 1860[a]

	South as Percentage of North	
	Variant A[b]	Variant B[c]
Output per unit of labor	79	79
Total nonlabor input per unit of labor	43	54
Total input per unit of labor:		
$\alpha = .2$[d]	84	88
$\alpha = .4$	71	78
Output per unit of input:[e]		
$\alpha = .2$	94	90
$\alpha = .4$	111	102

[a]The North includes only the Northeast and North Central states. For a description of the data see the text and footnote 36.

[b]Nonlabor input is the sum of cash value of farms, value of farming implements and machinery, and the value of livestock. Using value of farms amounts to assuming that differences in the price of land reflect quality differentials.

[c]Nonlabor input is a weighted average of improved acres and the sum of 20 percent of the cash value of farms, the value of implements, and the value of livestock. Land is weighted at 66.9 percent of nonlabor input. For the breakdown of the cash value of farms see Robert Gallman and Edward Howle, "Fixed Reproducible Capital in the United States, 1840-1900, Current Prices and Prices of 1860," unpublished paper presented to the Purdue University Seminar on Quantitative Methods in Economic History, 1965, p. 3. Improved acres per unit of labor in the South were 56 percent of the North's, and the relative for other nonlabor inputs was 49. If total acres were used rather than improved acres, the southern land input relative per unit of labor would be 104.

[d]α is the assumed output elasticity with respect to nonlabor input.

[e]Output per unit of labor divided by total input per unit of labor.

manufacturing) for the South was at least three-quarters that of the North.[38] These calculations suggest that, not allowing for the differing quantities of human capital embodied in each labor unit, the southern economy was in the neighborhood of at least 75 percent as "efficient" as the northern in the production of commodity output. This was not because the South was "inefficient" within either sector; it is the measured outcome of the South's unfavorable output mix.

Two main arguments are made to explain this lack of industrialization—three if we include the position that it was not the South's comparative advantage. One is that the southern social system did

38. Commodity output per unit of labor in the South relative to the North was 65 percent and capital per unit of labor, 55 percent. (Capital was measured as the value of farms, implements, and livestock in agriculture, plus capital in manufacturing). For a capital elasticity of 0.2, the southern relative input per unit of labor was 89, and output per unit of input was 74 percent of northern; for an elasticity of 0.4 the values were 78 percent and 83 percent, respectively.

not permit such a shift because to modernize would have imperiled the entire structure. The second concerns the proposition that the southern income distribution was such that the economy was incapable both of providing sufficient savings for modern growth and sufficient consumption to provide a demand for domestic manufactures. In general, our knowledge of southern income and wealth distribution is small, as is our information concerning the impact of any degree of skewness upon the rate of economic growth.[39]

39. Robert E. Gallman, "Trends in the Size Distribution of Wealth in the Nineteenth Century: Some Speculations," in Conference on Research in Income and Wealth, *Six Papers on the Size Distribution of Wealth and Income*, Studies in Income and Wealth Volume Thirty-Three (New York and London: Columbia University Press, 1969,) pp. 1–25.

Table 5.   Capital and Wealth Measures, 1860

	1860 National Total ($ million)	Southern Share (%)
True value of real estate and personal property:		
Gross:	$16,160	36.3
Net of Slaves[a]	14,500	29.6
Owner-evaluated:		
Real estate	10,930	27.9
Personal property	8,159	54.6
Personal-net of slaves[b]	4,474	21.5
Real + personal-net of slaves	15,404	26.0
By type:		
Agricultural:		
Farm values	6,645	32.2
Implements	246	36.7
Livestock	1,089	40.7
Manufacturing	1,010	11.5
Railroad (construction cost)	1,152	22.3
Bank capital	422	24.9
Specie in banks	84	38.0

Source: U.S. Census, Eighth (1860), *Statistics of the United States* (Washington, D.C.: Government Printing Office, 1866), pp. 292, 295, 331. U.S. Census, Ninth (1870), Vol. III, *Wealth and Industry* (Washington, D.C.: Government Printing Office, 1872), pp. 86, 393.

[a]A deduction of $1,660 million was made, as per the 1870 Census (p. 8), and distributed on the basis of the shares of slave population. That amount is a significant understatement based upon the slave prices of the time.

[b]Using Rose's estimates, slaves were valued at $3,685 million in 1860. Louis A. Rose, "Capital Losses of Southern Slaveholders Due to Emancipation," *Western Economic Journal*, 3 (Fall 1964), 39-51.

One usual basis for the presumed southern absence of capital formation, the citation of frequent examples of conspicuous consumption, ignores the evidence that large consumption expenditures and high savings ratios are generally positively correlated.[40]

Examination of census material indicates that southern wealth was not small relative to that of the rest of the nation. The frequent use of the level of industrialization as a proxy for capital formation is misleading. In 1860 total manufacturing capital was less than 10 percent of the estimated reproducible capital stock, and was less than the value of the inventory of livestock on farms.[41] The material in Table 5 suggests that any argument should be based not upon the lack of aggregate capital, but upon the specific composition of capital formation. Not only did the South have high shares of the broadly defined capital categories (relative to its 26 percent share of national income and its 33 percent share of population) but there were relatively high shares for railroad capital, bank capital, and specie in banks.[42] They do not suggest an economy lacking investment in key areas (with the exception of manufacturing) nor, for example, does the specie share suggest a heavy debtor about to topple over in bankruptcy.

It is unfortunate that we do not have detailed breakdowns on the composition of assets (or of their grossness) for the broad categories. Using the true value of property (net of slaves), the higher southern capital-output ratio means a lower average productivity of capital. But unless output elasticities differ significantly, the relative

40. Engerman, "The Effects of Slavery upon the Southern Economy: A Review of the Recent Debate," p. 89.
41. Gallman and Howle, "Fixed Reproducible Capital in the United States, 1840–1900, Current Prices and Prices of 1860." Unpublished paper presented to the Purdue University Seminar on Quantitative Methods in Economic History, 1965.
42. Fishlow's regional detail on railroad capital formation indicate a southern share of 25.1 percent. See Albert Fishlow, *American Railroads and the Transformation of the Ante-Bellum Economy* (Cambridge, Mass.: Harvard University Press, 1965), pp. 397–399.
Railroad construction during the 1850's was greater in the South than in the North. Southern banks were clearly more conservative than northern, with lower ratios of loans and circulation to specie. Since the southerners had access to northern banks and credit sources, the implications of this conservative banking structure are unclear. It has been argued that high shares in these specific categories represent only the persistence of a colonial economy in that railroads and banks were merely the instruments of the controllers of the traditional economy and not harbingers of progress. However, then any capital formation argument is redundant.

marginal productivity of southern capital cannot be markedly below that in the North.[43]

The 1850 share of the South in the true value of property (including slaves) was the same as the 1860 share.[44] If it is assumed that the value of slaves grew at the same rate as other capital, then the growth rate of total capital was the same in the South as in the rest of the nation. The average capital-output ratio was higher in the South than elsewhere. This would imply a ratio of capital formation to income greater in the South than in the rest of the nation. While this regional capital formation ratio can be little more than suggestive as to orders of magnitude, it would indicate that the southern savings ratio was not decidedly lower than that of the rest of the nation. This would be consistent with the hypothesis that savings: income ratios of free southerners (for nonslave capital) exceeded those of northerners.

HUMAN CAPITAL

It has often been argued that the South was wasteful of its human capital potential, both white and Negro. Negroes were legally barred from obtaining formal education and the nature of the sociopolitical system precluded expenditures for educating the large mass of whites. However, failure to consider human capital formation through on-the-job and other types of informal training and by migration understates human capital formation in the South. Informal training of Negroes would clearly have been in the economic interests of the plantation owner; indeed, occupational rosters and plantation records indicate that skills were developed in the slave labor force.[45] The level of white education in the South in 1860 was below northern levels as measured by both enrollment rates and expenditures per capita. However, Albert Fishlow's data show that education expenditures as a percentage of regional income were higher in the South than the North in 1860, and expenditures per white school-aged person were higher in the South. The lower southern enrollment rates meant a higher outlay per

43. The southern marginal product is about five-sixths of northern if output elasticities were the same in both regions.

44. U.S. Census, Eighth (1860) *Statistics of the United States* (Washington, D.C.: Government Printing Office, 1866), p. 295.

45. It can be argued that one of the wastes in the postbellum years, attributable to racism, was the failure of southern society to permit Negroes to use previously developed skills.

pupil. Southern increases in enrollment rates and expenditures between 1840 and 1860 were greater than those of the North, so education could be used to explain convergence of income levels rather than divergence.[46]

It is clear from regional shares of population that mobility was at a higher rate before the Civil War than in the later part of the century. Antebellum Negro migration was greater than in the post-bellum period, and the slave system was consistent with widespread geographic mobility into higher productivity areas. The owner-ship of human capital could have made for a better capital market than otherwise would have existed, and facilitated human capital formation through migration.[47]

IV. The South, 1860–1900

The magnitude of the decline in southern commodity output during the Civil War decade was shown in Table 3. This decline reflected not only social and economic disorganization, but also physical destruction of real capital.[48] The magnitude of this loss can be seen in comparisons of capital data in the 1860 and 1870 censuses. The undercount in the population census suggests that declines may be overstated, but it is doubtful if the undercount is so large as to distort the major conclusions. Not only did the cash value of farms decline by over 50 percent, but there were fewer improved acres counted in farms in 1870 than in 1860. The real value of farm implements similarly declined by over 50 percent, while the real value of livestock fell by more than 45 percent. The true valuation of wealth (net of slaves) fell to below 55 percent of its 1860 level. The southern share of this category of national wealth fell from 29.6 percent in 1860 to 11.8 percent in 1870.[49]

46. Albert Fishlow, "The American Common School Revival: Fact or Fancy?" in Henry Rosovsky, ed., *Industrialization in Two Systems: Essays in Honor of Alexander Gerschenkron* (New York: John Wiley, 1966), pp. 40–67.

47. Clearly it was a better capital market than that facing Negroes in the post-bellum South.

48. Easterlin, "Regional Income Trends, 1840–1950,"; Eugene M. Lerner, "South-ern Output and Agricultural Income, 1860–1880," *Agricultural History*, 33 (July 1959), 117–125; and James L. Sellers, "The Economic Incidence of the Civil War in the South," *Mississippi Valley Historical Review*, 14 (September 1927), 179–191.

49. Cash value of farms, value of livestock, and true valuation of real and personal estate were deflated by the Warren-Pearson wholesale price index averaged for 1859–60 and 1869–70. (The numbers of all livestock types declined sharply in this decade.) See U.S. Census, Ninth (1870), pp. 10, 81–82, and *Historical Statistics of the United States, Colonial Times to 1957*, p. 115.

While these may be attributable in part to declines in asset valuation, a substantial part must represent real capital loss. Thus, during the war decade southern capital declined, not only relative to northern, but also absolutely. So steep was the decline that even though the measured southern growth rates for most capital categories were close to those of the rest of the nation between 1870 and 1880, 1880 amounts remained below 1860 levels.

I shall make several comments about the state of the southern economy in the postbellum period. Because of the uncertainty concerning the 1870 census, the discussion will focus on a comparison between 1860 and 1880.

EFFICIENCY IN AGRICULTURE

Given the relative importance of agriculture to the southern economy, an analysis of changes in that sector will have strong implications for the region's overall position. Using accepted labor force measures, output per worker in southern agriculture in 1880 fell to about 95 percent of the 1860 level. As was noted above, these measures excluded most Negro females and children who had been counted in the labor force in 1860; thus they probably understate the true decline in output per worker during this interval.[50] Owing to the failure to recover from wartime destruction, there was a decline in capital per worker. Improved acres per worker rose only slightly, so that under either variant of nonlabor input the total input per unit of labor declined in this interval. When nonlabor input was defined as the number of improved acres plus the constant dollar value of building, livestock, and implements, there was a slight decline in output per unit of input between 1860 and 1880. The system of freed labor in 1880 therefore failed to provide for a

---

The deflator for agricultural implements was the unweighted average of Brady's indexes for agricultural machinery and agricultural implements. See Dorothy S. Brady, "Price Deflators for Final Product Estimates," in Conference on Research in Income and Wealth, *Output, Employment, and Productivity in the United States After 1800*, Studies in Income and Wealth Volume Thirty (New York and London: Columbia University Press, 1966), p. 111.

50. The labor force estimate is from Ann Ratner Miller and Carol P. Brainerd, "Labor Force Estimates," in Everett S. Lee, et al., *Population Redistribution and Economic Growth, United States, 1870–1950*, vol. I, *Methodological Considerations and Reference Tables* (Philadelphia: American Philosophical Society, 1957), pp. 363–633. The linking with the 1860 estimate from Lebergott yields a growth rate of 1.1 percent per annum, considerably below the growth rate of the population.

particularly more (or less) "efficient" economy than did the plantation system.[51] The major explanatory factor in the decline, however, varies with the output elasticities. For low nonlabor elasticities the more important factor was the decline in output per unit of input, while for high elasticities it was the decline in nonlabor input per worker.[52]

We can make a North–South comparison for 1880, similar to the one for 1860, to determine whether the explanation of southern backwardness differs from that of the antebellum period (see Table 6). It is clear that the southern relative amount of other factors per unit of labor fell. The Variant A decline is particularly sharp because of the decline in the value per improved acre in the South. The explanation of the lower output per unit of labor in the South with either variant is sensitive to output elasticities. Using the Variant B estimates, which seem more appropriate for these purposes, the comparison with 1860 indicates that the relative decline in output per unit of input explains the greater part of the South's relative decline in output per worker. At all output elasticity values southern efficiency relative to that of the North declined from the 1860 level. This suggests that there was a rise in output per unit of input in the North in which the South, because of social dislocations, did not share. Thus it was after the Civil War that southern agricultural backwardness became pronounced, and probably in the decade of the 1860's that most of the measured impact was to be found.[53]

51. The calculations were based upon Gallman's agricultural output in 1879 prices. The cash value of farms and livestock values were deflated by the Warren-Pearson index averaged for 1859–60 and 1879–80, and implements were deflated by the Brady index. See *Historical Statistics of the United States, Colonial Times to 1957*, p. 115, and Brady, "Price Deflators for Final Product Estimates," p. 111.

The deflated value of building, implements, and livestock per worker in 1880 was 62 percent of the 1860 value. Improved acres per worker rose 2.8 percent. Weighting the latter by two-thirds, nonlabor input per unit of labor was 89 percent of the 1860 value. Output per unit of input in 1880, based upon the accepted labor force estimates and using the number of improved acres to derive nonlabor inputs, is 96.9 percent of the 1860 level for $\alpha = 0.2$ and 99.2 percent for $\alpha = 0.4$.

52. If the 1880 labor force had been adjusted to include female Negroes at the estimated 1860 participation rate, output per unit of labor in 1880 would have been 76 percent of the 1860 level. For the range of elasticities used, the decline in output per unit of input is more important as an explanatory factor for the decline in output per unit of labor than the decline in nonlabor input per unit of labor.

53. Lave's technological change indexes for agriculture show no major differences in rates of increase of southern and northern regions in each decade from 1870 to 1900. See Lester B. Lave, *Technological Change: Its Conception and Measurement* (Englewood Cliffs, N.J.: Prentice Hall, 1966), p. 75.

Table 6. Southern versus Northern Agriculture in 1880[a]

	South as Percentage of North	
	Variant A	Variant B
Output per unit of labor	56	56
Total nonlabor input per unit of labor[b]	24	42
Total input per unit of labor:		
$\alpha = .2$	75	84
$\alpha = .4$	57	70
Output per unit of input:		
$\alpha = .2$	74	67
$\alpha = .4$	99	80

[a]For description see Table 4 and text. The nonlabor input data are from U.S. Census, Tenth (1880), vol. III, *Report on the Productions of Agriculture* (Washington, D.C.: Government Printing Office, 1883), pp. 3-4.

[b]In Variant B, the ratio of improved acres per unit of labor in the South to those in the North was 49, while that for other nonlabor input was 28. Land was weighted at 67.4 percent of nonlabor input.

Our knowledge of what occurred in southern agriculture during this period is limited. The South remained an agriculturally based economy through the early twentieth century, with cotton the most important crop. The cotton crop was still mainly for export purposes; postwar shares generally ran between 60 and 70 percent of cotton production compared to the antebellum 70–80 percent.[54] England, the major market, was recaptured by the late 1870's, and the United States held its share of that country's cotton imports through the 1920's. There was a slowdown in the rate of growth of English cotton imports after 1860, so that the very rapid expansion of cotton production in the early postwar period could continue only until the English market share was regained. However, the post-1875 price of cotton relative to the wholesale price index remained at the average level of the 1850's and above the levels of the 1840's.[55] It was only relative to the high prices of the immediate postwar period that "real" cotton prices declined.

The most marked changes in southern agriculture in this period were the sharp fall in farm size and the rise of the share-crop system.

54. M. B. Hammond, *The Cotton Industry: An Essay in American Economic History*, pt. I, *The Cotton Culture and the Cotton Trade* (New York: American Economic Association, 1897), Appendix 1.

55. *Ibid*; see also *Historical Statistics of the United States, Colonial Times to 1957*, p. 115.

The exact meaning to be attributed to the measured decline in farm size has been questioned by Roger Shugg, since the Census apparently counted each tenant-farm as a separate holding even if it was under some form of centralized control.[56] Thus some vestige of the plantation system remained, even if the direct control and supervision of the prewar version were missing.[57] Unless there was a marked shift of Negroes out of cotton production there must have been a decline in cotton output per Negro between 1860 and 1880, and possibly through 1890. This could account for the many complaints about the labor performance of the freedmen in the postbellum years.

INDUSTRY

There was some expansion of manufacturing in the late nineteenth century. As Eugene Lerner has noted, the Civil War decline in manufacturing was less sharp than that in agriculture and the recovery was more rapid.[58] However, the southern share of national value-added in manufacturing declined until the 1880's, and the 1860 share was not regained until the early 1900's.[59] While there were movements of some industries into the South—particularly cotton textiles and lumber—the end of the slave system did not lead to a marked acceleration in the rate of growth of southern industry.[60]

56. Roger Shugg, "Survival of the Plantation System in Louisiana," *Journal of Southern History*, 3 (August 1937), 311–325.

57. In 1900 cotton was the principal source of income on 71.8 percent of the southern farms operated by Negroes. Some form of tenancy was in effect on about three-quarters of these, with slightly more share tenants than cash tenants. See U.S. Census, Twelfth (1900), vol. V, *Agriculture*, pt. I (Washington, D.C.: Government Printing Office, 1902), p. civ.

The rise of sharecropping remains to be analyzed. Why this particular method of dividing price and output risks was chosen is unclear. The similarity to a piece wage system makes its incentive effects preferable to the owner to a straight money wage system, but presumably piece rates could have been introduced.

58. Lerner, "Southern Output and Agricultural Income, 1860–1880."

59. In the regional data on nineteenth-century manufacturing wages presented by Lebergott, southern relatives were higher before the Civil War than after, with the relatives from 1870 to 1900 showing little change. Lebergott, *Manpower in Economic Growth: The American Record Since 1800*, pp. 541–545.

60. Based upon the regional pattern of interest rate behavior, Davis has argued that the South was failing to attract sufficient capital and suggests various social and institutional reasons. This suggests that only the more lucrative investments attracted northern capital, and that perhaps the South wasn't enough of a "colonial economy." Lance E. Davis, "The Investment Market, 1870–1914: The Evolution of a National Market," *Journal of Economic History*, 25 (September 1965), 355–399.

It is usually argued that the emancipation of slaves merely re-distributed wealth from plantation owners to freedmen, with no change in its total value, but it may be that the value of human capital was reduced by the ending of the slave system and the racist aftermath. The economic organization of the plantation system was not reimposed (land and labor productivity being less in the early freedman years), and skills developed and used by Negroes in the antebellum period often were not employed. In this sense racial discrimination could have reduced the value of human capital. It is also possible that whatever redistribution did occur did not all accrue to the benefit of the freedmen, since the new land tenure arrangement and restrictions on mobility may have permitted landowners to capture part of the incomes which would have gone to the freedmen under a different set of institutions. Ending slavery also caused income redistribution among whites, depending upon prewar slave ownership and postwar land ownership.

With respect to formal education, it is necessary to define the appropriate measure before comparing changes in the stock of human capital in the North and the South. As measured by literacy and enrollment rates, southern growth was comparatively rapid. Negro literacy climbed to over 50 percent by 1900.[61] In that year public school attendance rates for southern whites (aged 5–20) had risen to about three fourths of those for the rest of the nation and that for Negroes to one-half.[62] Placed against this greater increase in numbers exposed to formal education were the shorter school year and lower expenditure per pupil in the South, as well as the more rapid rise in expenditures per pupil in the North.[63]

61. U.S. Census Twelfth (1900), vol. II, *Population* (Washington, D.C.: Government Printing Office, 1902), p. cv.

62. These ratios relate to school attendance and were derived from the Census. The Report of the Commissioner of Education shows higher enrollment rates for both whites and Negroes in the South relative to the rest of the nation. The white rate was over 90 percent that of the rest of the nation, and the Negro over 70 percent. See U.S. Bureau of Education, *Report of the Commissioner of Education for the Year 1899–1900* (Washington, D.C.: Government Printing Office, 1901), pp. lxvi, 2503; and U.S. Census, Twelfth (1900), vol. II, *Population*, pp. lxvii, 351.

63. See U.S. Bureau of Education, *Report of the Commissioner of Education for the Year 1899–1900*, pp. lxxi, lxxvii, liii, for 1870 to 1900. However, because of the sharp rise in southern enrollment rates, total southern expenditures on education, as well as expenditures per capita, rose more rapidly than those in the North. The relative costs of education in the South probably increased at a lower rate than measured by cash expenditures, since agricultural areas generally space their school years so as not to interfere with production, and, in any event, the cost of foregone opportunities was lower in the South than in the North.

In the case of the stock of human capital the major part of southern backwardness can be traced to the lower the level at the end of the antebellum period.

V. Summary

This paper has presented some measures of the relative southern income position between 1840 and 1960 and discussed several hypotheses about the causes of southern backwardness. The South has either converged upon or remained constant relative to national average per capita income throughout most of this period, with the exceptions of the 1860–1880 and 1920–1930 intervals. The material presented suggests that the first instance of divergence can be attributed to wartime destruction and to social upheaval which prevented rapid recovery from the impact of the Civil War, and not directly to the southern antebellum economic position.

Part V *Regional Models*

J. W. MILLIMAN

Large-Scale Models for Forecasting Regional Economic Activity: A Survey*

The art of building large-scale regional economic models is relatively new. In the last decade a number of major efforts have taken place to build complex models of regional demographic and economic growth for purposes of providing regional forecasts or projections. All indications point toward greater model-building efforts and to a proliferation of models and techniques in the future. It is now time for an appraisal.

The paper first discusses some of the general problems of developing regional economic projections and then concentrates upon developments in regional model-building in the United States. A survey of seven important regional forecasting models is pre-

* Helpful comments upon an earlier draft were received from Charles M. Tiebout, Arnold Zellner, and the members of the Seminar in Regional Economics at Harvard University.

sented with a catalog of important differences and a comparative analysis of alternative approaches. The final section presents some suggestions for further research and appraisal.

Regional Economic Projections and Model Building

Regional economic projections are useful to all sorts of groups, public and private, who need to have a better understanding of the likely course of future events. Yet, difficulties arise in specifying the exact relationship between regional planning and regional forecasting. On the one hand, regional economic forecasts must be tailored to meet the special needs of various kinds of regional planning agencies. On the other hand, the various regional planning processes are not clearly understood in terms of goals, scope, and institutional framework.

Undoubtedly a certain amount of circularity and ambiguity will always condition the relationship between regional planning and regional forecasting. The planner cannot plan without having some kinds of projections in mind. Similarly, the projector cannot forecast without making some assumptions about the plans and their estimated effectiveness. Moreover, the type of projections to be made, the extent of detail required, and the underlying policy assumptions employed will all depend upon the needs of the planning agency. In other words, projections must be related to the objectives and mission of the planning unit and to the policy instruments which that unit can employ.

No generally accepted procedures or rules of conduct for combining forecasting and planning have been devised. Clearly, both activities should be mutually supporting and must proceed in joint fashion. As a practical matter, initial planning guidelines must be established and then a preliminary forecast model may be constructed. Preliminary projections often will reveal the need for information about additional variables which in turn may modify the planning assumptions. The refinement of plans and forecasts is usually the result of an iterative nature of the process. However, this refinement may be hampered by the ever-present possibility of conflicts among objectives and by the sheer inability to assume a well-defined social welfare function.

Superficially, the matter of specifying goals for regional planning and development may appear to be a rather simple and obvious matter. Poor regions must grow to escape poverty, and rich regions desire to become richer. Growth of the region in terms of employment and income would seem to be a rather straightforward strategy for increasing the aggregate economic welfare of a region.

It is not the purpose of this section to explore the complexity of setting forth goals for regional development. It can be shown that one-dimensional evaluations of regional goals may be shortsighted; that a number of regional goals may exist that may not be compatible with each other. Second, it is also possible that there may not be a consensus on the ranking of goals among the various groups within a region. Third, pursuit of regional goals may not be optional for the development of the nation as a whole.[1]

The problem of congruency of goals may bear directly upon the choice of economic models for the projection of future economic activity. In particular, many mathematical models used in regional analysis employ a mathematical programming framework, which requires the specification of an objective function to be maximized—that is, the specification of a theoretical optimum. If goals cannot be uniquely specified, an objective function may be difficult or impossible to construct. Moreover, the complexity of the economic and social systems being analyzed may be so great that an optimal situation, even if it could be specified, could not be solved by present analytical techniques. Under these situations, regional models of the simulation type would seem to offer promise.[2]

It is usually desirable to construct a projection model in mathematical form that can be manipulated on a computer to illustrate the effects of alternative assumptions about goals, plans, and projections. The mathematical formulation serves to make alternative assumptions explicit and to provide a systematic framework for

1. See Charles L. Leven, "Establishing Goals for Regional Economic Development," *Journal of the American Institute of Planners*, 30: 2 (May 1964), 100–110; also Edgar M. Hoover, "Some Old and New Issues in Regional Development," Occasional Paper No. 5, Center for Regional Economic Studies (Pittsburgh, Pa.: University of Pittsburgh, 1967).

2. General reading on the use of simulation models is provided in a series of three articles published in *The American Economic Review*, 50:5 (December 1960): G. H. Orcutt, "Simulation of Economic Systems," pp. 893–907; M. Shubik, "Simulation of Industry and Firm," pp. 908–919; and G. P. E. Clarkson and H. A. Simon, "Simulation of Group Behavior," pp. 920–932. Broad philosophical and methodological treatment of the dynamic systems simulation approach is contained in Jay W. Forrester, *Industrial Dynamics* (Cambridge, Mass.: M.I.T. Press, 1961).

quantitative analysis. The technique of computer simulation is particularly wellsuited to this iterative relationship between planning and projection. We can simulate the consequences of alternative forecasts upon a given plan; we can simulate the consequences of various plans embodying different instruments and objectives upon future projections; and we can highlight important feedbacks between sectors. The model, then, is not a device for producing optimal or single-valued projections. Instead, it can be a means of facilitating understanding of complicated systems of relationships relevant to policy making. Generally, an optimal set of values can be specified only with an oversimplified model using one-dimensional goals. The planner needs to visualize sets of consequences likely to arise under many different assumptions about goals, plans, and the nature of the economy.

Regional forecasting techniques may be classified according to degree of sophistication. Less sophisticated techniques include trend extrapolation, share analysis, and simple economic base studies. More complex techniques are all the various kinds of mathematical models that make use of such tools as linear programming, input-output analysis, and complex regional accounting models.[3]

The various methods of regional economic forecasting all have a number of similarities, and each has different strengths and weaknesses. The best technique to use depends largely upon the need for completeness in the forecast and the budget and technical personnel available.[4] For many purposes the less sophisticated techniques are entirely adequate.

The sophisticated techniques generally involve the construction of complex economic models and the use of computers. Such models are costly in terms of time, talent, and date. Many of the less sophis-

---

3. The general reference is Walter Isard, *Methods of Regional Analysis: An Introduction to Regional Science* (Cambridge, Mass.: M.I.T. Press, 1960). For a discussion of economic base analysis, both simple and complex, see Charles M. Tiebout, *The Community Economic Base Study* (Supplementary Paper No. 16, Committee for Economic Development, New York, New York, December, 1962). Meyer discusses theoretical foundations and types of approach to regional studies. See John R. Meyer, "Regional Economics: A Survey," *American Economic Review*, 53:1, (March 1963) part 1 pp. 29–45.

4. Tiebout, p. 23, suggests that a community of 25,000 could carry out a *simple* economic base study using published data and indirect measures of the economic base at a cost in the $2,000–$5,000 range. Many of the models discussed in this paper, by contrast, had budgets in excess of $250,000 and required two to three years of construction time.

ticated techniques also have been incorporated to some degree in these ambitious attempts to build regional economic models. For example, one might attempt to forecast future income and employment for the state of Indiana by taking a simple percentage, or "share," of the Gross National Product and deriving an Indiana forecast from a more or less standard national forecast. The sophisticated model builder would probably attempt to formulate a complete model of the Indiana economy with all of its linkages and interdependencies; yet at several places in the model the analyst might resort to "share analysis" to derive some of the coefficients or parameters for his equations.

It is possible that the projections yielded by sophisticated models may not differ a great deal from those derived by less costly means. In fact, simple straight-line projections of regional economic trends may yield more accurate or more plausible results than a highly specified model taking into account interdependencies and various economic hypotheses.

Does the need for regional economic projections really require the construction of a costly, complex regional model? It would be interesting to compare the forecasts stemming from the sophisticated projection models with ones that might be derived by "naive" methods to see what variations in forecasting ability might be found. As far as can be determined, this sort of obvious comparison has not been done. In fact, very little post-audit research of any kind has been made upon these large-scale models to determine what might be learned about their reliability, their usefulness, and their theoretical underpinnings.

Very often a large-scale model effort is justified by the claim that the model is not just a device to grind out projections, but rather a tool to help understand how a complex economy works. In other words, the model attempts to portray relationships between variables within a framework designed to encourage consistency among complex relationships in line with present theories. This claim, however, is partially negated by the fact that no well-constructed theory of regional income generation exists. Moreover, there is not a common set of regions suitable for all types of regional analysis. Regions can be defined in many different ways, depending upon the types of questions we ask and the problems we attempt to solve. Consequently, regional models cannot be "all-purpose" in nature but, instead, must be constructed to deal with a particular region and a particular set of problems within a particular theory of regional growth. This means that the problem to be highlighted by the model must indeed, be important enough to justify a time-consuming, expensive model-building effort. Although asserting that models will advance our understanding of regional economic phenomena is helpful, particularly in permitting the planner or model builder to see the impact of alternative hypotheses and policies and thus to make conditional forecasts, the justification of large-scale model construction is not obvious or clear-cut.

To be fair, the issue is *not* one of having a model versus no model at all. The arguments here are clearly on the side of having a model, even a crude one, to make explicit the assumed relationships between variables. The issue, instead, depends on how complex the model should be. For example, if one were planning for the development of water resources in a river basin one would need to have a certain set of regional economic projections. If one could assume that the growth of the economy would create a demand for water resource investment in a *one-way* causation, generating economic projections very inexpensively in a "naive" fashion may be desirable. By contrast, if one had reason to believe that the water resource investment planned would change the mix and level of economic growth in the region, i.e., if the water sector would *feed back* upon the economy, then a much more complex model would be required to handle dynamic interaction between the various economic sectors in the model. No simple extrapolations of past trends could adequately account for dynamic feedbacks and new developmental growth. Of course this endorsement of complex model construction still would need to be considered against the ever-present constraints of budget, time, qualified personnel, and the need for a theoretical framework to "explain" the growth process.

Seven Regional Projection Models

During the past ten years a number of large-scale regional projection models have been developed. This section will discuss the general features of seven of these regional models to illustrate the general state of the art. This survey is not comprehensive either in terms of coverage or depth. The purpose is to set the stage for further appraisal and post-auditing of regional projection models. The seven regional models to be discussed are (1) The New York Metropolitan

Region Study by the Graduate School of Public Administration, Harvard University, for the Regional Plan Association; (2) The Upper Midwest Economic Study jointly undertaken by the Upper Midwest Research and Development Council and The University of Minnesota; (3) The Ohio River Basin Study by Arthur D. Little for the Corps of Engineers; (4) The California Development model for the state of California; (5) The Oahu, Hawaii, model for the state of Hawaii; (6) The Lehigh Basin simulation model by the Harvard Water Program; and (7) The Susquehanna Basin simulation model by the Battelle Memorial Institute.

These seven models are generally representative of current thinking. They offer a coverage that is sufficiently broad in scope in terms of the type of region analyzed and the particular study techniques to provide a general background. Some of the major regional models not covered in the survey are the Stockholm model, the Pittsburgh regional model, the Chicago Area Transportation study, The Penn-Jersey model, and the Philadelphia region input-output study.[5] A number of other state and metropolitan economic models are now under construction.

In 1956 the Regional Plan Association requested the Graduate School of Public Administration of Harvard University to undertake a three-year study of the New York Metropolitan Region, a 22-county expanse covering 7,000 square miles (in parts of three states) and constituting the most populous metropolitan area in

5. References for the major regional models not covered in our survey are (1) the Stockholm model, see Roland Artle, *The Structure of the Stockholm Economy* (Ithaca, New York: Cornell University Press, 1965); (2) the Chicago Area Transportation Study, see Irving Hoch, *Economic Activity Forecast, Final Report* (Chicago, 1959); (3) the Pittsburgh regional model, see Pittsburgh Regional Planning Association, *Region with a Future*, (Pittsburgh, Pa.: University of Pittsburgh Press, 1963); (4) the Penn-Jersey model, see Henry Fagin, "The Penn-Jersey Transportation Study: the Launching of a Permanent Regional Planning Process," *Journal of the American Institute of Planners*, 29:1 (February 1963); and (5) the Philadelphia input-output study, see Walter Isard, Thomas W. Langford, Jr., and Eliahu Romanoff, *Philadelphia Region Input-Output Working Papers*, vols. I and II, Regional Science Research Institute, Philadelphia, Pa., March, 1967. References to a number of European regional models can be found in H. Theil, *Economic Forecasts and Policy* (Amsterdam, North-Holland Publishing Co., Second Printing, 1965). Estimates of U.S. Regional export balances and regional incomes may be found in J. Thomas Romans, *Capital Exports and Growth Among U.S. Regions* (Middletown, Conn.: Wesleyan University Press, 1965).

the United States.[6] The study analyzed the major economic and demographic features of the region and made projections for 1965, 1975, and 1985. The results of the study were made public in ten separate volumes, but reference here will be confined to the summary volume and to the technical supplement dealing with methodology.[7] Many scholars view this study as the "grandfather" of large-scale regional models in the United States.

The New York Metropolitan Region model—as do all of the models considered here except the Susquehanna model—makes two independent projections of population and the labor force. Population projections were first made with standard demographic techniques, taking into account birth rates, deaths, and migration by age groups. Employment and population projections then were derived from a separate model of economic activity. Comparisons showed that the employment and population projections implied by the economic model were *higher* than those generated by demographic techniques. Reconciliation was achieved by allowing the economic projections to stand and by increasing the degree of response of inmigration in the demographic model. This "reconciliation," by changing the demographic projections to conform to the employment projections, was followed for each of the three projection years, 1965, 1975, and 1985.

The New York model is designed to forecast employment, output, and value added for 43 industrial groups for the years 1965, 1975, and 1985. It also generates estimates of employment for domestic servants and government employees, as well as disposable personal income and population. The complete system contains 47 linear equations for 47 variables (outputs of 43 industries, total population, disposable personal income, domestic servants, and government employees).

The formal economic model being described here was not put together until *after* eight earlier book-length studies of the New York region were completed. The projection model, then, was designed to utilize the data and incorporate the many special projections derived earlier and, if possible, to harmonize them and to

6. Nine counties in New Jersey, twelve counties in New York and one county in Connecticut.
7. Raymond Vernon, *Metropolis 1985: An Interpretation of the Findings of the New York Metropolitan Region Study* (Harvard Cambridge, Mass.: Harvard University Press, 1960); Barbara R. Bergmann, Benjamin Chinitz and Edgar M. Hoover, *Projection of a Metropolis: Technical Supplement to the New York Metropolitan Region Study* (Cambridge, Mass.: Harvard University Press, 1961).

make them consistent. Consequently, there was little opportunity to have the partial projections fitted into an overall model *before* they were made. Not all of these separate studies used the same background assumptions.

> This necessarily resulted in the employment of rough adaption of material developed by others. Furthermore, some of the ingredients for the model presented here simply were not developed in other parts of the study and had to be fabricated from scratch. Thus, some of the bricks were made with remarkably little straw. This is not to deny that the overall projections are of value. It may be, however, that the refinement of the method is somewhat in excess of the refinement of the data.[8]

The relation of data gathering to model building followed in the New York model is emphasized at this point to make the reader sympathetic to the difficult process of model construction and also to alert him to the thinking that went into the Susquehanna model which stressed initial model formulation *before* data gathering was started and *before* partial projections were developed.

The conceptual design of the New York model divides firms or industries into two groups: (a) those that sell on the "national market" and thus export goods and services outside the region; and (b) all other firms that are labeled as "local market" firms. These industries include those that sell exclusively to the local population and some that sell to the national market firms. In all, 43 industry groups were selected; 10 industries were completely local market and 25 industries served both markets. Total employment was conceived as the sum of employment in the 43 industry sectors plus employment in government and as domestic servants.

Essentially, total employment in the United States was projected by industry groups for 1965, 1975, and 1985.[9] Employment in national industries in the region was assumed then to be some constant "share" of the total United States employment in that industry. These exogenously derived employment demands for the national industries were then used to drive an input-output matrix for the region. The matrix multiplied the exogenously determined employment into total employment through the implied multipliers in the matrix based upon assumed local input demands, local

8. Bergmann et al., *Projection of a Metropolis*, p. 3.
9. This work was done separately by Robert M. Lichtenberg, *One-Tenth of a Nation* (Cambridge, Mass.: Harvard University Press, 1960).

consumption patterns, and local labor-force participation rates. Once total employment was found, the output and employment for each industry was derived as well as estimates of disposable personal income and total population.

Before analyzing some of the individual features of the input-output matrix, it should be noted that the factors influencing the location of the national market industries in the New York area were assumed to be *outside* the projection model. No internal devices were employed *within* the model to generate changes in the locational advantages of the region relative to other areas in the United States. In other words, the local firms serving national markets were assumed to have national market shares relatively unaffected by internal factors within the region or by the rise of competitive location sites elsewhere in the national economy. Price levels within the region were thus assumed to retain a constant relationship to national price levels so that substantial changes in the import-export mix were excluded.[10]

Conceptually the input-output framework divided the local market into three groups of buyers: business purchasers, consumers or households, and governmental units. Business purchases were subdivided into inputs for current production and purchases for investment to expand capacity. The coefficients for the purchase of interindustry inputs were derived from the 1947 input-output table compiled by the Bureau of Labor Statistics for the United States economy. Straight-line growth projections were made for purchases of capital goods.

The difficulties of using fixed input-output coefficients over time are well recognized, but it should be emphasized that the use of national coefficients at the regional level is even more perilous. There is usually little reason to expect regional and national production coefficients to be the same. The use of national coefficients at the regional level involves specifying not only the amount of inputs per unit of output, but also specifying the regional source.[11] Considering the data limitations involved, the builders of the New

10. These difficulties were recognized by the builders of the model. See Bergman et al., *Projection of a Metropolis*, p. 32.

11. For further discussions on the limitations of regional input-output models see Leon N. Moses, "The Stability of Interregional Trading Patterns and Input-Output Analysis," *American Economic Review*, 45:5 (December 1955), and Charles M. Tiebout, "Regional and Interregional Input-Output Models: An Appraisal," *Southern Economic Journal* 22:2 (October 1957).

York model had no other choice but to use national coefficients once they chose to use a regional input-output framework. Several of the models reviewed here also employed regional input-output analysis and were forced to use national coefficients at the regional level. A central preoccupation with each of these studies has been to adopt simplifications designed to reduce some of the difficulties associated with regional input-output models.

Consumption purchases from each of the 43 industry sectors were computed by a simple linear consumption function based upon population and disposable personal income. Parameters were derived from a least-squares fit to time-series data on national consumption expenditures for the period 1929-1956. Apparently, family interview data were used to modify estimates in some cate-, gories when consumption patterns in the New York area did not appear to follow estimates based upon national consumption patterns.

Government expenditures were treated as a linear function of the region's population. Purchases from each local market industry were considered to be a fixed proportion of total government expenditure. Equally simple formulations were used to derive disposable personal income and total population. Disposable personal income was taken as a direct function of total employment; total population was derived from total employment by single paramenter. In both cases the single parameters were used to approximate a whole host of economic relations that would affect the level of population and disposable personal income as a function of total employment. For example, the relation of disposable personal income to employment is affected by such variables as wage rates, productivity of labor, personal tax rates, transfer payments, indirect taxes, undistributed corporate profits of firms in the region, salaries of governmental employments, depreciation on capital equipment, and nonwage and salary incomes. All of these complex factors and relationships were expressed in a single constant.

Perhaps this survey of the New York Metropolitan Regional model will serve to illustrate some of the difficulties and anomalies that face a regional model builder. This model, a pioneer when constructed, has a number of strengths and weaknesses; model building can seldom be satisfying on all counts. Parts of the model seem incredibly simple or crude, while other features employed the most rigorous techniques then available. The final cautions of the Study Director, Raymond Vernon, are worth quoting:

This is the insubstantial stuff that our projection—that practically any economic projection—is made of. No projection of the economic and demographic characteristics of a metropolitan area can be free of the risk or error; no public or private planner can afford to assume that the potential error is small. From a policy standpoint, this may suggest that planners and investors should regard the preservation of flexibility as a virtue in itself, a virtue worth paying for at the seeming sacrifice of other standards of performance.[12]

THE UPPER MIDWEST ECONOMIC STUDY

The Upper Midwest regional study was designed to develop basic data for 1960 and to make projections of employment, income, population, and migration for 1975. The study was begun in 1960 as a joint venture between the Upper Midwest Research and Development Council and The University of Minnesota. The Upper Midwest region was taken as coincidental with the Ninth Federal Reserve District which included Montana, North Dakota, South Dakota, Minnesota, and 26 counties in northwestern Wisconsin and the Upper Peninsula of Michigan. In 1960 the region had a population of 6.3 million people and a land area of 411,999 square miles.

The component states shared many similar growth experiences, with employment closely tied to the processing of natural resources. Employment and growth rates were below the national trends, as was per capita income. The homogeneity criterion for "regionality" of the six states was derived from its common Federal Reserve District affiliation and apparently from a moderate degree of economic interdependence of the economic activities in the area.

The institutional framework for undertaking common regional policies in the Upper Midwest region would seem to depend upon cooperation between the various state and local governments and collateral help from the Federal Reserve Bank and private companies with developmental interests. Regional policies could not be extensively implemented based upon this sort of loose-knit institutional base, although this kind of cooperative regional action was assumed by the research team to influence economic development. However, the economic understanding of the problems and prospects of the region developed in the study can help the fragmented mix of public and private decision makers to deal more

12. Vernon, *Metropolis 1985*, p. 196.

effectively with their own individual, localized problems. The final study report was published in 1965.[13]

In common with most of the large-scale regional studies, the projections of the Upper Midwest group are not the product of one large overall model, the major exception being the Susquehanna model. Instead, the formal model utilizes the interregional multiplier[14] and is designed to provide estimates of income and employment under various exogenous or independent assumptions about population increase, migration, and unemployment.

The assumptions and the determination of the demographic variables do not evolve from the economic model itself.[15] Instead the model took as an input certain basic assumptions about population levels in 1975—that is, zero out-migration or enough out-migration to maintain 1960 unemployment rates in 1975, and then it projected the kind and level of employment needed to be consistent with the 1975 "targets." In this sense the projections are partial ones *not* designed to predict the future course of the variables but to show instead what economic trends are implied by certain exogenously derived assumptions about terminal (1975) unemployment and migration rates.

The basic set of projections for 1975 are labeled as "neutral" projections and are based upon five major planning assumptions:

(1) that projections made by the National Planning Association for regions outside the Upper Midwest will be realized;

13. A number of technical and study papers issued earlier by the Upper Midwest Economic Study are also available. Most of the discussion in this section is based upon the final report. See James M. Henderson and Anne O. Krueger, *National Growth and Economic Change in the Upper Midwest* (Minneapolis, Minn.: University of Minnesota Press, 1965).

14. The major formulation was by Lloyd Metzler, "A Multiple-Region Theory of Income and Trade," *Econometrica*, October 1950. A discussion of the interregional trade multiplier may also be found in Isard, *Methods of Regional Analysis*, pp. 205–213. In simple formulations exports of the various regions are considered autonomous magnitudes. Multiple regional incomes are a sum of regional investments and exports. The multiplier shows the change in regional income resulting from changes in regional investment and exports, i.e., $\Delta Y = k\Delta(I + E)$, where Y = regional income, k = the multiplier, I = investment, and E = exports.

15. This is not to suggest that the Upper Midwest Study failed to study migration, population, and employment. In fact, some excellent work on these matters was done in two study papers by Larry A. Sjaastad. Migration and population projections were made for 13 age groups for 31 state economic areas. Rural migration projections were based upon multiple-regression relationships between age, farm income, farm structure, and rural migration in the 1950–1960 period. Urban populations were projected separately. However, there were no feedback relationships between the demographic and employment and income sectors.

(2) that Upper Midwest sectors will maintain their 1960 shares of the regional and national markets that they serve;

(3) that Upper Midwest sectors will realize labor productivity increases at nationally projected rates;

(4) that Upper Midwest sectors will realize income increases at nationally projected rates; and

(5) that the labor force in each Upper Midwest State will increase at the same rate as total employment.[16]

Comments on some of the implications of these assumptions will be made below, although the reader will note that many of the relationships assumed initially are often the very things that many regional models attempt to project. For example, assumption (5) says that the unemployment rate for each state in 1975 will remain at its 1960 level.[17] Given this "neutral" assumption, the economic projections of the model are then used to derive population estimates based upon the amount of out-migration needed to reconcile natural population growth with the assumed 1975 unemployment rates. In other words, the problem of unemployment in 1975 is abstracted at the beginning and the projection concentrates upon predicting out-migration.[18]

The Upper Midwest model is one of the partial equilibrium variety, as well as being relatively static in its structural makeup. It projects economic activity with independent demographic variables affecting the size of the labor force determined outside the model. In addition, a large element of dynamic realism is lost when it assumes, as in number (2) above, that regional industries will maintain in 1975 the same national market shares they held in 1960.

The authors caution that if the assumption underlying these "neutral" projections are violated, the projections will not be

16. Henderson and Krueger, *National Growth*, p. 21.

17. The 1960 unemployment rates were: Montana 6.8 percent, North Dakota 5.6 percent, South Dakota 4.1 percent, Minnesota 5.0 percent, N.W. Wisconsin 6.1 percent, and Upper Michigan 10.4 percent. The corresponding national rate for 1960 was 5.0 percent.

18. Some attention was also paid to alternative employment projections needed to employ the labor force under various assumptions about the degree of out-migration. The less the amount of out-migration the greater the needed increase in nonagricultural employment designed to maintain 1960 unemployment rates. Henderson and Krueger, *National Growth*, pp. 27–28.

accurate. Yet there is no discussion of the "accuracy" of the five planning assumptions themselves. This position of "neutrality" is rationalized by stating, "Accurate predictors, however, would not be of much use for regional policy analysis since they could imply nothing much could be done about the future course of economic development."[19] One might respond that an attempt to be more dynamic, perhaps by developing changes in unemployment rates within the model or by systematically looking at variables likely to affect national market shares, might also be useful for the design of regional policy. It is not clear why attempts to introduce accuracy, realism, or dynamic factors would necessarily imply that nothing could be done about the course of economic development. Conceivably, policy actions would have a chance for greater effectiveness with more accurate predictions rather than with ones known to be less accurate. A more important test of a regional model is its ability to predict the impacts or outcomes of various regional policies.

The economic model itself is a variation on the interregional multiplier framework. The input-output approach involves setting up an interindustry matrix for the region. Influences from the outside would operate on the region either through an import-export sector[20] or through estimates of shares of national demands operating on specific industries, which then drive a regional input-output matrix.[21] In contrast, the Upper Midwest model concentrates upon interregional trade flows to specific regions instead of interindustry sales to specific industries. This means that the questions of the stability and size of interindustry coefficients needed for other types of input-output models can be put aside. However, the assumed size and stability of the flow coefficients governing trade flows to the various regions is now crucial; hence, the need for assumption number (2).[22]

The formal model uses 38 income-generating sectors, or "industries," plus exogenous estimates for agricultural and military

19. *Ibid*, p. 21.
20. See the Stockholm model in Artle, *Structure of the Stockholm Economy*.
21. See the New York regional study discussed above.
22. The income level of each Upper Midwest state is expressed in terms of a matrix of multipliers plus the external income components of each state. The six Upper Midwest states are endogenous; all other regions are exogenous. Different multiplier values were calculated for the 1960 and the 1975 neutral projections. Henderson and Krueger, *National Growth*; p. 161.

income. Sales for each of the 38 sectors are computed for each of the 6 states and for 9 regions (7 in the United States) encompassing the rest of the world, making a total of 15 regions. Income for each state and for each industrial sector is derived from total sales by a parameter specifying the proportion of sales accruing as income payments.

The flow of sales to the various regions was estimated from data in the 1958 Census of Manufactures. These sales formed the basis for estimates of flow coefficients tying the sectors and states to their various regional markets.[23] The flow coefficients were assumed to remain constant to 1975. Other coefficients were then used to convert sales estimates by sector and by state to employment categories. Levels of national demands for 1975 were computed exogenously. For example, national and foreign demands for 1975 were derived from projected values for personal income population and total sales of industries developed by the National Planning Association (NPA). With demand or purchase levels given, the interregional trade matrix was able to develop sales, employment, and income projections for each of the Upper Midwest states for 1975.

The formal model contained 690 equations, 921 variables, and 2,784 parameters and was said to be "far too large for convenient projection."[24] Therefore a greatly simplified model using only 6 equations (684 equations were collapsed) was used to get total state incomes expressed as direct functions of purchase levels (demands by external regions). Once total income levels by states were computed reference was then made to the expanded model to derive income and employments for each of the employment sectors.

Much of the validity of the model from a conceptual point of view hinges upon the stability of the coefficients describing interregional trade patterns, particularly the assumption that the Upper Midwest sectors will have the same shares of the regional and national market in 1975 that they had in 1960. Some observations on the New York regional model also apply here. Stability of market shares implies either that all of the many factors affecting relative price levels between regions and the other locational attributes affecting the ability of 38 sectors to sell in 15 regions must remain rel-

23. Sales are assumed equal to output, implying no inventory increases or decreases (Henderson and Krueger *National Growth*, p. 162).
24. *Ibid.* p. 160.

atively unchanged or that changes offset each other. These are heroic assumptions, especially when historical regional growth trends in the United States seem to show all sorts of dynamic shifts and changes.[25] On this same point, constant export market shares would seem to imply that as other regions (the rest of the world) grow they would continue to import from the Upper Midwest the same percentage of all of the various products over time. This would seem to deny the influence of import substitution and agglomeration economies in other regions outside of the Upper Midwest. These factors are important in explaining past shifts in the regional distribution of manufacturing activities. The Upper Midwest model also seems to imply that the imports into the Midwest from the rest of the world will not increase relatively as this region grows. In other words, the "neutral" projection allows manufacturing employment to increase equally with the increased demands for manufactured goods in the local markets, as well as the outside markets— and this despite the fact some of the six states lost failed to maintain market shares for manufacturing during the 1950–60 decade.

THE OHIO RIVER BASIN STUDY

The Ohio River Basin projections were developed by Arthur D. Little, Inc., for the Corps of Engineers as part of a comprehensive study of water development activities in the basin. The model was designed to provide 50-year projections (1960 through 2010) of employment and income for the entire Ohio River basin.[26] This area covered parts of 10 states and 400 counties. It included 163,000 square miles and one-tenth of the nation's population, second in size only to the Upper Midwest study. Because the drainage basin did not conform to state lines it was necessary to rely upon the county as the basic political unit for purposes of data sources. This feature along with the size of the area imposed difficult constraints upon data availability.

Can such a large area, defined in watershed terms, actually rep-

25. See Harvey S. Perloff, Edgar S. Dunn, Jr., Eric E. Lampard, and Richard E. Muth, *Regions, Resources and Economic Growth* (Baltimore, Md.: Johns Hopkins Press, 1960), pt. IV.

26. Arthur D. Little, Inc., *Projective Economic Study of the Ohio River Basin*, Appendix B. Ohio River Comprehensive Survey Volume III. Prepared for the Corps of Engineers (Washington, D.C.: U.S. Government Printing Office, 1964). Similar studies are now under way in 10 major river basins.

resent an economic region or integrated economy? With the exception of a few industries having direct dependence upon the river—access to water transportation or water supply, for example—it seems likely that much of the economy of the area is not tied in any important way to the Ohio River. It is even doubtful that some of the large cities located directly on the river, such as Pittsburgh, Cincinnati, and Louisville, have many economic activities that are interdependent. In other words, river basins may not be good regions for dealing with economic development even though rivers themselves may be "correct" regions for water-related activities and for dealing with water problems.[27]

The Ohio River study concentrated on developing equilibrium estimates of the supply of and the demand for labor by decades over a 50-year period. The supply of labor was projected separately in a standard demographic model based upon cohort-survival techniques involving estimates of births, deaths, and migration. Assumptions were then made concerning labor force participation rates and unemployment rates to determine the supply of labor.

The demand for labor was based upon a modified input-output model using 29 separate sectors, including 27 major industry groups, one government sector, and one nonclassified sector. The demands for each industrial sector were derived in turn from final demands for consumption, for capital formation, government, defense, net exports, and for interindustry demand. The total demand for labor was achieved by solving a set of simultaneous linear equations describing the demand sectors.

Reconciliation of the separate supply and demand for labor forecasts would not be undertaken unless the two estimates differed by more than 10 percent. This was not the case, and the differences ranged from +6.42 percent to −5.54 percent.[28] A consensus was achieved by simply averaging the two sets of projections for each preceding projection year and checking back to make all of the numbers consistent with the "equilibrium" projections. This feature, however, would make the model difficult to rerun with changed assumptions—for example, a different set of birth rates—because of the reconciliation problem.

27. However, this model does *not* contain a water sector.
28. The discrepancy was computed as a demand/supply projection ratio. For 1980 demand-based projections exceeded supply-based projections by 6.42 percent; for 2010 demand-based projections fell short of supply-based projections by 5.54 percent. Arthur D. Little, *Steady of the Ohio River Basin*, p. 118.

Total output in the basin was taken as the sum of demands for 29 sectors derived from six sources of demand: the five final demand sectors of consumption expenditures, investment expenditures, government expenditures, defense expenditures, and net exports, plus the interindustry demands. Consumption and interindustry demands were derived endogenously within the model. The estimates of demands for investment, government spending, net trade balances, and for defense expenditures in the basin were derived exogenously from national projections by the National Planning Association. These exogenous demands were used to drive a modified input-output matrix to generate interindustry demand and consumption employment and thus finally arrive at total employment.

For the modified input-output framework, Arthur D. Little used only 81 interindustry coefficients instead of the 729 that would have been required by a full 27-industry matrix. They hoped that the data from the 1958 input-output study would be available for use in constructing the model. The 1958 study was not published until the fall of 1964[29] so Little had to "update" coefficients from the 1947 input-output study. In other words, the Ohio River study was not only forced to use national coefficients at the regional level—a somewhat shaky procedure itself—but the coefficients used were seriously out of date. The "updating" of the 1947 coefficients proved to be a difficult task. As a short-cut, Little used the region's share of national employment at the one-digit level of the Standard Industry Classification Code (SIC) to modify the 1947 interindustry coefficients. The use of 81 coefficients (27 × 3) also was a short-cut device that allowed for substitution among inputs *within* each subtotal as long as the *sum* of inputs remained a fixed proportion of total output.

In the Ohio River study the basin's investment demands were derived from national projections for investment by assuming that the basin's share of investment was the same as its share of total national output. Net exports demands for seven industries, which were large exporters, were related directly to national growth trend projections. For the other 21 industrial sectors Little estimated net-trade balances by assuming them to be a constant share

29. Morris R. Goldman, Martin L. Marimont, and Beatrice N. Vaccara, "The Interindustry Structure of the United States: A Report on the 1958 Input-Output Study," *Survey of Current Business*, 44:11 (November 1964).

of total output for each of the industries. Consumption functions for the Ohio River basin were derived by assuming that the consumption expenditures were the same functions of disposable personal income in the region as they were for the national economy.

In some ways this model is a clear example of the general tendency among regional models employing input-output frameworks to take a great deal of care in devising frameworks depicting fairly sophisticated structural relationships within the region, but spending relatively little time assessing the exogenous or independent variables which are assumed to drive the matrix to generate total employment. This is not just a matter of attempting to secure data for elusive regional coefficients of intermediate demands; it is also a matter of philosophy concerning model building. Leven pointed toward this apparent inconsistency when he argued:

> . . . it seems fair to ask whether it is easier to predict the independent variables in a system than to predict directly these dependent variables in which one is specifically interested. It is not clear that the independent variables can be predicted more easily. And, if not, the moral should be clear: there is a legitimate basis for skepticism about the use of sophisticated analytical systems simply for the purpose of obtaining more accurate predictions of such major regional economic aggregates as employment, population or income.[30]

A proper response to this argument is that the use of a sophisticated system, such as a regional input-output matrix, is probably justified when we wish to predict in fine detail and to describe complex interrelationships between sectors. However, the smaller the region and the more "open" the economy the less important will be the internal interindustry relationships and the more important will be interregional trade flows of imports and exports to the rest of the world. Nevertheless, the point seems well taken that accurate predictors depend equally upon the derivation of valid exogenous estimates as well as sophisticated structural frameworks.[31]

Another question concerning the use of the input-output framework in this case is whether the interindustry coefficients *really*

30. Charles L. Leven, "Establishing Goals for Regional Economic Development," *Journal of the American Institute of Planners*, 30:2 (May 1964), 101.

31. The sophisticated structural framework in the Ohio study, however, is limited to the economic sector. As indicated earlier, no attempt was made to explicitly tie the demographic and economic sectors together.

show regional interdependencies among the 27 industrial sectors. This reservation is separate from the question that the regional coefficients may differ from national ones. Assume for the moment that the national coefficients do, in fact, hold for the same industries in the Ohio River basin. In that case a given increase in demand for output A would not necessarily generate the same demands for inputs to A *in the region*, even though the amount of inputs to produce a unit of A were correctly specified. As stressed earlier, the Ohio basin was defined in river basin terms, and the economic interdependencies between various parts of the region appear to be weak. Arthur D. Little did *not* conduct a separate trade-flow analysis. As a result, the regional multipliers and spatial linkages, so important for regional analysis, could well appear stronger in the input-output framework used in this study than actually would be the case. Regional input-output multipliers, therefore, involve two factors: the amount of inputs used to produce given outputs (the technical coefficients) and the locations where these inputs are purchased (interregional and intraregional trade flows).

Separate projections were also provided for 19 subareas in the basin. These were done by fitting least-square regression equations to each subarea's share of total employment for each of the 29 employment sectors from six historical observations. A lag of time was employed to damp the effect on growth implied by historical trends. This means that the projections for individual subareas were *not* made independently of the projections for the basin as a whole and therefore did not take into account internal factors influencing subarea growth.

Ostensibly, the purpose of the Ohio River projections was to provide guidelines and back-up data to the Corps of Engineers and to public agencies interested in various kinds of water resource-related investments in the region. The projections that were developed did *not* consider water qualities or water quantities for any of the activities specified. This is a river-basin model that does not contain a water sector. In fact, the Corps instructed Arthur D. Little to make its projections on the explicit assumption that *water would be available at all times in sufficient quantities and qualities to support the projected economy.*[32]

Perhaps some of the implications of this assumption should be

32. Arthur D. Little, *Study of the Ohio River Basin*, p. 3.

spelled out. On the one hand, it could be inferred that the threshold cost of water in terms of quantities and qualities would *not* rise in the future despite the growth of population and production in the basin. This, in turn, would imply *either* that no future water shortages would occur *or* that possible water constraints in terms of quantities or qualities would be modified or removed in such a way as not to affect water costs in the basin. The first alternative is a possibility, of course, but it is not one which the Corps of Engineers usually endorses. The second possibility would mean that additional investments on the river (public and private) would be made at no cost to the region. This possibility does not seem very plausible despite the fact that river works construction by the Corps of Engineers is largely subsidized in relation to the region in which the works are built.

On the other hand, it could be inferred that water resources, even though a necessary input to all kinds of economic activity, are not in themselves important factors in determining the economic growth of a region. In this case, increases in the threshold cost of water might influence the use and consumption of water somewhat, but the economic growth of the region would depend upon more fundamental factors determining the location of economic activity and the rate of growth of the national economy.[33] It is not likely that the Corps of Engineers would endorse this possibility either, because it suggests that river basin investment would be an unlikely candidate for accelerating economic growth in the Ohio River basin.

Of course the river works construction *itself* might have some feedbacks to the economy and thereby affect employment and income projections. For example, in the Susquehanna model, river works construction generates employment during the actual period of construction. A second feedback may occur if the projects themselves generate *new* employment opportunities in the long run in the region—employment for example, stemming from recreation. In general, it would seem desirable for river basin projection models to build a water sector into the model in the beginning to take into account possible feedbacks from the economy to the water and possible feedbacks from the water sector back on the economy.

33. For some evidence on this point see Charles W. Howe, "Water Resources and Regional Economic Growth in the United States, 1950–60." Mimeographed paper (no date) at Resources for the Future, Inc., Washington, D.C.

Otherwise it may be difficult to formulate valid regional employment projections and even more difficult to determine the economic feasibility of prospective water investments in the basin.

THE CALIFORNIA DEVELOPMENT MODEL

The California Development model was designed to forecast personal income and employment on a quarterly basis by major industry groups for the state of California from 1960 to 1975. The projections were commissioned by the State Office of Planning in connection with the preparation of a State Development Plan. The study was financed jointly by the state of California and by a 701 planning grant from the Housing and Home Finance Agency.[34]

The California model has two different versions. The Phase I model was developed by Arthur D. Little under contract with the Office of Planning. This model was widely anticipated in the profession but references to it have been largely confined to one journal article because the final report describing the model was never made public.[35]

Subsequently, a Phase II model was constructed under contract with the Institute for Urban and Regional Development at the University of California at Berkeley. This second model was completed in January 1966.[36] Model construction for each version was directed by John W. Dyckman and Richard P. Burton. Widespread rumors of difficulties in the Phase I model were partially confirmed by publication of the Phase II report, which described some serious conceptual and statistical problems in the earlier formulation.

The Phase I model projected personal income and employment for

34. By 1963 planning efforts in 22 states and 3 territories were being supported by 701 grants. For a discussion of California planning see John W. Dyckman, "State Development Planning: The California Case," *Journal of the American Institute of Planners*, 30:2 (May 1964), 144–152.

35. The Phase I report by Arthur D. Little to the State Department of Finance in 1964 was not made available for public distribution. For a general account of the model see John W. Dyckman and Richard Burton, "The Role of Defense Expenditures in Forecasts of California's Economic Growth," *Western Economic Journal*, 3:2 (Spring 1965), 133–141.

36. Richard P. Burton and John W. Dyckman, *A Quarterly Economic Forecasting Model for the State of California*, Center for Planning and Development Research: Institute of Urban and Regional Development, University of California, January 1966.

53 industry sectors by quarters (60 quarters) for the period 1960 through 1975. The basic economic framework reflected the tradition of the quarterly econometric models developed earlier for the Netherlands by Tinbergen, for Norway by Frisch, and for the United Kingdom by Klein.[37] Yet the model also combined elements of input-output analysis coupled with an export-base theory of regional growth. This amalgamation of model concepts created difficulties in the role of the interindustry sectors. The Phase I model apparently was an uneasy compromise between features requiring simultaneous solutions and procedures requiring sequential or recursive solutions.

Wages and salaries served as proxy variables for output. Multiple regressions for income and employment for each of the sectors were derived from a sample of 40 quarterly observations for the period 1950 to 1960. Explanation of patterns of trade flows for the demand sectors was thus inferred from correlative changes in wages and salaries. Constant ratios between the industry demand sectors and total output were assumed in estimating interindustry demands.

Three types of demand sectors were used: export demands, interindustry demands, and local final demands. Exports for seven categories were determined from national economic projections prepared by the National Planning Association. Once these were determined, interindustry and local final demands were developed endogenously. Local final demands consisted of local consumption demands, local investment demands, and local government demands. The model first produced estimates of wages and salaries for the various demand sectors, and employment figures were derived from these estimates. Simultaneous equations were used in the Phase I system with the claim that the model yielded "highly reliable individual industry and total industry forecasts" based upon forecast results for 1960–1962.[38]

When work on the Phase II model began in 1964, it was reported that the Phase I model would be expanded to develop an inter-

37. Jan Tinbergen, *An Econometric Approach to Business Cycle Problems* (Paris: Hermann et cie, 1937); Ragnar Frisch, *Statistical Confluence Analysis by Means of Complete Regression Systems* (Oslo, Norway: University Economics Institute, 1934); and L. R. Klein et al., *An Econometric Model of the United Kingdom* (Oxford, England: Basil Blackwell, 1961).

38. Dyckman and Burton, "The Role of Defense Expenditures in Forecasts of California's Economic Growth," p. 136.

regional model. The first phase was essentially a one-region model depicting California and the rest of the world without feedback from California to the rest of the world. California exports to the rest of the world were the generator of state economic growth. The Phase II model, as originally proposed, was to divide California into four regions so that there would be a four-region model plus the rest of the world. Again, as in Phase I the primary driving force for the California economy would come from the rest of the world through the influence of exports, but the interregional model would then generate local final demands, interindustry and interregional demands for *each* of the regions. If successful, this would have been the first operational interregional model developed for use in regional economic forecasting.

In order to secure data for this ambitious attempt, a comprehensive survey of California firms was carried out. Each enterprise was asked to apportion its sales by five geographical regions—four California regions and the rest of the world—and also by industry classification. The survey was actually conducted, but apparently the difficulties of constructing the interregional model proved to be too great because the Phase II model that actually appeared is largely a reconstruction of the Phase I one-region model and not an interregional one.[39]

The Phase II model both expanded the scope of the Phase I effort and introduced important changes in statistical methodology. The following additions were made: period of observation was lengthened to 52 quarters (13 years); the personal income section was expanded to 59 industries; some of the predetermined variables influencing the volume of exports were disaggregated; and forecasts were now provided for some miscellaneous categories—for example, types of taxable sales, which are important for estimating state revenues.

The methodological changes involved in the Phase II effort centered around attempts to reduce serial correlation and multicol-

39. The promise of delivery of an interregional model was given by John W. Dyckman and Richard P. Burton, "Some Interregional (Intra-State) Problems in the California State Development Studies," mimeographed paper presented to the Regional Science Association, Ann Arbor, Michigan, November, 1964, 17 pp. The Phase II report makes no mention of the failure to produce an interregional model except to indicate that such a model was given some trial runs that seemed promising (Dyckman and Burton, *A Quarterly Economic Forecasting Model for the State of California*, p. 9).

linearity which plagued the structural equations of the Phase I model. A second modification was the removal of triangularity in the interindustry sector.[40]

The Phase II model abandoned the triangular ordering. This model is largely recursive; that is, the structural relations are not decided simultaneously but are expressed in lags which are unidirectional with respect to time. The Phase II model was expanded to 130 equations.

In most other aspects the Phase II model retained the features of Phase I; (1) it is linear in variables and in coefficients; (2) it forecasts to 1975 by quarters; (3) it continues to use NPA projections to forecast export variables; and (4) it uses wage and salaries as proxy measures of industry output.

The summary forecast results for the Phase II model are presented for 1963–64 using actual values for the exogenous variables. Comparison of actual versus forecast values for the eight quarters (1963–64) show low-percentage deviations for such aggregate classifications as total wage and salary disbursements, personal income, and total employment; however, no comparisons were presented for individual industry figures (actual versus forecast values). In addition, the report describing the model does not apply sensitivity analysis to important assumptions of the model, nor is there any discussion of the "reasonableness" and meaning of the forecast results for the period 1964 to 1975.

Copies of the Phase II report are difficult to obtain. As far as can be learned, the model is not being used by state officials, and one can only speculate whether or not the model actually does "run" and is appropriate for its intended uses. A postaudit on the California Development model by economists might be useful to see what lessons may be offered to future model-building efforts.

THE OAHU, HAWAII, PLANNING MODEL

In cooperation with the University of Hawaii and with the assistance of a 701 planning grant from the Housing and Home Finance Agency, a team of economists developed a model for economic planning and growth for the island of Oahu, Hawaii. The study

40. For an extended discussion of these modifications see, Dyckman and Burton, *A Quarterly Economic Forecasting Model for the State of California*, pp. 36–47.

began in 1963 and the first phase of the program was completed in 1965. At that time a decision was made to extend the model to the state of Hawaii as a whole—that is, Oahu and the Neighbor Islands—and the model was taken over by the Department of Planning and Economic Development for Hawaii. In March 1966, a report of the model containing projections of the Hawaiian economy to 1985 was submitted to the Hawaii State Legislature.[41] The report was given only limited circulation and is now out of print. As a result, general knowledge of the model is limited to one journal article describing the early Oahu model and to several very general nontechnical articles on the complete model.[42] The discussion here will be confined to the Oahu model, as no major structural changes were made in the extended model.

The novel feature of the Oahu model was the attempt to quantify and to integrate planning goals *within* the model itself. The model projected the economic growth and the types and levels of certain kinds of exogenous spending necessary to achieve four planning goals. These goals, specified in quantitative terms, were related to the shape of income distribution, to desired levels of population, to external payments outside the island, and to combines budgets of state and local governmental agencies. For example, not only did the model predict total incomes but it distributed these incomes among three household categories—low-income, middle-income, and high-income households. Labor demands from the industrial, household, and government sectors were divided into demands for unskilled, medium-skilled, and skilled labor, with income used as a proxy measure of skill levels. No discussion was provided on how the planning goals themselves were to be derived. The report describing the second phase model for the entire state indicates that primary attention was given to the achievement of certain levels of population in 1985 and the ability of the economy to produce a sufficient number of jobs.

41. Department of Planning and Economic Development, *The Hawaiian Economy: Problems and Projects, A Report on the Economic Foundations of the General Plan Revision*, Honolulu, Hawaii, March 1966. 100 pp.

42. The Oahu model was described by its principal designer, Ronald Artle in "External Trade, Industrial Structure, Employment Mix and the Distribution of Incomes: A Simple Model of Planning and Growth," *The Swedish Journal of Economics*, 1965, pp. 1–23. Nontechnical articles on the complete model may be found in the *Hawaii Economic Review* published by the Department of Planning and Economic Development, State of Hawaii, Honolulu, Hawaii, for Spring 1966 and Summer 1966.

The conceptual framework of the Oahu model was quite simple. The local economy was conceived as a household sector plus 16 industry sectors, *which* included a service sector and state and local expenditures. Public investment spending was excluded from state and local expenditures. The relatively isolated nature of the island economy enabled the model builders to have more data on exports and imports than would be expected in most "open" regions. The local economy was viewed as being driven by exogenous spending divided into the following categories: (1) federal defense spending in Oahu; (2) tourist expenditure in Oahu; (3) research and development expenditures in Oahu; and (4) public and private investment in Oahu. The usual orientation for regional projections was reversed. Instead of assuming certain levels of exogenous spending to drive for local economy, this model assumed certain planning goals to begin with and then derived as an output the levels of exogenous spending in these four categories necessary to achieve the planning goals. Possible tradeoffs between types of exogenous spending and between types of goals seem not have been considered.

In contrast with many other regional models, exports of goods to the rest of the world were given a rather minor role. Exports of sugar and pineapples were predetermined outside the model, based upon trend projections over the preceding two decades on the plausible assumption that these sales were not likely to change much over time. The values of other exports were generated endogenously within the model under the assumption that given proportions of total outputs would be exported. Initially import coefficients for each household and industry were assumed to remain at their 1960 levels. Apparently future model runs were to imply sensitivity analysis on this assumption.

Coefficients for most of the equations were determined on the basis of time-series estimates. Weights assigned to variables were often allowed to vary with time; shift variables were used which allowed for some nonlinearities—as, for example, scale economies and relative price changes. Business taxes and business savings were viewed as linear functions in time. For such industries as public utilities in which products were used widely among the 16 industry sectors, sales and outputs were viewed as fixed proportions of total interindustry demand, relaxing the assumption of fixed input-output coefficients for individual demand sectors. For other industries ordinary input-output coefficients were estimated on the basis of local sales data. Noncapital expenditures for state and local governments were viewed as a linear function of total household incomes earned locally.

Total population in Oahu was derived from a sum of total employment adjusted by coefficients measuring unemployment (4 percent was used) and labor force participation rates. This population estimate was viewed as an "artificial" one, that is, a parametric constant, to be compared with side assumptions and calculations dealing with such demographic factors as birth rates, deaths, and net migration.

In pleasant contrast to many, perhaps most, regional studies, the Hawaii model apparently will not be "put on the shelf," nor will its initial projections be kept intact. The Department of Planning and Economic Development of Hawaii hopes to use the model as a planning tool and a learning device. Plans are under way to keep the model in operation and to see that it is revised and updated in the light of new information. Also, the model will be used to test the likely effects of alternative hypotheses and programs relating to such things as changes in tax rates, growth of exports, and fluctuations of public expenditures. If the model is used in this way it may improve the understanding of the Hawaiian economy and pinpoint crucial areas for further study. In addition, we might hope that model itself and the experience gained in using it will be made available for study by future model builders.

THE LEHIGH BASIN SIMULATION MODEL

The Lehigh model is included in this survey of regional models for two reasons. First, it is a river basin model that emphasizes the river and its hydrology, in contrast to the Ohio River Study. The study recommends procedures for planning, designing, and operating a system of river works to meet various kinds of economic demands. Second, the model relies upon simulation techniques. Therefore it will be important to contrast the simulation attempted in the Lehigh model with the systems simulated in the Susquehanna model. Because the Lehigh model is an outgrowth of the Harvard Water Program and the earlier study, *Design of Water-Resource Systems*,[43] a brief overview of the earlier study will be presented before turning to the Lehigh model.

43. Arthur Maass, *et al., Design of Water-Resource Systems: New Techniques for Relating Economic Objectives, Engineering Analysis, and Governmental Planning* (Cambridge, Mass.: Harvard University Press, 1962).

Design of Water Resource Systems described an ambitious attempt to integrate economic, engineering, and governmental planning and to devise new techniques for designing multipurpose, multiunit water systems. Probably the most important contribution of the book was the development of two techniques of system design—the simulation of a simplified river basin on a digital computer and the development of mathematical models for programming river systems.

The hypothetical river system involved 12 design variables consisting of reservoirs, power plants, irrigation works, target outputs for irrigation water and hydroelectric power, and specified allocations of reservoir capacity for active, dead, and flood storage. The study used monthly hydrological data on normal inflows and six-hour data for floods. These flows are then routed through the reservoirs, power plants, and irrigation systems for various periods of stream flows. The basic hydrologic data were for a 32-year period. A separate computer model was employed, however, to synthesize flows for longer periods of time, and these synthetic flows were also routed through the model. Fixed operating procedures, in conjunction with *predetermined benefit and loss functions*, were used to generate outputs and the resulting net benefits.

Although the Harvard study is an important milestone in river basin planning, it contains a number of limitations most of which are also found in the Lehigh basin model. For one thing, despite the emphasis on simulation, the study attempted to specify optimal design and optimizing procedures. The optimizing procedures were based in large part upon linear programming techniques and specified objective functions. These programming techniques necessarily required considerable simplification of the original problem, which meant target outputs and benefit functions were highly restricted and simplified and a rigid system of priorities had to be imposed. Operating procedures for facilities were fixed, and many sorts of dynamic feedbacks had to be omitted.

The attempt to find optimal solutions, then, forced the problem into channels that could be solved by linear programming techniques. Thus the study was limited even within its own framework of how to design a water system. More important, however, was the fact that the model was one of hydrology and engineering design that took the regional economy as given. All regional economic variables were fed into the model from the outside. The emphasis was placed on engineering and water management, not upon regional growth and development.

The Lehigh basin simulation extends and refines the methodology developed in the earlier Harvard study to a real world situation, namely the Lehigh River basin in Pennsylvania. The model is later extended to the entire Delaware River basin and is described in a book by Maynard M. Hufschmidt and Myron B. Fiering,[44] two of the authors of the first study. The project was largely financed by the Corps of Engineers under a contract with the Harvard Water Program. The book contains detailed reports on the steps and procedures used and is intended to serve as a guide to others who wish to design water resource systems.

The simulation analysis described in the book is designed primarily "to utilize long synthetic streamflow traces derived by statistical analysis of parameters of the historical record."[45] The planning problem is viewed as a detailed analysis of engineering and management alternatives leading to the identification of an optimal design or designs. Although in theory the model could be modified to deal with other purposes, only four uses for water were studied: water supply, hydroelectric power, flood control, and recreation. The model simulates mean monthly flows and three hour flows at flood peaks measured at six reservoir sites.[46] The major construction elements in the system are six reservoirs and nine hydroelectric power plants.

There is an associated unique optimal operation policy with each system design. In terms of priorities for the use of minimum flows, first priority is given to minimum flows for flood storage space at each reservoir; minimum recreation storage is given second priority; water supply output is given third priority; and fourth priority is given to hydro-energy production. Given certain initial conditions, the inflows to the system, and a set of targets, the essence of the simulation is to trace the behavior of the system over time.

Economic benefit functions associated with the targets for water

44. Maynard M. Hufschmidt and Myron B. Fiering, *Simulation Techniques for Design of Water Resource Systems* (Cambridge, Mass.: Harvard University Press, 1966).

45. *Ibid.*, p. 14.

46. In contrast, the Susquehanna model deals with water supplies, water qualities (primarily dissolved oxygen), and recreation. The Susquehanna model uses 7-day–5-year low flows and computes water qualities and quantities at various "critical points" in relation to changing economic growth patterns generated by the model.

supply, flood control, recreation, and power are then used to evaluate the results and point toward the optimal design. Benefit functions used in the model in theory combine two elements: (1) benefits which result when the system exactly meets a predetermined target, and (2) losses associated with undershooting or overfulfillment of targets in any time period. In theory the program can handle different types of investment programs, both static and dynamic, different methods of discounting benefit streams, and differing lengths of simulation periods. The term "in theory" is used because the actual model produced does not deal with many of the complexities and variables discussed in its theoretical chapters. Even with simplification and short cuts the Lehigh model represents "an enormous coding effort" and computer program (FORTRAN):

> It consists of a main routine and 22 sub-routines, and the compiled or binary object program occupies 32, 744 memory locations, leaving a scant 24 registers of the IBM 70904 computer unused.[47]

Apart from the need for simplifications and short cuts that plague all model builders, there is an important question of philosophy regarding planning for river-basin development. The Lehigh simulation model does an excellent job of tackling the problem of optimal design and optimal management of a river system under highly specified external conditions (especially output targets and benefit-cost functions) and when the system is only moderately complex. If the model is placed within this perspective it represents a very useful piece of work.

Two possible points of difference in philosophy can be highlighted regarding river-basin planning efforts in particular and simulation analysis in general. Turning to the latter point first, the use of optimizing and programming techniques often limits the researcher in the complexities of problems he can tackle. The mathematics for programming under many complex situations simply do not exist. In addition, basic difficulties of public policy stem from a lack of congruency of goals for development and an inability to specify social welfare functions.

Second, with regard to regional model building and river-basin planning, it can be argued that the two strands of analysis—regional economic growth and river works construction—are parts

47. Hufschmidt and Fiering, *Simulation Techniques*, p. 89.

of the same general system. Regional economic analysis and large-scale river-basin planning should take into account the effects of the economy upon the water and also the possible feedbacks from the water sector back upon the economy. In this view, one would be incorrect to plunge into river-basin planning by designing optimal management systems for the water variables without *first* having a general regional economic model of the basin that includes a water sector. Thus, models of the Lehigh basin type should *follow*, not precede, the more general approach.[48]

THE SUSQUEHANNA BASIN SIMULATION MODEL

The Susquehanna model is an outgrowth of a series of reports attempting to define the possible role water resources investment might play in the economic growth of the Susquehanna River Basin. The study was conducted by the Battelle Memorial Institute over a four-year period and was financed by a group of utility companies serving the region. Following the publication of the final Battelle report in 1966,[49] a book-length analysis of the Susquehanna model was prepared by six authors who served as employees or consultants to Battelle during the study.[50] The discussion here is based upon the description of the model contained in the book.

The Susquehanna model is interesting because it appears to break new ground by tying together the employment, demographic, and water sectors of a large region within a systems simulation framework. The Susquehanna model is the only large-scale model to tie the demographic and economic sectors together in one model. This means that changes in economic activity feed back upon the demographic sector and induce changes in birth rates, migration, and labor-force participation rates. The simulation-type model is

48. A short cut of interest to water economists is the case of point estimates of the "requirements" for water made by the Corps of Engineers for the years 1965, 1980, and 2010. For example the Corps estimated that flow requirements at Bethlehem, Pennsylvania, will be 570,000 acre-feet in 2010. Also, unit costs for alternative water supplies are assumed to remain constant ($88,000 per cubic feet per second) over the entire 50-year period. See Hufschmidt and Fiering, *Simulation Techniques*, pp. 35–61.

49. H. R. Hamilton et al., *A Dynamic Model of the Economy of the Susquehanna River Basin* (Columbus, Ohio: Battelle Memorial Institute, August 1, 1966).

50. H. R. Hamilton, S. E. Goldstone, J. W. Milliman, A. L. Pugh, E. B. Roberts, and A. Zellner, *Systems Simulation for Regional Analysis: An Application to River Basin Planning* (Cambridge, Mass.: M.l.T. Press, Fall 1968).

dynamic in the sense that explicit feedbacks and lagged variables exist within and between the various sectors. Finally, it is the only river-basin model to combine the economic and water sectors. Projections of water quantities and qualities are derived along with the usual economic projections. The model is also capable of showing possible feedbacks from water resources development upon the economy. In keeping with most river-basin studies, projections are made for a 50-year period.

The Susquehanna River starts in New York and flows 450 miles across Pennsylvania and Maryland into the Chesapeake Bay. In general, the Susquehanna basin is not densely populated. The entire drainage basin (27,500 square miles) had a 1960 population of 3,267,000 or which 2,630,000 were in Pennsylvania. The study area's population in 1960 was 5,220,800, the difference being mainly the presence of Baltimore in the study area but not in the basin (the city of Baltimore draws upon the river for part of its water supply).

The Susquehanna model pays much attention to subregionalization. The study area is divided into eight subregions made up of blocks of counties based upon labor market commuting patterns and retail trade areas.[51] The river flows through most of the subregions rather than providing a boundary between them. This fact allows demands upon the river at most geographical points to be related to the economy of a single subregion; thus, regionalization permits demands for water to be related to specific stretches of the river. Further, it allows for greater disaggregation in treating local differences in demographic and economic behavior. The local economies have greatly different growth rates and different economic structures—for example, agriculture, bituminous and anthracite coal mining, lime and limestone production, and a wide variety of manufacturing and processing activities.

Each of the eight economic subregions is modeled separately but in a similar fashion. The total projections, then, are a sum of the eight subregional models. In contrast, the Ohio River Study first computed total employment projections for the entire Ohio basin and then allocated shares of the total employment to each of the 19 subareas in the basin.[52] Each subregional model is composed of three

51. The eight subregions are Binghamton, Elmira, Williamsport, Sunbury, Wilkes-Barre-Scranton, Altona, Harrisburg, and Baltimore.
52. These 19 subareas were defined in terms of drainage basins and not in terms of local economic regions.

major sectors: demographic, employment, and water sectors. The demographic and employment sectors are tied together mainly through the unemployment rates generated in the economic sector that feed back upon migration, birth rates, and labor-force participation rates.

The model is limited because there are no economic feedbacks between subregions. Although the subregions were selected to minimize the possibility of economic interdependence between regions to simplify the model, some distortions may possibly have been introduced for some industries purchasing inputs outside a particular subregion but still within some part of the study area. Multiplier effects from household expenditures, however, would appear to be fairly well captured by the labor force commuting patterns used in the subregionalization.

The water sectors of the subregional models are not independent, because each region's water sector must reflect economic activity upstream as well as in its own subregion. In turn, this activity alters the quantity and quality of water available in all downstream regions. The water sector should be viewed as a "technical" section. In theory it could be replaced or augmented by other technical sectors that might be studied in relation to economic growth—for example, a minerals sectors or a transportation sector. However, this particular region was selected because it is river basin-oriented. Thus, although one might want to pull out the water sector and substitute a transportation sector to see its relation to economic growth, the results might not be very interesting unless the region itself were redefined.

This rather elaborate and interesting model of regional economic growth, with the potential for redesign because of its modular construction, unfortunately will be necessarily limited in its application to more general problems of economic growth because the Susquehanna region is defined in basin terms. The formal model, therefore, has only limited application to problems of regional economic development not related to water resource policies or to this particular region. This observation may be even more important if we find that water resource investment itself is a poor tool for stimulating economic growth, as the Susquehanna model seems to show. Perhaps greater attention should be directed toward defining regions that have economic meaning for a greater range of technical sectors. This problem will become more acute and important when future developments make it possible to link together several regional growth models.

The model for each subregion contains approximately 200 equations to describe the demographic, economic, and water sectors. Thus, the complete Susquehanna model contains 1600 equations. The model, although large in size, is relatively simple in makeup. Most of the individual equations are simple, and the subregionalization and modular construction also serve to reduce the complexity that often comes with large models.

The simulation technique employed in the Susquehanna model is one of the "industrial dynamics" variety.[53] It employs continuous simulation. With the digital computer, a set of simultaneous differential equations are approximated by a set of nonsimultaneous difference equations. It is possible, of course, to simulate "conventional" econometric models, but the primary obstacle lies in the difficulty of solving large sets of nonlinear simultaneous equations.[54]

The demographic sector of each subregional model is disaggregated into six age classes that appear to have homogeneous birth, death, and migration characteristics. People enter an age class by aging from the previous age category or by in-migrating; people leave the age class by aging, dying, or out-migrating. The demographic sector is viewed as the "supply of labor," and the employment sector provides "the demand for labor." The major equilibrating mechanism tying labor supply and demand is migration. In the model, migration is specified as a function of the difference between subregional and national unemployment, and national unemployment is specified exogenously at 5 percent.

For most subregions it was found that a zero differential in unemployment compared to the national rate still produced out-migration. The migration functions vary a great deal between age classes. This differential response in turn alters overall per capita birth and death rates. Because migration is so volatile and because of its feedback on births and deaths, it is potentially the most dynamic element causing population change in a region. Clearly, migration is influenced by factors other than regional unemployment

53. Forrester, *Industrial Dynamics.*

54. Irma Adelman and Frank Adelman, "The Dynamic Properties of the Klein-Goldberger Model," *Econometrica*, 27 (October 1959), 596–625. In the Susquehanna study, more than 200 major simulations of the model were made.

rates. One is also haunted by the knowledge that measurements of unemployment rates are subject to error. Further refinements on the Susquehanna migration functions appear necessary. Yet the demographic formulations in the Susquehanna model are interesting for their direct and dynamic ties with the employment sector and for their disaggregation by subregions.

In addition, the Susquehanna model contains some preliminary work on the relation of skill levels and education to key variables such as labor force participation rates and migration. In several simulation runs, the model migrated highly educated people more rapidly, and this in turn affected the skill level of the entire subregion. It was also postulated that skill levels affect labor productivity in such a way as to change wage costs in a subregion relative to the nation. Simulation runs over a 50-year period proved very sensitive to assumptions about the impact of build-ups or declines in skill levels. These results appear to suggest that expanded treatment of skills may enhance understanding of regional growth.

The employment sector of the Susquehanna incorporates the export-base theory of regional growth. Total employment is a sum of export employment, business-serving employment, and household-serving employment. An income sector is "tacked on" to the employment sector. This sector computes a version of personal income in terms of 1960 dollars, based upon wages, salaries, and selected transfer payments. Unfortunately, the income sector does not feed back upon the economy in the present model.

As might be expected, some problems are involved in classifying industries into the three major groupings. Some arbitrary decisions are usually necessary; for example, in most two-digit SIC manufacturing industries, numbers 20 through 39 are classified as export industries. Household employment is considered as a linear function of total population. Some students would rather see per capita income play a more direct role in determining this type of employment, even though a trend factor increases the percentage of service employment over time. Business-serving employment is specified as a linear function of total employment minus business-serving employment. Parameters for both relationships are estimated by cross-sectional analysis of subregional data. No explicit employment multipliers tie business-serving and household-serving employment directly to export employment.

The interesting feature of the employment sector is the attempt to treat endogenously various locational cost influences on the ability of export industries to compete in outside markets. The relative attractiveness of a subregion to industry in relation to other areas where it might locate is treated explicitly through a relative cost index embodying transportation and labor costs. Market area demands, for a subregion's exporters, are specified exogenously and are derived from national projections made by the National Planning Association.

This attempt involves a fairly high degree of aggregation and a number of simplifying assumptions. The manufacturing industries are divided into four industry groups thought to have homogeneous cost characteristics with regard to wages and transportation costs: capital-intensive processors, labor-intensive processors, durable fabricators, and nondurable fabricators. For each industry group a cost index is developed that measures the relative cost of conducting operations in a particular subregion. The cost indices incorporate simple measures of labor costs, transportation costs of raw materials, and transportation costs of product to market. For example, the ratio of total payroll to value of shipments is used to indicate the importance of labor costs, and the value of shipments per ton of product shows the importance of transportation costs. The cost indices are modeled to change over time to reflect changes in the comparative costs of production in a subregion in response to its own pattern of growth.

This attempt to show the effect of feedbacks from a change in the level and mix of activity in a subregion on its employment growth in subsequent time periods is an extremely complicated matter. It is fair to observe that the Susquehanna model is only partially successful in implementing this concept. As presently conceived, only the region's relative wage level (a surrogate for labor costs) is modeled to respond to changing industry mix (low-wage versus high-wage industries) and to the degree of local unemployment. Other potential feedbacks from a region's industrial growth pattern on its comparative costs are not included in the model.

The dynamic approach taken in this model can be contrasted with procedures used to estimate export employment over future periods in other models which often extrapolate regional export activity as some share of national demand projections. These procedures implicitly assume that the comparative advantages of a region in terms of its cost characteristics will not change over time even though the growth patterns themselves are changing. The Susquehanna model makes only a small beginning, but does attempt to place industrial location theory within the context of a regional growth model and to depict the feedback nature of growth on comparative costs.

The water sector in the Susquehanna model simulates conditions in the river relating to water quantities and qualities as the economy grows, as different levels of treatment of effluents are applied, and as different levels of river works construction are assumed. That is, the water sector shows the economy acting on the river. It is capable, also, of showing feedbacks from the water sector upon the economy in terms of possible cost increases resulting from increased water use that might affect employment and household demands; however, few such feedbacks are identified. Largely because the Susquehanna economy is small in relation to the flow of the river, various simulations of economic activity over a 50-year period disclose only a few potential trouble spots in terms of organic pollution, as measured by dissolved oxygen. As far as water quantities are concerned, no potential shortages are uncovered. These results are insensitive to alternative assumptions about regional growth and about water consumption.

Two feedbacks from the water sector to the economy are identified, the economic impact of river works construction activity and employment generated by increased recreation at reservoirs that might be constructed in various subregions. Construction activity is converted into employment (both local and imported workers) during the period of construction. Three levels of river works are assumed, ranging from low scales to an elaborate system of works. The impact of construction activity for particular subregions is quite dynamic in terms of unemployment rates and local activity. Although the unemployment rates fall dramatically during the period of construction, they soon rise again and usually return to levels previously attained in simulations without elaborate construction.

Multiple regression analysis is employed to predict recreational attendance for reservoirs that might be built. Attendance is then converted to employment by multiplying each 1000 visits by 0.142. It is assumed that "local-serving" recreational employment represents a diversion of funds from other local-serving activities. Thus, the economic growth in the model is related only to the percentage of visitors a given reservoir is assumed to attract from outside its region. Under an elaborate system of reservoirs, a measurable effect upon economic growth from recreational attendance is observed. The results, although far from perfect and only preliminary, do suggest possibilities for further research on the possible relation between recreation investment and regional economic growth.

A complete audit of "all" present water uses and an attempt to predict "all" future uses in a major river basin are often suggested when river basins are to be studied. Such comprehensiveness is clearly very costly; yet there is a question of whether such comprehensiveness is actually needed in designing a water sector as part of a regional growth model. The Susquehanna study adopts a "critical point" concept as a way to identify critical water problems and critical points in a river system. This approach concentrates initially on finding points that appear most likely to create water problems in a subregion, such as a large user on a small tributary. Separate critical points are used in relation to quantity and quality considerations. The basic premise of the critical point concept is that, if no problems appear to develop at critical points during various simulated runs of future activity, problems will not develop at less critical points. This assumption greatly simplifies the task of river modeling.

In contrast to the Lehigh model, the Susquehanna water sector is relatively simple, because the Lehigh model is designed to simulate the hydrology so that an optimal management scheme of river works and operating procedures might be devised. The emphasis in the Susquehanna study is the relation of the river to economic growth. For example, the Susquehanna model treats demands on the river only in relation to low flow periods (7-day, 5-year flows calculated by the U.S. Geological Survey) under the assumption that flows of the river at other stages will not create problems. This assumption, while plausible, is one which can be questioned. Moreover, many basic features of traditional river development, such as flood control, hydropower production, irrigation, and navigation are not modeled. The potential feedbacks of these types of water-related investments and outputs on economic growth in the Susquehanna basin are thought to be minimal or nonexistent and therefore are not considered. No evidence is presented to support these omissions. It is possible that some readers, particularly those concerned with water resource management, will find the water sector less complete than desired. Yet, comprehensiveness of a technical sector is not necessarily a virtue for its own sake when one is concerned with constructing a model of regional economic growth with limited resources and with limited "handles" on a satisfactory theory of regional growth.

Perspectives on Regional Projection Models

This paper has surveyed seven large-scale models designed to forecast regional economic activity. The models differ a great deal in their theoretical structures, in their purposes, and in the types of projections provided. Just as a general all-purpose set of regions cannot exist, models cannot be all-purpose. Instead, they are designed to answer specific sets of questions and to reflect specific kinds of approaches. Regional models, therefore, do some things better than others. As noted, each model has a number of strengths and each has some features that can be criticized. All seven models were expensive to construct. Reports on several of them have not been available for professional study and criticism. It appears that most of the models have not been kept running and operative to be studied in light of both their past projections and changing economic conditions in the study regions.

What are some of the lessons and principles relating to large-scale regional projections that seem apparent from this survey? Perhaps the most important suggestion is the need to have further appraisal and postauditing of large-scale regional models. This survey has not been sufficiently detailed in coverage or depth to provide a definitive assessment of the state of the art. To date, outside observers have expended surprisingly little effort in evaluating regional models. In addition, model builders themselves appear to have given relatively little attention to model validation. Considering the vast amounts of funds and talent expended in the past and the great potential for improvement of future modeling efforts, a definitive appraisal seems required. Our preliminary conclusion is that regional model building is an art full of promise, but one that is not very well mastered or tested.

The evaluation of regional models should be carried on at several levels. First, there seems to be a need for a "summit-meeting" or a definitive assessment of the entire state of the art to serve as a basis for seeing where we are and where we might go from here. Next, there is a continuing need to build in auditing, or evaluation, procedures to monitor individual modeling efforts as they evolve in the future. These continuing evaluation efforts, in turn, can be carried out at two levels. One is an attempt to provide evaluation and criticism by outside observers so that the model-building profession can be kept abreast of new developments.

A second kind of continuing evaluation can be provided through greater effort on the part of the model builders themselves to validate and improve their own models. It seems fair to say that most of the large-scale regional model-building efforts surveyed here concentrated all of their resources upon constructing a model and producing a set of projections. In many cases the model and the set of projections were turned over to a sponsor, and the model-building team was disbanded or shifted to new tasks. Few resources were set aside for running the model with new data to see how the model or its projections could be improved or revised. It may be a wiser strategy to build simpler and less expensive models that might be kept operative and updated over time than to embark upon an expensive all-out attempt to construct a "grand" model that is not to be kept operative, used, and useful.

This matter is more complicated than the need and ability to provide revised sets of projections to sponsors and regional planners with the related need to understand why projections may change. A major rationale for keeping models operative is internal model validation. Model builders need to rerun their models many times in order to become intimately familiar with the dynamic properties of their own models. Most statistical analysis is concerned with estimating parameters in given models. Relatively little work has been done on how to validate or find the "right" model in the first place. Proper research budgeting policy would seem to require that funds be provided for extensive validation, for reruns on the model in subsequent time periods, and for revision and improvement in model structure.

Some other preliminary observations may be in order. Most regional models surveyed here used projections provided by the National Planning Association as exogenous estimates of national demands. Although there is no apparent reason to question the NPA projections, it would seem proper that an independent assessment of the validity of the NPA projections would serve future regional model-building efforts. Second, models of regional activity would appear to profit from greater attention to subregionalization and disaggregation. Third, further attempts to tie together demographic and economic sectors appear promising. Fourth, the technique of simulation also appears to offer promise. Fifth, in the future several regional models might be tied together so that understanding of the complex problems of regional interdependence may be enhanced. Perhaps we may finally get a better picture of the regional impacts of various national fiscal and monetary policies, as well as an appraisal of the effects of regional investment programs on regional economic growth.

In summary, large-scale regional forecasting models have come of age, but there is need for a definitive assessment of the state of the art. The lessons learned will be valuable in future model-building efforts. The many possible uses for regional models suggest that an expansion of model-building efforts will be of great benefit to society.

JAMES C. BURROWS AND CHARLES E. METCALF

The Determinants of Industrial Growth at the County Level: An Econometric Analysis*

I. Formulation of the Model

This paper describes an econometric investigation of the determinants of employment by industry at the county level, the purpose

* This paper is based on a study prepared by the authors for Charles River Associates Incorporated (CRA). A complete description of the study is presented in Charles River Associates Incorporated, *Area Employment Prediction to Determine Public Facilities Requirements*, for the Economic Development Administration, U.S. Department of Commerce, Washington, D.C., under Contract C–315–65, January 1968. At the time of this study, the authors were research staff members of Charles River Associates. The authors are specially indebted to Robert Miki of the Economic Development Administration (EDA), who was Project Monitor for the study, to John B. Kaler, who coordinated the project and contributed in many ways to the final product, and to Gerald Kraft and Franklin M. Fisher, who were instrumental in the development and statistical estimation of the model presented here. Other members of CRA, especially Alan R. Willens and Thomas A. Domencich, offered many helpful suggestions.

of which is to obtain ten-year projections of employment by industry for every county in the United States.

Attempts to study the determinants of local or regional employment have utilized such techniques as base theory (multiplier analysis), regional input-output analysis, linear programming, and location analysis. In certain important respects, however, all these approaches are inadequate.[1] As an alternative, we propose the following "structural" equations for the determinants of employment in industry j in county i:

$$E_{1,t}^{ij} = f_1^{ij} (\overline{Q}_t^i, P_t^i, V_{t-1}^i); j = 1, \ldots, f \tag{1}$$

$$E_{2,t}^{ij} = f_2^{ij} (\overline{Q}_t^i, P_t^i, E_{2,t-1}^{ij}, V_{t-1}^i); j = 1, \ldots, f \tag{2}$$

$$E_t^{ij} = E_{1,t}^{ij} + E_{2,t}^{ij}; j = 1, \ldots, f \tag{3}$$

$$P_t^i = h (\overline{E}_{t-1}^i, \overline{Q}_{t-1}^i, \ldots, \overline{E}_{t-s}^i, \overline{Q}_{t-s}^i); \tag{4}$$

$$V_{t-1}^i = g (\overline{E}_{t-1}^i, \ldots, \overline{E}_{t-n}^i); \tag{5}$$

$$Q_{1,t}^i = g^1 (\overline{Q}_{t-1}^i, V_{t-1}^i); \tag{6a}$$

$$\vdots \qquad \vdots \qquad \qquad \vdots$$

$$Q_{m,t}^i = g^m (\overline{Q}_{t-1}^i, V_{t-1}^i); \tag{6m}$$

where

$E_{1,t}^{ij}$ = employment in period t for county i, industry j, in new establishments not present in period $t-1$;

$E_{2,t}^{ij}$ = employment in period t for county i, industry j, in previously established firms;

P_t^i = labor force, or "size", variable for county i in period t;

V_t^i = industrial structure indicator for county i in period t;

$\overline{E}_t^i (E_t^{i1}, \ldots, E_t^{if})$ = an f-dimensional vector of employment rates by industry in county i in period t;

1. A summary and critique of these techniques is contained in Charles River Associates Incorporated, *Area Employment Prediction to Determine Public Facilities Requirements*, for the Economic Development Administration, U.S. Department of Commerce, Washington, D.C., under Contract C–315–65, January 1968, chap. 3. The interested reader is also referred to Walter Isard, *Methods of Regional Analysis: An Introduction to Regional Science* (Cambridge, Massachusetts: the MIT Press, 1960).

and

$$\overline{Q}_t^i = (Q_{1,t}^i, \ldots, Q_{m,t}^i) = \text{an } m\text{-dimensional vector of socio-economic}$$
$$\text{characteristics of county } i \text{ in period } t.$$

The model is recursive in form with autocorrelation of the error terms likely. Furthermore, the recursiveness may be a misspecification if some of the socio-economic variables are related to *current* economic activity and other *current* socio-economic variables. For example, variables such as the wage level are probably dependent on both current and lagged (predetermined) variables.

The first two equations are essentially reduced-form relationships between the derived demand for labor and the determinants of industrial location. Alternatively, the equations may be viewed directly as specifying determinants of industrial location with employment serving as a proxy for activity or production levels. For this latter view to be appropriate we must assume a constant output-labor ratio within an industry.

In equation (1) we are concerned with location theory: why does a new plant locate in County A instead of County B? If we postulate rational profit-maximizing behavior, the sole criterion of location is long-run maximization of profits. Under this assumption all we need to consider are costs (of manufacturing, transporting and marketing, and so on) in order to determine location. Unfortunately, the cost data required for such prediction are not available. The required data go far beyond such conventional items as freight and power costs for a region. For example, the socio-economic characteristics of a region sometimes can be very important in determining costs. A highly educated, skilled labor force may enable firms to produce at a lower cost even though they must pay higher wages, or the physical, social, and cultural attractiveness of an area may be an important determinant of the cost of obtaining efficient managerial talent.

Costs of production may also be lowered as a result of economies of scale and of external economies. For example, the study of the New York Metropolitan Area by Vernon[2] highlights the role of agglomeration economies for supporting the growth of New York, an area that is otherwise poorly endowed. (It has a lack of raw

2. Raymond Vernon, *Metropolis 1985: An Interpretation of the New York Metropolitan Region Study* (Volume 9 of the New York Metropolitan Region Study, Cambridge, Mass.: Harvard University Press, 1960).

materials, a poor location relative to the national market, and a high average wage rate.) The Los Angeles study by Pegrum[3] also confirms the fact that agglomeration factors are quite significant for location decisions. In equation (1) the variables V_{t-1} and P_t represent some of these agglomeration economies. The size variable, P_t, also serves as a scaling factor.

Equation (2) relates employment in already established plants to characteristics of the county. With the exception of lagged employment, the same variables (socio-economic characteristics, industrial structure, and size) appear in equation (2) as in equation (1), but there is no reason a priori to expect the coefficients to be the same. The presence of lagged employment in equation (2) basically reflects inertia and economies of agglomeration. Because the costs of a locational change are not trivial, a plant that does not move, even though *de novo* other counties might be superior locations, may be acting completely rationally. Similarly, an establishment may not relocate until absolutely forced to do so, though relocation might be economically rational even with moving costs included. In this case, lagged employment is a surrogate for decision-making inertia. The lagged employment variable also serves as a proxy for the cumulative effect of past Q's and the unique characteristics making a county a desirable place to locate that have not been accounted for by other variables in the regression. Finally, the lagged employment variable may be regarded as a proxy for an industry's viability in a county.

Direct estimation of equations (1) through (6) raises a number of problems. For example, the data required to segregate employment in new plants from employment in old plants are not available except in cases where an industry is represented in a county for the first time; as a result we are forced to aggregate equations (1) and (2). Furthermore, it would be extremely difficult to construct an adequate formal model to determine the size of the labor force by county [equation (4)], the previously existing industrial structure [equation (5)], or the vector of socio-economic characteristics of each county [equations (6a)–(6m)]. Consequently, we simplified the approach by substituting equations (6a)–(6m) for the socio-economic variables into the two employment equations and then

3. Dudley Frank Pegrum, *Urban Transport and the Location of Industry in Metropolitan Los Angeles*, Los Angeles Bureau of Business and Economic Research, 1963.

aggregating to form the following "partially reduced form" equation:

$$E_t^{ij} = h\ (\overline{Q}_{t-1}^i, P_t^i, E_{t-1}^{ij});\ j = 1, \ldots, f. \tag{7}$$

Because of the prohibitive cost involved, we did not attempt to deal with autocorrelation of the error terms, as autocorrelation would not affect the accuracy of predictions, although as a result of the presence of a lagged dependent variable estimation of individual coefficients would be biased. Because the structural model is rather loosely specified, and because P_t is not an exogenous variable, equation (7) is not in an ideal form for estimation. However, data are available for the variables included in the specification; the direct inclusion of P_t^i removed the need for data lagged more than one period.

Equations (1) through (7) are almost certainly not linear. To assert linearity would be to assert, for example, that the absolute effect on employment of a one-year increase in average years of schooling is constant for all counties, independent of all other variables, including such "size" variables as lagged employment or total labor force.

As an alternative to linearity, we have specified the model in the following form:

$$\ln E_t^{ij} = a_j + b_{1j} Q_{1,t}^i + \ldots + b_{mj} Q_{m,t}^i + \gamma_j \ln P_t^i$$
$$+ \mu_j \ln E_{t-1}^{ij} + \ln e_1^{ij};\ j = 1, \ldots, f \tag{8}$$

$$Q_{1,t}^i = c_1 + d_{11} Q_{1,t-1}^i + \ldots + d_{1m} Q_{m,t-1}^i$$
$$+ \rho_1 V_{t-1}^i + \epsilon_{11}^i \tag{9a}$$

$$\vdots \qquad\qquad \vdots \qquad\qquad \vdots$$

$$Q_{m,t}^t = c_m + d_{m1} Q_{1,t-1}^i + \ldots + d_{mm} Q_{m,t-1}^i \tag{9m}$$
$$+ \rho_m V_{t-1}^i + \epsilon_{1m}^i$$

$$\ln E_t^{ij} = \alpha_j + \beta_{1j} Q_{1,t-1}^i + \ldots + \beta_{mj} Q_{m,t-1}^i + C_j V_{t-1}^i$$
$$+ \gamma_j \ln P_t^i + \mu_j \ln E_{t-1}^{ij} + \ln \epsilon_1^{ij} \tag{10}$$
$$+ b_{1j}\epsilon_{11}^i + \ldots + b_{mj}\epsilon_{1m}^i.$$

In equations (8) through (10), ln indicates a natural logarithm and ϵ_1^{ij} and ϵ_{11}^i through ϵ_{1m}^i are the error terms of equations (8) and (9), respectively, for county i.

Rewriting the model in nonlogarithmic form, we have:

$$E_t^{ij} = (E_{t-1}^{ij})^{\mu_j}(P_t^i)^{\gamma_j} \, exp \, \{a_j + b_{1j}Q_{1,t}^i + \ldots + b_{mj}Q_{m,t}^i\} \cdot \epsilon_1^{ij};$$

$$j = 1, \ldots, f \tag{8'}$$

$$E_t^{ij} = (E_{t-1}^{ij})^{\mu_j}(P_t^i)^{\gamma_j} \, exp \quad \{a_j + \beta_{1j}Q_{1,t-1}^i + \ldots$$

$$+ \beta_{mj}Q_{m,t-1}^i + C_j V_{t-1}^i + b_{ij}\epsilon_{11}^i + \ldots$$

$$+ b_{mj}\epsilon_{1m}^i\} \, \epsilon_1^{ij}; j = 1, \ldots, f. \tag{10'}$$

A difficulty of any nonlinear model is that linear aggregation of nonlinear functions destroys the functional form of the model unless very special assumptions are made. If the true relation is nonlinear, we have no recourse other than to fit what we believe is the true relationship to the data. If μ is close to 1 [see equation (10)], the bias from aggregation over industries will not be very serious, and if μ and γ are close to 1, the bias from aggregation over counties will not be serious.[4]

To insure that the forecasts would be roughly correct in the aggregate, as described below, the individual industry forecasts were summed and compared with national totals forecast for each industry by Clopper Almon using input-output techniques.[5] The employment forecast for each county was scaled by the percentage deviation of this sum from Almon's forecast for the comparable industry.

The aim of the model, as just developed, is to explain changes in an area's industrial activity by the presence or absence of certain socio-economic factors. For some industries, however, it should be clear that locational decisions rest largely upon the presence or absence of natural resources. Activity will be located near the re-

4. Of course, if we have reason to believe that one particular size unit is relevant, to avoid aggregation bias we would have to estimate the equations for regions of that size. The aggregation problem is therefore directly related to the correct choice of the range and domain of the function estimates. As happens so often in empirical economics, we are constrained to examine economic relationships with data that are in all probability for areas different from those relevant to the functions being examined. The two areas that we could have used for our study are state economic areas and counties. Data do exist for other small area classifications, such as metropolitan areas, but the data do not exist on a national scale in a consistent, mutually exclusive, and exhaustive form. Facing a lack of information of the relevant functional area, we chose the county as the unit of analysis, since this is the area size most relevant for EDA policy.

5. Clopper Almon, Jr., *The American Economy to 1975—An Interindustry Forecast* (New York: Harper & Row, 1966).

sources, and changes in activity will be a function of both the local supply of and the national demand for the resource. Examples of such resource-based industries are Agriculture, Mining, and Forestry and Fisheries.

An area's relative advantage in supporting a resource-based activity is dependent upon its ability to supply the "resource" at a low cost relative to other suppliers. For example, the South's relative advantage as a producer of cotton was maintained until technological innovation made the large, level lands of the Southwest more productive. Similarly, high transportation costs may prohibit an area from being a source of supply even though it possesses the necessary resources. Thus, transportation innovations can create new areas of low-cost supply, or an area's composition of "resources" itself may change. A decline or inactivity in production may, of course, be the result of depletion of natural resources.

It should be clear that one useful method of explaining variation in employment by county in industries such as Mining and Agriculture is to disaggregate these industries into as many subindustries as possible. For example, the decline of coal in relation to petroleum might explain the fact that mining employment in Arizona has been increasing more rapidly than mining employment in Pennsylvania. Disaggregation can also account for differences caused by changes in labor productivity. Some types of farming and mining have experienced greater increases in labor productivity than others.

As a consequence of these special considerations, employment projections for the resource-based industries (Agriculture, Mining, and Forestry and Fisheries) were constructed in an ad hoc fashion outside the framework of the general model. For similar reasons, ad hoc projections for the transportation industries were also made. The procedures used in these cases are described in Appendix A.

II. Data Used in the Analysis

It must be stressed that in selecting data our objective was to provide 1970 estimates of county employment by industry. The necessity of providing county estimates required that both the industrial employment measures and the social and economic explanatory variables be available in machine-processable form and be compatible over the time span being examined.

The county industrial employment data were taken from the 1950 and 1960 Censuses of Population published in *Growth Patterns in Employment by County 1940–1960* by Office of Business Economics (OBE), U.S. Department of Commerce. These data are disaggregated into 32 broad industry groups.

As the industry employment data are drawn from the Censuses of Population, they are collected by place of *residence* and are therefore not necessarily equivalent to data collected by place of *employment*. This can be a particularly acute problem at the fringes of large metropolitan areas and in counties where a major population center lies near the county border, making a significant disparity likely between the actual level and mix of industrial activity in a county and the level and mix of industrial activity in the county in which the county's residents are employed.

The list of 32 industries contains significantly more defining detail for service industries than for primary and manufacturing industries. For example, a single category, Other and Miscellaneous Manufacturing, includes such diverse industries as manufacturing of tobacco, watches and clocks, and blast furnaces.

What is included in a particular industry in one area of the nation may be quite different from what is included in the same industry in another area. A clear example is the Forestry and Fisheries category, which is likely to be mostly forestry in Idaho and mostly fisheries in New Jersey. Industry 14, Other and Miscellaneous Manufacturing, may be predominantly tobacco manufacturing in North Carolina and predominately leather products in Massachusetts.

To approach the problem of industry definition we obtained from OBE a disaggregation of state census data to 118 industries for 1950 and 1960. As described below, we used this finer breakdown in certain instances when we felt that a given classification was too broad for our purposes.

A final problem is the heterogeneous nature of the county unit. Georgia, for example, has 157 counties, while Arizona, with nearly double the land area, has only 14. Alpine County, California, had a population of 397 in 1960 when Los Angeles County had over 6 million. Although these examples may not be typical, they serve to illustrate the lack of uniformity in county characteristics and can be extended to almost any descriptive variables reported.

For our model the Office of Business Economics (OBE) 32-industry list was compressed into a 24-industry list by aggregating service-oriented industries into two groups. Table 1 shows the correspondence between the OBE industry classifications and our (CRA) industry classifications as used in this study. For our 24 industries, no econometric relationships were estimated for Mining, Forestry and Fisheries, the Armed Services, or Industry not Reported. Further, Agriculture and the Transportation Industries were estimated by special ad hoc procedures described in Appendix A.

Industry 20 includes all the industries that we felt were population-oriented. Most of the observations evidently are for bank offices, small loan offices, and local insurance and real estate agencies, which exist to serve both business and the general populace.

In many respects the activities in Industry 21 are much like those in Industry 20. We felt, however, that the activities in Industry 21, particularly Advertising, Miscellaneous Business Services, Medical Services, some of the Educational Services, and Legal, Engineering, and Miscellaneous Professional Services, require a higher degree of professionalism than the Industry 20 firms. Industry 21 firms are supported by a different type of community and require different personnel than Industry 20 firms. The former exist predominantly in communities of above-average wealth and educational attainment.

The public sector (CRA Industry 22) would be almost wholly population-oriented and, to a lesser extent, business service-oriented, were it not for the presence of Federal Public Administration employees in the data. These employees "sell" to the nation and they tend to be concentrated in large Federal Administration centers. Unlike the output of Postal Service and State and Local Public Administration, the output of Federal Public Administration is not highly correlated with population.

For the final two OBE–32 industries, Armed Forces and Industry not Reported, we made no attempt to allocate projected employment. We have no faith in our ability to develop a model that can explain the physical distribution of Department of Defense installations. Industry not Reported can hardly be considered an industry, unless one assumes that the people listed therein have some common denominator (for example, they are rugged individualists, unwilling to respond to the census-taker). In effect, we have distrib-

Table 1. Correspondence Between CRA and OBE Industries

CRA 24 Industry List		OBE 32 Industry List	
No.	Title	No.	Title
1	Agriculture	1	Agriculture
2	Forestry and Fisheries	2	Forestry and Fisheries
3	Mining	3	Mining
4	Contract Construction	4	Contract Construction
5	Food and Kindred Products	5	Food and Kindred Products
6	Textile Mill Products	6	Textile Mill Products
7	Apparel	7	Apparel
8	Lumber, Wood Products, and Furniture	8	Lumber, Wood Products, and Furniture
9	Printing and Publishing	9	Printing and Publishing
10	Chemical and Allied Products	10	Chemical and Allied Products
11	Electrical and Other Machinery	11	Electrical and Other Machinery
12	Motor Vehicles and Equipment	12	Motor Vehicles and Equipment
13	Other Transportation Equipment	13	Other Transportation Equipment
14	Other and Miscellaneous	14	Other and Miscellaneous
15	Railroads and Railway Express	15	Railroads and Railway Express
16	Trucking and Warehousing	16	Trucking and Warehousing
17	Other Transportation	17	Other Transportation
18	Communications	18	Communications
19	Utilities and Sanitary Services	19	Utilities and Sanitary Services
20	Population-oriented Services–A	20	Wholesale Trade
		21	Food and Dairy Products Stores
		22	Eating and Drinking Places
		23	Other Retail Trade
		24	Finance, Insurance and Real Estate
		25	Hotels and Other Personal Services
		26	Private Households
21	Population-oriented Services–B	27	Business and Repair Services
		28	Entertainment and Recreation Services
		29	Medical and Other Professional Services
22	Public Administration	30	Public Administration
23	Armed Forces	31	Armed Forces
24	Industry Not Reported	32	Industry Not Reported

uted Industry not Reported employment over the other industries in proportion to their projected employments, a reasonable thing to do given a complete lack of knowledge of its composition.

EXPLANATORY VARIABLES

The variables used to explain the changes in employment by industry were also required on a county basis in machine-processable form. The basic sources were tapes of the *County and City Data Books* for 1962 and 1952, published by the Bureau of the Census, containing primarily 1960 and 1950 data respectively.

Other data available in the required form for analysis included data on

(1) the availability of transportation facilities, by air, water, rail and highway;

(2) climate, soil and terrain;

(3) the distance to nearest metropolitan areas of various sizes;

(4) agricultural activity;

(5) mining activity; and

(6) the cost of oil, gas and electricity at the state level.

The form of our model required us to predict 1960 employment as a function of 1950 employment and 1950 socio-economic variables, stated in such a way that they are scale-free (i.e., proportions, averages, and so on). The following selection criteria were used:

1. Variables that represented a linear combination of other included variables were eliminated as redundant (with the exception of the dummy variables).

2. Because the models were ultimately to be used with 1960 data to predict 1970 values, variables were not used for which comparable values were unavailable for both 1950 and 1960.

Table 2. Explanatory Variables

Variable number	Variable name
1–11	Ln of 1950 employment of corresponding industry sector
23–44	Ln of 1960 employment of corresponding industry sector
45–110	Dummy variables indicating 0 employment in 1950 or 1960 for all industries
111	Ln of special constructed variable for agriculture
112	Ln of special constructed variable for railroads
113	Ln of special constructed variable for trucks
114	Ln of special constructed variable for other transportation
115	Population growth (1950 population ÷ 1940 population)
116	Proportion of population nonwhite
117	Population density (population ÷ area)
118	Proportion of population urban
119	Proportion of population rural farm

Table 2. (continued)

Variable number	Variable name
120	Proportion of population aged 21–64 years
121	Ln of population ages 21–64 years
122	Live births (one year) per family
123	Proportion of persons 25 years and over with less than five years education
124	Proportion of persons 25 years and over with less than twelve years education
125	Proportion of labor force male
126	Proportion of labor force unemployed
127	Proportion of total employed persons employed in mining
128	Proportion of total employed persons employed in manufacturing
129	Proportion of total employed persons employed in wholesale-retail trade
130	Average family size
131	Median family income
133	Proportion of dwelling units built after 1940
134	Time and savings deposits ÷ population
135	Normal maximum temperature, annual
136	Normal precipitation, annual
137	Distance to nearest SMSA of over 250,000
138	Distance to nearest SMSA of over 1,000,000
139	Terrain variability index
140	Relative extent of unionization in state, 1953
141	Railroad line variable (number of railroad lines running through a county)
142	Highways variable (number of major highways serving the largest population center in each county)
143	Cost of oil in state
144	Cost of gas in state
145	Cost of electricity in state
146	Water availability variable (variable to indicate existence of seacoast or navigable waterway in county, having a value of one if it exists and zero otherwise)
147	Median age of population
148	Land area
149	Ln of total employment
150	Employment in manufacturing ÷ number of establishments
151	State proportion of CRA industry 5 engaged in dairy products (OBE industry 10)

Table 2. (continued)

Variable number	Variable name
152	State proportion of CRA industry 5 engaged in canning (OBE industry 11)
153	State proportion of CRA industry 8 engaged in furniture manufacturing (OBE industry 27)
154	State proportion of CRA industry 11 engaged in the manufacture of office and electrical machinery (OBE industries 33 and 35)
155	State proportion of CRA industry 13 engaged in the manufacture of aircraft (OBE industry 37)
156	State proportion of CRA industry 15 engaged in the manufacture of ships (OBE industry 38)
157	State proportion of CRA industry 14 engaged in the manufacture of tobacco products (OBE industry 40)
158	State proportion of CRA industry 14 engaged in the manufacture of petroleum and petroleum products (OBE industries 44 and 45)
159	State proportion of CRA industry 14 engaged in the manufacture of products of blast furnaces, and other metal industries (OBE industries 56 and 57)
160	Variable 158 plus Variable 159
161	Variable 151 times Variable 137
162	Variable 152 times Variable 137
163	Variable 153 times Variable 123
164	Variable 154 times Variable 123
165	Variable 155 times Variable 123
166	Variable 156 times Variable 140
167	Variable 157 times Variable 123
168	Variable 160 times Variable 123

3. When a group of variables existed that could be expected to measure the same factor, the group was reduced to one or two chosen on the basis of a priori examination.

Two variables, the logarithm of population aged 21–64 (a labor force availability proxy) and total employment, were retained for use as scaling measures. The set of socio-economic variables chosen for inclusion in the preliminary analysis is summarized in Table 2. Space limitations preclude a complete description of each variable; a detailed description however, is available in the full CRA report.

As mentioned above, internally consistent forecasts provided by the Almon model of total U.S. employment in major industries were used to scale the CRA projections.

Almon presents his results in terms of growth rates of employment in the 90 sectors of his model. These growth rates were converted to 1970 estimates of employment in the 24 sectors of our model.

In order to make the projections comparable to the Census data used in out study we applied the Almon growth rates to 1960 data to obtain the 1970 projections. However, as Almon's sectors do not correspond exactly to ours we were not able to use his growth rates directly. In all cases except the transportation sectors, our industry sectors are composed of several Almon industries. Fortunately, in no case does an Almon industry overlap more than one of our industries. By using the Almon growth rate projections we were able to obtain weighted growth rates that could be applied to our industries.

Special assumptions had to be made for two industries in our model: Armed Forces (23) and Industry not Reported (24). We assumed that Armed Forces employment would remain constant at its 1960 level and that Industry not Reported would maintain its 1960 proportion of total employment. Essentially, we applied Almon's growth rate for total civilian employment to Industry not Reported.

In the case of transportation our procedure was somewhat different. Almon has only one transportation sector (Industry 71 in his model), while we have three (Sectors 15 through 17). We constrained the growth rate of the total employment of Sectors 15, 16, and 17 to be equal to the growth rate of Almon's Industry 71 and thus allowed our model to assign different growth rates to each transportation sector.

III. Special Problems

A number of problems had to be solved before the general model and the special industry models outlined above could be estimated. The most important problems were (a) the presence of observations of zero for some of the variables; (b) the excessively aggregated character of some of the industry data; (c) the presence of heteroskedasticity in the error terms; (d) the ambiguities involved in attempting to use cross-section regressions for projection; and (e) changes over time of the structural relationships.

THE "ZERO PROBLEM"

Both theoretical and mathematical problems arise when the data vector for the dependent variable (employment in a given industry for every county) contains zeros. As we use the logarithmic form of the dependent variable—employment—we must handle the mathematical difficulties that arise when an attempt is made to use the log of zero as an observation in the regression. The same problem, incidentally, arises with lagged employment, an independent variable, which is also used in logarithmic form. Other difficulties arise from the fact that zero is the lowest value that employment may take: negative employment is impossible. It should be noted that these last difficulties arise in linear as well as logarithmic models.

To handle the zero problem we separated the county data for a particular industry sector into four categories: (1) those counties with no employment in either 1950 or 1960; (2) those counties with no employment in 1950 and positive employment in 1960; (3) those counties with positive employment in 1950 and 1960; and (4) those counties with positive employment in 1950 but no employment in 1960.

As the basic model does not adequately treat zero observations, we must correct for the existence of zeros before applying it. Therefore, on the basis of 1950 and 1960 data we wish to predict which counties will pass from no employment in 1960 to a positive level of employment in 1970, and which counties will pass from a positive level of employment in 1960 to a zero level of employment in 1970.

We therefore wish to discriminate between counties in categories (1) and (2) above, on the one hand, and between counties in categories (3) and (4) on the other. That is, in the first case we wish to distinguish the socio-economic factors that are associated with counties that passed from zero employment in 1950 to positive employment in 1960; and, in the second case, to distinguish the socio-economic factors that are associated with counties that passed from a positive level of employment in 1950 to a zero level of employment in 1960. For prediction purposes we then assume that the relationships found to be relevant for 1950 and 1960 are relevant for 1960 and 1970.

We chose discriminant analysis to distinguish between the relevant categories. Discriminant analysis isolates the linear combination of variables that "best" distinguishes the elements in one set (e.g., those counties with positive employment) from the elements in another set (e.g., those counties with zero employment).

The actual procedure by which this is done is to assign a value of 1.0 to all counties in the first set and a value of 0.0 to all counties in the second set. A regression is then calculated using the vector of ones as the dependent variables and the set of socio-economic variables as the independent variables. The calculated equation then provides a linear combination of the socio-economic variables by which the counties may be ranked.

As shown in Table 3, two discriminant analyses (D_1 and D_2) were performed for each industry. In the first (D_1) we discriminated between counties in categories (1) and (2) and in the second (D_2) we discriminated between counties in categories (3) and (4). The forms of the discriminant equations were the same as the form of the model presented earlier, except that lagged employment obviously could not be included as a variable in the first set of discriminant analyses.

For those counties in the two sets for which positive employment was predicted we then calculated regressions (R_1 and R_2) to predict the magnitude of employment. The R_2 equations are identical in form to equation (10), described earlier. The R_1 equations are identical except that lagged unemployment cannot be included.

Table 3.

			Employment		Regression used
			1950	1960	
D_1	Discriminant	Case 1	0	0	
	Set 1	Case 2	0	>0	R_1
D_2	Discriminant	Case 3	>0	0	
	Set 2	Case 4	>0	>0	R_2

The purpose of the two discriminant functions was to isolate those counties which are expected to have zero employment in a given industry for 1970. An average of 377 counties (out of 3,097) had zero employment in a given industry for 1950. Of these, about 18.3 percent moved to a positive level of employment for 1960. Of the remaining 2,595 counties (average) having positive employment in a given industry in 1950, only 8.0 percent moved to a position of zero 1960 employment. In projecting to 1970 for the subset of counties with zero employment in 1950, we estimated a function to predict those counties from among the zero employment counties in 1960 that are expected to have nonzero employment for a given industry in 1970. To be selected, we required that a county's discriminant score be significantly greater than zero at a 5 percent one-tail t-test level. In predicting zero cases from among those having positive 1960 employment we required that the discriminant score be significantly less than 1.0 at a similar test level.[6]

AGGREGATION PROBLEMS

A major disadvantage of the data available for this study is that many of the industry categories are quite heterogeneous in composition. While more disaggregated data are not available by county, they are available by state. If each state had the same industry composition in each of the 32 OBE industries, state data would not add any information. Industry composition does, however, vary by state. For example, if we divide Industry 14 into tobacco manufactures, light industry, and heavy industry (primarily

6. It should be pointed out, however, that the choice of a 5 percent one-tail t-test value as a discriminant cutoff is rather arbitrary when we consider that in all likelihood we do not have error distributions approaching normality. If each distribution has error terms that are normally distributed about a mean of zero, with both having the same variance, then a t-test based on the equation standard error of estimate would be equivalent to a t-test on one section of the distribution. If the above assumption is violated only to the extent that the two parts of the distribution have different variances, then the t-test is still appropriate except that the confidence level is incorrect. It is likely, unfortunately, that the violation of the above assumptions is more severe. Not only may the error distributions be skewed, but there is no assurance whatsoever that each part of the distribution has a mean error of zero. With these problems added to a general lack of separation of the two discriminant groups, there are no clear criteria to follow in choosing a score cutoff. In setting the cutoffs, however, it is apparent that we have biased the analysis in favor of a county retaining its current status. In the absence of valid evidence such a bias is probably warranted.

oil refineries and metal works) for 1960, we find that in North Carolina 38.92 percent of Industry 14 employment is in tobacco, 45.45 percent is in light industry, and 15.63 percent is in heavy industry; in Maine 0.11 percent is in tobacco, 95.06 percent is in light industry, and 4.83 percent is in heavy industry; and in Wyoming, 0 percent is in tobacco, 15.35 percent is in light industry, and 84.65 percent is in heavy industry.

To adjust for "excess" aggregation in industries such as Industry 14, we used intercept dummy variables and coefficient dummy variables for selected variables. The procedure used for coefficient dummies is very similar to that used for intercept dummies.[7] We constructed the dummies by multiplying the data vector for the selected variables by the percentage distributions of employment by subindustry.

The basic model postulates that the socio-economic variables have a marginal impact on the logarithm of employment which is measured by their slope coefficients in the regressions. The use of ordinary slope and intercept dummies tests the hypothesis that the mere presence of tobacco, for example, alters the functional relationship. The use of slope coefficients which take into account the percentage composition of an industry in each state tests the effect of a percentage increase in, say, employment in tobacco manufactures, rather than the effect of the mere presence or absence of tobacco manufacturing.

By attributing state percentages to each county, we were able to test the following intercept-affecting dummies in the relevant industry equations:

(a) state proportion of Food and Kindred products employment engaged in dairy products and canning, respectively;

(b) state proportion of Lumber and Wood products employment engaged in furniture manufactures;

(c) state proportion of Machinery and Equipment manufactures employment engaged in the manufacture of office and electrical machinery;

(d) state proportion of Transport Equipment employment engaged in the manufacture of aircraft and in the manufacture of ships; and

7. See J. Johnson, *Econometric Methods* (New York: McGraw-Hill, 1963), pp. 221–228.

(e) state proportion of Miscellaneous Manufactures employment engaged in the manufacture of tobacco products, petroleum and petroleum products, and blast furnaces and other metal industries, respectively.

It was not feasible to use coefficient dummies for all the socio-economic variables. We therefore limited our testing to one socio-economic characteristic for each of the cases in which we had used intercept dummies. In most cases we assumed that the most crucial difference among industries would be skill requirements. Since we found that the proportion of the adult population having less than five years of education served as a useful proxy for the skill level of the local labor force, we generally tested for homogeneity of that coefficient. Food products, for which we used distance to nearest SMSA with a population of at least 250,000, and shipbuilding, for which we used a water availability dummy, were exceptions to this general rule.

THE CROSS SECTION PROBLEM

Certain special problems arise because we wish to use cross-section regressions to make projections over time. In particular, a problem arises of how to interpret the $B_j Q_j$'s. For example, in the cross-sectional equations the following two interpretations of the median income coefficient are indistinguishable.

(a) Employment differs according to differences in median income *relative* to the national average.

(b) Employment varies with the absolute changes in median income. Within a single cross section, only relative differences can be distinguished. In projecting to 1970 employment, however, the two interpretations yield different results.

If we are to accept interpretation (a), the median income coefficient should be scaled down by the ratio of the 1960 to the 1970 national median incomes. If each coefficient is interpreted in this manner, the values of the coefficients for 1970 will change relative to each other compared to 1960. If interpretation (b) is accepted, the absolute coefficient values are to be retained, but such a decision would increase the *relative* importance of variables with a positive trend such as income or education compared to variables with mean levels which are invariant over time.

There is a third interpretation which allows the absolute values of Q variables to be significant, but which has the same operational significance as interpretation (a) above. Suppose that the absolute value, say, Q_A, is relevant, where

$$Q_A = Q_N Q_R, \qquad (11)$$

$$Q_N = \text{national } Q \text{ level}, \qquad (12)$$

$$Q_R = \text{local relative } Q \text{ level.} \qquad (13)$$

If we specify that in our logarithmic function $\ln E_{60}$ is linearly related to Q_N and Q_R, we have the following:

$$\ln E_{60} = \ln c + \mu \ln E_{50} + \overline{\beta}_N \overline{Q}_N + \overline{\beta}_R \overline{Q}_R \qquad (14)$$

$$E_{60} = c E_{50}{}^{\mu} \exp [\overline{\beta}_N \overline{Q}_N + \overline{\beta}_R \overline{Q}_R] \qquad (15)$$

$$E_{60} = (c \exp [\overline{\beta}_N \overline{Q}_N]) E_{50}{}^{\mu} \exp [\overline{\beta}_R \overline{Q}_R] \qquad (16)$$

$$E_{60} = c^* E_{50}{}^{\mu} \exp [\overline{\beta}_R \overline{Q}_R] \qquad (17)$$

Similarly, if we had specified $\ln E_{60}$ to be logarithmically related to Q_A, we obtain the following:

$$\ln E_{60} = \ln c + \mu \ln E_{50} + \beta_A \ln Q_A \qquad (18)$$

$$= \ln c + \mu \ln E_{50} + \beta_A \ln Q_N + \beta_A \ln Q_R \qquad (19)$$

$$= (\ln c + \beta_A \ln Q_N) + \mu \ln E_{50} + \beta_A \ln Q_R \qquad (20)$$

$$= \ln c^* + \mu \ln E_{50} + \beta_A \ln Q_R \qquad (21)$$

In either case the effect of the absolute level of Q, as opposed to its relative level, is included in the constant, if an additive relationship is specified in the logarithmic form. Since the adjustment of our forecasts to certain control totals takes the form of adjusting the constant terms in each equation, the amount of absolute effect creates no problem and we can therefore assume that the *relative* level of Q is the relevant factor, while not ruling out a certain class of absolute Q effects.

Given the acceptance of the above criteria, we must still decide whether to hold relative coefficients constant, or whether to hold relative beta weights constant. If the variance of a given Q_R^i increases from 1950 to 1960, the assumption of a constant coefficient implies that this particular Q_R^i will have a greater impact on the variance of $\ln E_{70}$ than it did on $\ln E_{60}$. Given possible changes in the variance of all Q_R^i's, such an interpretation allows for a possible change over time in the relative power of different Q_R^i's, as well as a different predicted variance for $\ln E_{70}$ than was the case for $\ln E_{60}$.

If we hold relative beta weights constant, on the other hand, we restrict each variable to have a fixed influence on the variance of $\ln E_{70}$. While neither assumption is likely to be correct as a polar extreme, the first alternative is less restrictive as an approximation.

We therefore chose to interpret each Q_j as a value relative to the national average, with β_j to be scaled such that $\sum_{i=1}^{n} \beta_j Q_j^i$ is invariant from 1950 to 1960 for each Q_j, where $i = 1 \ldots n$ refers to the 3,097 counties in the model. Any discrepancies with the control totals are then to be corrected by making an appropriate uniform adjustment in the logarithmic constant.[8]

The standard regressions thus involve two types of adjustment: first, the coefficient adjustment just described, and, second, a consistency adjustment in the constant term to coordinate the results with the Almon control totals. This second adjustment also absorbs any absolute effects which were omitted from the model specification. When dealing with our discriminant functions, however, we do not have this second adjustment available as a safeguard. If we specify that the Q_j's are important only in their relative effects, there is no way in which absolute effects can have an impact without seriously distorting the discriminant functions. While we expect that a relative value assumption is reasonable, it is on less secure ground for the discriminant functions than for the regressions.

In treating lagged employment (or some other scale variable) in an absolute manner, we are saying that if all counties increase in absolute size (population or employment), the appearance of a zero observation for a given industry classification is thereby less likely. This assumption is probably more reasonable than the alternative assumption that a county of a given *relative* size has a given likelihood of yielding a zero observation regardless of its absolute size.

PROBLEMS INVOLVING CHANGES IN THE RELATIONSHIPS OVER TIME

The assumption that future time periods are governed by the same structural relationships which have been estimated from

8. Since $\ln E_{50}$ is a scale variable, it seems reasonable to assume that its coefficient should retain its absolute value. Relative adjustments were therefore made only in the Q variables.

historical data creates a well-known problem in statistical estimation. Two aspects of this general problem are especially worthy of note.

First, we have specified that employment in 1960 is a function of 1950 variables. Our implicit assumption is that the speed of response to lagged variables will remain the same in the 1960–1970 period as it was in 1950–1960. A specialized violation of this assumption would be a situation in which the speed of response to each lagged variable increased by a uniform rate. If this were to happen we would have not a prediction of the 1970 employment distribution, but rather a prediction for some earlier year. A more likely violation of the assumption would be that the speeds of response to lagged variables have changed in a diverse manner.

Second, the predicted range of discriminant scores for 1970 might be substantially different from the 0–1 range of 1960. A number of explanations might be advanced for such a result, each of which must be kept in mind when interpreting the results. For example, the basic structural relationships may have changed, in which case the discriminant scores become meaningless unless we can determine the nature of the structural changes. Alternatively, our treatment of relative and absolute socio-economic effects may have been incorrect, resulting in incorrectly scaled discriminant scores, or, finally, the discriminant structure may have remained the same, with differences in the score distribution reflecting legitimate changes in the likelihood of zero and nonzero observations.

HETEROSKEDASTICITY

There is reason to believe that the two regression sets may have heteroskedastic error terms; specifically there is probably a systematic relationship between the size of the variance and the population (or employment) size of the county. Fortunately, the possible presence of heteroskedasticity affects only the efficiency of the estimates, not their accuracy.

The choice of a logarithmic estimating equation should roughly correct for heteroskedasticity, in that the smaller observations have a heavier weight. In relative terms, the upper ranges of the error structure are scaled down by the logarithmic transformation and the lower ranges of the error structure are scaled up.

IV. Results of the Analysis

As indicated earlier, our method of projection to 1970 is a two-step procedure. First, we adapted our regressions of 1960 employment on 1950 data to the 1960 socio-economic data to obtain a raw estimate of 1970 employment by industry for each county. Second, we scaled all employment estimates to the 1970 industry totals projected by Almon. To do this, four basic equations were estimated for each industry: (1) a discriminant function choosing counties having positive 1960 employment from the subset of counties having no employment in 1950; (2) a discriminant function choosing counties continuing to have positive 1960 employment from the subset of counties having positive 1950 employment; (3) a regression predicting 1960 employment for those counties actually moving from zero 1950 employment to positive 1960 employment; and (4) a regression predicting 1960 employment for those counties having positive employment in both 1950 and 1960.

Our final model contains 63 equations, with 39 variables appearing at least once. Accordingly, it would be difficult, if not impossible, to present a readable presentation in detail of the estimated equations. We have therefore attempted to consolidate the results without eliminating important information. A complete description of the system of equations is presented in Appendix E of the CRA report. We will discuss first the four sets of equations (the two discriminant and the two regression sets) and then the individual variables found to be correlated with employment.

DISCRIMINATION FUNCTIONS: CASES WITH ZERO EMPLOYMENT IN 1950

The first set of discriminant functions is designed to separate those counties which had positive 1960 employment in a given industry from those which did not, within the subset of counties which had no employment in 1950. For a number of industries there were no counties with zero 1950 employment. On the average, an industry had 277 zero observations in 1950, of which an average of 69 (or 24.9 percent) moved to positive 1960 employment.

In general, the correlations for this first set of discriminant functions were highly significant according to an F-test criterion, although the values of R^2 were rather low. In 10 of the 14 industries for which the discriminant functions were estimated, an F-test rejected the hypothesis that all coefficients were equal to zero at a 0.1 percent confidence level. Of the remaining four industries, three had correlations significant at a 1.0 percent level, while Industry 17 had a correlation significant only at a 2.5 percent level.

By observing the coefficient sign pattern in Table 4, we can make some observations about which county characteristics are associated with high discriminant scores. The first conclusion is that the larger a county is in population or employment size, the less likely it is to remain at zero employment in a given industry. In Industries 5 through 13 we found a strong positive relationship between either lagged total employment or population aged 21–64 and a county's discriminant score. Since our industry categories are relatively broad, it is extremely unlikely that a county with high total employment will have any zero industry observations.

Certain other tendencies are apparent in the socio-economic data: given the population size of a county, the discriminant score tends to rise with the rate of population growth and with proximity to SMSA's in excess of 250,000 population. A surprising negative correlation was found with median family income. The gas cost variable (144) was positively correlated with the emergence of employment in the three equations in which it appeared, while the electricity cost variable (145) was negatively correlated in the three equations in which it appeared. Other tendencies were scattered across industries, as indicated by the pattern of coefficient signs in Table 4.

While the discriminant functions are highly significant by standard test criteria, there is a serious question whether they can predict nonzero observations with any degree of power. Our criteria were discussed earlier: in order to predict a movement away from zero, we require the discriminant score to be significantly greater than zero at a 5 percent one-tail test level. If the number of observations is sufficiently large, the required discriminant cutoff is about 1.65 times the standard error of estimate. The question to be answered is whether any counties will be given a score which exceeds this cutoff.

The beta weight on each right-hand variable indicates the number of standard deviations movement in the discriminant score associated with a one-standard deviation movement in the right-hand variable. Similarly, the sum of the absolute values of

Table 4. Signs of Socio-economic Variable Coefficients, First Discriminant Set

Variables						Industries								
	5	6	7	8	9	10	11	12	13	14	15	17	18	19
115 Pop. 1950/Pop. 1940	+					+	−				+			+
117 Pop. Density														
118 Prop. Pop. Urban			+		−			+						
119 Prop. Pop. Rural Farm			+						−		+		+	
120 Prop. Pop. Aged 21–64										+				
122 Births/Family					+									
124 Prop. Pop. > 25, > 12 yrs. educ.			−											+
126 Prop. Unemployed				+										
127 Prop. Empl. Mining		−												
128 Prop. Empl. Mfg.														+
129 Prop. Empl. Whole-Retail					+									
130 Avg. Family Size										+			+	
131 Med. Family Income			−					−				−		
133 Prop. Dwellings Built Since 1940						−								
134 Time & Savings Deposits/Pop.					−	−								
136 Normal Precipitation	+								+					
137 Distance to SMSA > 250,000			−				−	−				−		
138 Distance to SMSA > 1,000,000								−		+				
139 Terrain Variability Index									+					+
140 Rel. Extent of Unionization 1953								+						

142 No. National Highways				+			
143 Oil Cost $/barrel	−						
144 Gas Cost $/1000 cu. ft.	+	+					+
145 Elec. Cost $/1000 KWH	−			−		−	
147 Median Age			+				
148 Land Area					−		
150 Employees/Estab. in Mfg.	+						
168 Prop. Heavy Industry in				+			
#14 × Prop. Educ. < 5 yrs.		+		−			
1–22 Ln of 1950 Employment	+	+	+	−		+	+
121 Ln of Population Aged 21–64	+	+	+	+		−	−

Source: See complete equations in Appendix E of CRA Report.

the beta weights, multiplied by the standard deviation of the discriminant score, gives the amount by which the discriminant score is increased by the movement of all variables by one standard deviation in the direction of improving that score. The larger this potential movement relative to the difference between the mean and the discriminant cutoff, the more likely are we to find discriminant scores in excess of the cutoff. In only four of the fourteen equations did the beta weight "score" exceed the above difference. In one of these four cases (Industry 14) the absolute beta-weight sum is misleading because of the presence of two highly correlated scale variables with opposite signs. Thus, while the discriminant functions are significant in a statistical sense, they do not appear to be performing their task effectively.

DISCRIMINANT FUNCTIONS: CASES WITH NONZERO EMPLOYMENT IN 1950

The second group of discriminant functions involves counties with employment in a given industry in 1950 that moved to the zero category in 1960. This movement in absolute terms was much larger than the opposite flow.

While an average of less than five variables per equation was found to reduce the standard error of estimate in the first discriminant set, an average of almost eight variables per equation was found to reduce the standard error in the second set. The values of R^2 again appeared to be rather low, but every equation was found to pass an F-test at a 0.1 percent confidence level. In seven industries, compared to only four in the first discriminant set, the absolute sum of the beta weights multiplied by the standard deviation of the left-hand variable exceeded the difference between the cutoff and the mean of the discriminant scores: in two of the seven industries, however, the presence of highly correlated scale variables with opposite signs contributed to the large beta-weight value. Still, by this test, the second discriminant set is far superior to the first.

As shown in Table 5, virtually all industries displayed a strong positive correlation between discriminant scores and lagged scale variables. In thirteen out of fifteen industries lagged industry employment had a positive coefficient, indicating the rather obvious point that the larger lagged employment is, the less likely is a zero observation in the current period. More general size variables were also significant.

Relations to socio-economic variables are more pronounced in the second discriminant set than in the first. There is an extremely powerful negative relationship between the discriminant score and the distance to an SMSA in excess of 250,000 population. There are rather consistent relationships between the discriminant score and the rate of population growth, the proportion employed in wholesale-retail trade, normal precipitation, the proportion of the population over 25 years of age with less than twelve years of education, and oil cost per barrel. There tends to be a negative relation with terrain variability, and Industries 14 through 19 are negatively related to the proportion of the population aged 21-64 and the proportion of the labor force which is male, and positively related to the proportion of the population in rural and farm areas. The complete discriminant functions appear in Appendix E of the CRA report.

REGRESSION FUNCTIONS: CASES WITH ZERO EMPLOYMENT IN 1950

The first set of regression functions was estimated for those counties which, for a given industry, had positive 1960 employment but no 1950 employment. The purpose of these equations is to assign specific 1970 employment values to those counties predicted to move from zero in 1960 to a positive employment level in 1970.

By definition, none of the counties in this subset had lagged employment for use as a variable, although other scale variables were available. In half of the fourteen industries for which we have equations the employment level was positively related to a scale variable.

In only five equations did we have more than 100 observations. Five equations in all passed an F-test at a 0.1 percent significance level, including four of the five equations with more than 100 observations. The primary reason for our consistent failure to find a well-fitting relationship may very well be that no significant relationship exists. For example, consider the means of the dependent variables, which in logarithmic terms range between 1.46 and 2.25. In employment terms this is equivalent to a geometric mean ranging from 4.3 to 9.5 employees per county. This indicates that the typical county moving from zero to positive employment

Table 5. Signs of Socio-economic Variable Coefficients, Second Discriminant Set

Variables							Industries								
	5	6	7	8	9	10	11	12	13	14	15	16	17	18	19
115 Pop. 1950/Pop. 1940			+			+			+		+				+
116 Prop. Pop. nonwhite	+		+	−										+	
117 Pop. Density								−							
118 Prop. Pop. Urban	−				+										
119 Prop. Pop. Rural Farm					+						+	+	−	+	+
120 Prop. Pop. Aged 21-64					−					−		−	−	−	−
122 Births/Family							−								
123 Prop. Pop. > 25, < 5 yrs. education				+	+		+				+	+			+
124 Prop. Pop. > 25, < 12 yrs. education													−		−
125 Prop. L.F. male		−								−		−			
127 Prop. Empl. Mining					+	+			+					+	
128 Prop. Empl. Mfg.				+	+	+			+						
129 Prop. Empl. Whole-Retail														+	
130 Avg. Family Size	−		−		+	−	−	−			+	+		+	
131 Med. Family Income							+								
133 Prop. Dwellings built since 1940															
134 Time & Savings Dep./Pop.					−									−	
136 Normal Precipitation	+				+					+		+			
137 Distance to SMSA > 250,000														+	

Variable										
138 Distance to SMSA > 1,000,000	−	−	−	−	−	−	−	−	−	−
139 Terrain Variability Index	−	+		−			−		−	
140 Rel. Extent of Unionization, 1953	+									
142 Number of Nat'l. Highways	+	+	+	+					+	
143 Oil Cost $/barrel	+	−				+				
144 Gas Cost $/1,000 cu. ft.	+									
145 Elec. Cost $/1,000 KWH						−				
147 Median Age					+	+				+
148 Land Area										+
154 State Prop. Elect. Mach. in #11		+	+	+	+	+	+	+	+	
164 (Var. #154) × (Var. #123)	+	+	+	+	+	+[a]	−[b]	+[a]	−[a]	
1–22 Ln of 1950 Employment in Industry	+[a]	+[a]	+[a]	+[a]	+[a]	+[c]	+[b]	+[b]	+[c]	−[b]
Other Scale Variable										

Source: Appendix E of CRA Report.
[a] Ln of total 1950 employment.
[b] Ln of population aged 21-64.
[c] Special transportation variable discussed in Appendix A.

has an industry employment level of less than ten in the nonzero period. Given the overall small size of these counties, both the fact of movement to a nonzero level and the size of this movement may very well have a large element which can be legitimately regarded as random. This may be particularly true because our data are based on residence and not on plant location.

We can therefore hypothesize that for the relatively broad industry classifications which we are using the zero status of a county is to a large extent a random occurrence which becomes less likely as the absolute size of a county's population increases. There is some size at which the probability of a zero observation in *any* of our industries becomes effectively zero. As an extreme instance, whatever our conception may be of New York County (Manhattan) as a strictly urban county, it does *not* have literally zero employment in Agriculture (569) or Forestry and Fisheries (35).

As we are restricting ourselves in this set of equations to those counties which moved from literally zero employment to a positive level of employment, our sample set is a heterogeneous mixture of counties which made either a trivially random movement from zero to, say, three, or a significant movement from zero to some number which is large relative to the county size. Furthermore, counties which moved from some trivially small level of employment to a far greater level were omitted altogether from our discriminant analysis (and first regression set). Such counties would instead be in the second regression set, which includes a vast majority of the counties. In the converse case a county with a movement from high employment to a trivially small level would be assigned a positive score in the second discriminant set.

This raises the question as to whether it would have been wiser to have chosen some point other than zero to distinguish between significant and insignificant employment levels. Such a procedure might have worked, but the arbitrariness of such a cutoff would have raised many of the same problems, unless a band of counties on the margin were explicitly omitted from the analysis. Such a possibility is overridden by our need to include an exhaustive set of counties in our analysis, and by our a priori suspicion that in many cases the presence of a zero observation may have more significance than its random difference from a number such as one or two.

It was felt that the weakness of this link would be relatively unimportant. First, the chances are that a county which moved from zero to a high employment level will still be picked out by the first discriminant function-regression sequence, for extreme observations usually do "much of the work" in determining regression coefficients. Second, if a movement from zero to four is truly random, it should not make too much difference whether, on the one hand, the county fails the discriminant test and is predicted to have zero employment, or, on the other hand, passes the discriminant test and is assigned some small employment value.

Turning to the socio-economic variables generally found to be correlated with employment, Table 6 indicates that population growth, proportion of population rural-farm, proportion employed in manufacturing, and normal maximum temperature are all generally positively correlated with employment in the first regression set. No other variables appeared in the equations for more than two industries.

REGRESSION FUNCTIONS: CASES WITH CONTINUING POSITIVE EMPLOYMENT

The second regression set includes the vast majority of counties which had positive employment for a given industry in both 1950 and 1960. Because of inertial factors the tendency is for the prior existence of an industry in an area to increase strongly the likelihood of that industry's continued existence. For this reason the availability of lagged employment as a variable improved the fit of our regression set considerably.

Tables 7 and 8 present the basic data for this regression set. Of the twenty industries for which regressions were calculated, thirteen industries had continuing positive employment in at least 92 percent of the counties of the contiguous United States. The seven industries which did not have continuing positive employment as often were Textiles, Apparel, Lumber and Wood Products, Chemicals, Machinery, Motor Vehicles, and Other Transportation Equipment. As columns (5) and (6) of Table 7 indicate, the equations for these seven industries performed worst in terms of goodness of fit.

These same seven industries (6 through 8 and 10 through 13) are also becoming more concentrated in two senses. First, the number of counties in which each of these industries appears has been diminishing in every instance except Industry 13. Second,

Table 6. Signs of Socio-economic Variable Coefficients, First Regression Set

Variables	Industries											
	5	6	7	8	10	11	12	13	14	17	18	19
115 Pop. 1950/Pop. 1940	+		+	+					−		+	
116 Prop. Pop. nonwhite			−		−							
117 Pop. Density									−			
118 Prop. Pop. Urban	−											
119 Prop. Pop. Rural Farm	−		+	+			+	+			−	
122 Births/Family				+								
126 Prop. Unemployed	−											+
127 Prop. Empl. Mining				+								
128 Prop. Empl. Mfg.			+		+			+		+		
129 Prop. Empl. Whole-Retail	−						+	+				
131 Med. Family Income							+					
133 Prop. Dwellings since 1940				+			+	+				
135 Normal Max. Temp.							−		−			
137 Dist. nearest SMSA > 250,000								+				
138 Dist. SMSA > 1,000,000				+								
139 Terrain Variability		−										
140 Extent of Unionization		+	+									
142 National Highways	+									+		
143 Oil Cost $/Barrel		+										
144 Gas Cost $/1,000 cu. ft.				+								−
145 Electric Cost $/1,000 KWH	+						+					
148 Land Area			+									
150 Empl./Estab.								−				
165 (State Prop. of #13 in Aircraft) × (Prop. Pop. > 25 with < 5 years educ.)												

among the subset of counties with continuing positive employment, the distribution of employment is becoming more concentrated in the sense that the logarithmic standard deviation fell between 1950 and 1960. An examination of columns (3) and (9) in Table 7 can verify this observation.

The remaining thirteen industries performed far better in terms of values of R^2 and F, and also in terms of the size of the standard error of estimate. Furthermore, we were generally able to find more statistically significant explanatory variables for the former thirteen industries than for the latter seven.

Columns (10) and (11) of Table 7 present the coefficient values for scale variables. While in most cases the sum of the coefficients is quite close to one in value, we must emphasize the clear presence of an aggregation problem. While we anticipated this earlier, there is no effective way of dealing with the problem except to warn of its existence. In eighteen of the twenty industries, we found scale variables which remained significant in the presence of lagged industry employment. The coefficients of these variables are reported in column (11); test statistics for all coefficients appear in Appendix E of the CRA report.

Table 8 presents a tabular summary of the signs of socio-economic variables as they appear in the regressions. As we found in the previous regression sets, the rate of population growth (variable 115) had a very strong positive impact on employment location. The distance to SMSA's with populations exceeding 250,000 had a fairly strong negative impact on a large number of industries. In nine industries a high proportion of the population engaged in mining was associated with a smaller level of employment for 1960. Employment in Industries 16–20 (Transportation, Communications, Utilities, and Population-oriented Services) was positively related to the proportion of dwelling units built since 1940. Proportion of population over 25 years of age with less than twelve years of education was in general negatively correlated with employment, as was the proportion of the labor force unemployed and normal maximum temperature. Gas cost and electricity cost, on the other hand, were positively correlated with employment in those equations in which they appeared. Other variables were somewhat less systematic in their correlations.

DISCUSSION OF INDIVIDUAL VARIABLES

In general, it would be unwise to attempt to derive cause-and-effect relationships from our results. One can only say that in the past a particular variable has been associated with a particular level of employment, holding the values of all other explanatory variables constant. If such associations will remain constant in the future, then we can make predictions of employment by observing the present values of the socio-economic variables.

The most effective variable was population growth, which was, with only one exception, positively associated with employment in the regression and the discriminant equations in which it appeared. This variable appeared in equations for both manufacturing and

Table 7. Results of Regression Functions, Nonzero Employment 1950 and 190

Industry number	(1) Number observations	(2) Mean	(3) Standard deviation	(4) Number of right-hand variables	(5) R^2
1	3097	6.8314	.9922	19	.9195
4	3097	6.0542	1.2914	12	.9366
5	2920	4.8886	1.6806	12	.8896
6	1486	4.1307	2.2528	7	.7898
7	1965	4.6259	1.7729	9	.7224
8	2664	4.8789	1.6112	8	.8669
9	2916	4.0430	1.6669	10	.9085
10	2151	3.8600	1.9012	6	.7087
11	2607	4.5084	2.1545	9	.8419
12	1438	3.6161	1.9770	8	.7690
13	1480	3.9971	1.9699	7	.6773
14	2869	5.3666	2.0805	11	.8816
15	2874	4.2368	1.6086	9	.9159
16	3023	4.4257	1.4057	13	.8858
17	2926	3.9532	1.4528	8	.8627
18	2870	4.1208	1.5362	12	.8905
19	3016	4.4509	1.4229	7	.8977
20	3097	7.4640	1.3623	14	.9638
21	3097	6.7011	1.3790	11	.9784
22	3097	5.5481	1.3295	14	.9496

[a]All significant at 0.1 test level.
[b]Ln of total 1950 employment.
[c]Ln of population aged 21-64.
[d]Special transportation variable, discussed in appendix.

service industries. In the R_2 equations, the coefficient of this variable ranged from 0.2 for Railroads to 0.9 for Chemicals, with the average value of the coefficient being about 0.5. In other words, using the average coefficient value of 0.5, a doubling of population growth indicates that the *logarithm* of future employment will increase by one (0.5 times 2), or that the value of future employment will be, other things equal, 2.72 times larger than the value of present employment. Thus, those counties with a high growth in the past are likely to exhibit a high growth in the future.

Distance to nearest SMSA with a population greater than 250,000

	1950 Employment			
(6)	(7)	(8)	(9)	(10)	(11)
	Standard error of estimate	Mean	Stand. Dev.	Coefficient	Coefficient of other scale variable
F-test[a]					
,3077) = 1849.35	.2824	7.3851	0.9230	.9575	.0165[f]
,3084) = 3796.77	.3258	5.9854	1.2331	.7038	.2761[c]
,2907) = 1951.48	.5596	4.4366	1.7410	.7338	.3258[b]
,1478) = 793.51	1.0352	3.9865	2.5889	.7200	.1886[b]
,1955) = 565.30	.9362	3.7651	2.1758	.6297	.3997[b]
,2655) = 2162.08	.5886	4.9533	1.7102	.8599	—
,2905) = 2885.64	.5050	3.6662	1.6486	.5950	.4156[c]
,2144) = 869.15	1.0276	3.3934	2.0172	.6669	—
,2597) = 1536.45	.8582	3.6640	2.2305	.6723	.3510[c]
,1429) = 594.57	.9529	1.9672	2.2584	.6890	.2596[c]
,1472) = 441.34	1.1217	2.5960	2.1749	.6212	.2867[c]
,2857) = 1933.08	.7174	4.8163	2.2424	.7568	.2719[c]
,2864) = 3466.78	.4672	4.7173	1.5524	.9290	.0787[d]
,3009) = 1794.52	.4761	4.2501	1.3092	.6207	.2674[b], .1285[d]
,2917) = 2291.08	.5391	3.8211	1.5398	.6226	.2858[c], .0706[d]
,2857) = 1936.04	.5094	3.9893	1.4916	.6019	.3846[b]
,3008) = 3772.57	.4555	4.2444	1.4425	.7033	.2767[b]
,3082) = 5864.84	.2597	7.2822	1.3601	.2353[e]	.7751[b,e]
,3085) = 12674.29	.2033	6.3996	1.2931	.8723	.1171[c]
,3082) = 4145.42	.2992	5.3148	1,2799	.8855	.1033[c]

[e] Industry 20 erroneously regressed against lagged employment for industry 21. The predictive power is not significantly altered, however, since E_{50}^{20} and E_{50}^{21} have a zero order correlation coefficient of .975 and E_{50}^{20} and E total/^{50} also have a zero order correlation of .975. Note that E total/^{50} takes up the slack left by the omission of the proper lagged employment variable.

[f] Special agricultural variable discussed in appendix.

also appeared in more than half the equations, including both manufacturing and service industry equations. As expected, this variable was in general negatively correlated with employment: it appeared with a positive sign in only two equations. This variable appeared more often than any other in the discriminant equations. The value of the slope coefficient in the R_2 equations varied from $-.0003$ in Population-oriented Services–B (21) to $-.003$ in Other Transportation Equipment (13). Thus, taking $-.001$ as the average coefficient,

Table 8. Signs of Socio-Economic Variable Coefficients, Second Regression Set

Variables	Industries																			
	1	4	5	6	7	8	9	10	11	12	13	14	15	16	17	18	19	20	21	22
115 Pop. 1950/Pop. 1940	+	+	+	+		+	+	+	+		+	+	+	+	+	+			+	+
116 Prop. Pop. nonwhite	−		−	−	−		−			−		−		−		−			+	−
117 Pop. Density	+			−										−		−		+		−
118 Pop. Urban	+					+										+		+		−
119 Prop. Pop. Rural Farm			+			+	−				+									+
120 Prop. Pop. Age 21-64																				+
122 Births/Family			+				−								+				+	+
123 Prop. Persons > 25, Educ. < 5 yrs.					+							+							+	−
124 Prop. Persons > 25, Educ. < 12 yrs.	+						−		−									−	−	+
125 Prop. LF Male		+																		
126 Prop. Unemployed	−	−	−						+			−		−		−		+	−	+
127 Prop. Empl. in Mining	−	+	−	−	−									+	−				+	
128 Prop. Empl. in Mfg.	−	+	−	−	−			+						−	−	+		+	+	+
129 Prop. Empl. in Whole-Retail		+				+	−				+			+			+			+
130 Avg. Family Size	−																			
131 Med. Family Income	+	+	−					−	−	−	−			−		−		−	−	+
133 Prop. Dwellings built since 1940	−	+		−				−				+		+	+	+	+			−
134 Time & Savings Deposits/Pop.	+	+		−			−									+		+	+	+
135 Normal Max. Temp.						−				+		+	+	+			+			
136 Normal Precipitation		+						+	+		+					−	+		+	+
137 Dist. SMSA > 250,000	+	+					−	−	−	−	−		+	+	+	−	−	−		
138 Dist. SMSA > 1,000,000	+	+				+	+	+				−	+			+			+	
139 Terrain Variability	−	+	−				−							+						
140 Extent of Unionization 1953										+									−	
142 National Highways						+		+	+									+		
143 Oil Cost, $/barrel	−	+	+	−	+			−	+						−		−			−
144 Gas Cost, $/1000 cu. ft.	+	+	+	+	+	−	+	+	+											
145 Elect. Cost, $/1000 KWH	−	+									+					+			+	+
147 Median Age										+				+		+		+		
148 Land Area							+											+		
152 State Prop. #5 in Canning		+	+																	
159 State Prop. #14 in Metal Mfg.												+								
169 State Prop. #14 in Metals &												−								

an increase of 1,000 miles in the distance from a large SMSA is needed to decrease the logarithm of employment by 1, and the effect is therefore relatively weak. Curiously, distance to an SMSA with a population greater than one million (Variable 138) entered few equations, and often with the wrong sign. Variable 138 entered eight equations in all, and in five cases the sign was perverse. Thus, there appear to be external economies from being near a small city, but as the size of the city approaches a population of one million these external economies diminish.

Variable 127 (Proportion Employed in Mining) appeared in ten R_2 equations, although it appeared only once in each of the other sets of equations. Except for the equation for Industry 16, mining employment was negatively correlated with employment. As we have stated above, however, the reason for the negative correlation is undoubtedly that mining-intensive counties possess a constellation of socio-economic characteristics that contribute to economic stagnation and which we have been unable to identify with the other variables.

Variable 128 and Variable 129 (Proportion Employed in Manufacturing and Proportion Employed in Wholesale-Retail) each appeared in eight R_2 equations. These two variables also appeared in a number of D_2 and R_1 equations, though each appeared only once in the D_1 equations. However, no clear pattern can be discerned among the coefficients.

The results for the three fuel and power cost variables, Variables 143, 144, and 145 (Oil Cost, Gas Cost, and Electricity Cost) illustrate the simultaneous equation bias present in our system. These three variables appear often in the equations, but more often than not they appear with a positive sign—that is, greater fuel costs are associated with higher levels of employment. Obviously we are not observing the true causal sequence—we cannot conclude that we can increase employment by increasing fuel or power costs. We are in fact observing two offsetting tendencies: lower fuel or power costs would be an incentive for greater employment, but on the other hand greater employment in an area would tend to drive up fuel and power costs.

A number of the intercept and slope dummies worked well in some of the equations for Industries 5, 11, 13, and 14, indicating that these industries are not homogeneous. For example, Variable 152 (State Proportion of Industry 5 in Canning) had a positive coefficient of 0.6 in the R_2 equation for Industry 5, indicating that there is an upward shift of the entire function for Industry 5 for states which have a high proportion of canning in Industry 5. Similarly, Variable 159 (State Proportion of Industry 14 in Metal Manufacturing) had a negative coefficient in the R_2 equation for Industry 14, indicating that the functional relationships for metal manufacturing differ from those for other Industry 14 activities. Again, the presence of Variable 168 (Proportion Heavy Industry in Industry 14 times Proportion Education $<$ 5 years) in the R_2 and D_1 equations for Industry 14 indicates that the effect of the educational level of the population on employment is different for Heavy Industry from what it is for Industry 14 activities.

The results for other variables are so mixed that it is difficult to derive any pattern. In general, therefore, we found that location near a center of population with greater than 250,000 but fewer than one million people has a strong positive effect on industrial growth, and that the size variables (lagged total employment, lagged population and lagged industry employment) have strong positive effects on future employment. Economies of scale and external economies are therefore key factors in industrial growth. Furthermore, counties which have exhibited a large growth of population in the past tend to have large growths of employment in future decades.

PROJECTIONS OF EMPLOYMENT

As mentioned above, certain corrections were made in the regression equations before they could be used in the projection analysis. Specifically, in order to correct for the bias of using absolute cross section regression coefficients of variables which are significant only in determining relative county orderings, we assumed that only the scale variables, lagged employment and size of labor force, have an absolute effect on employment. All other variables were assumed to be relative variables, and therefore were adjusted in proportion to their respective increases or decreases in the country as a whole between 1950 and 1960; that is, we multiplied the coefficient of every relative variable by the ratio of the national mean in 1960 to the national mean in 1950. It should be pointed out that the mean value in the United States as a whole for a particular variable often differed considerably from the mean of the values for all counties. Such an anomaly may arise because the distribution of counties is not random—for example, the percentage of counties that are rural is far higher than the percentage of employment in rural areas. Presumably, however, relative variables should be interpreted in relation to a national norm.

In general, the projected employments by industry for each county presented in Table 9 appear to be quite satisfactory—at least the 1970 county employments are almost always of the same

Table 9. Projected State Employment Growth Rates Between 1960 and 1970

State	Growth rate of total employment %	State	Growth Rate of total employment %
Alabama	9	Nebraska	11
Arizona	47	Nevada	22
Arkansas	0	New Hampshire	11
California	40	New Jersey	22
Colorado	36	New Mexico	35
Connecticut	23	New York	12
Delaware	25	North Carolina	9
D. C.	25	North Dakota	2
Florida	60	Ohio	20
Georgia	14	Oklahoma	13
Idaho	6	Oregon	14
Illinois	16	Pennsylvania	11
Indiana	15	Rhode Island	13
Iowa	8	South Carolina	9
Kansas	18	South Dakota	2
Kentucky	5	Tennessee	10
Louisiana	15	Texas	19
Maine	3	Utah	27
Maryland	34	Vermont	3
Massachusetts	19	Virginia[a]	23
Michigan	19	Washington	13
Minnesota	15	West Virginia	− 4
Mississippi	2	Wisconsin	12
Missouri	15	Wyoming	3
Montana	1		

[a]Adjusted to compensate for an error in the projection of Industry 17 (Other Transportation).

Table 10.

County	Industry	1960 Employment (actual)	1970 Employment (projected)
Alpine, California	Utilities	0	109,239
Brevard, Florida	Chemicals	35	1,679
Schley, Georgia	Other transportation	0	3,444

magnitude as the 1960 employments. Furthermore, implied state growth rates seem to accord well with a priori expectations. For example, the three states with the largest projected growths were Florida (60 percent), Arizona (57 percent), and California (40 percent), while the five states with the smallest projected growths were West Virginia (−4 percent), Montana (1 percent), Mississippi (2 percent), North Dakota (2 percent), and South Dakota (2 percent).

While the overall projections are satisfactory, the model made poor projections in several cases. For example, we projected employment in Industry 17 (Other Transportation) in Buena Vista City, Virginia to grow from 0 in 1960 to 481,012 in 1970. The reason for this was that the R_1 equation for Industry 17 had a very high coefficient (22.5517) for Variable 128 (Proportion Employed in Manufacturing). While all of the counties that went from 0 employment in 1950 to positive employment in 1960 in Industry 17 had a low proportion of manufacturing employment, employment in 1960 was strongly correlated with this proportion, and therefore the slope coefficient of Variable 128 was very high. Unfortunately, Buena Vista City, which has a high value for Variable 128, was picked by the discriminant equation to have positive employment. Therefore, when the R_1 equation was applied to this county, the estimated employment was absurdly large.

Since the projections were scaled so that their sums would equal Almon's projections, there is no easy way to correct for errors of this nature. An overestimate of employment in an industry in one county means that employment in that industry in all other counties will be underestimated. The example of Buena Vista City cited above is the worst overestimate we were able to find in the projections. However, we also found the three other grossly overestimated projections shown in Table 10. Two of these implausible projections are caused by R_1 equations (for counties predicted to pass from zero employment in 1960 to positive employment in 1970).

In addition to the overestimates resulting primarily from the R_1 equations, the model in several instances substantially underestimated 1970 employment in the "home counties" of highly concentrated industries. For example, employment in Industry 12 (Motor Vehicles Manufacturing) in Michigan was projected to decrease from 377,163 in 1960 to 229,554 in 1970. The declines projected for counties with a large 1960 employment in Motor Vehicles are given in Table 11.

These obviously inaccurate results are undoubtedly caused by the fact that in the equation for Industry 12 we have been unable to account sufficiently for such things as decision-making inertia and economies of scale. In all probability there is nothing in Genessee, Ingham, Macomb, Oakland, Saginaw, and Wayne counties which makes them uniquely suitable as centers of the automobile industry other than that, partly because of historical accident, the automobile industry has been concentrated there in the past. Given this concentration, however, these counties are able to retain employment in automobile manufacturing, partly because of decision-making inertia, partly because of the high costs of moving elsewhere, partly because of economies of scale, and partly because of the external economies arising from other industries which have been attracted to these counties (or to neighboring counties) by the presence of the automobile industry. Since there is no reason to believe that the counties mentioned would be inferior, *ceteris paribus*, to other counties for automobile manufacturing, the latter

Table 11.

County	1960 Employment (actual)	1970 Employment (projected)	Decline %
Genessee	54,900	28,029	−48
Ingham	12,081	8,402	−29
Macomb	24,222	14,236	−40
Oakland	48,801	28,610	−40
Saginaw	8,340	5,990	−27
Wayne	173,428	89,244	−48

two reasons are probably the most important. In our equations we tried to account for the economies of agglomeration mentioned above by the use of lagged employment as an explanatory variable. Apparently, however, this variable was not powerful enough to pick up all the effects of agglomeration economies.

When one considers, however, that our model generated 74,328 separate employment projections (24 industries in 3,097 counties) it is remarkable how few implausible projections were made. Of course, for the reasons discussed above, the projections for any one county may be inaccurate, but such an outcome is almost inevitable given the ambitious nature of our task.

Estimation Procedures for Resource-based and Transportation Industries

Agriculture. The data shown in Table A-1 were available for analysis

Table A-1.

Symbol	Description	Source
E_5^i	Employment in agriculture in county i in 1950	*Census of Population*
E_6^i	Employment in agriculture in county i in 1960	*Census of Population*
R_{A6}	Percent of farmers growing crop A in 1959	*Census of Agriculture, 1959*
I_{Aj5}	Index of production of crop A in region j in 1950	Supplement I to *Changes in Farm Production and Efficiency,* 1967 (CFPE)
I_{Aj6}	Index of production of crop A in region j in 1960	
M_{Aj5}	Index of farm production per man hour in crop A in region j in 1950	Supplement IV to *Changes in Farm Production and Efficiency,* 1967 (CFPE)
M_{Aj6}	Index of farm production per man hour in crop A in region j in 1960	

These data were available for the following crops:

CRA Definition	Definition on CFPE Basis
Cash grains	Food grains
Tobacco	Tobacco
Cotton	Cotton
Other Field Crops	Hay and Forage
Vegetables	Vegetables
Fruits and Nuts	Fruits and Nuts
Poultry	Poultry
Dairy	Milk Cows
Other Livestock	Meat Animals
General	All Farm Output
Miscellaneous	All Farm Output

The farm production regions used in the CFPE reports are shown in Table A-2.

Table A-2

Region	States included
Northeast	Maine, New Hampshire, Vermont, Massachusetts, Rhode Island, Connecticut, New York, New Jersey, Pennsylvania, Delaware, and Maryland
Lake States	Michigan, Wisconsin, and Minnesota
Corn Belt	Ohio, Indiana, Illinois, Iowa and Missouri
Northern Plains	North Dakota, South Dakota, Nebraska, and Kansas
Appalachia	Virginia, West Virginia, North Carolina, Kentucky and Tennessee
Southeast	South Carolina, Georgia, Florida, and Alabama
Delta States	Mississippi, Arkansas, and Louisiana
Southern Plains	Oklahoma and Texas
Mountain	Montana, Idaho, Wyoming, Colorado, New Mexico, Arizona, Utah, and Nevada
Pacific	Washington, Oregon, and California

A five-step procedure was used to project agricultural employment by county:

(1) The regional indexes of the CFPE ($I_{Aj6}, I_{Aj5}, M_{Aj6}, M_{Aj5}$) were first converted to corresponding county indexes ($I_{Ai6}, I_{Ai5}, M_{Ai6}, M_{Ai5}$). Thus we implicitly assumed that production and productivity trends are the same for all counties in a given region.

(2) Using the county indexes calculated in step (1), the estimated 1960 employment $\hat{E}_6^i$ was calculated from 1950 employment under the assumption that changes in output and labor productivity are invariant with respect to county. That is,

$$\hat{E}_6^i = \sum_A (E_5^i \cdot R_{A6}) \frac{I_{Ai6}}{I_{Ai5}} \cdot \frac{M_{Ai5}}{M_{Ai6}}. \tag{A-1}$$

In equation (A-1) total employment in county i is multiplied by R_{A6}, the percent of farmers growing crop A in 1959, to obtain an estimate of employment in crop A in 1950:

$$E_5^i \cdot R_{A6}.$$

This figure is then multiplied by the ratio of the index of production of crop A for 1960 to the index of production of crop A for 1950 to obtain an estimate of employment in crop A in 1960, assuming that there is no change in composition of employment and no change in productivity:

$$(E_5^i \cdot R_{A6}) \frac{I_{Ai6}}{I_{Ai5}}.$$

To adjust for productivity change, this figure is then multiplied by the ratio of the index of farm production per man-hour in crop A in 1950 to the index of farm production per man-hour in 1960:

$$(E_5^i \cdot R_{A6}) \frac{I_{Ai6}}{I_{Ai5}} \cdot \frac{M_{Ai5}}{M_{Ai6}}.$$

This estimate is then summed over all crops to obtain $\hat{E}_6^i$.[9]

(3) E_6^i was then regressed on the vector of socio-economic variables ($\overline{Q}$) and $\hat{E}_6^i$.

$$\ln E_6^i = \alpha + \overline{\beta}\,\overline{Q}_5 + \gamma \ln \hat{E}_6^i. \tag{A-2}$$

9. We were forced by lack of data to assume that the composition of employment by crop was the same in 1950 as it was in 1959. This assumption is contradicted by our own procedure of using different indexes of production and productivity for each crop. However, the relative movements of the indexes are not sufficiently different for this assumption to bias the results seriously.

$\hat{E}_6^i$ thus plays, in a sense, the same scale variable role as lagged employment does in the equations for nonresource-based industries.

(4) Using the regressions calculated in step (3), employment in 1970 was projected, using the following equations:

$$E_7^i = \alpha + \overline{\beta}\,\overline{Q}_6 + \gamma \hat{E}_7^i;$$ (A-3)

$$\hat{E}_7^i = \sum_A E_6^i \frac{I_{Ai7}}{I_{Ai6}} \cdot \frac{M_{Ai6}}{M_{Ai7}} \cdot R_{A6}.$$ (A-4)

Estimates of I_{Ai7} and M_{Ai7} were calculated, using data available through 1966. The productivity indexes (M_{Ai7}) were projected by graphing the historical data and projecting visually. With the exception of the production of "Fruits and Nuts," which in most regions had erratic movements, there were strong trends for all crops.

The production indexes for 1970 were derived by projecting on the basis of regressions of the historical indexes on "Total Personal Consumption" and on time. The consumption variable was picked because Almon presents a 1970 projection for it and because it is a good proxy for total personal income. The two independent variables are naturally highly collinear, but this fact does not affect the accuracy of prediction. In the cases with insignificant fits (that is, cases in which the F-statistic was not significant at the 5 percent level of significance) the 1966 value of the index was used as the prediction for 1970. In those cases in which the regression was significant we still checked the prediction of the equation against the most recent history of the crop. If the prediction seemed out of line with recent history, we again used the 1966 value as the estimate for 1970.

(5) The projected county employments from step (4) were scaled so that their sum equaled the Almon projection for agriculture.

Mining. Our procedure was to disaggregate the county mining employment into as many mining categories as possible and then to project mining employment on the assumption that each county will maintain its share of national production in each category of mining.

County employment data are available only for mining as an aggregate. OBE's 118 industry data by state divide mining into four groups: metallic mining, coal, oil and gas, and nonmetallic mining. However, this still conceals very important differences in growth rates. Almon's model projects growth until 1970 for six categories:

1. Nonferrous
2. Coal
3. Oil and gas
4. Nonmetallic
5. Ferrous
6. Chemical

We were fortunately able to obtain an estimate of the percentage distribution of mining by type for these six activities by county from the *Census of Mineral Industries* for 1958. Volume II (*Area Statistics*) of this census presents data on mining for each state. At the beginning of the tables for each state there appears a set of maps on which employment by county is represented by means of circles of different sizes. The maps are published for metal mining, coal mining, oil and gas extraction, and nonmetallic minerals mining. Exact figures for each category could not be determined, but as we were only interested in the percentage composition of mining employment by county, the data available from the maps were adequate for our purposes. To make the data comparable with the Almon mining categories, we used census Table 4 for each state to distribute metal mining to ferrous and nonferrous mining and nonmetallic minerals mining to chemical and other nonmetallic minerals mining. Table 4 of each state report in the *Census of Mineral Industries* presents county data on the distribution of firms by size class by type of mining, but because the size classes are very broad, (e.g., 0–19 employees, 20–99 employees, 100–249 employees, etc.) precise estimates could not be made. Unfortunately, we could not update the data with the 1963 *Census of Mineral Industries* because it does not present maps of employment by type of mining for each state.

Using the estimated 1958 composition of mining employment for each county, we then projected total mining by county by applying the distribution data to the 1960 employment data and using the Almon growth projection for each mining category. As in the case of all other industries, the projected employments were then uniformly scaled so that the total predicted mining employment by sector in 1970 equaled the Almon prediction for mining employment by sector.

It must be stressed, however, that national trends are not the only factors explaining slow growth of employment in mining-intensive counties. Thus, such factors as depletion, the emergence of new competitive areas and materials, and changing access to markets are important in determining local county employment.

Forestry and Fisheries. Because natural resources are obviously of overriding importance for forestry and fisheries and because data on past and future employment are very sparse, we assumed that each county will maintain its share of national growth in forestry and fisheries, as projected by Almon.

Transportation Industries. Employment in several of the CRA industries is in a sense directly dependent on economic activity in the other industries. The industries that might be termed dependent industries are Contract Construction (4), Railroads and Railway Express (15), Trucking and Warehousing (16), Other Transportation (17), Communication (18), Utilities and Sanitary Services (19), and the two population-oriented industries (20 and 21).

The models for the industries dependent primarily on local economic activity were generally estimated with the same variables as the national industries, although it was expected that the size and income variables would prove to be more significant. The major exception to this generalization is that special variables were constructed for the models of the transportation industries (Industries 15 through 17).

Employment by county is provided by the OBE 32 industries classification for the modes of transportation listed in Table A-3.

We projected employment in each of these categories by means of the following equation:

$$\ln E_{it} = \alpha + \beta \overline{Q}_{i,t-1} + \gamma \ln W_{it}, i = 15,17; \qquad (A\text{-}5)$$

where

$$W_{it} = a_{i1} E_{1t} + \ldots + a_{in} E_{nt}, i = 15,17. \qquad (A\text{-}6)$$

In other words, W is a weighted average of projected employment in every other industry, with the weights being the use of transportation mode i by industry j in a base year divided by employment in industry j in a base year. The transportation data are available in the 1963 *Census of Transportation, Commodity Transportation Survey*; 1960 data were used for employment.

A possible objection to the procedure adopted for the transportation industries is that current employment by industry (E_{1t} through

Table A-3.

OBE 32 Industries Code	Content	OBE 118 Industries Code
15	Railroads and Railway Express Service	062
16	Trucking Service	063
	Warehousing and Storage	064
17	Streets Railways and Bus Lines	065
	Taxicab Service	066
	Water Transportation	067
	Air Transportation	068
	Petroleum and Gasoline Pipeline	069
	Services Incidental to Transportation	070

E_{nt}) is in turn a function of lagged Q's and lagged industry employments and that therefore these latter variables should replace the constructed variable W_{it} in equation (A-5). However, too many variables are involved—in theory, in a reduced-form equation every lagged variable and every exogenous variable should appear. If the assumptions involved in constructing W_{it} are correct, using W_{it} increases the efficiency of estimation. Furthermore, to the extent that E_{it} is not explained by $E_{i,t-1}$ and the vector of socio-economic variables, prediction is improved by using W_{it}, which is constructed from actual E_{it}'s.

Index

Area development: need for programs of, 24–25

Area Redevelopment Act (ARA), 21; emphasis on business capital, 35; subsidized plant location under, 169–170; effects of on local unemployment, 183

Area Redevelopment Administration (ARA), 3, 163

Arizona, 359, 392

Arkansas, 93, 262, 265; garment factory in, 180, 183

Assumptions underlying growth model, 209–217; influences on rate of growth of income, 209–210; demand for region's exports, 210–214; composition of regional output, 214; full employment, 215; migration, 215–217

Automobile financing, 225

Back-migration, 147

Backwardness, southern: causes of, 279–280; results of in later years, 280–284; lack of, pre-Civil War, 284–289. *See also* South; Southern development

Baltimore, Md., 342; science-based industry in, 111

Bank borrowing, 225

Bank loans, small, 10

Battelle Memorial Institute, 315, 341

Baty, Gordon, 135n

Baumol, W. J., 150

Bentham, Jeremy, 47

Birth rate, southern rural, 267

Bolton, Roger, 137–160; summary of paper by, 6

Borrowing: analysis of, in growth model, 191; range of, 220; divisions of, 223; household, 223, 224–225; business, 223, 225–227; government, 223, 227–228

Borts, George H., 141n, 189–217; summary of paper by, 8; on structural change, 283

Boston, Mass.: science-based industry in, 5, 107, 111; engineers and scientists in, 118; availability of capital in, 133–135

Buena Vista County, Virginia, 392

Buffalo, N.Y., 252

Burrows, James C., 352–394; summary of paper by, 15–18

Burton, Richard P., 331

Business capital, under Economic Development Act, 35

California, 92, 392; government-sponsored research in, 124; cotton-growing in, 246

California, University of, 331

California Development Model, 13, 315, 331–334; Phase I, 331–332; demand sections in, 332; Phase II, 332–334; similarities of two models, 334

California Institute of Technology, 113, 116

Cambridge, Mass., and science-based industry, 113

Capital: for science-based industry, 133–135; formation of in South (1860), 298–299; decline of in South after war, 300–301

Capital coefficient, 190

Capital flows, regional, Borts on, 8, 189–217

Capital markets, regional, 8–9, 218–239; structure of, 219–223; lack of data for studying, 222–223; extent of compartmentalization in, 223–232, 237–238; short-run changes in credit conditions, 232–237; summary of, 237–239

Casualty life insurance companies, 228

Certificates of deposit, 9, 227, 230, 234–235

Charles River Associates (CRA), 352n; industry list of, 260–261

Chemistry, distribution of specialists in, 118

Chenery, H., 55n

Chesapeake Bay, 342

Chicago, Ill., 252

Chicago Area Transportation study, 315

Chinitz, Benjamin, 18, 21–39; summary of paper by, 2–3

Cincinnati, Ohio, 252, 326

City, large vs. small, 389, 390

Civil War, related to southern backwardness, 12

Classification: of areas, 60–65; cost of, 61

Cleveland, Ohio, 252

Coal, 246

Cobb-Douglas production factor, 194

Cochran, Thomas, 292

Coleman Report. See *Equality of Educational Opportunity*

Commercial banks, 224; home mortgages by, 225; consumer credit by, 225; business loans by, 226; regional variation in loans by, 226; as financial intermediaries, 228–230; time deposits in, 229; investment problems of, 234; effects of CD's on, 235

Commercial mortgages, 9, 224, 225

Commercial paper, 227, 233

Commodity output, estimates of, ca. Civil War, 290–291

Communications, necessity of for technical companies, 128–133

Compartmentalization, regional, of capital markets, 219–223; extent of, 223–232; in private domestic borrowing, 224–228; in financial sector, 228–232; trend away from, 237. *See also* Capital markets

Complementarity, 140

Complex, nature of, 111–112

Computer simulation models in analysis of goals, 15

Congress: detrimental limitations imposed by, 2; aid to depressed areas by, 21–22; support for planning, 32–33

Consumer credit, 224, 225, 238

Consumer finance companies, 224, 232

Core, or Deep, South: crop changes in, 246; poverty in, 248; Negro migration from, 253–256; Negro education in, 257; expenditure for education in, 264–266. *See also* Appalachia or Border South; Heterogeneous South

Corporate bonds, 221, 223, 225, 232

Corporate external financing, 225; long-term, 225; short-term, 225–226

Cost-benefit analysis, 147–150

Coastal Plains, 29

Cotton: growing of, 246, 358; price, post-Civil War, 291; southern export of, 303

Counties: determinants of growth in, 16, 352–394; drawbacks in study of, 17; as units for federal aid, 28–29, 31; measurement of unemployment and income in, 66–73, 84; location of most depressed, 84–89, 91, 92–94; heterogeneous nature of, 359

Credit: regional impact of changes in, 8; new institutions for, 220–221; short-run changes in, 232–237

Credit instruments, 221

Cross-section problem in county model, 366, 370–372

Danilov, Victor J., 134

Dealer loans, 227

Debt instruments, new types of, 220

Defense, research for, 118

Defense spending: and labor-surplus areas, 137–160; importance of regional effects, 138–141; causes of immobility, 142–144; role of subsidized employment, 144–147; cost-benefit analysis, 147–150; adjustments possible in, 151–152; estimating regional impact of, 152–153; effect of military payrolls, 153–155, 158; effect of procurement, 155–156; input-output studies of, 156–159; conclusions concerning, 159–160

Delaware, 245, 266

Delaware River Basin, 339

Demand deposits, 229

Denison, Edward F., 283

Denver, Colo., 134

Department of Labor, 162

Department stores, consumer credit by, 225

Depreciation, rate of, in growth model, 199–201

Depressed areas: disadvantages of defense spending in, 6; designation of, 58–60; classification of, 60–65; pros and cons of research-based industry for, 108–110. *See also* Designation of depressed areas

Design of Water-Resource Systems, 337–338

Designation of depressed areas: problems of, 58–60; determining welfare criteria, 58; specifying criteria, 59; classification of, 60–65; sample and variables, 65–73; discriminant functions for, 73–96; physical variables of, 80, 81; income-related variables of, 80, 81, 84; educational variables of, 80, 81; labor-market variables of, 80, 82; basic explanatory variables, 97–104. *See also* Depressed areas

Detroit, Mich., 252

Deutermann, Elizabeth P., 134

Development District, 29, 31

Direct public investment, 161, 162n, 183

Disaggregation of industries, 359

Discriminant functions in county model: cases with zero employment in 1950, 374–378; cases with nonzero employment in 1950, 378–379, 380–381

District, 29. *See also* Region

District of Columbia, 245

Douglas, Senator Paul, 22

Dummies: intercept, 369; coefficient, 369, 370

Dyckman, John W., 331

Easterlin, Richard A., data on ante-bellum incomes, 12, 280–285, 289
Economic Development Act (ERA), 2, 163; objectives contrasted with ARA, 183; limitations of, 184
Edgerton, Germeshausen, and Greer, 114
Education: improvement of in South, 11; facilities for, related to professional employment, 123, 135; of employees in market-induced plant location, 165–168; of employees in subsidized locations, 170; of southern migrants, 256–264; causes of underinvestment in, 264–266; need for improvement of, in rural South, 269; contrasts in, in North and South, 305
Educational variables of depressed areas, 80, 81
Efficiency: national income growth as, 4, 41; as goal of national economic growth, 42; paradigm of equity and, 49–56
Efficiency frontier: defined, 51; in paradigm, 50–56
Eisenhower, Dwight D., 22
Electronics: in Boston complex, 111, 113; in metropolitan areas, 112; in New York, 115; distribution of experts in, 118
Eligibility for federal aid, 30–31
Employment: equal opportunities for, in South, 270; county, by industry, 358; related to population growth, 385–386; and distance to nearest SMSA, 386–387; projected growth rates of, 390–394
Engerman, Stanley L., 279–307; summary of paper by, 11–13
Engineers: in technical firms, 116–124; mobility of, 120
Engineers, Corps of, 315, 325, 339
England, as market for cotton, 303
Entrepreneurs, for science-based industry, 116–124
Entropy, measures of, 44
Environment, as factor in unemployment, 24–25
Equality of Educational Opportunity (Coleman Report), 259
Equity: measurement of, 4, 44–47, 49; as goal of national policy, 40, 42; normative vs. statistical measures of, 46; paradigms of efficiency and, 49–56
Equity frontier: defined, 52; in paradigm, 50–56
Equity issue, 225

Eurodollars, 227, 236–237
Evaluation of regional models, 349–350
Expectations, techniques for setting of, 45–46
Extractive industries, and unemployment, 59

Family income: as criterion for federal aid, 30; as discriminant in distressed areas, 95
Farm capital financing, 226
Federal assistance: by local programs, 26; by direct payments to poor, 26; by subsidies to local government, 26, 28–32; local participation in planning for, 32–35; tools for, 35–39
Federal government: and aid to depressed areas, 22; criteria for aid from, 29–32
Federal Home Loan Bank Board System, 230, 231
Federal Housing Authority (FHA), mortgages by, 9, 231
Federal land banks, 226
Federal Reserve System, 234
Federal Savings and Loan Insurance Company, 230
Fellner, William, 139n
Fiering, Myron B., 339
Finance companies, 221
Financial intermediation, 220; regional differences in, 223; thrift institutions, 223, 230–232; large institutional lenders, 223; consumer finance companies, 224, 232; commercial banks, 224, 228–230
Financial sector, 228–232; commercial banks, 228–230; savings institutions, 230–232; insurance companies, 232; consumer finance companies, 232
Fishlow, Albert, 299
Florida, 93, 245, 392
Flow-of-funds accounts, 222; submarkets revealed by, 223
Forecasting: related to planning, 14–15; sophisticated vs. naive, 15
Four Corners, 29
Fredrickson, E. Bruce, 198
Friedmann, J., 50n
Frisch, Ragnar, 332
Fuchs, Victor, 272
Funds flows, effects of changes in, 232–237

Gallman, 290
Garment industry, cluster of in New York, 112, 115
Gemeinschaft, 48

Genessee County, Mich., 393
Geographic spectral analysis, 45
Georgia, 92, 93, 262, 359
Gesellschaft, 48
Gini index, 44
Goals, specifying of, 14
Gordon, Robert A., 201
Government: spending by for R & D, 124–125, 135; as market for science-based industry, 126–127. *See also* Federal assistance; Federal government
Government securities, 221, 223, 227; national markets for, 9; bank holdings of, 236
Great Britain, policy of on plant location, 184
Greenberg, D. S., 109n
Gross National Product as criterion of rate of growth, 42
Growth models: in analysis of regional economics, 8, 190; borrowing, lending, and net factor income, 191–193; simple model, 193–199; more sophisticated model, 199–209; assumptions underlying, 209–217; and regional differences in income, 219, 237. *See also* Regional models; Simple growth models; Sophisticated growth models
Growth rate, 190

Hall, Max, 113n
Harvard University: relation to cluster of science-based industries, 112, 113; spin-off companies from, 114; regional study by Graduate School of Public Administration, 315–320
Harvard Water Program, 315; basis of Lehigh Basin model, 337, 338–339
Haveman, Robert, 148
Hawaii, University of, 334
Heterogeneous South: poverty in, 246–247, 248; expenditure for education in, 266. *See also* Appalachia or Border South; Core or Deep South
Heteroskedasticity, 336, 373
Hirschman, A., 50n
Households, capital financing of, 224–225; mortgages, 224–225; consumer credit, 224
Housing and Home Finance Agency, 331
Hufschmidt, Maynard M., 339
Human capital: in Civil War South, 299–300; postbellum, 305–306

Immobility: causes of, 142–144; preference for, 160
Income: size of, related to unemploy-

ment, 4; inequality of northern and southern, 11; related to equity, 46–47; and education, 256; and expenditure for education, 264–266; per capita (1880–1960), 282; per capita (1840–1860), 287. *See also* Low income
Income, area: measurement of, 66; 15-variable discriminant analysis of, 74, 76
Income and product accounts, 222
Income transfers, alternatives to, 4
Indian reservations, federal aid for, 30
Industrial development: impact of, 1; Shimshoni on, 5, 107–136; Bolton on, 5–6, 137–160; Miernyk on, 7–8, 161–185
Industrialization, lack of in South, 295–299, 304
Industries, OBE and CRA lists of, 360–361
Inequality, regional measure of, 43
Information, costs of in capital market, 9, 220
Infrastructure, emphasis on, 37
Ingham County, Mich., 393
Input-output analysis, 312
Input-output studies of defense spending, 156–159
Installment credit, 225
Institute for Urban and Regional Development (University of California), 331
Instrument industry: location of, 117–118; government sponsorship of, 125
Instrumentation Laboratory, 118, 120
Insurance companies, 225, 232. *See also* Casualty life insurance; Life insurance
Intelligence tests, 258
Interbank balances, 235, 236
Interest rate, 190; regional variations in, 226–227
Investment effects, 152–153

Jordan, Max, 179–180, 183

Kain, John F.: summary of paper by, 11; on North's stake in southern rural poverty, 243–278
Kaiser Aluminum and Chemical Corporation, 166–168, 181
Kaler, John B., 58–96; summary of paper by, 4–5
Kennedy, John F., 168
Kentucky, 92, 93, 271, 290
Klein, L. R., 332
Kraft, Gerald, 18, 58–96; summary of paper by, 4–5
Krutilla, John, 148

Labor: migration of, 239; demand for, in Ohio River study, 326

Labor-market variables of depressed areas, 80, 82

Labor surplus, and defense spending, 137–160

Legislation to aid depressed areas, rationale and objectives, 23–28

Lehigh Basin Simulation Model, 13, 315, 337–341; extension of Harvard Water Program, 337, 339; problems of river-basin planning, 340–341

Lending: analysis of, in growth model, 191; varieties of, 220; new institutions for, 221

Leontief, Wassily, 156

Lerner, Eugene, 304

Leven, Charles L., 328

Life insurance companies, 221; home mortgages by, 225, 226, 232. *See also* Casualty life insurance; Insurance companies

Lincoln Laboratory, 113, 118, 134

Linear programming, 312

Literature, as source of technical information, 130–131

Little, Arthur D., 315, 325, 331

Local labor markets: effects of new plants on, 7, 161–185; market-induced plant locations, 164–168; subsidized plant locations, 168–170; effects of market-induced vs. subsidized, 181–182

Locke, John, 47

Lorenz index, 44

Los Angeles, Calif.: center for technical industry, 107, 111, 113; Negro migration to, 253; Pegrum study of, 355

Los Angeles County, 359

Louisiana, 92, 94, 265, 271

Louisville, Ky., 326

Low income: as criterion for areas of redevelopment, 59, 83, 88, 90, 92–94, 95; indiscriminating distressed areas, 95. *See also* Income

Maass, Arthur, 337n

Machlup, Fritz, 108n

Macomb County, Mich., 393

Maine, 369

Manhattan project, 114

Map generalization, 45

Marginal propensity to save, 190

Market-induced plant locations, 164–168; age and education of employees in, 165; effects of, compared with subsidized, 181–182

Markets, for technical firms, 129–130

Maryland, 245, 266, 342

Massachusetts Institute of Technology, 135; relation of to cluster of science-based industries, 112, 113; spin-off companies from, 113–114; government sponsorship of research in, 124. *See also* Radiation Laboratory

McKay, Raymond, 161n

Mean deviation, drawbacks in use of, 27

Memphis, Tenn., 109

Mental deficiency, rates for, 258

Metcalf, Charles E., 352–394; summary of paper by, 15–18

Metropolitan areas, large: Negro migration to, 251

Metropolitan areas, medium: white migration to, 251; growth of in South, 272–274

Meyer, John R., 58–96, 110n; summary of paper by, 4–5

Michigan, 181, 393

Michigan, University of, 113. *See also* Ann Arbor

Middle West, scientists in, 122–123

Miernyk, William H., 161–185; summary of paper by, 7–8

Migration: economic effects of, 4; between South and West, 11, 253; studied in paradigm, 50–56; of labor, 239; southern, 249–256; education of southern participants in, 256–266; prognosis for, 266–268

Military personnel, payrolls of, 153–155

Milliman, J. W., 309–351; summary of paper by, 13–15

Milwaukee, Wisc., 252

Minneapolis, Minn., 107, 113

Minnesota, University of, 315, 320

Misclassification of areas, costs of, 62

Mississippi, 262, 264, 392

Missouri, 92, 94

Mobility: lack of, and regional policy, 139; as social question, 160; of workers at subsidized plant, 173–175

Model for determinants of employment by industry at county level: formulation of, 352–358; data used in, 358–365; explanatory variables, 361–364; derivation of scaling factors, 365; special problems in, 365–373; results of analysis, 374–394; discriminant functions, 374–381; regression functions, 379, 383–385; individual variables discussed, 385–390; projections of employment, 390–394

Models. *See* Regional models

Money markets, compartmentalization of, 8

Montana, 392

Mortgages: FHA, 9, 231; small, 9, 223, 224, 232, 238; large commercial, 9, 224, 225, 238; by savings and loan associations, 225, 230; farm, 226; restrictions on, 230; by mutual savings banks, 231

Multiplier effects of defense spending, 152–153

Mutual savings banks, 235; home mortgages by, 225, 231, 238

National goals for regional policy, 41–49; efficiency, 41, 50–56; equity, 41, 50–56; occupation of territory for defense purposes, 41; occupation of frontier regions, 41; civil stability, 41; support for cultural or ethnic groups, 41

National Planning Association, 327, 350

Negroes: and poverty, 243; in Core South, 247; migration of, 251–256; education of, 257–264; entrance into labor force of, 266–268; need for improvement of education of, 269–270; equal employment opportunities for, 270–274

Neighborhood adjustment capital, 142–143, 144

Net factor income, 190; in growth model, 191

New England, 29; scientists in, 122–123

New Orleans, La., 290

New plant locations: effect of on local labor market, 161–185; market-induced, 164–168; subsidized, 168–170; worker characteristics at, 170; employment and labor force statistics of, 171–181; market-induced vs. subsidized, 181–182; policy implications for, 183–185

New York City: mortgages in, 231; Negro migration to, 252

New York County, 382

New York metropolitan area: science-based industry in, 112; industry clusters in, 115; Vernon study of, 354

New York Metropolitan Region Model, 13, 315–320

New York State, 342

Normative measures of equity, 49

North, the: migration from South to, 10, 251, 254; stake of in southern rural poverty, 11, 247–249, 269; education

of Negroes in, 259; compared with South before Civil War, 285–287; postwar growth in, 292; agriculture in contrasted with Southern (1880), 302–303

North Carolina, 92, 94, 369; appliance factory in, 246; expenditure for education in, 266

North Dakota, 392

Northeast corridor: center for technical industry, 107; mutual savings banks in, 231

Oahu, Hawaii, Model, 13, 315, 334–337; conceptual framework of, 336

Oak Ridge, Tenn., 115

Oakland County, Mich., 393

Office of Business Economics (OBE): U.S. Dept. of Commerce, 359; industry list of, 360–361

Office of Economic Opportunity (OEO), 25, 162

Office of Scientific Research and Development (OSRD), 113

Ohio River Basin Model, 13, 315, 325–331; demand for labor in, 326; sources of demand in, 327; problems of input-output framework, 328–329

Oklahoma, 245, 262

Opportunity costs, 145, 147–148, 150

Out-migration, as criterion for federal aid, 30

Overall Economic Development Plan (OEDP), 2–3, 33

Ozarks, 29

Palo Alto, Calif., 113; technical industry in, 114

Pareto optimum, 55

Payrolls: of military personnel, 153–155; of civilian employees, 155

Pegrum, Dudley Frank, 355

Penn-Jersey model, 315

Pennsylvania, 342

Pension funds, 221, 225; private, 232

Persky, Joseph J., 243–278; summary of paper by, 11

Petersen, John, 180

Philadelphia, Pa.: availability of capital in, 135; Negro migration to, 252; input-output study of, 315

Physical variables of depressed areas, 80, 81

Physics, distribution of experts in, 118

Pittsburgh, Pa., 115, 252, 326; regional model of, 315

Planning: as prelude to federal assist-

tion, 128
Shadow prices, 145
Shapero, Albert, 110n, 134
Share analysis, 312
Share-crop system, rise of in South, 303-304
Shimshoni, Daniel, 107-136; summary of paper by, 5
Shugg, Roger, 304
Simple economic base studies, 312
Simple growth model, 193-199; assumptions of, 194; relationships in, 195-197; statistical tests of, 197-199. *See also* Sophisticated growth model
Slavery: and antebellum income in South, 12-13; and economic development of South, 280, 288-289
Smith, Adam, 48
Snyder, Arthur F., 135n
Social capital, 142
Social overhead capital, 162, 183
Socioeconomic variables correlated with employment, 383, 384, 385, 388
Solow, Robert, 8, 191
Somers, George, 166
Sophisticated growth model, 199-205; place of depreciation in, 199-201; gross savings function in, 201; gross investment in, 201-202; effects of individual parameters on state debtor position, 203-205; sensitivity analysis, 205-206; regression analysis, 206-209. *See also* Simple growth model
South, the: scientists in, 122; commercial banks in, 229, 235; interbank deposits in, 236; definition of, 245-246; subregions of, 247; education in, 257-258; need for metropolitan development in, 270-274; economic condition of (1880-1960), 280-284; pre-Civil War, 284-289; impact of Civil War on, 289-293; economy of (1860), 293-300; economic decline in (1860-1900), 300-306. *See also* Appalachia; Core South; Heterogeneous South; Rural poverty
South Carolina, 265
South Dakota, 392
Southern development, special problems of 2, 10, 241-307; Kain and Persky on 11, 243-278; Engerman on, 11-13, 279-307, *See also* Rural poverty; the South
Spending for defense, regional impact of, 6-7
Spiegelman, Robert C., 112
Spin-off companies, 113, 129; from MIT, 113-114; from Harvard, 114

Standard Economic Areas (SEA's), 17
Standard Industry Classification Code, 327
Standard Metropolitan Statistical Areas (SMSA's), 17
Stanford Research Institute, 134
Stanford University, 114
States, projected employment growth rates in, 390-394
Stein, Jerome L., 141n, 214; on structural change, 283
Stockholm model, 315
Straszheim, Mahlon R., 218-239; summary of paper by, 8-10
Subsidized employment: role of, 144-147; dangers of, 146; cost-benefit analysis of, 147-150
Subsidy: effect of on hiring practices, 7; kinds of, 144-145; vs. income maintenance, 149; for plant locations under ARA, 168-170, 181-182, 183-185. *See also* New plant locations; Subsidized employment
Susquehanna Basin Simulation Model, 13, 315, 341-349; new features in, 341-342; subregionalization in, 342-343; simulation technique of, 344; employment sector of, 345-347; water sector in, 347-349
Swan, T. W., 8, 191

Technical assistance, under EDA, 38
Technical industry, U.S. centers of, 107
Technological change, rate of, 239.
Tennessee, 92, 93, 290
Teplitz, P., 110n
Terman, Frederick, 114
Texas, 92, 94, 245, 246, 286
Textiles, 246
Tight money, 232-236; regional effects of, 234
Time, changes in relationship over, 366, 372-373
Time deposits, 229-230, 234
Tinbergen, Jan, 332
Tobacco: as crop, 246; price of, 291
Tolley, G. S., 147
Trade credit, 225
Trend extrapolation, 312
Trusts, 232
Tucker, George, 285
Tucson, Ariz., 134

Unemployment: relation of to low income, 4, 7, 59, 96; effect of subsidized firms on, 7; personal vs. environmental variables in 24; as criterion for federal aid, 30; substantial, 30; persistent, 30; as measure of equity, 44, 46–47; as criterion for areas for redevelopment, 59, 83, 86, 90, 92–94, 95; measurement of, 66; 15-variable discriminant analysis of, 75; regional, 140–141; vs. subsidized employment, 144; reduction of national, 162; local and national, 163, 181–182

U. S. Chamber of Commerce, 163

Universities: attitude toward science-based industries, 5, 113–115; government sponsorship of research in, 124; role of, in industrial complex, 133, 135. *See also* universities by name

University of California at Los Angeles, 113

Upper Great Lakes, 29

Upper Midwest Economic Model, 13, 315, 320–325; major planning assumptions of, 321–322; weakness of, 324–325

Urban poverty, 244

Urban renewal, fallacies in, 26

Urbanization, paradigm of equity and efficiency in relation to, 50–56

Vernon, Raymond, 116, 319, 354

Veterans Administration, mortgages by, 231

Virginia, 92, 94

Wages: of workers at subsidized plants, 175–177; in South, 272

Wainer, Herbert A., 110n, 134

Washington, D.C., science-based industry near, 107, 111

Water development, 325

Water resource investment, study of, 148–149

Wayne County, Mich., 393

Weinberg, Alvin, 115

Welfare need, indices of, 4–5

Welfare payments vs. procurement costs, 145

West, the: migration from South to, 10, 253; certificates of deposit in, 230

West Virginia, 246, 271, 292

Whites, southern: migration of, 253, 256; education of, 257

Willens, Alan R., 58–96; summary of paper by, 4–5

Workers, at subsidized plants: age of, 170; education of, 170; previous employment of, 171–173; occupational mobility of, 173–175; earnings of, 175–177; place of residence of, 177–179

World War II, electronics research during, 113

Wright, Earl, 180

Wyoming, 369

"Zero problem" in model at county level, 365, 366–368